THE PROPHET MUḤAMMAD

IN FRENCH AND ENGLISH LITERATURE

THE PROPHET MUḤAMMAD

in FRENCH *and* ENGLISH LITERATURE, 1650 *to the present*

AHMAD GUNNY

THE ISLAMIC FOUNDATION

Published by
THE ISLAMIC FOUNDATION
Markfield Conference Centre, Ratby Lane, Markfield,
Leicestershire LE67 9SY, United Kingdom
E-mail: publications@islamic-foundation.com
Website: www.islamic-foundation.com

Qur'an House, PO Box 30611, Nairobi, Kenya
PMB 3193, Kano Nigeria

Distributed by: Kube Publishing Ltd.
Tel: +44 (0) 1530 249230, Fax: +44 (0) 1530 249656
Email: info@kubepublishing.com

A Cataloguing-in-Publication Data record for this book is available from the British Library.

ISBN: 978-0-86037-478-7 *casebound*

Cover design: Nasir Cadir
Typesetting: Naiem Qaddoura

Contents

Transliteration Table

Arabic Consonants

Initial, unexpressed medial and final:

ء	ʼ	د	d	ض	ḍ	ك	k
ب	b	ذ	dh	ط	ṭ	ل	l
ت	t	ر	r	ظ	ẓ	م	m
ث	th	ز	z	ع	ʻ	ن	n
ج	j	س	s	غ	gh	هـ	h
ح	ḥ	ش	sh	ف	f	و	w
خ	kh	ص	ṣ	ق	q	ي	y

Vowels, diphthongs, etc.

Short:	ـَ	a	ـِ	i	ـُ	u
Long:	ـَا	ā	ـِي	ī	ـُو	ū
Diphthongs:			ـَوْ	aw		
			ـَىْ	ay		

Preface

Logic would have required me to complete the investigation I began years ago, on the images of Islam in European writings, with another volume dealing with the same subject in the modern period. This would have meant a complete shift in emphasis: issues such as politics, economics, and the environment, all of increasing importance in our times, would have had to be tackled. However, when Professor Ann Jefferson (New College, Oxford) sent me some material relating to a twentieth-century biographer of Muḥammad, I began to think that perceptions of the Prophet, independently of other topics in Islam, might prove an equally valid subject of enquiry, even if apparently more limited in scope. Evaluating the responses of European writers to Muḥammad over a reasonably long period has proved to be a stimulating challenge.

The Oxford Centre for Islamic Studies has been building bridges between Islam and the West. I hope that the present study will contribute to its effort. I, however, bear sole responsibility for the opinions expressed here.

My warm thanks also go to the Islamic Foundation for accepting this volume for publication, which attempts to trace the fortunes of the Prophet Muḥammad in French and English literature over the last three-and-a-half centuries.

I am indebted to my family for their continuing support.

Ahmad Gunny

Preface

[illegible] would have ventured to [illegible] by my [illegible] friend, [illegible] [illegible] Muhammad [illegible] and [illegible] volume dealing [illegible] the same subject [illegible] the work [illegible] retired. [illegible] [illegible] Mohammedan [illegible] [illegible] and the [illegible] of any [illegible] importance would have had to be added. However, when [illegible] [illegible] sent me some material relating to [illegible] I began to think this [illegible] independently of other [illegible] [illegible] subject [illegible] opportunity [illegible] examples of [illegible] of Muhammad [illegible] [illegible]

The [illegible] Centre for [illegible] Studies has [illegible] [illegible] I hope [illegible] the present [illegible] [illegible]

[illegible] [illegible] the Prophet Muhammad [illegible] and [illegible] [illegible]

[illegible] Cummings[illegible]

[illegible]

Introduction

The period examined in my previous works on perceptions of Islam in European literature began from the late seventeenth and ended with the nineteenth century, covering about a hundred years at a time in one volume. The present study begins a little earlier, concentrating on perceptions of the Prophet Muḥammad from the mid-seventeenth century to the twentieth century and beyond. Its longer chronology is justified by the fact that the evaluation of perceptions of Muḥammad over more than three centuries is not as broad a subject as a study of Islam would have been over the same period; after all, many of the crucial events affecting Muḥammad's life cover a period of only some twenty-two years, from the first revelations in 610 to his death in 632. While there is no Islam without Muḥammad, it does not follow that he and Islam are the same thing, as some Westerners seem to think.

The earlier start should allow me to fill in the gaps I had left in the previous studies, especially with regard to the attitudes of English Protestants to the Prophet in the seventeenth century (see Chapter 1). For the sake of convenience, the chronological divisions adopted here broadly follow those of the previous books. The emphasis is, however, different. There is now room for a discussion of authors such as Ibn Ṭufayl, du Ryer, Alexander Ross, Joseph Morgan, Sale, Carlyle, Garcin de Tassy, and William Dalrymple on Indian Islam. New material on the eighteenth century concerning the *Traité des trois imposteurs* (1719) and on Lamartine's *Vie de Mahomet* (1854) is also introduced. At the same time, only those few travellers and diplomats who deal specifically with Muḥammad or his family are included. For the same reason only the works of some oriental scholars are subject to scrutiny. Reference to articles on Muslim personalities other than Muḥammad in d'Herbelot's

Bibliothèque orientale (1697) is brief, as the focus here is on the latter. The last chapter (on the modern period) is completely new territory.

Even older territory, if approached from a slightly different angle, may yield interesting results. In any case, it is unthinkable that the Enlightenment (earlier periods too, provided one does not go as far back as the Middle Ages which were not able or unwilling to engage seriously with Islam and Muḥammad) could be overlooked. Going back to a fairly distant past certainly exposes readers, especially Muslim readers, to the painful experience of reading incessant denunciations of Muḥammad as an impostor. Yet this experience is unavoidable unless one is embarking on an exercise in hagiography. Moreover, only by examining past responses to Muḥammad can one avoid giving the impression that he had always been recognized as a Prophet. Previous centuries could show if there has been an evolution in his fortunes in the French and English literature of modern times.

If the study as a whole appears to be unevenly weighted, with slightly more space devoted to the seventeenth and eighteenth centuries than the nineteenth and twentieth centuries, it is not because the latter are deemed to be less important; while even-weighting is a reasonable target to aim at, it should not, however, be pursued at any cost. If, for example, attention were devoted to some aspects of the works on Qur'ānic studies by scholars such as Theodor Nöldeke in the nineteenth century, or Richard Bell and Régis Blachère in the twentieth century, this might result in a confusing situation for many Muslims. These writers, in their attempts to renew Islamic studies, propose a re-ordering of the *Sūra*s of the Qur'ān, which may be of interest to non-Muslims, but which would leave the majority of Muslims bewildered.[1] The latter are more comfortable with the traditional ordering, which European writers of the early period do not attempt to disturb. Fidelity to European thought surely does not require me to give full exposure to an end product that is not recognized by Muslims? On the other hand, the recommendation, by many Orientalists, that Muslim sources should be jettisoned in favour of non-Muslim sources (that prove to be unreliable on close examination) will be discussed without prioritising the latter.

To make Muḥammad the sustained centre of attention for much of the time, rather than the rest of the Arab-Muslim civilisation, is to face a daunting task which, nevertheless, has its rewards. Keeping the discussion within strict chronological boundaries, desirable as this may be, is also quite difficult. Moreover, an assessment of the 'man' is to a large extent governed by external factors and attitudes to a world religion, which has renewed its challenge to the Christian West in terms of ideology and space. Of note is the reversal of roles and fortunes that has taken place over the last four centuries. The Ottoman Empire was extending into central Europe in the sixteenth century, attacking Mediterranean outposts such as Malta, Cyprus, Rhodes, and Crete. The end of the seventeenth century, however, marked the end of an era in its history. Following the defeat of its forces at the gates of Vienna (1683), and the signing of the Treaty of Karlowitz, Croatia (in 1699), the Ottomans were left with only a third of their Hungarian possessions. They were no longer the aggressive, expanding military power that had been feared for more than three centuries by Christian countries. The decline in their fortunes, which continued until 1923, undoubtedly had some impact on the image of Muḥammad in the West.

Islam as a subject has developed much in recent years, such that in addition to traditional approaches of history, philosophy, theology, and culture, it now also requires increasing attention to politics, economics, the environment, military, and social matters. For this reason, the field of enquiry needs to be limited. Although it may not always be possible to develop an argument entirely around Muḥammad, the narrowed focus on him and his message is justified. Western writers have been reacting to him for some fourteen centuries, producing a proliferation of biographies and shorter essays in European languages. In order to obtain a balanced appraisal, the discussion therefore has to concentrate on a number of carefully chosen writers, texts, and ideas. This may leave less room for an assessment of Muḥammad in popular literature, despite the fact that this literature may have been influential: giving it more exposure than I do here might have ensured the predominance of fantasy over reality, which is unnecessary, given that the historical figure of Muḥammad is available. Two further points are worth noting in relation to the scope of this study. One is that no individual writer is likely to offer a sound evaluation if their survey stretches from the beginning of Islam to the present. The other is that despite much talk of multidisciplinary studies in our times, few authors demonstrate a deep knowledge of both the European and Islamic material on the theme 'Muḥammad and the West', and this knowledge is, in my view, an essential requirement for understanding Islam

J. M. Buaben has published a work entitled *Image of the Prophet Muhammad in the West* (1996). However, its subtitle 'A Study of Muir, Margoliouth and Watt' indicates how limited it is in scope. Moreover, this book does not take into account some crucial studies by Montgomery Watt on Muḥammad. Similarly, two books published subsequently, while highly stimulating, have not managed to avoid the pitfalls of a long chronology: Norman Daniel's *Islam and the West* (1960, revised 1993) and Edward Said's *Orientalism* (1978). Clinton Bennett examines reactions to Muḥammad by the West in two chapters of *In Search of Muhammad* (1998): 'Non-Muslim lives of Muḥammad: from the 7th to the 16th centuries' and 'Non-Muslim lives: from the Renaissance to Today'. It is unlikely that a study covering some fourteen centuries of Western reactions to Muḥammad, compressed into two chapters, would be able to produce a satisfactory result. While fair in his evaluation of English–speaking writers, Bennett is less satisfactory when he comes to examine Boulainviller's and Voltaire's perceptions of Muḥammad, for example.[2] The titles of his chapters are useful, however, because they remind us that his book deals primarily with the attempts of non-Muslim writers to assess the Prophet, and less with those of Muslims who, for example, write in English or French about him. I follow a similar approach on the whole. However, Muslim writers who live in the West and who have distinguished themselves in their analysis of the relations between Islam and the West cannot be ignored.

Another book is *Muhammad in Europe* (2000) by Minou Reeves, which has as its subtitle 'A Thousand Years of Myth-Making': both title and subtitle are far too ambitious. Given its long chronology, the survey was bound to evidence many gaps. Moreover, it reads like defensive Muslim apologetics against the European Orientalists, theologians and missionaries who passed on errors and thus presented an erroneous image of Muḥammad.[3] This is not to suggest that Muslims do not have the right to interpret Islam according to their convictions[4]: they do indeed, but they must be seen to be faithful to European thought as well. Fidelity to both at the same time is perhaps the biggest challenge facing writers who engage in multidisciplinary appraisals of Muḥammad. Although Reeves' approach to the German contribution to studies on Islam is sound, especially in relation to Goethe's attitude to Muḥammad and on the impact of German thought on Carlyle, her scholarly approach is weaker in relation to French assessments of the Prophet. She puts perhaps too much emphasis on *Mahomet* at the expense of other important works by Voltaire on Muḥammad. Strangely enough, she offers no discussion of d'Herbelot or Rousseau.[5]

Writings on Islam and the Prophet have been dominated by Western writers who are not well-disposed towards them, and who have therefore sought to impose their perspectives on the Muslim world. There is hope that such cultural hegemony will gradually recede when more (and better-trained) scholars from the Arab-Muslim community come forward. Fortunately, this is increasingly the case, with growing numbers of contemporary scholars from this community demonstrating knowledge of both European and Islamic material.

It is true that these scholars do not all follow the traditional approach to Islam and the Prophet. Specialists in their own fields of study, they are also very much at ease with modern European languages, even if many of them are not also specialists of French and English thought. It is not enough to have a reading knowledge of these languages, rather it is essential to have actually read the texts written in them:[6] For instance, an author cannot be assessed simply on the basis of one article or text, yet this is what seems to have happened when the Arab-Muslim world delivered its verdict on d'Herbelot and Renan, for instance (see below). It is deplorable that the rhetoric against Islam and its Prophet (usually associated with the West) has in this instance been superseded by Arab-Muslim rhetoric against the West.

Nabil Matar, Professor of English at the University of Minnesota, has published works of considerable merit. These are *Islam in Britain, 1558-1685* (1998), followed by *Turks, Moors and Englishmen in the Age of Discovery* (1999) and a third volume *Britain and Barbary, 1589-1689* (2005).[7] Matar's first volume sacrifices chronology in order to present a persuasive framework, which makes it difficult to detect an evolutionary pattern in English attitudes. Nevertheless, his work as a whole is essential reading for anyone interested in the relations of Britain with the world of Islam in the sixteenth and seventeenth centuries. Matar's chapters on aspects of the representation of Muslims in early modern English drama are complemented by Daniel Vitkus's *Turning Turk: English Theater and the Multicultural Mediterranean, 1570-1630*

(2003). This explores English conceptions and misconceptions of the Turkish and Islamic perspectives against a background of cross-cultural encounters conducted through trade, rather than empire building, in the Mediterranean space.[8]

With regard to the modern period, Tariq Ramadan's work includes two impressive volumes: *To be a European Muslim* (1999) and *Islam, the West and the Challenges of Modernity* (2001).[9] In the first of these, Ramadan argues that European Muslims inhabit *dār al-shahāda* (abode of testimony) rather than *dār al-ḥarb* (abode of war). Indeed, the West is no longer *dār al-ḥarb* since Muslims are able to practise their religion openly, even though the political or executive authority is not Muslim. Ramadan adds that the life of Muslims must be a *testimony* to a permanent involvement and an infinite self-sacrifice for social justice and the environment, and that Muslim people must promote good and equity within and through *human brotherhood* (p.150). Unfortunately, his noble ideals have to some extent been undermined by the events of 9/11, which brought the West and Islam (or to be precise, a very tiny fraction of the latter), once again into direct conflict. Relationships have to be reassessed, and there is a widely-felt need to counteract the image of the Muslim *jihādī* who moves from Saudi Arabia to the US and back with great speed in order to destroy.

Aziz Al-Azmeh is the author of many books and has contributed significantly to studies on Ibn Khaldūn (1332-1406), the Tunisian historian and philosopher who was regarded by nineteenth-century French writers as an authority on the Qur'ān and who still commands much respect in the modern world. Al-Azmeh's two volumes on him, entitled *Ibn Khaldun in Modern Scholarship* (1981) and *Ibn Khaldun* (1982 and 1990),[10] are matched by the studies of the Moroccan scholar Abdesselam Cheddadi, who has an established reputation as an Ibn Khaldūn specialist due to works published in both Morocco and France. Cheddadi has probably produced the best edition of the *Muqaddima* (2002), the first volume of Ibn Khaldūn's monumental *History* (*Kitāb al-'Ibar*).[11] His historical study, *Les Arabes et l'appropriation de l'histoire* (2004) opens new perspectives on our understanding of the Prophet's life.

Mohammed Arkoun, formerly Professor of the history of Islamic thought at the University of Paris III, has published many books in France since the 1980s. His aim is to renew Islamic studies, judging by the title of one of his works, *Ouvertures sur l'Islam* (1989). However, in his publications and lectures, he gives the impression of being a neo-Orientalist, sometimes taking up the controversial positions dear to the Orientalists. Thus one of his theses is that Islam is a religion made up by people in a social context, reminiscent of the Orientalist view that Islam was created by Muslims some centuries after the Prophet. Such a view recalls the position of the authors of clandestine literature in the eighteenth century (see Chapter 2), and does not take into account the significance of revelation in Islam.

The term 'the West' or 'Europe' denotes too wide a geographical area: so many European nations are involved in Western reactions to Islam and its Prophet that one might achieve a better balance by dealing with writers from one or two countries, without overlooking the contribution of other nations.[12] For this reason, I refrain from using the word 'European' in my title, although the use of 'European' or 'the West' is often unavoidable within the text. I thus do not raise an expectation in the reader that he or she will find here an in-depth discussion of the perceptions of all European writers, including Russian and German ones. However, the importance given to French-speaking and English-speaking writers does require some explanation. From the sixteenth century onwards the interaction between England and France in the sphere of relations with the Islamic world, as in many others, is quite noticeable. One is sometimes struck by the similarity of French and English writers with regard to techniques used and treatment of Islam and Muḥammad.

In A Report of 1810, Bon-Joseph Dacier, *Secrétaire perpétuel* of the Institut de France, made the bold claim that France had done as much for Arabic literature as the rest of Europe put together. Although this should be treated with scepticism, one should nevertheless readily acknowledge that not only has France had a longer association with the world of Islam than any other European nation, but also that her writers have also produced some of the most distinguished works on Islam and the Prophet. In 1538, François I founded the first Chair of Arabic in France at the Collège Royal, and it was not until about a century later that the English established Chairs of Arabic at Cambridge and Oxford. Despite a later loss of momentum in these studies (which allowed other countries such as Holland and Germany to increase their contribution), there is no denying the fact that France played a major role in spreading knowledge of the Arabic, Turkish, and Persian languages and of the Islamic religion and civilisation from the sixteenth century onwards.[13]

For example, the reputation of Ibn Khaldūn in the world today owes much to the sustained efforts of nineteenth-century French-speaking Orientalists, prominent among whom were A-I Silvestre de Sacy (1758-1838), Professor of Arabic at the Collège de France, and his students A. F. E. Coquebert de Monbret, F. E. Schultz, E. Quatremère, W. MacGuckin de Slane (Irish by birth, but French by culture and principal interpreter of the French army in Algeria) and Garcin de Tassy. Their contribution to the rediscovery of Ibn Khaldūn in the West is a significant achievement, considering that when the *Muqaddima* appeared in Arabic for the first time in Tunis (in 1381), it did not give rise to any thorough discussion, and it failed to arouse any enthusiasm.[14] Silvestre De Sacy also promoted interest in the Islamic religion and civilisation in many of his works, including the *Chrestomathie arabe* (1806, 1826), a huge anthology of texts from all branches of Arabic literature, theology, and history (which he methodically arranged in order of rising difficulty and enriched by French translations), and historical, literary, and philological commentaries in French.[15]

The initial impetus for this research was provided by the diplomatic relations France enjoyed with the Ottoman Empire in the sixteenth century, when the latter's impact was felt in Europe. The dispatch of an ambassador to Istanbul by King François I (1515-1547) in 1535 led to France later acquiring military alliances.[16] François I pursued a policy of military collaboration with the Ottomans, despite the fact that three popes had invited him to participate in the Crusades. In 1535, he suggested a joint campaign with Suleyman the Magnificent (1520-1566) against the Hapsburgs. His offer led (a year later) to the first of a series of capitulations: treaties defining the status of foreigners in the Ottoman Empire and granting commercial and religious privileges to the French.[17]

The longest encounter with Muslims, after the French, was that of the Spanish in Al-Andalus. They maintained a lively interest in Islam, such that in the late fifteenth century (and throughout the sixteenth) many versions of the Qur'ān were produced in *aljamiado* (that is, Spanish texts using the Arabic alphabet) among the Mudejars and Moriscos. The Mudejars were Muslims in the Iberian Peninsula, who acquired the status of a protected religious minority, and the Moriscos were crypto-Muslims who were forced to pretend to be Christian converts.

The first Spanish translation of the Qur'ān was carried out under the Christian patronage of Spanish cleric Juan de Segovia (perhaps with polemic purposes in mind), by Muslim scholar Yça Gidelli, who was learned in Qur'ānic sciences and Islamic sources. Yça Gidelli was commissioned to produce a complete translation of the Qur'ān into Spanish, and this appeared in 1456. However, only Juan's Latin prologue to the work survives. A complete Spanish rendering of the Qur'ān (albeit in manuscript form, with a few interpolated commentaries) remains in Toledo. This uses Latin letters and was copied by an anonymous Morisco in 1606.[18]

The first complete published translation of the Qur'ān in the vernacular (French) was by André du Ryer (c. 1599-1672) in 1647. This later proved to be the model for translations in other European languages. Du Ryer was a remarkable diplomat, writer, and avid collector of oriental manuscripts, which eventually found their way to the Bibliothèque Nationale de France.[19] In 1623, his protector Savary de Brèves (Henri IV's former Ambassador to Istanbul) appointed him as vice-consul in Egypt. He fell into disgrace, but on Savary's recommendation du Ryer served as interpreter and secretary to the French Ambassador in Istanbul, Henri de Gournay, in 1631. Du Ryer must have been exceptionally well-favoured by Sultan Murad IV to be appointed as his ambassador extraordinary to France in 1632. Certainly, however, no conflict of interest was noted and du Ryer's friendly dealings with Ottoman officials in Istanbul must have created the feeling that he was a Turcophile.

Du Ryer's preface to his Qur'ān translation was off-putting, as he pandered to European prejudices against Islam in his summary of the religion. Nevertheless, these were perhaps techniques used to disguise his real sympathies, and the translation provides a reasonable rendering of the text. Du Ryer's translation was in turn anonymously translated into English in 1649, and though attributed to Alexander Ross (1592-1654), it was not by him. It gained greater currency through its indirect use in mid-seventeenth century England (see Chapter 1). In France, Montesquieu drew the attention of the reading public to it in four of the *Lettres Persanes* (1721). One of du Ryer's great achievements is his pioneering exposition of well-known commentaries on the Qur'ān, such as those of Al-Bayḍāwī and the Jalālayn (al-Maḥallī and al-Suyūṭī), which would otherwise have remained unknown to the general public. Marracci, Sale, and Edward Lane (in *Selections from the Kuran*, 1843) followed his lead, as did Antoine Galland and Barthélemy d'Herbelot when they used the vernacular in their oriental works and celebrated the cultural successes of the Arabs, Persians, and Turks.

The impact of Britain on the Arab-Muslim world has also been firmly established since the seventeenth century, with relations between Britain and the Barbary States steadily developing over a period of about a hundred years. The Barbary States formed part of a vast territory stretching between Egypt and the Atlantic, consisting of the Ottoman regencies of Algeria, Tunisia, and Libya and the kingdom of Morocco (although the latter was independent). In the seventh century, this region was ruled by the Arabs, who had introduced Islam. Many Britons, including traders, soldiers, sailors and travellers, had dealings with the Moors, Turks, Arabs, Moriscos, Jews, Armenians, and European renegades who lived there. Commercial, trade, and diplomatic exchanges actually started in the sixteenth century: a list of diplomatic agents is available at the Public Record Office, London, which shows that agents were sent to Barbary from 1577.[20] The defeat of the Spanish Armada in 1588 must have encouraged Mūlāy Aḥmad al-Manṣūr, king of Morocco, to view Elizabeth I as a possible military and diplomatic ally.

Cultural relations also developed between Britain and the Barbary States at this time. George Peele's *The Battle of Alcazar* (1589) was one of the first plays to show North African Moors on the London stage, and it depicted their encounter with Europeans during the 1578 battle of Alcazar in a historical framework and rather positively. However, when in 1689 John Dryden published *Don Sebastian*, a play revolving around the same battle (although using more fantasy), he gives a very negative image of the Moor; this may also be due to the fact that years earlier a large number of English captives had been seized and transported to North Africa. In *Britain and Barbary* Matar concludes that after this, the impact of the Barbary States on England became religiously and politically destabilising to the region (p.8).

In England, there seems to have been a deliberate policy of publicising the horrors of captivity in North Africa, while silence prevailed over captives taken in North America. A gloomy picture of British captives taken by corsairs on the high seas and near the Barbary coasts, and the horrors suffered by many of them was a subject of much discussion. In fact, an Act of Parliament was passed in 1641 for the 'Relief of Captives taken by Turkish, Moorish and other Pirates'. The modern reader is amazed to learn how dangerous these times were: hundreds of men, women and children were seized on the coasts of Britain and Ireland and taken to the slave-markets of Salé, Algiers, and Tunis. However, this horror was partly attenuated by the relatively good treatment some received. By 1650 there was no forcible conversion and intermarriage was not unknown.

The picture becomes more balanced when account is taken of the Barbary corsairs who were captured, taken to England and executed (often by poor European soldiers who had become well-paid *rais* or captains), although it is difficult to give the exact numbers of captives on either side. There may be some truth in the remark made in 1729 by John Morgan, the British trading agent in Algiers, that the seizing of European captives and their use as galley slaves, was an approach that had been learnt by the 'Barbarians' from the Christians themselves (Matar, *Britain and Barbary*, p. 113). The issue of captives becomes less important in the second half of the seventeenth century, when the naval supremacy of the British and the French meant that fewer captives were taken. Freed from this concern, these nations were among those that then turned their attention to empire-building.

This study dealing with the impact of Muḥammad on French and English literature begins with the period around the mid-1650s, after the publication of the English translation of the Qur'ān in 1649 (which was a landmark in the history of British perceptions of Islam and the Prophet). Whatever its weaknesses, this translation had an enormous impact on Britain from the mid-seventeenth century onwards (see Chapter 1). It was followed a year later by the publication of Edward Pococke's influential *Specimen Historiae Arabum*, which includes a brief biography of the Prophet. With the retreat of the Ottomans from Vienna in 1683, there followed renewed curiosity about Muḥammad: a curiosity that was just beginning to displace traditional hatred. From then on, and continuing to the present, interest in Islam and the Prophet has remained constant in the Western world. The timescale adopted in this study should help avoid the hasty generalisations that mar the efforts of those writers whose single-volume studies range from the earliest periods to present times.

There are two questions that are of particular relevance to this study: has there been any evolution in the status and perception of Muḥammad over the centuries? And if so, why did it take so long for Muḥammad to acquire the status of Prophet? The search for an evolution in attitude probably requires emphasis to be placed on a chronological (as opposed to a thematic) approach, although throughout the study (apart from Chapter 2 perhaps), Muḥammad and his message provide the centre on which everything else converges. Through this convergence, one may note the recurrence, at various points in the study, of two significant episodes involving Muḥammad: 1) the Night Journey and 2) his meeting with the monk named Baḥīra in Syria. The latter episode in particular has given rise to numerous conflicting interpretations.

What weight must be given to studies on Muḥammad by Orientalists? Jacques Berque stated in his *Leçon inaugurale* (1956) at the Collège de France that the Western scholar must work in partnership with those who know their societies and cultures from within.[21] It is a clear acknowledgement of the contribution that a Muslim scholar could make, for example, to studies on the Prophet, and of the fact that one could be objective about him. On the other hand, the corollary also seems true, that the Muslim scholar must work in partnership with the non-Muslim scholar. Nevertheless, this partnership remains difficult when Orientalists (who are more influential than other Western scholars) militate in favour of a complete rejection of Muslim sources. Conversely, the extent to which non-Muslim writers are fair, balanced, and accurate in their evaluation of Muḥammad is uncertain in light of the information available.

The most important events that have taken place in the Middle East have occurred in the last few decades of the twentieth century and thereafter, and are therefore still fresh in our minds. In this study, earlier events too need to be examined to provide a broad picture of the relations between Europe (particularly France and England) and the Arab-Muslim world. Relations between Europe and the rest of the Muslim world, important and interesting as they may be, are beyond the scope of this book. Historical landmarks might act as an injection of reality into a study where some attention is paid to literature of the imagination (Chapter 2).

Evaluations of the life of the Prophet are certainly not carried out in a vacuum: these require context. The increasing interest in Islam and its Prophet shown by French and English writers is partially due to penetration in the Middle East and North Africa by their compatriots, who had a variety of objectives in mind. Some of the historical events revolve round the occupation of Egypt by Napoleon (in 1798-1801); this is one of the ambivalences that characterize French relations with the world of Islam. Despite the fact that France and Islam came into direct conflict in Egypt, Egypt's French connection was strengthened later by Muḥammad Ali (1805-49), *vālī* of Egypt, who saw the benefit of having Egyptian military officers, doctors, and engineers trained in France and elsewhere in Europe. Thus relations were continually reassessed.

Napoleon's invasion cannot simply be viewed as an episode in the war between Britain and France: it had long-lasting repercussions and it marked the beginning of the Anglo-French domination of the Middle East for some two hundred years. After the Napoleonic wars, European armed power and influence over the Islamic world increased considerably as a result of growth in factory production, and rapid changes in means of communication. Europe needed raw materials for its factories and food for its increasing population. From about 1820, much of Egypt's cultivable land was used for the production of cotton, which was exported to the mills of Lancashire. Under Khedive Ismail (1862-79), Egypt severed its administrative links with the Ottoman Empire, only to become a cotton plantation serving the needs of the European market. Despite revenue accruing from the Suez Canal (which was built with French and Egyptian capital and opened in 1869), Egypt was unable to pay off its debts to European creditors. Egyptian nationalist struggles against European interests finally led to intervention by Britain in 1882.[22]

After its expulsion from Egypt by a British expeditionary force in 1801, the French army was keen to establish French power overseas, and was encouraged by a report on Algeria suggesting that Arabs and Berbers would, in their dislike of the Ottoman authorities, welcome the French, so long as they respected the religion, women, and property of Islam.[23] They therefore invaded Algeria in 1830: purporting to liberate it from Ottoman oppression, they actually began a brutal colonisation of the interior, under General Bugeaud. Local resistance under 'Abd al-Qādir (1808-83) finally crumbled in 1847. In 1863, in an attempt to reconcile various interests, the then ruler of France, Napoleon III, reversed the policy of dividing village lands and recognised the rights of cultivators to the land.[24] While the Arabs of Algeria were generally despised, the French (including de Tocqueville), thought that the Kabyles could be assimilated, as they appeared less devoted to Islam. French justifications of empire exist in the nineteenth century, for example those of de Tocqueville, author of *Rapport sur l'Algérie* (1847), and Jules Ferry (1832-97), the French Left leading champion of empire.

One may also note the Algeciras Convention of 1906 in which the 'Great Powers' determined the fate of Morocco. With the backing of Britain, France established a protectorate over Morocco in 1912. The Sykes-Picot Agreement of May 1916 divided the Arab provinces of the Ottoman Empire into zones of permanent influence, and the Treaty of Versailles (1919) stipulated that these countries could be recognised as independent, provided they accepted a 'mandate' from the European powers, which would give them assistance and advice.[25] French influence in the Islamic world expanded with the introduction of the mandates from the League of Nations into Syria and Lebanon.[26] France, which had invested heavily in Lebanon in the second half of the nineteenth century, departed half-heartedly from it in 1946, and the France-Morocco joint declaration of March 1956 provided for the independence of the Kingdom of Morocco. At nearly the same time (March 20, 1956), the Franco-Tunisian Treaty was signed, making Tunisia an independent country. After a long crisis, the Evian accords of 1962 ended more than 130 years of French rule in Algeria.

Some allowance may be made for the difficulties faced by French and English writers wanting to assess Islam and Muḥammad in the seventeenth century (see Chapter 1). Although they had du Ryer's and the 1649 English translations of the Qur'ān, access to Arabic dictionaries, grammar books, and other Arabic texts was limited. In the eighteenth century they could consult George Sale (c. 1697-1736), whose English translation of the Qur'ān (published in 1734) was actually preferred by writers such as Voltaire. Sale may, however, have been suspected of being a crypto-Muslim; in the *Essai sur les moeurs* (1756) at any rate, Voltaire invented a story that the latter spent twenty-five years in Arabia. As Chapter 1 of the present study shows, there is certainly no justification for concluding that all Protestant writers were champions of Islam and Muḥammad. Sale was better disposed towards the latter than major Roman Catholic writers such as Pascal, Bossuet, and the Arabists d'Herbelot and Gagnier. Little could be expected from Roman Catholic missionaries travelling to the Middle East in the seventeenth century and later, and there was no official statement from their Church on Islam to guide them. Nevertheless, they at least came face to face with Islam as practised, and their reports complemented the texts of those who stayed at home.

It will be noted that even those who speak well of Muḥammad in late seventeenth-century France often have an ulterior motive. For example, there is the attempt of Bayle (1647-1706), in the article 'Mahomet' of the *Dictionnaire historique et critique* (1697), who defends the Prophet from various charges; however, this must be seen as a camouflage adopted to attack the extremism of the Roman Catholics. Bayle, however, had enormous influence on later writers, including Veyssière de la Croze and Voltaire.

Works of the imagination do not of course have to satisfy the strict criteria of fairness, accuracy, and balance. In *The Satanic Verses* (1988), Salman Rushdie seems to have taken this idea beyond its limits. He is briefly mentioned here because he is a major novelist belonging to the English literary canon, who shows a fair knowledge of Islam in his book. Although he exhibits craftsmanship by very successfully blending various layers of material issuing from his own background, this is used to satirise Muḥammad's life and deeds in a way that is most offensive to Muslims. The vilification of Muḥammad (Mahound) and his wives through a travestied biographical novel, using stock medieval imagery, masks other issues such as alienation, loss of faith, and identity. Like Voltaire, Rushdie uses earlier materials, tales, and images to demonise Muḥammad. He has been excluded from other writers of imaginative literature dealing with Muḥammad (Chapter 2) because he has contributed nothing new to the formation of the image of Muḥammad in the West. He will, however, be remembered as the author of *Midnight's Children* (1981).

Voltaire's attack against Muḥammad through the character Mahomet somehow seems to provoke less outrage than Rushdie's, perhaps because Rushdie is seen to be attempting, single-handedly, to defy the whole Muslim world through a work which scholarly research does not support and which is not likely to blaze a trail. Viewed by many in the Western world as a hero for some two decades now and as a champion of free speech, he puts forward ideas that are figments of his imagination, but shows no originality in his use of Islamic material. Voltaire, on the other hand, articulates the inner convictions of large parts of eighteenth-century European civilisation through *Mahomet*: namely that Muḥammad was an impostor. Despite this, he does make amends to Islam and the Prophet elsewhere.

Unlike Rushdie, Marana and the authors of clandestine texts leave a progeny after them. While the age of the epistolary novel may be gone, the pioneering nature of Marana's masterpiece is important in terms of the stimulus it provides to the techniques of presenting ideas. Marana undoubtedly influenced Montesquieu in the *Lettres Persanes* (1721). For their part, the authors of clandestine literature invite readers to look at Islam and its Prophet with new eyes. In our times, their message is considered so significant that they have given rise to a dynamic and substantial output of critical editions of their works by international scholars (particularly from France and Britain), and thus these texts continue to contribute to a better knowledge of the Enlightenment.

In his thought-provoking book, *Les Arabes et l'appropriation de l'histoire*, A. Cheddadi has made some pertinent remarks on the nature of Arab historiography (p. 182). Following Bravmann,[27] he points out that *Sīra* (discussed in Chapters 4 and 5), especially in the phrase *Sīrat Rasūl Allāh*, does not mean biography, but the practice of the Prophet: that is, his way of dealing with particular situations or questions. In other words, biography is a secondary meaning of *Sīra*. Instead of questioning the reliability of the *Sīrat Rasūl Allāh* (the *Life of Muhammad*), by Ibn Isḥāq (704-767), as the Orientalists do, Cheddadi concentrates attention on an analysis of its contents in the version edited by Ibn Hishām (d.833). In his view, the central part of the text puts more emphasis on the message than on the messenger (and consequently on those to whom it is addressed) such that the personality of Muḥammad is eclipsed by the book he reveals (p. 200). It is as recipient of the message and as divine instrument that Muḥammad appears throughout his mission. To Cheddadi, Muḥammad's death is not so much the triumph of an individual as that of a community.

Although Boulainviller's *Vie de Mahomed* (Chapter 3) was read as a polemical work against Christianity in the eighteenth century, and despite the fact that the author did not have direct access to Arab sources, he must have had the intuition that Muḥammad's message was what mattered most. For this reason he focuses on the Prophet's teaching of religion, without emphasizing mystery. So too does Voltaire who (in works other than *Mahomet*) insists that Muḥammad spreads the idea of the unity of God. He also conveys the essential elements of Muḥammad's teaching. Despite their scepticism about religion and their more brief encounters with Islam, both Diderot and Rousseau (who are ambivalent towards Muḥammad) have their own contributions to make when they introduce him to a cultured public. Diderot highlights Muḥammad's achievement in extirpating idolatry among the pagan Arabs, while Rousseau (at his best) admires the legislator in Muḥammad. One, however, needs to become used to the contradictions of these three masters of the French Enlightenment.

Up to the second half of the eighteenth century, the use of Arab sources was not widespread (aside from d'Herbelot, Gagnier, and Sale). This situation changed in the latter part of the century and in the next (Chapter 4). In the works of Savary, Desvergers, and Murray, the Arab historian Abū al-Fidā (1273-1331) assumes increasing importance despite the fact that the biographical information he provides on the Prophet is late. The brevity of his account of the life of Muḥammad, and its balance, were particularly appreciated in the nineteenth century. However, Caussin de Perceval, Sprenger, and Muir gave greater weight to biographical material from earlier Arab authors such as the *Sīrat* of Ibn Isḥāq and the *Kitāb al-Maghāzī* by al-Wāqidī (d. 822). The *Tārīkh* (or *Annals*) of al-Ṭabarī (d.923) was used extensively, even by Lamartine who benefited from Zotenberg's translation of a shortened version (see Chapter 4). Important personalities in England and France (such as the non-Arabists Gibbon, Pastoret, and Barthélemy St-Hilaire) managed to present Muḥammad in a more favourable light, as a legislator, reformer, and leader of his people.

The extreme scepticism as to the worth of Muslim sources, displayed at the beginning of the twentieth century by L. Caetani, created a long tradition of challenging them, adopted by subsequent French- and English-speaking Orientalists, and led by the learned Jesuit Henri Lammens (Chapter 5). Lammens is clearly motivated by religious prejudice against Islam, and he does everything to discredit Muḥammad and his family. It is refreshing, then, to note the more moderate stand of Emile Dermenghem in *La Vie de Mahomet* (1929). Although Dermenghem admires Lammens's knowledge of Islamic sources, he points out the latter's antipathy to Islam. He appreciates the honesty of Muḥammad's biographers who do not hide his weaknesses, and so Dermenghem's contributions to the *Sīra* are much more than merely providing an example of hagiographical work (a failing which the more extreme among the Orientalists see in Muslim biographers of the Prophet)

In the 1950s, Régis Blachère (a translator of the Qur'ān), gives us a French view on the problems involved in the biography of Muḥammad, by boldly calling his work *Le Problème de Mahomet.* To a degree, he upholds the tradition inaugurated by Caetani and Lammens, but he does this with a certain restraint and dignity. Despite his opposition to Muslim Tradition, he does not engage in a blanket condemnation of all it has to offer. Worthy of note too is the work (in 1961) of the Marxist biographer of Muḥammad, Maxime Rodinson, who gives a critical but stimulating account of the Prophet. The Romanian Orthodox priest Virgil Gheorghiu is even more sympathetic towards Muḥammad in his *Vie de Mahomet* (1962).

Monsignor Virgil Gheorghiu seems happy with Muslim sources. He has some affinity with Montgomery Watt, Joseph Van Ess, and Hugh Kennedy, who on the whole accept the more traditional accounts of Islamic history. Others who are equally prolific but more radical in their approach such as Patricia Crone and Michael Cook continue the precedent set by John Wansbrough in *Qur'anic Studies* (1977) and *The Sectarian Milieu* (1978). Their book *Hagarism* (1977) is rather sensational: it raised an outcry when it first appeared because of its extreme theses, such as the origins of Islam being traceable back to the Fertile Crescent rather than the Hijaz.[28] Although this book provides a negative evaluation of Muslim accounts of Muḥammad, it is highly desirable to set *Hagarism* alongside other accounts to gain a more comprehensive view of the image of the Prophet in English writings, as its undoubted influence may be seen on G. R. Hawting's *The idea of idolatry and the emergence of Islam* (1999) and J. P. Berkey's *The Formation of Islam* (2003), although Berkey's theories sound a little more plausible and moderate. It would be surprising if more books coming from this 'school' were not in the pipeline. Even if one does not agree with the iconoclastic reinterpretations of Islamic history to be found in some French and English books, one cannot afford to bypass them completely. However, the time has now come for us to begin the investigation of Christian writers' attitudes to Muḥammad from the mid-seventeenth century.

Notes

1. Nöldeke, *Geschichte des Qorans* (Leipzig, 1860), Bell, *The Quran: Translated with a critical re-arrangement of the Surahs* (Edinburgh, 1937, 1939), 2 vols. and Blachère, *Le Coran: Traduction selon un essai de reclassement des Sourates* (Paris, 1947-51), 3 vols. See the chapter entitled 'The chronology of the Quran' in M.Watt's *Bell's Introduction to the Quran* (Edinburgh, 1970).
2. He takes *Futūḥ al-Shām* (*The Conquest of Syria*), translated by Simon Ockley as *History of the Saracens* (1708), to be the name of the author! See *In Search of Muhammad* (London, 1998), p. 98.
3. I use the word Orientalists throughout the book to mean writers (usually non-Muslim Europeans) who are engaged in scholarly studies of Islam, Arabic, Persian, and Turkish texts, without any of the pejorative connotations associated with Orientalism.
4. Hamilton Gibb argued in *Modern Trends in Islam* (Chicago, 1947) that it was not for Protestant Christians to refuse to Muslims, either as a community or as individuals, the right to reinterpret the documents and symbols of their faith in accordance with their own convictions (p. xii). Gibb's argument should of course extend to other non-Muslims.
5. Even stranger is the fact that she uses pages of an article of mine on French images of Islam, appearing in *British Journal for Eighteenth Century Studies* (1991) as if it was published anonymously!
6. Reviewing my book *Perceptions of Islam in European Writings* (Markfield, 2004) in the *Times Literary Supplement*, October 2004, Robert Irwin felt that my predecessors in the field did not bother with reading the writers they referred to.
7. See my review of it in *Journal of Islamic Studies*, 18, no. 1, Jan. 2007, pp. 147-49.
8. See Andrew Duxfield's review of the book in *Early Modern Literary Studies* 12.3 (January, 2007).
9. His *Life of Muhammad* (2007) is a traditional Muslim biography.
10. In his volume on *Islams and Modernities* (1993, 1996) he seeks by the use of the plural in the title to establish *inter alia* that Islam is not a monolithic religion. That may well be, but to write of 'Islams' when he has in mind the varied practices prevailing in Muslim societies does not take sufficient account of the unifying factors in the religion.
11. See *Le Livre des Exemples*, text translated and annotated by A. Cheddadi (Paris, 2002).
12. The Germans are particularly important from the eighteenth century onwards. For J. J. Reiske's edition of Abū al-Fidā's *Life of Muhammad* under the title *Annales Muslemici* in 1754, see Chapter 1.
13. A major contribution to Qur'ānic studies was that of the German scholar Theodor Nöldeke, winner of the prize of Académie des Inscriptions et Belles-Lettres in 1857 for *A Critical History of the Text of the Coran*. Revised and

enlarged, it was published in 1860 as *Geschiste des Qorans* and became the foundation of later European studies of the Qur'ān. L. Krehl enriched studies on the Traditionist Al-Bukhārī with his edition of the *Ṣaḥīḥ*, under the title of *Le Recueil des traditions mahométanes* (Leiden, 1862-68), 3 vols. Vol. 4 was edited by Th. W. Juynboll (Leiden, 1908).

14. See Cheddadi's edition, p. xxxvi.
15. Equally important was the work of Noël des Vergers, another French Orientalist who has been unduly neglected in the modern period. He complemented de Slane's account of Maghrib history when in 1841 he published a translation of select passages of Ibn Khaldūn's *History* dealing with North Africa under the title *Histoire de l'Afrique sous la dynastie des Aghlabites et de la Sicile sous la domination musulmane*, with Arabic text and translation.
16. England too realised the importance of having diplomatic relations with the Ottoman Empire, but it was some fifty years later that the first English Ambassador, William Harborne, was sent to Istanbul.
17. See William Watson, *Tricolor and Crescent, France and the Islamic world* (Westport, 2003), p. 10.
18. See Consuelo Lopez–Morillas, 'Lost and Found? Yça of Segovia and the Qur'ān among the Mudejars and Moriscos', *Journal of Islamic Studies*, 10.3 (1999), pp. 277-292.
19. An outstanding book on du Ryer by Alastair Hamilton and Francis Richard is entitled *André du Ryer and Oriental Studies in Seventeenth-Century France* (Oxford, 2004). See my review of it in *Journal of Islamic Studies*, 16, no. 3, September 2005, pp. 409-411.
20. See N. Matar, *Britain and Barbary, 1589-1689* (Gainesville, FL, 2005), pp. 3-4.
21. See Albert Hourani, *Islam in European Thought* (Cambridge, 1991), p. 130.
22. See Albert Hourani, *A History of the Arab Peoples* (London, 1991), pp. 260-287.
23. See D. Hopwood, *Sexual Encounters in the Middle East* (Reading, 1999), p. 87.
24. Hourani, pp. 270-71.
25. The Arabs who had supported the Allies against the Turks in World War I were bitterly disappointed by the peace negotiations, which did not provide for their independence, but rather for French and British mandatory rule over many Arab territories. French mandatory rule was established in Syria and Lebanon, while British mandatory rule was established in Iraq, Kuwait, and Palestine. See W. E. Watson, *Tricolor and Crescent: France and the Islamic World* (Westport, 2003), p. 204.
26. In *Western Imperialism in the Middle East, 1914-1958* (Oxford, 2006), D. K. Fieldhouse concludes that the best achievement of the mandates was the creation of 'a system of states with viable western-type governmental institutions with the potential to develop into nations' (p. 347). See Jennifer M. Dueck's review of the book in *French Studies*, vol. LXI, no. 4 (2007), pp. 542-43.
27. M. M. Bravmann, *The Spiritual Background of Early Islam* (Leiden, 1972).
28. P. Crone's book, *Meccan trade and the rise of Islam* (1987) is unashamedly polemical. It was written against Montgomery Watt, who had linked the rise of Islam with spice trade in Makka before the Prophet.

1

Muḥammad in Christian Thought, 1650-1750

In the times of Emperor Charles V (1500-1558), church bells rang in German towns to remind people of the Turkish menace. Turkey (or, more accurately, the Ottoman Empire), although later considered moribund by Europeans, had, at that time, a greater standing than Arabia in politico-economic affairs. Many Western writers referred to 'Turk' and 'Turkey': these terms were not used by the Ottomans themselves but are often unavoidable. The 'dread of the Turks' did not disappear completely even after 1571, when their navy was crushed at the battle of Lepanto by the Holy Alliance of Spain, Venice, and the Papacy. Such a defeat did not necessarily lead to a decisive shift in the balance of sea power, since the Ottomans retained Cyprus, forced the withdrawal of Venice from the Christian alliance in 1573, and conquered Tunisia in 1574.[1] More significant was the failure of the Ottomans to capture Vienna in 1683, when they were driven from it for a second time by a coalition of Christian forces. With the ensuing retreat, the long-standing Muslim threat to Europe ended.

Islam and its Prophet did not, however, suddenly disappear from the scene. After the religious animosity of the Middle Ages and the end of the Ottoman threat, a period of relative calm followed, just before the colonial expansion of the nineteenth century. This period may have provided the right atmosphere for a balanced evaluation of the Prophet by the West. It was certainly conducive to a revived interest in the Ottoman Empire and Sunnī Islam (which was the dominant religion of its various peoples). We shall see in Chapter 4 that, despite appearances, the colonial period was not inimical to the diffusion of knowledge about Islam and the Prophet. In the latter part of the seventeenth century, however, European attention began to shift from the Qur'ān to Muḥammad himself, who continued to be perceived as the 'author' of the book.

European interest in the 'other' was not confined solely to the Ottoman Empire. Although Persia (arch rival to the Ottoman Empire) was late in developing its relations with European countries, it made great strides in the seventeenth century. Persia is of special significance from a theological point of view. At the outset, some Europeans might have been interested in Persia as the birthplace of Zoroaster (founder of the ancient religion of Zoroastrianism) and later as the home of Manes (the heresiarch founder of Manichaeism in the third century A.D.). In the seventeenth century, however, European missionaries primarily encountered Shī'ī Islam within Persia (this version of Islam had been established there since the beginning of the sixteenth century). It is worth mentioning that Shī'ī Muslims are to be found in other countries, including Arabia, Iraq, India, and Pakistan, however, only in Persia was this the state religion.

During the reign of Shāh 'Abbās I (1587-1618) of the Safavid dynasty (1501-1722), ambassadors came from France to take up residence in the capital, Isfahan. The reign of Louis XIII (1610-1643) in France witnessed a constant exchange of ambassadors between the two countries. 'Abbās also allowed European missionaries to settle in the main towns of his empire. Like travellers and diplomats, Roman Catholic missionaries sought to gain a foothold in the Middle East, but their aims were naturally different from the former; as they were particularly interested in the conversion of Muslims, they were looking for ways to show how misguided these people were. Their activities in the Middle East had been boosted by the foundation of the Sacra Congregatio de Propaganda Fide (in 1622), which was established by the Council of Trent (1545-1563). The conversion of 'infidels' formed part of a grand design that had been elaborated in Rome, and the missionaries who were sent to the Orient under the auspices of the Congregatio belonged to various orders: Carmelite, Capucine, Dominican, Augustinian and Jesuit. Eager to specialise in the languages of the countries where they had been posted, some of them acquired a thorough grasp of Persian, Turkish, and Arabic. In the Ottoman Empire, the missionaries were tolerated, and exempt from capitation, but they made few converts among the Muslims and the non-Catholic Christian minorities. They did not meet with any greater success in Persia, although they were welcomed with much courtesy by the Shāh.[2]

Europeans who came into contact with the Persians (that is, travellers, traders, diplomats, and missionaries), could not fail to be impressed by the affection the Persians showed for members of the Prophet's family, especially his cousin and son-in-law 'Alī and his daughter Fāṭima. The greatest sign of affection was, however, reserved for his grandson Ḥusayn, who has always been regarded as a martyr by Shīʿites. For Ḥusayn died tragically and heroically on the battlefield at Karbala in Iraq in 680, while fighting an army of the Umayyads with a handful of men. To Christian missionaries and others, Muḥarram (the festival which is celebrated during the first ten days of the same month with such gusto by Shīʿites) must have recalled memories of passion plays. Travellers could easily note its special significance in the Shīʿite calendar, which is marked by celebrations to commemorate the death of Imām Ḥusayn.[3] But their visits, like their interest in the Middle East and its main religion of Islam, were often fleeting. They had different motives from those of the missionaries, and little time or inclination to undertake a thorough evaluation of Islam and its Prophet. So it fell to the Roman Catholic missionaries, who generally stayed longer in the Middle East, to show a more sustained curiosity about Islam and Muḥammad.

Roman Catholic writers

It should be pointed out that missionaries within the Roman Catholic Church were not the only people to develop an interest in Islam and Muḥammad. Indeed, Roman Catholic writers can be divided into two categories: 1) those who never travelled to Muslim lands of the Middle East and elsewhere, yet happily made their observations from home on the basis of (received) textual information and 2) members of the clergy (such as missionaries) who did travel. The latter had the opportunity to encounter aspects of living Islam on their trips abroad. We may, however, begin with one of the most distinguished in the first category, Pascal.

The brilliant Jansenist polemicist, who in the *Lettres Provinciales* (1656) had denounced laxity in Jesuit thinking, and who was such a keen apologist of the Christian faith, was not likely to let Muḥammad off lightly in the *Pensées* (1669, 1670). So, in article IX of the text entitled 'La Perpétuité', he begins by claiming that all religions other than Christianity are false, because they have no witnesses. He argues that since Muḥammad is lacking in authority, the reasons he supplies rely solely on their own merit and must therefore be powerful to be effective. Pascal proceeds by asking a number of rhetorical questions in the manner of the *Lettres Provinciales*, and making various statements, which tend to show Muḥammad in a bad light.[4]

An objective approach is always difficult when one personality is set against another. Pascal asks: 'Who bears witness to Muḥammad?' The reply he gives is Muḥammad himself. Pascal wants to judge Muḥammad not by what is obscure in him, but by what is clear, such as his teaching on paradise, which Pascal claims is what makes Muḥammad ridiculous. Pascal reasons that, given the assertion that these less obscure teachings are untenable, it is therefore not possible to take Muḥammad's obscurities for mysteries. He then begins a series of comparisons between the Qur'ān and the Bible, Muḥammad and Jesus. He admits that obscurities as strange as those of Muḥammad may exist in the Bible, but argues that the Bible also contains admirable truths and clear prophecies that have been accomplished.

Pascal carefully lays the ground for the climax of his argument: a straightforward comparison between Jesus and Muḥammad, the purpose of which is to show how inferior the latter is to the former. On three occasions he harps on the idea that Muḥammad, unlike Jesus, has not been foretold. Apart from repetition, Pascal's rhetoric consists of a number of antitheses: Muḥammad kills people whereas Jesus has his disciples killed, and Muḥammad chose to be successful in a human way, while Jesus chose to die in the same way. According to Pascal, one should not conclude that since Muḥammad was successful Jesus too could have been, but rather that since Muḥammad was successful Jesus had to die. He claims that anyone could have done what Muḥammad did (that is, that he did not perform any miracles) and that no one can do what Jesus did. He hints that Muḥammad had himself called prophet without having taught any mystery, and that he did not engage in any moral teaching. He finally seeks to reinforce the myth that Muḥammad forbade his disciples to read the Qur'ān. One recognises here some of the medieval criticisms levelled against Muḥammad, which included the accusations that he preached ignorance, propagated Islam by force, and did not perform any miracles. In fact, Muḥammad never claimed that he could perform miracles, and far from forbidding his disciples to study the Qur'ān, he made some of them memorise it in his lifetime so that an authorised text would remain for posterity.[5] Thus numerous commentators of the Qur'ān have appeared since the earliest times.

On the whole, Roman Catholic missionaries in the Middle East, on encountering living Islam, appeared to have little interest in commenting on the visual aspects of religious ceremonies and contemporary events they witnessed.[6] They tried rather to explain the historical factors that lay behind the divisions in Islam and to give a partial evaluation of Muḥammad's role in history. Among these missionaries was the Capucine friar Gabriel de Chinon, who spent twenty years in Isfahan from 1640. He learned Armenian, Turkish, Persian, and other oriental languages, speaking them with ease. Having set up a mission of his order at Tauris and another in the mountains of Kurdistan, he wrote his observations of Persia during his stay there. After Gabriel de Chinon's death in 1670 Louis Moréri revised his work and published it in 1671 under the title *Relations nouvelles du Levant ou Traités de la religion des Perses, des Arméniens et des Gaures*. Chinon's account of Islam and the Prophet is written entirely from a Shī'ite point of view, and it betrays prejudice against Sunnīs. He traces the origin of the split between Shī'ites and Sunnīs to the time of the Prophet's death, and although this cannot be challenged, the statement that Muḥammad proclaimed 'Alī his successor before forty thousand people at Ghadīr al-Khumm (the pond of Khumm between Makka and Madīna near al-Juḥfa, on the trade route between Syria and Yemen) is inaccurate. Rather, after the campaign in the Yemen, the Prophet made a farewell pilgrimage to Makka (in 632) and then returned to Madīna. On his way back, one of the troops bitterly complained of 'Alī to the Prophet. Later on the journey, when they had halted at Ghadīr al-Khumm, Muḥammad gathered all the people together and, taking 'Alī by the hand, said: 'O God, be the friend of him who is his friend, and the foe of him who is his foe', after which the protests against 'Alī stopped.[7]

Chinon has some understanding of the importance of the *imāms* to Shī'ite believers, although he exaggerates when he says that before his death Muḥammad, on God's commandment, transmitted his authority to twelve *imāms* and to twelve grandsons or nephews, descendants of

Ali. He echoes a Shīʿite viewpoint here. The Shīʿites claim that if the imāms are not given proper recognition by Muslims, the latter commit an act of rebellion punishable by God in the next world. They even say that God has given signs of his indignation by making the last *imām* invisible (p. 32). Chinon sounds authentic here, as the Shīʿites believe that the twelfth *imām* suddenly disappeared in the year 874 without leaving a successor, and that he is not dead, but hidden somewhere, so that on a day appointed by God he will come back among the people in order to convert everyone to Islam. In an earlier period, the idea gained ground among some Shīʿites that Muḥammad ibn al-Ḥanafiya, their *imām* (who had seemingly died in 700), was not dead but in concealment, and that at the proper time he would return as the *mahdī* (the nearest Judaeo-Christian equivalent to this term would be Messiah). The conception of the hidden *imām* was used by the Imamites about the end of the ninth century and applied to the twelfth and last of their *imāms*.[8] A belief in the coming of the *mahdī* is not restricted to Shīʿites, as many Sunnīs also share this belief. According to the Traditionist Abū Dāwūd (d.889) in his *Sunan*, the Prophet is reported to have said that the *mahdī* would be of his stock, and would fill the earth with right and justice and would reign seven years.

Ange de Saint-Joseph (1636-1697), a Carmelite missionary and a possible source of information on Persia to Jean Chardin, author of the famous *Voyages en Perse* (1686), spent some fourteen years in Persia, Iraq, and Turkey from 1664 to 1678. In 1684 he published the *Gazophylacium linguae Persarum*, a dictionary written in Italian, Latin, French, and Persian.[9] Although not the first Persian dictionary published in Europe, it gave serious European readers some assistance in coping with a difficult language. The small in-folio has the unusual merit of reflecting simultaneously European images of the Orient and of Christian Europe. Its image of Islam and the Prophet, based on both the author's experience and his reading of oriental and European sources, contains a mixture of the expected and of the unexpected. In the entry entitled 'Mahomet' (pp. 140-141, ed. Bastiaensen), the most sensational information relates to the dates of Muḥammad's birth and death.[10] After quoting Arab authors, who trace his genealogy back to Ismāʿīl, son of Abraham, the missionary states categorically (but without giving any source) that Muḥammad was born in 578 A.D. and that he lived for sixty-three years. This would make the year of his death 641, whereas history accepts the event as occurring in 632. Both the European and Persian versions observe that Muḥammad lived for forty years before he claimed to be a Prophet.

The article also refers to the belief by Muslim scholars that there is an allusion to Muḥammad in Deuteronomy 33:2, where Moses said to the Israelites: 'The Lord came from Sinai/ and shone forth from Seir./ He showed himself from Mount Paran' (*Souvenirs de la Perse safavide*, ed. M. Bastiaensen, pp.140-141). Jewish and Islamic traditions consider these three regions as the symbol of the three great monotheist religions. Sinai recalls Moses and Judaism, Seir was the dwelling place of Esau (ancestor of the Christians) and Paran is the name of the desert where Hagar was sent back with Ismail, ancestor of the Arabs.[11] In *Gazophylacium linguae Persarum*, 'Mahomet' mentions the assertion by Muslim scholars that the verse aludes to the descent of the Pentateuch on Moses, the Gospel on Christ and the Qur'ān on Muḥammad. It also alludes to another verse of the Psalms (50:2): 'God shines out from Zion, perfect in beauty'. According to Bastiaensen (p. 208, n. 284), this interpretation becomes possible if one plays on the root *ḥ-m-d* (meaning praised), and its derivative *Muḥammad.*

Another Roman Catholic missionary to the Levant was Father Michel Nau (1631-1683), superior of the Jesuit mission in Aleppo. In *L'Etat présent de la religion mahométane* (1684) Nau provides a caricatured account of the nature of God in Islam, and further denigrates Islam by exaggerating its Prophet's status in the eyes of Muslims who, allegedly, turn him into 'le chef-d'oeuvre des mains de Dieu, le premier des prédestinés et l'homme incomparable en toute sorte d'excellence' (p. 8) In an approach that is later adopted by d'Herbelot, Nau attributes to Muslims the false idea that God created all people, and the whole universe, only with Muḥammad in view, and that people would be saved and be able to enter Paradise only through him. Another inaccurate idea of Nau is that on Judgement Day the prayers of all saints other than his will be rejected, although it is true that Muḥammad's intervention on behalf of sinful members of his community is generally accepted by Muslims.

According to Nau, people reproached the latter with believing in a Prophet who could not perform miracles, and this sense of shame made them invent the fabulous stories that are to be found in his biography. As an example, he quotes the episode in which the young Muḥammad is taken by his uncle Abū Ṭālib with a merchant caravan to Bostra, Syria. There Muḥammad meets the monk Baḥīra who foretells his future prophethood, asking Abū Ṭālib to protect him from his enemies. This episode appears in the earliest biography of Muḥammad and Muslims have never objected to its inclusion there.[12]

Nau, in *L'Etat présent de la religion mahométane*, shows astonishment at the expansion of Islam throughout the world, on the grounds that it is so visibly false (p. 28). In his view, Muḥammad himself would have found it difficult to explain the progress of his religion. Nau claims that judging by what one sees in the Qur'ān, Muḥammad had no intention of extending it beyond Arabia. He quotes lines from *Sūra* 42 ('The Counsel') to prove that Islam was intended for a restricted public, and indicates that he does not find any instruction from Muḥammad to his disciples that Islamic doctrine should be spread throughout the world. Nau, of course, fails to quote *Sūras* 7, l. 158, and 34, l. 28, in which it is clear that Muḥammad's mission is addressed to all humankind. Nau further argues that since Muḥammad was encountering Arabs who were not very enlightened and given over to sensual pleasure, he had simply pandered to their lust. While there is some restraint in Nau's reference to sensuality, there is less restraint in the reason he puts forward to explain the ban on alcohol to Muslims. The origin of the prohibition, according to Nau, can be traced back to a day when the drunkard Muḥammad killed one of his best friends, looked for the murderer in his intoxicated state and learnt that it was himself! (I,136). There is absolutely no foundation in Islamic history for this story.

The Jesuit missionary nevertheless tried to do some justice to the Prophet. He claims that shortly before his death, Muḥammad wished to repair the injury he had done to Christians: thus Muḥammad drew up a will in their favour, commanding his followers to live in friendship with them, render them services, and even help them build their churches and monasteries. Nau suggests that it is perhaps because of the last wishes of their Prophet that Muslims have some consideration and respect for Christian priests and monks.[13] He may be referring to the fact that a deputation of Christians from Najran (Yemen) came to make a pact with Muḥammad. The latter signed a favourable treaty, according to which (in return for the payment of taxes), they were to have the full protection of the Islamic state for themselves, their churches, and other possessions.

One writer who did not travel to the Middle East, but who was probably more distinguished in the Roman Catholic Church hierarchy, was Bossuet (1627-1704), Bishop of Meaux. He was known for his didactic and polemical writings in defence of Catholic faith and morals. Unfettered in his day by any official declaration of the Church (the Vatican Council statement on Islam was to be made some three centuries later in 1965), Bossuet spread his negative thoughts on the Prophet without the slightest hesitation, although he would have been able to claim that he was writing in a personal capacity and that the Catholic Church was not involved in his pronouncement.

In the *Discours sur l'histoire universelle* (1681) he mentions, very briefly, the arrival of the Prophet on the world stage, although not in approving terms. While the power of the Persians under Chosroes II had been held in check, Bossuet claimed that 'a greater evil rose against the Roman Empire and against the whole of Christendom': this evil was Muḥammad, who 'declared himself a prophet among the Saracens' (p.132). Bossuet adds that the false prophet provided his victories as the only mark of his mission to make the whole of Arabia submit to him willingly or by force within nine years and thereby to lay the foundations for the empire of the caliphs (p.132). With such laconic observations on Islam and Muḥammad he could not, of course, sum up Islamic civilisation in its entirety, but he had done enough to strengthen the Christian perception of Muḥammad as an evil force and an impostor.

A close contemporary of Bossuet was Louis Moréri (1643-1680), who studied theology at Lyon and took his orders there. He published the first volume of his *Grand Dictionnaire historique* in 1673, but the second volume was published in 1681, after his death. The article on Muḥammad in his book makes painful reading: he starts by describing him as the famous impostor and false prophet, and then claims that Muḥammad's father was a pagan and his mother a Jewess (both of them being the most abject from the dregs of society), despite the claims by Muḥammad's disciples of his royal ancestry and genealogy traceable to Adam. In the account of Moréri, Muḥammad was a liar and a vindictive villain who committed all sorts of crimes: poverty forced him to serve a rich merchant, and on the latter's death he cajoled the merchant's widow into marrying him, thereby becoming her heir and using her wealth to aggrandise himself. There is no basis for Moréri's allegations about Muḥammad's suspicious dealings with the widow he married, Khadīja. Generally, Moréri circulated all the medieval myths about Muḥammad (such as his falling into epileptic fits and using a pigeon to whisper things into his ears). It is no wonder that Pierre Bayle wanted to refute all these myths in his *Dictionnaire historique et critique*.

Barthélemy d'Herbelot (1625-1695), like Pascal, Bossuet, and Moréri, had experienced no direct contact with the Middle East, although he had made long stays in Italy. Nevertheless, he more than made up for his lack of contact with his extensive knowledge of Arabic, Persian, and Turkish. Indeed, in the *Discours pour servir de préface à la Bibliothèque Orientale* (1697) Antoine Galland (1646-1715), destined to become Professor of Arabic at the Collège Royal from 1709, paid a glowing tribute to d'Herbelot's mastery of these languages. Galland asserted that this was a necessary ability because Arab, Persian, and Turkish authors each deal better with the affairs of their respective nations. D'Herbelot was able to use the oriental manuscripts which Galland had been collecting for the Bibliothèque Royale (Nationale) on Colbert's instructions in the period 1679-1685. He thus studied oriental history, geography, and theology at its source, although he chose rather late Arab and Persian authors such as Al-Zamakhsharī (1075-1144), the Qur'ānic commentator, Abū al-Faraj (1225-1286), the Christian Arab historian, Abū al-Fidā, and Ḥusayn Wā'iẓ (d. 1505). His most important source, however, was Ḥajjī Khalīfa (1608-1657), the Ottoman historian and bibliographer whose *Kashf al-Ẓunūn* listed and described some 14500 books in Arabic, Persian, and Turkish.[14] Ḥājjī Khalīfa's alphabetical arrangement may have provided a model for d'Herbelot, and the latter managed to compile the oriental dictionary which Galland had planned but which he never completed. In the *Discours*, Galland also lavished high praise on d'Herbelot for being an excellent Christian theologian. Given the extent of the prejudice prevailing against Islam at the time, Galland's eulogy of d'Herbelot as theologian might make one feel somewhat apprehensive about the presentation of Muḥammad in the *Bibliothèque orientale*, published in 1697 after its author's death.[15]

Before becoming Professor of oriental languages at the Collège Royal in 1692, d'Herbelot had been sent to Italy in 1656 by the Archbishop of Aix, Cardinal Jérôme Grimaldi. In Rome he met Queen Christina of Sweden (1626-1689) who made a solemn appearance there after her conversion to Roman Catholicism. As a faithful son of the Catholic Church in the seventeenth century, d'Herbelot could not be expected to be neutral towards Muḥammad. Yet his account of some Muslim personalities (other than the Prophet) in the *Bibliothèque* was not unfair. He may have felt that there was no harm in raising the status of other Muslims at Muḥammad's expense. Like other devout writers, d'Herbelot knew too well Muḥammad's crucial role in spreading Islam.

In line with the above technique, d'Herbelot pays the highest compliment to Abū Bakr, when he claims that *Sūra* 92 was revealed in honour of a memorable act performed by him during Muḥammad's lifetime. Apparently, when Abū Bakr had purchased Bilāl (the Ethiopian slave who had been tortured on account of his faith), the enemies of Islam stated that he did this only out of self-interest. In response to this, d'Herbelot suggests that the description in *Sūra* 92, l.18-20 ('Those who spend their wealth/ For increase in self-purification,/ And have in their minds/ No favour from anyone/ For which a reward / Is expected in return,/ But only the desire/ To seek for the countenance/ Of their Lord Most High'), admirably fits Abū Bakr. For his description of Abū Bakr's qualities, d'Herbelot was using material from the late commentator Ḥusayn Wā'iẓ, although the earlier commentator of the Qur'ān and great Sunnī theologian, Fakhr al-Dīn al-Rāzı (1149-1209), had also referred to Abū Bakr's sincerity, fidelity, disinterestedness, and generosity.[16] D'Herbelot also devotes a long article to 'Alī, the fourth Caliph of Islam. In fact, he gives 'Alī lengthier treatment than he does to Muḥammad in a separate article on the Prophet life. This is not because his aim was to project Shī'ite views of Islam: if he appears to have given more importance to 'Alī than to the Prophet it is because a major part of the entry is taken up with 'Alī's military struggles.

As the *Bibliothèque orientale* is an enormous and erudite compendium, one cannot fully do justice to it by commenting on only one article, and should mention the existence of balanced articles such as 'Din' and 'Eslam'. Towards the end of the latter, d'Herbelot refers to what he calls one of the *authentic traditions*, according to which, Jesus, at his second coming, will unite all religions and sects into Islam. He has no doubt that Muslims really mean Christianity when they talk of Islam. According to the commentator al-Ṭabarī (839-923), on the return of Christ, the triumph of Islam will be complete: the Jews will believe in him and Christians will renounce the Trinity.[17] D'Herbelot takes the opportunity to criticise both Muslims and Muḥammad, for he adds that it would be very convenient for their false Prophet to unite all religions to 'Mahométisme'. What he fails to appreciate is that by referring to the second coming of Jesus, Muslims actually elevate his status, as they do not extend the same honour of attributing a second mission to Muḥammad.

Although d 'Herbelot's achievement in other articles cannot be denied, the focus has to be on the article 'Mohammed'. Here, the devout Catholic writer destroys the delicate balance that characterises the articles 'Din' and 'Eslam' and refuses to give Muḥammad the title of Prophet. He instead bluntly describes him as the famous impostor, founder of the heresy which assumed the name of religion called Mohammedan. In this, he seems to echo sentiments of the polemical work of John of Damascus.[18]

In 'Mohammed', d 'Herbelot perversely (but conveniently), forgets the correct definition of the religion proclaimed by Muḥammad, which he had himself given in the article 'Eslam'. He castigates the Qur'ānic commentators and other Muslim doctors for having transferred to Muḥammad all the praise that the Arians, Paulicians, and other heretics bestowed on Christ, while stripping him of his divinity. By attributing to these commentators the notion that Muḥammad was created before time, that the world was created only for him, and that he is the only mediator between God and humanity, d'Herbelot projects an image of Muḥammad with which the majority of Muslims are unfamiliar. The Qur'ānic commentators are made to say that the first thing created by God was light, which is very much in harmony with holy scripture, but they also claim that this light was a substance from which Muḥammad's soul was extracted and thereafter those of other creatures, including those of the patriarchs and prophets. D'Herbelot is not particularly interested in Muḥammad's personality, claiming that everyone has readily available copies of Eutychius' *Annals*, Abū al-Faraj's *Dynasties*, and Erpenius' *History of the Saracens*. Although he gives details about Muḥammad's genealogy that are accurate, d'Herbelot attributes to all Muslims, quite inaccurately, the belief that the Caliphate should more appropriately have gone to the Hashimite family, and that the Umayyad Caliphs were therefore usurpers. His main aim, however, is to denounce Muḥammad's supposed ignorance and imposture.

D'Herbelot takes particular objection to *Sūra* 7, l. 157, where Muḥammad is described as 'the "unlettered" Prophet whom they find written down with them in the Torah and the Gospel'. To him, this is the coarsest imposture used by the false Prophet to convince the Jews and Christians of the truth of his mission. He suggests that Muslims claim that the word 'Paraclete' (John xiv, 16) meaning comforter, is the same as 'Muḥammad', meaning worthy of praise.[19] In fact, Muslims read 'Periklutos' (that is, illustrious) instead of 'Paracletos'. According to d'Herbelot, in *Sūra* 61, l. 6, Muḥammad wanted to strengthen this belief (as the certainty and truth of his mission depends on this) when he makes Jesus say, when addressing the Jews: 'I am the apostle of God/ Sent to you confirming/ The Law (which came)/ Before me, and giving/ Glad tidings of an Apostle/ To come after me,/ Whose name shall be Aḥmad'. D'Herbelot takes delight in pointing out that the proof that Muḥammad adduces to authorise his mission is not found in the texts to which he refers his disciples. Thus, d'Herbelot asserts that the imposture will not carry weight with anyone who uses the light of their reason. The irony of this is that in 'Din', d'Herbelot seemed to approve of the Muslim writers who frowned upon the use of reason as a path to God.

To achieve his aim of presenting Muḥammad in a grotesque light, d'Herbelot attributes the most exaggerated traits to him. Thus he quotes one mystic who has reportedly said that Muḥammad contains in his person all perfection created and uncreated, that he holds the balance between all the proportions and links that are to be found in the three forms, angelic, human, and animal. Moreover, this mystic claims that the world is but a discharge of Muḥammad's qualities, and all men are in relation to him like conquered subjects and slaves, who simply exist to extol his graces. Based on this, d'Herbelot claims that Muḥammad had the impudence to proclaim loudly that he was the lord of the children of Adam, and that Adam and his children have to fight under his banner!

It seems that d'Herbelot does distinguish between mystics and the main body of Muslims (who do not bestow such qualities on Muḥammad). Nevertheless, he argues that the latter, although less likely to extol such lavish praises, see miracles where there are none, and that they turn Muḥammad's memorable acts into miracles. He notes that among these 'miracles' are the battles Muḥammad fought, which d'Herbelot indicates show the character of the 'false' Prophet (about whom, he claims, only an imperfect idea has been given up to now) and therefore should be discussed at length. He does not see fit to point out that Muḥammad fought battles (in self-defence) only in the last eight years of his life, and so instead of discussing the achievements of Muḥammad as social and moral reformer (about which he maintains almost complete silence), he focuses attention on his military campaigns.

In his description of Muḥammad as a military leader, d'Herbelot chooses an episode of the battle of Badr (a location fifty miles to the south-west of Madīna) in 624, in which the Muslims were fighting superior numbers of Makkans. Purportedly, Muḥammad threw a handful of small pebbles at the enemy as he turned towards Quraysh, saying 'Foul be those faces!', which had a powerful psychological effect, and this was followed by a successful battle: 'Then he ordered his companions to charge. The foe was routed. God slew many of their chiefs and made captives many of their nobles'.[20] According to d'Herbelot, the pride of the Muslims became so inflated that Muḥammad 'published' *Sūra* 8, l. 17, which insists that it was God who threw dust at the enemy and slew them. D'Herbelot embellishes this account by suggesting that the dust literally covered the faces of the Makkans and prevented them from fighting, and that Muḥammad's troops then attacked the enemy. Although there is mention of a thousand angels at l. 9, the Qur'ānic commentator Fakhr ad–Dīn al-Rāzī (1145-1209) rejects the intervention of angels and gives the line a metaphorical interpretation that is supported by *Sūra* 3, l. 124-125, where there is a reference to three and five thousand angels.[21]

D'Herbelot argues that like Jews and Christians, Muslims recognise that victories come from God and do not depend on the number and the worth of troops. To illustrate this, he narrates what happened to Muḥammad at the battle of Ḥunayn (about fourteen miles to the east of Makka), after the conquest of the city in 630. Muḥammad had set out with an army of about 12,000 troops to face a smaller army of about 4000. Some Muslim tribes who boasted of their strength and military skill were reprimanded by Muḥammad. The superior numbers of the Muslims proved to be of no avail and they had to retreat. D'Herbelot's account is fairly accurate up to this point, and he states that when Muslims had recourse to God, He at last gave them victory. However, while the text of the Qur'ān (*Sūra* 9, l. 26) actually reads: 'God poured His calm on the Apostle and on the believers and sent down forces which ye saw not', d'Herbelot states that it is claimed that God sent invisible troops of angels to Muḥammad's rescue.

In 'Mohammed', d'Herbelot also takes shelter behind the Prophet's enemies to depict him as a fickle man, who passed a few laws only to abrogate them. He quotes, as examples, the change of the *qibla* (the direction Muslims face in prayer) from Jerusalem to Makka, and the fact that Muḥammad retained all the ceremonies practised by the idol-worshippers in the temple of Makka, although he had supposedly suppressed idolatry (for a further discussion of idolatry, see chapter 5). The final picture of Muḥammad that emerges in the article is that, apart from being a man full of contradictions, he played the role of comedian up to the time of his death. The flimsy evidence adduced by d'Herbelot to prove this last point is that Muḥammad, being consumed by poison and fearing a violent death, caused the *Sūra al-Naṣr* (110), called by Muslims the 'Farewell' *Sūra*, to descend from heaven, because it was the last that he received before his death (Muḥammad's death is alleged by d'Herbelot to have taken place two years later, in fact, Muḥammad died only a few months later). D'Herbelot quotes al-Zamakhsharī, who is alleged to have said that Muḥammad summoned his daughter Fāṭima after this *Sūra* was revealed and informed her that he had received a letter from heaven announcing his return there: and that he was thinking of going and sending his luggage in advance! Contrary to d'Herbelot's statements here, Muslim historians do not record that Muḥammad died from a poison administered by a woman in the pay of his enemies.

We can now determine if the first half of the eighteenth century made any difference in the perceptions of Muḥammad by French Roman Catholic writers. It seems that there was, at first, a wish to maintain the tradition of the seventeenth century, when some writers made their evaluation of the Prophet not in full-length biographies but in shorter texts (such as a dictionary article, a dissertation, a *discours* or a 'notice'). For instance, when the abbé de Vertot (1655-1735), a member of the Académie des Inscriptions et Belles Lettres, read a 'Dissertation sur l'Auteur de l'Alcoran' at the end of a session of the Académie on the 14 November 1724, there was absolutely no doubt in his mind that Muḥammad was the author of the Qur'ān. His address is characterised by some of the clichés that came to be associated with Muḥammad from the Middle Ages: that Muḥammad favoured loose morals and the Qur'ān was lacking in divine inspiration and originality.

These clichés reached a wider readership, since the *Mercure de France* of December of that year gave a full account of the *Dissertation*. The readers of the journal learnt from Vertot that the illiterate Muḥammad had dealings with people who were apparently even more ignorant than himself, and that the wealth he acquired through marriage enabled him to increase his standing among the Makkans. The *Dissertation* stressed Muḥammad's alleged hypocrisy and that all the austerity he affected in his external conduct, including his retreat to a solitary place, masked his true intention of studying the contents of the Old and New Testaments and of drawing from them what might suit his project of founding a new religion. In this account, the self-contradiction of the abbé is glaring, for he is reconstructing the picture of an illiterate Muḥammad who reads the Bible! Even those who have doubts about Muḥammad's illiteracy have at least recognised that he was 'unscriptured'.[22] While many Western writers refer to the assistance Muḥammad is supposed to have received from a Jew and a Nestorian monk (Sergius), Vertot further invents a story about Muḥammad closeting himself with these two men over a period of two years.

Muḥammad's licentiousness is repeatedly stressed in the *Dissertation*, which is reproduced at the end of Volume I of the *Histoire des Chevaliers de Malte* by Vertot.[23] He devotes a number of pages to Muḥammad at the beginning of the later work. Here the 'infidel' Persians of Bossuet's *Discours sur l'Histoire universelle* have become the barbarians who were being challenged by the Roman Emperor Heraclius. The greatest challenge, however, was provided in the deserts of Arabia by 'one of those restless and ambitious men who seem born just to change the face of the world' (p. 4). This reference to changing the face of the world is not meant as a compliment: it infers a change for the worst. Vertot sees Muḥammad as the most skilful and dangerous impostor to appear in Asia, and claims that it was marriage to a rich widow (Khadīja) that fostered Muḥammad's ambition for glory and independence. He further suggests that wealth without domination proved insufficient to Muḥammad; thus Muḥammad used religion to achieve his aim, 'a device used by many an impostor before' (p. 5). It does not occur to Vertot that Muḥammad never proclaimed that he was setting up a new religion. Muḥammad, before his 'revelations', is represented as a voluptuous man who eventually abandoned his licentious companions to 'turn over a new leaf'. To Vertot, the 'revelations' were nothing but epileptic fits, which the clever impostor passed off as ecstatic trances.

Nevertheless, Vertot feels the need to redress the balance slightly in favour of Muḥammad by outlining his more positive qualities. To do this, he relies on Ibn al-'Amīd, (that is, George El-Makin, 1205-1273), a Coptic Christian whose world-encompassing *History* was translated into Latin in 1625 (as *Historica saracenica*) by Erpenius (Thomas van Erpe (1584-1625)), Professor of oriental languages at Leiden. It was also translated into French in 1657 (as *L'Histoire mahométane*) by Pierre Vattier (1623-1667), Professor of Arabic at the Collège Royal. El-Makin had used Muslim historians, mainly al-Ṭabarī, and that is perhaps why Vertot's study is occasionally favourable to Muḥammad. The picture of the Prophet that emerges through this source is of a man with noble bearing, gentle and modest looks. He is also pictured as persuasive, quick-witted and possessing all the qualities required of a party leader. In accomplishing his designs, he displayed a firm spirit and courage that triumphed over the greatest dangers.

What strikes Vertot above all is that Muḥammad excelled in a type of oriental eloquence, consisting of parables and allegories, with which he bedecked his speech. Vertot sees this eloquence reflected in what he calls 'the bombastic and figurative style' of the Qur'ān, where Muḥammad attempts to imitate the sublime features of the beginning of the Book of Genesis and the pathos of the true Prophets. At the risk of contradicting himself, Vertot now says that Muḥammad did not claim to have founded a new religion, but to purify that which was corrupt in older religions. He refers to the Muslim belief that Muḥammad was the last of the Prophets, but inaccurately attributes to him the claim that he was greater than Moses and Jesus. The discourse ends on a negative note: that Muḥammad borrowed from the Jews the principle of the existence and unity of God in order to consolidate his religion. The Christians had provided Muḥammad with the examples of fasting, the frequent use of prayer (which he fixed to five daily),[24] charity towards the poor, and forgiveness of one's enemies. Vertot insinuates that to propagate his errors the clever impostor spoke a few truths and even put on an air of great virtue, and the only evolution he sees in Muḥammad is that after having been a robber he became a conqueror.

Another Roman Catholic priest (and a former member of the Académie française), the abbé de Saint-Pierre (1658-1743), contributed to the formation of the image of Muḥammad in French writings of the first half of the eighteenth century. Admitted to the Académie in 1695, but expelled from it in 1718 for his criticism of Louis XIV in the *Polysynodie*, the abbé de Saint-Pierre published the *Discours contre le mahométisme* with his *Ouvrages de politique* in 1733. In the *Discours*, Saint-Pierre puts forward the (at that time novel) idea that Muḥammad was a fanatic of good faith for some time, and that he would never have succeeded in converting his wife, relatives, and neighbours to believe in the truth and reality of his visions if he had begun as an impostor; Muḥammad was apparently the first to be deceived and that made him more disposed to deceive others. According to Saint-Pierre, Muḥammad recognised his errors afterwards, but he refrained from undeceiving others. So, from being a fanatic, he became an impostor in order to exploit the errors into which he and his followers had fallen: the abbé concludes that there was nothing remarkable about this. Saint-Pierre does not, of course, explain how Muḥammad continued to deceive millions of people after his death.

Two factors which he emphasises in his attempt to account for the rise of Muḥammad are those of climate and imagination. Since the climate of Arabia is particularly hot, he argues, the imagination of the Arabs is consequently more fertile. Saint-Pierre argues that as imagination in hot countries represents more vividly the good and evil to come, whoever has the talent and the eloquence to portray visions of a great future evil to the ignorant can lead them to believe in it. Thus the persuasive Muḥammad had a natural advantage in depicting the delights of an eternal Paradise and the woes of Hell, because no men could be more ignorant than the Arabs! Saint-Pierre forgets to mention that the temperate climate of Europe did not prevent Virgil, Dante, and Milton from representing the torments of Hell so vividly. Since he attaches so much importance to climate, he argues that the region that is more likely to foster various types of fanaticism is the one that is most affected by the sun. He does not, however, state whether the fact of living in equatorial latitudes and being the most exposed to a torrid sun turns some communities into fanatics: unlike Vertot, Saint-Pierre finds in Muḥammad's patriarchal religion no trace of Christianity, but a coarse mixture of the old paganism and Judaism.

According to Saint-Pierre, Muḥammad begins by having dreams in which he thinks he is talking to the angel Gabriel, and he ends up believing that his dreams are revelations. This insistence on divine revelation induces him to lie, and he then decides to exploit the illness of those whom he has made ill with this lie. Saint-Pierre then makes the surprising comparison between Muḥammad (on the one hand) and Descartes and Malebranche (on the other). He argues that although the latter Frenchmen surpassed Muḥammad a thousand times in knowledge, it is highly unlikely that they would have had Muḥammad's power of persuasion (to convince the ignorant Khadīja about Gabriel's revelations). Saint-Pierre writes that the ignorant Muḥammad 'made ill by his visions, easily does with his contagious disease what Descartes would never have been able to do with his great mind , through surprise and fear' (p.123). Saint-Pierre sees hypocrisy everywhere in Islam, arguing that Muḥammad was not the only hypocrite. He cites as an example Abū Sufyān, Muḥammad's former enemy who converted to Islam, and who won the confidence of others and gained much through hypocrisy.[25] In the abbé de Saint-Pierre's text, the fundamental teachings of Muḥammad are only indirectly given to the reader. Even this is only a fleeting glimpse where Muḥammad apparently imagines in a dream that an angel shows him repeatedly how to avoid Hell and obtain Paradise by renouncing idolatry, observing justice, fasting, practising charity, and pilgrimage.

In view of their negative attitude towards Muḥammad, Vertot and Saint-Pierre had never given any thought to the idea that Muslims might actually be converted through their texts. Ange de Saint-Joseph, on the other hand, was entitled to hope that his dictionary of spoken Persian would not only help Europeans converse with Iranians, but also facilitate the preaching of Catholicism among the latter. There was even the hope that the Shāh might convert to Christianity, although this did not materialise. Earlier on, the diplomat André du Ryer, despite having little interest in religion, had produced the first complete translation of the Qur'ān into the vernacular (French). He too seems to have had the missionaries in mind (he claimed that the translation would be helpful to them). However they do not appear to have taken much notice of it.

Protestant writers

While the French Roman Catholic missionaries were busy trying to convert people in Persia, the English Protestants did not remain completely inactive. In England, a partnership was being forged between members of the clergy and laymen, in order to bring about the conversion of Muslims. Following the French and the Dutch, the English eventually established chairs of Arabic at Cambridge (1632) and Oxford (1636) Universities. Founder of the Cambridge chair, Thomas Adam (a prosperous draper), hoped that it would help convert Muslims; and that apart from disseminating widely the treasures of the Arabic language, the chair would contribute 'in God's good time to the enlarging of the borders of the Church and the propagating of the Christian religion to them who now sit in darkness'.[26]

William Laud, Archbishop of Canterbury from 1633 to 1645, was interested in oriental languages partly because he believed that Arabic (for example) could be of some use in clarifying obscurities in Hebrew grammar. When he founded the Oxford Chair of Arabic that bears his name, his protégé Edward Pococke (1604-1691) was the first to be appointed to it in 1636. Pococke finished his tour of duty in Aleppo as chaplain to the Levant Company from 1630 to 1636, and afterwards spent three years in Constantinople, looking for manuscripts. In Syria he had devoted all the time he could spare from his ministerial duties to the study of Arabic, Hebrew, Syriac, and Ethiopian. This led to the publication of his monumental *Specimen historiae Arabum* (1650), which was later to inspire many writers. The book was made up of an excerpt from the Arabic chronicle *Tārīkh mukhtaṣar al-duwal*, by the Syrian Christian writer Bar Hebraeus (Abū al-Faraj ibn al-Ibrī, 1225-1286) with a translation and some 300 pages of notes in Latin.

In his notes to the biography of the Prophet (included in the text), Pococke poured scorn on the miracles attributed to him by Christian writers. What may be even more significant for Christian-Muslim relations of the period is Pococke's Arabic translation of Hugo Grotius's *De veritate religionis Christianae* in 1660.[27] Copies of the translation containing only the Arabic text were specially prepared for the Arab world and distributed afterwards by R. Huntington, chaplain at Aleppo, from 1670.[28] Its purpose was the conversion of Muslims who were well-disposed towards Christianity.

Grotius, a Dutch Arminian apologist, enjoyed the reputation of a best-selling author when his *De veritate religionis*, first published in 1627, was republished in French translations in 1649, 1659, and 1692, and in English translations from 1680 onwards. Its vogue continued into the eighteenth century. Grotius agreed to excise some puerile fables regarding Muḥammad that had been falsely attributed to Muslims, at the insistence of Pococke, who asked for permission to make changes in his Arabic translation when he visited Grotius in Paris. However, the latter remained hostile to Islam and Muḥammad and Pococke himself continued to look on Muḥammad as the great impostor and Islam as the religion of the false prophet.

The six books of *The Truth of the Christian Religion* deal *inter alia* with the 'confutation' or refutation of the 'religions opposite to Christianity', and Islam is included among these religions. The sixth book is devoted to a 'Confutation of Mahumetanisme' (English tr., p.164). Grotius anticipates the authors of clandestine texts (see below) by comparing Jesus and Muḥammad, although his aim is different to theirs: while the clandestine writers later attempt to negate the influence of both, Grotius wishes, like Pascal, to elevate the former at the expense of the latter. Starting with a comparison of the two 'in their person' (p.207), he argues that Muḥammad himself accepts that Christ was the Messiah as promised in the Law, and that he calls Christ the word of God. To Sunnite Muslims, the word of God is the Qur'ān, and to all Muslims Jesus is 'a word from God'. The confusion between 'a word' and 'the word' is in itself not such a terrible mistake; what is deplorable is that in his desire to demonstrate the superiority of Christ over Muḥammad, Grotius denigrates both the public and private life of the latter. The mere fact that Muḥammad was buried in Madīna is used against him: Grotius remarks that Muḥammad is still in his tomb, whereas Jesus is in heaven. This contrast between Muḥammad and Christ is sharpened by reference to their deeds. Christ's raising of the dead, Grotius argues, has no parallel, and Grotius quotes Muḥammad as saying that he was not sent to perform miracles, but that whatever miracles were attributed to him by his followers were such as could be done by humans. This comparison is a device used by Grotius to belittle Muḥammad, by concentrating on the legends that grew up around him. Bayle, on the other hand, took an entirely different stand by dismissing these legends (see below).

In England, Alexander Ross showed that he had other aims than those of Grotius. Although he did not know Arabic, the translation of the Qur'ān which went under his name (based on du Ryer's), was read by all sections of English society, including Oliver Cromwell, who made good use of some of its teachings. Matar quotes a letter to the ruler of Algiers in June 1656, in which Cromwell referred to Algerians as men who had declared themselves 'hitherto in all things to be men loving righteousnesse, hating wrong and observing faithfulnesse in covenant'.[29] As he points out, these words are reminiscent of a Qur'ānic injunction, although he is rather vague about the precise wording of the Qur'ān. Several times the Qur'ān orders Muslims to do what is just and forbids them to do wrong: for example, in *Sūra* 7, l. 157, the Prophet himself is presented as the author of the injunction which Cromwell appears to echo. In our times, this has inspired Michael Cook to produce a monumental work of scholarship entitled *Commanding Right and Forbidding Wrong in Islamic Thought* (2000), where he attempts to chart the history of Islamic reflection on this duty.

Ross made some additions to du Ryer, including a 'Life and Death of Mahomet' at the end of the work. In the 1688 edition of the translation, after his death, these were moved to the beginning of the text. The 'Life', definitely by Ross, reproduced legendary stories betraying anti-Muslim chauvinism. Yet the result is not entirely negative, for Ross inaugurated a tradition of juxtaposing Qur'ān translation with an account of the life of Muḥammad, and this was later perfected both by Sale and Savary (see below).

There is an apparent link in the attitudes of some French and English writers towards Muslims in the seventeenth century. Ross gives the impression that he appreciates the zeal 'Mahometans' show in works of devotion, piety, and charity, although the extent to which this admiration is genuine remains questionable. Pétis de La Croix, on the other hand, who was Secretary to Ambassador De Nointel at the French Embassy in Constantinople, seems more sincere in his eulogy of Turks, when in an unpublished *Mémoire* (dating from 1682) he claims that they put Christians to shame when it comes to devotion to religion, and he is clearly moved by their approach to prayer.[30] De La Croix seems to have had no polemical purpose, whereas Ross, as a staunch Royalist in the English Civil wars, used Muslims to combat the regicides of his country and did not hesitate to appeal to the Qur'ān in his attack on Commonwealth authority.

A work that attracted much attention in late seventeenth-century Europe, especially in England, was *Ḥayy Ibn Yaqẓān* ('Alive Son of Awake') written by Ibn Ṭufayl (c.1105-1185).[31] The latter, a mentor of Ibn Rushd or Averroes (1126-1198), was born in the small town of Guadix, north-east of Granada. Like Averroes, he was keen to reconcile religion and philosophy.[32] His romance was translated from the Arabic into Latin as *Philosophus autodidactus* in 1671 by Edward Pococke the Younger, and into English from the Latin by the Quaker George Keith in 1674 and George Ashwell in 1686. In 1708 Simon Ockley translated it from the Arabic as *The improvement of human reason*.[33] One of its ideas is that humanity carries within the potential for finding truth without the help of an established church. This idea had a strong appeal to Quakers who were also believers in 'inner light', and their leader, Robert Barclay, even used it in his *Apology for the True Christian Divinity* (1678). Although Ibn Ṭufayl's romance belongs, more appropriately, to the domain of Islamic philosophy (as it is a blend of Aristotelian and Neo-Platonic thought), the use of the text had a bearing on the mentality of the age with regard to Muḥammad.

As N. Matar has shown, the appeal of *Ḥayy* was possible only because the text had been 'de-Islamicised': allusions to the Prophet were removed from the Latin and English versions.[34] In the opening epistle of the Arabic original, Ibn Ṭufayl concludes his invocation by referring to Muḥammad as God's servant and messenger, which is followed by three lines of praise for the Prophet and his family. I do not, however, share Matar's view that the character Ḥayy, having examined the natural world around his island, ascended through the seven stages of reason to obtain knowledge of God that was exactly similar to Qur'ānic principles (p. 98). This would effectively turn the character Ḥayy into a deist, whereas Islamic teaching on reason is finely balanced. In the seventeenth and eighteenth centuries many European deists saw Islam as a form of deism.

Unlike these European deists, D'Herbelot understands well the position of Muslims on the limitations of reason, and he restricts deistic views to only a few Muslims in the article 'Din' of the *Bibliothèque orientale*. Seemingly authentic in his projection of a Muslim distrust of reason, he refers to unnamed Arabic and Persian poets, who denounce belief in one's own light as leading to impiety, and who conclude that one must abandon this attachment to it as this is self-idolatry. After relying on commentators who suggest that those who already believe through the demonstrative reason of faith should now believe by virtue of the supreme truth, he quotes a fifteenth-century writer, 'Umar Naqshbandī. This writer says that in verse 136 from *Sūra* 4 ('You who believe! Believe in God and his Apostle'), believers are commanded to abandon their own reason, in order to adhere to the supreme reason of God.

However interesting, *Ḥayy* is not primarily about Muḥammad, so we must return to the latter and note the gap that separates Grotius from Henry Stubbe (1632-1676) in their writings on the subject. The work of Stubbe, a physician and friend of Thomas Hobbes and Sir Henry Vane, was probably composed around 1673. It circulated in manuscript form for a long time and was published only in the twentieth century. The printed version is entitled *An Account of the rise and progress of Mahometanism with the Life of Mahomet. And a Vindication of him and his Religion from the calumnies of Christians.*[35] Although Stubbe relies heavily on Pococke, he offers a favourable account of the early life of Muḥammad, mentioning that 'during his infancy, he gave pregnant signs of a singular nature, great art and good behaviour' (Sloane 1709, f.97), and reiterating that at age twenty Muḥammad gave proof of his valour in a fight between the Quraysh and another tribe. Stubbe defends Muḥammad against the charge that he was a mere camel driver, and clearly has little doubt about the nobility of Muḥammad's birth. Criticism of Muḥammad for this employment, Stubbe argues, is a sign of envy, considering that camels in the times of Muḥammad were closely associated with the wealth of the Arabs.

Stubbe pays glowing tribute to the character of Muḥammad who, in his view, was provided with 'all the qualifications requisite in a person cut out for great achievements and equally qualified for actions of war or the arts of peace and civil government'.[36] Stubbe claims that Muḥammad was not ignorant of the teaching of the various Christian sects then living in Arabia (such as the Trinitarians, Jacobites, Nestorians, Arians) and Jews. He notes that Western writers, ignoring this fact, gave Muḥammad two assistants, 'Abdullāh (a Jew), and Sergius (a Nestorian monk) and represented him as an ignorant person, who was unable to evaluate what had been instilled into him. In a relation of some years travaile (1634), for instance, Thomas Herbert claimed that Muḥammad 'concocted'the Qur'ān from Sergius (p.152). However, having decided to dispel some of the myths that circulated about Muḥammad, Stubbe proceeds to invent a few of his own: thus the Prophet's first wife Khadija is made to live in Syria and to employ her cousin, Warakah ibn Naufal, a Christian, to teach Muḥammad to write, since (in Stubbe's view) there were few among his tribe who could write. While Stubbe makes a fair point about the lack of literacy among the Quraysh, his information regarding Khadīja's stay in Syria (p. 77) or the tutoring of Muḥammad by Waraqa, has no foundation in Islamic history (although it is true that Waraqa could read). Waraqa had made a study of the scriptures and of theology and felt, like Baḥīra, that the coming of the prophet would be in his lifetime.[37]

Another myth suggested by Stubbe concerns Muḥammad's travels abroad: he apparently travelled to Africa and from there passed into Spain in 605. Again, there is nothing in the sources to justify this claim. This alleged trip to Spain, however, served Stubbe's purpose of identifying Muḥammad as exploiting the divisions among Christian sects. Stubbe seized the opportunity to denounce the Spanish king for forcing his subjects to become Trinitarians, pointing out that much of the population were of Gothic origin, and that they had always been staunch Arians; Muḥammad nevertheless, according to Stubbe, tried to inculcate some of his teachings into them. The myth of Muḥammad's journey to Spain and his preaching to the Spanish people who were opposed to the Trinity may have led P. M. Holt to the conclusion that Stubbe's work is merely an anti-Trinitarian tract.[38] However, although it was certainly anti-Trinitarian, it also tries to present Muḥammad in a positive light. Stubbe, for example, admires Muḥammad's quick repartee and 'sublimity of thought and quaintness of speech' (f. 98).

No such admiration was felt for Muḥammad by Jacques Abbadie (d.1727), who was perhaps the best known French Protestant apologist of the late seventeenth century. There was a truly European dimension to his career as preacher and minister of religion and in his writings one certainly finds a good example of the interaction between England and France. While spending part of his life in England and in Ireland (where he became dean of Killaloe in 1689), Abbadie continued to write in French. He had been a pastor in Berlin (in the 1680s) before moving back to London in 1690, and he came across as a type of spiritual leader within the Protestant community in England and Ireland.[39] His *Traité de la vérité de la religion Chrétienne*, which was first published in 1684, was translated into English, German, Dutch, and Italian and was reprinted many times. It is worth a close examination because of the high acclaim its author received from both Roman Catholics and Protestants.

Abbadie says in it that his definition of true religion (being knowledge and love of God, obedience to Him and the practice of virtue for His love), may create some difficulty in people's minds, since by espousing these same qualities, Muḥammad is supposed to have spread knowledge of the true God everywhere, although he was an impostor. Abbadie, however, finds no difficulty in accepting this, and suggests that there are two factors in Islam that need to be taken into consideration: (1) it is based on something that is true and even divine. This divine element is a legacy from the Christianity, which Muslims used to profess (Islam being simply a corrupt version of this) and (2) it is also, on the other hand, based on something that is false and human: namely, that which Muḥammad has added to Christianity. Abbadie's reputation as writer and preacher relies heavily on rhetoric, and here we see an example of it in the antithesis that he uses to divide Islam into two component parts.

He introduces into the debate arguments that have no historical foundation; contrary to his assertions, the Arabs Muḥammad converted were not primarily Christians, but rather pagans. Abbadie claims that Christianity has the exclusive right to proclaim knowledge of the true God. In his view, it is a mistake to say that Muḥammad established this knowledge; rather it would be more accurate to say that he corrupted what had been secured before him. Thus an unflattering image of the Prophet emerges in some Protestant writings: the robber gives way to the corrupter.

The idea that Christ and Muḥammad were moved by the same spirit seems contemptible to Abbadie. Somewhat like Grotius, but even more like the Pascal of the *Pensées*, he focuses on what he calls the 'essential differences' between the two religious leaders. He begins with a series of negatives: that Muḥammad did not claim to establish his religion by miracles and did not leave behind prophecies that had been fulfilled; and that Muḥammad is surrounded by soldiers, while Christ is surrounded by martyrs (the former produces death, the latter receives death for us). There is nothing new in much of Abbadie's attack, since it rests on old fallacies about the Prophet, such as his encouragement of loose morals and the suppression of books which could enlighten people. The pastor stresses the fraudulent nature of the mission of Muḥammad who, he says, at first promises to tolerate other religions and is pleasant towards Christianity, but then attempts to destroy them. What is original in Abbadie's thinking is the idea that Muḥammad must adopt the same methods of self-justification as Jesus. He would have liked Muḥammad to die and then to resurrect so as to show that he had won God's approval. Abbadie forgets completely that he had himself admitted that Muḥammad did not justify his religion by miracles.

Whereas other writers (such as Montesquieu in the *Lettres Persanes* (1721) and Lamartine in the *Voyage d'Orient* in 1836) hint that Muḥammad teaches Muslims to neglect this world and to concentrate on the next , Abbadie unambiguously depicts him as a preacher who places excessive emphasis on material progress in this world. Through his use of rhetoric, he suggests, with scarcely concealed irony, that Muḥammad may be divinely inspired if it is true that those who enjoy prosperity in the world are loved by God. On that reckoning, the wicked, the unjust, and tyrants must be God's favourites. More seriously, he suggests that to establish the basis of his calling, Muḥammad should have used scripture instead of casting doubts on it. To a certain extent, Abbadie acknowledges Muḥammad's achievement as legislator by saying that he cared for the protection of the most sacred rights and, therefore, retained the idea of a true God. But this praise is immediately qualified, for he attributes to Muḥammad the desire to pander to people's inclinations as a means to attract them to his faith: he borrows from Christianity to mortify passions and from paganism to flatter the baser instincts.

The attack against Muḥammad is pursued even more vigorously in the *Traité de la divinité de notre seigneur Jésus Christ* (1690). Abbadie assumes that everyone acknowledges Muḥammad to be an impostor whose technique rests on a number of unproved suppositions. Thus he wonders, if indeed Muḥammad has opened people's eyes about Christian idolatry, (he ironically suggests Christian worship of Jesus would be idolatry if the latter is not the supreme God), by what means he accomplished such a great task: was it through God or through the

Devil? If it was through the Devil, it is difficult to comprehend how Muḥammad was successful in abolishing idolatry; and if it was through God, it seems contradictory that Muḥammad could be an impostor.

To resolve these issues, Abbadie points out the difference between principles assumed by Muḥammad and those established by Muḥammad. According to Abbadie, Muḥammad takes knowledge of the true God and the destruction of pagan idolatry for granted, but it was Christ, not Muḥammad, who produced these two results in the world. Thus, Abbadie suggests that the true God was known everywhere and that pagan idolatry was completely abolished many centuries before Muḥammad, this being an effect of the preaching of Christ's Apostles. However, Abbadie ignores one of Muḥammad's achievements and distorts early Islamic history. It is generally agreed (except among some Orientalists), that Muḥammad converted the Arabs (who were pagans) and that in the course of this conversion he met with so much opposition from his pagan compatriots that he was forced to flee to Madīna. Muslims would, however, agree with Abbadie, since they also believe that Islam and knowledge of the true God existed before Muḥammad. This is illustrated in *Sūra* 3, l. 67 which is addressed to Abraham as a Muslim, that is, one who had submitted to God's will, and one of pure faith. Abraham was clearly neither a Jew nor a Christian because his message came before the Old and New Testaments were written.[40]

Much of the *Traité de la divinité* is devoted to a refutation of Muḥammad's teaching on idolatry and Christ. Relying mainly on unconfirmed suppositions and on an irony lacking in subtlety and persuasive force, Abbadie argues that Muḥammad taught men that Christians were idol worshippers because they worshipped Jesus Christ as sovereign God. Abbadie refers to the Qur'ān in order to describe Muḥammad's mission, which consisted in bringing back to the right path those who had gone astray and who under the name of the Trinity served many gods. He suggests, with evident sarcasm, that Christ and his Apostles acted as reformers of the pagan world: destroying (by their preaching) pagan idolatry, but leaving the world to be reformed by Muḥammad. This takes another twist when Abbadie refers to Christ's words in the Gospel, implying that doctors of the law are known by the results of their work. He suggests that, judging by this principle, one could not have but a high opinion of Muḥammad and recognise him as a great Prophet, if indeed it is true that he taught men not to confuse the sovereign God with a created being.

The 'afterthought' of the conditional clause (a useful polemical device which challenges the statement of the main clause), leads to another rhetorical device: the antiphrasis. Abbadie claims that Muḥammad enlightened many nations throughout many centuries, put God on the throne, and situated the created being in its proper place (p.16): What could be more legitimate and holier than such an achievement? What could be nobler and greater than such a work? Abbadie assures us that one would be wrong in depriving Muḥammad of all the titles granted him by Muslims, if he indeed enlightened the world by removing all superstition from it. However, the implication of the conditional clauses functioning as an afterthought device is clear: that Muḥammad never accomplished any of these acts. Abbadie adds with increasing irony that Muḥammad should be considered greater than all the prophets of the law, in fact greater than Christ himself. He is, of course, aware that these are strange and shocking paradoxes. However, his suggestion is that they will be certain and evident truths, if Christ is not the sovereign God. At this stage, all the praise that Abbadie has showered on Muḥammad seems to become meaningless.

One of Abbadie's facetious suppositions is that Muḥammad may be regarded not only as a Prophet, but as the greatest of Old Testament Prophets (p. 19). As evidence of this 'greatness', Abbadie suggests that whereas the ancient prophets addressed themselves to the people of Israel alone, Muḥammad spoke to the most beautiful and the most extensive part of the world. Contrary to Abbadie's insinuation that Muḥammad had deviated from the path of the prophets, companions and successors were necessary to remove idolatry from the countries where his religion was received. Abbadie then changes his tactics of denigration by making a bogus comparison between Muḥammad and Moses, then between Muḥammad and Christ. He claims that if Moses has been honoured with the glorious title of 'friend of God', one must appreciate even more the status of Muḥammad, who is claimed to not only know God's will but also to have made it clearly known: the possibility that Muḥammad had this special knowledge is only put forward to be rejected, for it is clear that Abbadie really believes that Christ alone knew God and made Him known.

Abbadie turns Muḥammad into a deist who founded his religion on the principle of natural religion (that is, the idea that a created being like Christ, simple in its nature, cannot be worshipped as the supreme God). In his view, Muḥammad is presented as not only a doctor of truth, but also a doctor who claims to reinstate all truths, at any rate all truths that are important and essential to religion. Abbadie's method of counteracting this reputation is to rely on traditional views of Muḥammad, which relate to his sexual morality, and Abbadie arranges this target so that he can hit at it as often as he likes. Abbadie becomes the mouthpiece of Christian apologists and expresses what he considers justifiable surprise that so much truth should be allied to so many defects. He does not hesitate to rely on rumour in attempting to justify his attack. Posing as a naïve person, he claims to be baffled by rumours and entitled to ask questions, such as: If Muḥammad is an impostor, how can an impostor make God's cause thrive, destroy idolatry and enlighten the world? He argues that if this man who is an impostor has been chosen by Providence to restore true religion, it follows that Providence must have wished either to discredit religion by having it restored by an impostor or wished to consecrate imposture by choosing it to restore religion. Both propositions are equally blasphemous.

The apologist says facetiously that one cannot but conclude that Muḥammad is more truthful, wiser, more charitable, and keener to defend God's glory than Jesus Christ. At one point he puts himself in the place of the Muslim opponents, by arguing that the lack of miracles does not weaken Muḥammad's position, for it is not essential for a true prophet to perform miracles (p.45), and he quotes the example of John the Baptist in this connection. In the end, all Abbadie's irony does not suffice to clinch the argument in favour of Christ in the way that he clearly intended. The questions he asks leave the issue unresolved, and the arguments he puts forward do not prove that Muḥammad acted out of political motives nor that Christ alone acted through persuasive arguments. From his description of Christ and Muḥammad, one cannot decide who is more governed by a worldly spirit: Christ, who assumes all the essential truths belonging to God's glory or Muḥammad, whose real aim in establishing his religion is to glorify the true God by showing that one must not associate with Him a simple created being.

As popular as Abbadie's treatises were, *The true nature of imposture fully display'd in the life of Mahomet* (1697) by Dr Humphrey Prideaux, Dean of Norwich, was even more so. Although he lists a number of Arab authors, his knowledge of them was second-hand. The most authoritative of his sources was Pococke, but the rest comprised anti-Muslim polemicists from the twelfth to the fifteenth century.[41] There is a sense that the 'true nature of the imposture' referred to in the title is Prideaux's pretence to be an Arabist.[42]Although he may have intended to refute Stubbe (a fellow pupil at Westminster), his main target was the deists. In his 'note to the reader', he expresses his fear that 'God may raise up… some Mahomet against us for our utter Confusion… And by what Socinianism, the Quaker, and the Deist begin to advance in this Land, we may have Reason to fear, that Wrath hath some Time since gone forth from the Lord for the Punishment of these our iniquities and gainsayings and that the Plague is already among us' (p. vii). Grotius before, and Boulainviller later, saw in the rise of Muḥammad in Arabia a form of punishment by God for the sins of Christians in the East.

Prideaux argued that Muḥammad drew up a scheme of imposture and, by a ' Medley made up of Judaism, the several heresies of the Christians then in the East, and the old Pagan Rites of the Arabs, with an indulgence to all Sensual Delights' (p. 13), drew people of all sorts to embrace his design. To illustrate this point about sensuality, Prideaux mentions the 'multitude of women' (p. 35) that Muḥammad had dealings with. However, he also shows some understanding of Muḥammad's teaching; Muḥammad, he admitted, did not maintain that he was introducing a new religion but reforming an old one.

Prideaux perhaps enjoyed the dubious honour of having had a negative impact on Pierre Bayle (1647-1705), the French Protestant thinker, who wrote a substantial article on 'Mahomet' in his monumental *Dictionnaire historique et critique*, first published in 1697. Bayle recognises his debt to Prideaux in the second edition of the *Dictionnaire* (1702), where he states that whoever wants to know in chronological sequence the acts and adventures of the false prophet simply has to read Prideaux's work, which has been translated into French.[43] He adds that one finds many proofs that Muḥammad was an impostor and that he made his imposture serve his cupidity. Yet to take Bayle's statement at face value, and as a ringing endorsement of Prideaux's evaluation of Muḥammad, would be rather simplistic, for a different picture of Muḥammad emerges when the article 'Mahomet' is fully assessed.

An understanding of Bayle's stance therefore requires more than a brief reference to this and to one or two remarks appended by Bayle to the body of the article (as often happens among commentators), but rather a survey of the totality of the remarks. Otherwise, one runs the risk of a fragmented view of Bayle's reading. He appears to be engaged in a debate with himself on the true worth of Muḥammad. Toward this debate he lists the positive and negative aspects of Muḥammad (whom he insists on calling the 'false prophet' or the impostor throughout). He tries (with little success) to add an original note to Muḥammad's biography. In 'Remarque D', he states that the first husband of Khadīja, Muḥammad's wife, was still alive when Muḥammad entered her service, and that perhaps the agent had qualities missing in the master. In 'Remarque E', in a reference to Khadīja's conversion, Bayle claims that Muḥammad was unlike other religious leaders who surround themselves with 'dévotes' and use the intrigues and zeal of a few women in order to succeed in their scheme, for Muḥammad did not win the affection of his wives: it was they, so rumour has it, who took away his life. Nevertheless, there is no evidence to support Bayle's claims in these two remarks.

Although not versed in oriental languages, and therefore with no access to source material in the original, Bayle nevertheless read Abū al-Fidā and El Makin (in translation) as well as Pococke, Hottinger, and d'Herbelot. He tries to be fair to Muḥammad, and strikes the right balance by separating the man from his detractors and his overzealous admirers. As he points out, it is difficult to authenticate all the details of Muḥammad's actions: while Muslim writers have invented countless fables to honour him, there is no doubt that his opponents also did not hesitate to invent lies against him. Bayle states that (as far as possible) he will protect Muḥammad's reputation from the damage done to him by enthusiastic friends and foes alike. So, in 'Remarque H', Bayle criticises Grotius for describing (in the version of the text prior to its revision, in Arabic, by Pococke) an alleged miracle of a portion of the moon that fell into Muḥammad's sleeve, where Muḥammad sent this back to heaven so that the moon might not lose its roundness.

Bayle convincingly argues that one must regard as fable references to the pigeon that came to eat from Muḥammad's ear, and to the bull that would eat only from his hand. His argument is that such tales are the product of the excessive zeal of some Christians against the impostor, and he condemns both Christians and some Arabs for their indiscreet and Romanesque zeal. Bayle is attempting, with some success, to dispense with the legendary Muḥammad so as to concentrate on the historical figure. His attitudes to Islam and the Prophet also need to be understood against the background of his own polemical purposes, of attacking the Roman Catholics by showering praise on Islam and Muḥammad.

Compared with that of Abbadie, Bayle's assessment (although not always fair) contains some positive elements up to this point. Having disposed of a few myths regarding Muḥammad, Bayle is now in a position to lay down his own criteria for evaluation of the Prophet, who is to be judged by his own acts. This is where the latter falls considerably in Bayle's esteem. Bayle stigmatises his marriage to Zaynab following her divorce from his adopted son Zayd, as incestuous. The finer points of Islamic sociology and history were no doubt beyond Bayle's comprehension, for Muḥammad's real aim was to break the hold of a pre-Islamic idea over a person's conduct. As Zayd was not a blood relative, his divorced wife had Qur'ānic sanction to marry Muḥammad, whose marriage was regarded as politically desirable, since Zaynab's family supported his enemies.[44] Bayle also states that Muḥammad was convinced about the infidelity of another wife, 'Ā'isha (with Ṣafwān), but as he could not bear to repudiate her, he made the machinery of his revelation intervene to silence slanderous gossip.[45]

The article sometimes gives evidence of Bayle's wit at the expense of Christians. Thus in 'Remarque K', it appears that all Christians agree the Devil is the true author of 'Mohammedanism', and that he used Muḥammad simply as an instrument to establish a false religion. Bayle's witty conclusion is that Muḥammad must have been handed over to the Devil by the Providence of God, and that the power that God gave the Devil over this wretch was far more extensive than the power the Devil had over Job: for God did not allow the Devil to pervert Job's soul, whereas he enabled the devil to use Muḥammad's soul to deceive mankind. These Christian writers, Bayle continues, imagine that the Qur'ān is the work of a fanatic, and that everything in it is disorderly and confused. Bayle refuses to adopt this long-standing approach, but chooses to stress the positive aspects of Muḥammad's mission, concluding that Muḥammad was not the instrument of the Devil. Nevertheless, he does assert that Muḥammad was an impostor, with ingratiating manners, who used religion as a means of self-aggrandisement.

To do justice to Muḥammad, Bayle takes great care to emphasise his teaching. He therefore challenges the view that Muḥammad attracted so many followers because his moral code pandered to corrupt morals. He strongly defends the moral teaching of Islam, which he identifies as being in harmony with the Gospel. He is most persuasive in 'Remarque L', where he argues that far from pandering to loose morals, Muḥammad makes the burden more difficult to bear. He lists 'Muḥammad's' commandments: circumcision (which is difficult for adults to endure), abstention from certain meats and wines, inopportune fasts and ablutions, and constant prayers (which can be physically painful or mentally taxing). He adds that one has simply to consider his moral teaching as laid down in aphorisms, where one finds everything that is most opposed to corrupting the heart: precepts such as patience in adversity, not slandering one's neighbour, charity, renunciation of vanity, and especially, doing to others what you would want done to you. Bayle can therefore draw a clear conclusion that the claim that Muḥammad's law gained ground quickly and widely because it removed from man the burden of good works, painful observances, and condoned the practice of corrupt morals, is untenable. Always careful not to appear too well disposed towards Islam and Muḥammad, Bayle admits that, without flattering Muḥammad as a person, the religion Muḥammad espouses contains excellent precepts for the practice of virtue and the chastisement of vice.

The article rejects the notion that the progress of Islam was due to the promise of a sensual paradise made by Muḥammad. In 'Remarque M' Bayle admits that such a promise could attract the pagans, who had confused ideas about happiness in the next world, but he doubts whether it could have any impact on Jews and Christians. Yet he does indirectly use this to attack Muḥammad's attitude to wives. In 'Remarque Q' he deplores the fact that in this world the odds are weighted against wives in favour of women slaves, who can inherit the wealth that should be given to the wives. To strengthen his criticism of Muḥammad, Bayle is here misinterpreting Islamic laws of inheritance, as there is no question in these of diversion of funds from one woman to another. Bayle insists that wives cannot expect anything better in the next world, and he admits that the 'Habiles Mahométans' do not claim that women will be excluded from Paradise; rather, though not excluded from Paradise, women will be deprived of its joys and reduced to the humiliating position of peeping through fences while others are enjoying themselves. Despite its wit, this voyeurism associated with the Islamic Paradise is lacking in authority, for the delights of paradise, based on Qur'ānic teaching, are meant for husbands and wives together.

It is not surprising that the Orientalist Mathurin Veyssière De La Croze (1661-1739), a Protestant convert and friend of Bayle and Leibniz, who became Librarian to the King of Prussia in 1697, should continue in Bayle's steps in the 'Réflexions historiques et critiques sur le Mahométisme et sur le Socinianisme'.[46] These were translated and grouped together with other well-known texts to form the *Four treatises concerning the worship of the Mahometans*.[47] Though perhaps lacking Bayle's depth, Veyssière still has some affinity with Bayle in that he is interested in the personality of Muḥammad and in the legends that grew up around him. Like the abbé Vertot later, his partial use of El Makin had a positive effect on him: he found material there which enabled him to pay homage to the natural talents of the Prophet. The latter is described as pleasant, polite, taking delight in obliging people, and fit to converse with people throughout the entire world.

When he argues that Muḥammad's disciples exaggerate his ignorance, Veyssière touches on a difficult problem, namely the extent of the Prophet's lack of learning. The argument he puts forward is not without merit; he argues that as Muḥammad prayed and preached in mosques, it is difficult to conceive how he could do so without being able to read. Veyssière seeks support for his point of view in one of the *Traditions* quoted by Pococke in the *Specimen historiae Arabum*. When the illness that he eventually died from became more severe, Muḥammad is believed to have said, according to the *Tradition*: 'Bring for me (writing) paper and I will write for you a statement after which you will not go astray'. The *Tradition* is attributed to Ibn 'Abbās (619-686), who is considered to be one of the greatest of the first generation of Muslims and a pioneer in Qur'ānic exegesis. Muḥammad was apparently prevented from writing this statement, and when 'Umar said that the Prophet was seriously ill and that the Qur'ān was sufficient for them, there was disagreement among the Companions. Muḥammad's statement was not authenticated since Ibn 'Abbās had not witnessed the event personally.[48] The debate on Muḥammad's learning would have been more balanced if Veyssière had taken into account two verses of the Qur'ān, *Sūra* 7, l. 157 and *Sūra* 62, l. 2, which describe Muḥammad as '*ummī*', that is , the 'unlettered' Prophet. According to Islamic tradition and exegesis, these verses mean that Muḥammad is ignorant only in an intellectual sense, that is, he cannot read or write. He is not ignorant in a moral sense which would have earned him the epithet '*jāhil*'.[49]

Veyssière's evaluation of Muḥammad is weakened by the fact that he does not distinguish between authentic and doubtful sources. For instance, he relies on the doubtful source of Juan Andres, a Muslim converted to Christianity at Valencia in 1487. According to Andres' account, commentators of the Qur'ān acknowledge that Muḥammad had had dealings with two Christians who were slaves in Makka, and heard from them many stories from the Old and the New Testament. However, no authentic Islamic source mentions this point. Thus, it is an unconvincing deduction when Veyssière traces the origin of Muḥammad's miraculous flight to heaven back to Christ's words: 'No one ever went up into heaven except the one who came down from heaven' (John, iii: 13).

The 'Réflexions' give Islam a more central role than Socinianism. Veyssière links Muslims and Socinians, since both groups maintain that the texts of the New Testament are corrupt (although the Socinians go about it with more circumspection). Veyssière claims that Muḥammad's suppositions conform more to his teaching, and that this places his followers in a better position than the Socinians to accept from the New Testament just what is useful to support their beliefs. However, defying almost all logic, Veyssière suggests that Muḥammad's technique is preferable on the grounds that it does not force his followers to distort the real meaning of biblical texts, whereas the Socinians, with their caricature of Christian teachings on the Trinity and other articles of faith, stray even further from the truth than Muslims. Sozzini (Socinus) is cited by Veyssière as saying that the spirit of anti-Christ introduced no error into the Church of Christ more dangerous than the dogma that puts many distinct persons in the essence of God. Veyssière then asks whether this is not the same as Muḥammad's words, which echo parts of the Qur'ān, including *Sūra* 112: 'God has not begotten; he is not begotten. Do not talk of the Trinity'.

There is some affinity between Veyssière and Muḥammad Rabadān (a Morisco who came from Aragon) in their approaches to the attributes of God. In 1603 Muḥammad Rabadān wrote a religious text in *aljamiado* script, that is, in Spanish with Arabic characters, for his coreligionists in Spain.[50] This was annotated and partly translated by the historian Joseph Morgan in 1723, under the title *Mahometism fully explained,* and was followed by a sequel in 1725, *Mahometism explained.* Morgan had spent twenty years in Barbary, and wanted to draw the attention of English readers to a contribution on Islam and the Prophet from a Spanish Muslim. His intention in translating Rabadān's manuscript was, he claimed, to give English readers a fairer notion than they had hitherto received. He also believed that Rabadān had many strange and original ideas, and that these should not be buried in a little-known language, which Morgan was one of the few Europeans capable of translating (I, iv, viii).[51] Morgan invokes Prideaux, but his attitude towards him is ambivalent. Basing his conclusions on those of Adriaan Reland (1676-1718), Professor of oriental languages at the University of Utrecht, and author of *De religione mohammedica libri duo* (1705), Morgan states that Prideaux's sources are unreliable and that many stories that circulated about Muḥammad are dubious (ii, p. liii).

Morgan's translation of the first volume of Rabadān lists thirteen articles of faith which every good Muslim is bound to believe in. In particular, the article relating to unity of God is given prominence, and the words used by Veyssière (God not begetting and not begotten) recur. Surprisingly, Muḥammad's intercession on Judgement Day on behalf of his community has been raised to the level of an article of faith, although it would be more appropriate to say that Muslims simply believe in Muḥammad's intercession. The second volume devotes a number of chapters to the biography of Muḥammad, and focuses especially on his early life, which is greatly exaggerated in this account. There is emphasis on the cult of Muḥammad's mother, who purportedly exceeds the moon in brightness: from her chaste womb shall proceed, Rabadān tells us, 'the very quintessence of Purity and Perfection' (ii. p. 30). This account corresponds in many ways to the cult of the Virgin Mary. Miracles accompanying Muḥammad's birth are also duly recorded. Yet Rabadān criticises the miracles attributed to Jesus. In an editorial note, Morgan explains that while the doctrine may be anti-Christian, this is because these are the words of a Moor and not of a Christian.

Although Christ is described as a beatified Prophet whose miracles were performed through divine grace, Rabadān is critical of his disciples for neglecting 'Him from whom he received power: (they) fell to adoring the Messenger, taking him for their Lord' (i, p. 215-216). By making Christ a simple messenger, Rabadān is acting in harmony with Islamic teaching. In his note, Morgan explains that Rabadān inherited the prejudices of his ancestors, who in turn inherited these from their subtle legislator, the impostor Muḥammad (i, p.214). Morgan's frequent reference to 'the impostor Muḥammad', made in the spirit of Prideaux (to whom he addressed a letter on the 12 August 1723), may be a device to divert attention from his denunciation of the Inquisition and the 'bigotry and mistaken zeal of the Romish clergy' (i, p. 8). Yet Morgan clearly appreciates Muḥammad's hatred of idolatry and insists that despite his methods of teaching, Muḥammad taught worship of the only true God who exists of Himself (ii, p. lvii). This echoes *Sūra* 2, l. 255 where God is described as the 'Living/ The Self-subsisting, Eternal'.

Mahometism explained has a short description of the Night Journey, wherein Muḥammad, during his ascent to the heavens, leads other Prophets to prayer in the sight of God. Nothing, however, is said about the significance of Muḥammad's ascension. Yet there is mention of the impious Abū Jahl, who challenges the Prophet to ascend again to heaven in full view of the unbelievers, in order to convince them of the truth (ii, p. 102). In contrast with Rabadān's account of the early life of Muḥammad, the account of the last part of Muḥammad's life is described in far more realistic terms. Overall, despite Morgan's recurring reference to Muḥammad as 'the impostor', his editorial work generally gives a favourable view of Muḥammad.

A completely different account of Muḥammad was given in the same year (1723), in the Arabic edition by Jean Gagnier (c. 1670-1740) of some chapters on the biography of Muḥammad taken from the *al-Mukhtaṣar fī akhbār al-bashar* (*The Concise History of Man)* by Abū al-Fidā, together with a Latin translation, under the title *De vita et rebus gestis mohammedis*. Having converted to Anglicanism and settled in England in the early 1700s, Gagnier became an Anglican clergyman. In his academic career, he vacillated between Cambridge and Oxford Universities and was eventually appointed to the Lord Almoner's professorship of Arabic at Cambridge in 1724. Early in his career he wrote a book entitled *L'Eglise Romaine convaincue de dépravation, d'idolâtrie et d'anti-christianisme* (1707) in which he adopted the tone of Pierre Jurieu's *Histoire du Calvinisme et celle du papisme mises en parallèle* (1683). He also translated the preface of the Arabic manuscript 'The Doctrine of the Apostles' on behalf of the Unitarian William Whiston, Newton's successor at Cambridge. These two publications (the anti-Catholic *L'Eglise Romaine* and the translation of the pro-Unitarian preface) might with some justification raise expectations of a positive approach to the Prophet in his work; however, this was not the case.

Although Chapters XVIII and XIX of the *De Vita*, which deal with Muḥammad's Night Journey, contain an element of the marvellous in embryonic form, Gagnier stated in the French version that this was not enough to 'satisfy the curiosity of those who could not read Arabic or Latin'.[52] This led him to make greater use of the unreliable Muṣṭafa Jannabī (d. 1590), the author of a *History*. Gagnier turned a work of moderate length (160 pages) into a substantial and popular two-volume novel (873 pages), purporting to be a biography, which gives free rein to his predilection for the marvellous. The two thin chapters on the Night Journey in the *De Vita* are expanded into twelve chapters, where Gagnier indulges in lengthy descriptions of the miraculous events said to have accompanied the birth of Muḥammad or to have been accomplished by him. Although Gagnier's scholarship was sound, the transformation of the work into a popular biography occurs at the expense of the historical Muḥammad, and this approach by Gagnier justifies categorising him within the ranks of Protestant apologists.

Gagnier relies mainly on the *Traditions*, some of which are of doubtful authenticity, to show the development of a legendary Muḥammad, and not a word is said about the Prophet as legislator or even the victorious leader. Gagnier explicitly claims that his purpose is not to depict Muḥammad as he really was, but to acquaint European readers with what orthodox Muslims say about him. However, if he had been genuine in this undertaking, he would surely have used the biographies of Ibn Isḥāq, al-Wāqidī, Ibn Sa'd, and al-Ṭabarī: Muslims preferred all of these accounts to Jannabī's, and Gagnier was well aware of this (see Chapter 4). While in the main text he is less scathing, Gagnier undertakes a violent attack against Muḥammad in the preface to this work, identifying him as the 'most villainous of men and God's most mortal enemy' (p. xvi).

Gagnier boldly claims to have steered a middle course between Dr. Prideaux and others who allow themselves to be carried away by insult and invective in order to make Muḥammad appear offensive. He even claims to have shown scrupulous neutrality, although quite the opposite impression emerges from a perusal of his biography of the Prophet. Nevertheless, when he lets Abū al-Fidā speak, the Prophet's personal qualities come out clearly: the Arab historian depicts Muḥammad as judicious in his answers, just in his manner of expressing himself, sincere in his words and deeds, and careful to eschew whatever was indecent and dishonest. Muḥammad's compatriots are said to have called him 'al-Amīn', that is, the trustworthy, and it is stated that God had endowed him with the most excellent qualities 'qui font l'honnête homme' (i, p. 96).

If, in general, the Prophet's reputation suffers in Gagnier's *La Vie de Mahomet,* it is likely that professional jealousy was a contributory factor. Gagnier's earlier *De Vita* was, on the whole, a dedicated work of scholarship, but this serious approach and the Arabic text and Latin translation meant that it could never hope to reach more than a limited public. Gagnier therefore tried to redress the balance in his favour, by producing a work in French that would eclipse Boulainviller's (see below). He admitted that his own biography was no less Romanesque than his rival's, but claimed that it contained nothing invented by himself, and was instead entirely based on authentic material and cited the best Muslim authorities (p. xxxix).The last claim was certainly not true.

In the *Oxford Dictionary of National Biography*, Michael J. Franklin's entry on Gagnier claims that he had established an 'enlightened historicist objectivity', and had produced a pioneering yet accessible work of historiography, which found Muḥammad to be neither impostor nor hero. A more sound view, perhaps, was that expressed by the author of the original article in the DNB, who judged the *Vie de Mahomet* to be unworthy of Gagnier's reputation. Although the *Annales muslemici* (the title under which the German Arabist J. J. Reiske published his Arabic edition and Latin translation of Abū al-Fidā in 1754) must have had as limited a readership as Gagnier's pioneering *De Vita*, it arguably deserves greater acclaim, as it contains nothing fanciful and offensive and Reiske faithfully recounts Abū al-Fidā. A five-volume second edition of the work by I. G. Adler was published between 1789 and

1794. In this, the 'Life' is equally divided between the Arabic text and Latin version, and occupies only some two hundred pages of the first volume, which contains events up to the overthrow of the Umayyad caliphate (that is, from 661 to 750). The chief merit of Reiske's edition was its concise approach, in comparison with the prolixity of Gagnier's *Vie de Mahomet.* Due to this, Abū al-Fidā was to reach the peak of his popularity in the late eighteenth and in the nineteenth century (see Chapter 4).

George Sale (c. 1697-1736) nevertheless drew extensively on Gagnier's edition and Pococke's *Specimen historiae Arabum.* Sale did not belong to a religious order, being a solicitor by profession, although his Christian affiliation was never in doubt. His literary activity occurs in the context of a general movement toward the conversion of Arabs, in the later seventeenth and the first decades of the eighteenth century; for example, Leibniz, in a letter to Veyssière dated 2nd December 1706, agreed with the stated need to translate the Bible into Arabic so as to convert the Arabs.[53] Among those who taught Arabic to Sale may have been a Syrian Christian, Suleiman Alsadi, whom the Patriarch of Antioch had sent to the Society for Promoting Christian Knowledge.[54] In 1726, Sale offered his services to the Society, helping to correct its version of the Arabic New Testament, and he soon became its chief translator. In 1734, Sale published a fairly reliable translation of the Qur'ān which is greatly indebted to Marracci's Latin translation, and to the commentary on the Qur'ān by al-Bayḍāwī (d. 1286), one of the few Arab sources Sale consulted firsthand. Sale owed his reputation not only to the translation but also to his substantial preface to this volume, the 'Preliminary Discourse'. This preface was often translated and published separately in the eighteenth century with the title *Observations historiques et critiques sur le mahométisme* (1751).

Voltaire expressed great admiration for the English version, stating in a letter to Thieriot (dated 14 August 1738) that it was more beautiful than all the Alcorans in the world.[55] There was much to interest Voltaire in the eight sections of the 'Discourse'; however, of special significance to him (and to his contemporaries) was Section II, which very briefly traces the Prophet's career. In his remarks to the reader, Sale claims that the 'Protestants alone are able to attack the Koran with success' and that 'for them Providence has reserved the glory of its overthrow' (p. v).[56] Although there is a touch of bravado here, Sale tries to strike a delicate balance by bringing out Muḥammad's personal qualities. To achieve this, he enlists the support of Spanhemius (that is, Friedrich Spanheim (1632-1701), Professor of Theology at Heidelberg and Leiden), translating Section VII of the latter's *Ecclesiae Historiam*, and reproducing the text in Latin at the bottom of the page. Sale praises the balanced approach of Spanheim who, despite believing Muḥammad to be a wicked impostor, also acknowledges him as 'richly furnished with natural endowments, beautiful in his person, of a subtle wit, showing liberality to the poor, courtesy to everyone, fortitude against his enemies ... a great preacher of patience, charity, mercy, beneficence and a frequent celebrator of the divine praises' (p. vii). Some of these attributes of Muḥammad correspond with those suggested by Abū al-Fidā, whom Sale often quotes in his Section II.

By choosing to limit his account to the manner in which Muḥammad carried on his enterprise, rather than providing a full description of Muḥammad's life, Sale can eliminate the details of the Prophet's subsequent battles and expeditions, which may have been tedious to some non-Muslim readers. He does say, however, that some of these will be noted when he explains several passages of the Qur'ān. He thus spares the reader the excessive emphasis on the military aspect of Muḥammad's career, which writers such as d'Herbelot were unable to avoid. Sale therefore has the opportunity to focus on other aspects of the biography: he chooses to highlight Muḥammad's marriage to Khadīja as the determining factor in the formation of his scheme to establish a new religion, being the time when he began to 'live as his ease' (p. 30). Here, Sale corrects himself by identifying a further determining factor: the desire to restore the only true and ancient religion (as professed by the prophets, from Adam to Jesus) by destroying the gross idolatry into which his countrymen had fallen, and by removing the corruption and superstition introduced by later Jews and Christians into their religion, thereby restoring religion to its original purity, namely the worship of only one God.

While Sale shows some fidelity to Muḥammad's aims in this account, as finding the original plan of bringing the pagan Arabs to knowledge of the true God to be both noble and highly commendable, he rejects Prideaux's suggestion that Muḥammad traded idolatry for an equally blasphemous religion. Indeed, in Section I he argues that it was from 'this gross idolatry, or the worship of inferior deities, or companions of God, as the Arabs continue to call them, that Mohammed reclaimed his countrymen, establishing the sole worship of the true God among them; so that how much so ever the Mohammedans are to blame in other points, they are far from being idolaters' (p. 13). He finds it logical for Muḥammad to attempt to rescue the world from ignorance and superstition, as his 'warm imagination'(supposedly a typical trait of the Arabs), had made him believe that he was destined to achieve this great reformation. Nevertheless, Sale does not accuse Muḥammad of being a 'hot-brained religionist' (p. 31), rather, he suggests that the damage done by Muḥammad to Christianity was a result of ignorance rather than malice. Sale posits a simple explanation for this: that Muḥammad had no proper understanding of the pure doctrines of Christianity.

While Sale does not neglect to mention the stereotyped image of Muḥammad as a 'great lover of women' (p. 31), this is put forward to reject the argument of sensuality as evidence of imposture. He counteracts these accusations with the suggestion that polygamy was not deemed immoral, and was often practised in other parts of the East, by referring to Jewish precedents. While critical of the excessive commendation of Muḥammad's frugality by Muslim authors (whom he suspects of partiality), he is willing to concede that Muḥammad was a man of 'at least tolerable morals' (p. 32).

Quoting Abū al-Fidā from Gagnier's *Vita*, Sale describes Muḥammad as 'a person of few words, of inoffensive behaviour towards his friends and of great condescension towards his inferiors' (p. 32). Sale seems to approve of Muḥammad's approach to conversion that begins with his own household. His account of Muḥammad's life in part accords with Muslim tradition, as his sources include al-Bukhārī and Abū al-Fidā. He also references Pococke, Prideaux, and even Bayle. The latter's name, used in connection with the peaceful establishment of Christianity, gives Sale the opportunity to show that 'Mohammedism' was no other than a human invention, which owed its progress almost entirely to the sword. Nevertheless, quoting Machiavelli's *The Prince*, he points out that Moses, Cyrus, Theseus, and Romulus would not have been able to establish their institutions had they not been armed (p. 38). In this way he is effectively able to argue that Muḥammad had a right to take up arms in defence against his unjust persecutors

Roman Catholic and Protestant views of Muḥammad

Henri Baudet makes a strong case for separating Protestant from Roman Catholic writings.[57] There is, however, little to justify his claim that Protestantism presents Muḥammad as an exemplary apostle of tolerance in opposition to the views of the Roman Catholic Church. Notably, the only official statement of the Roman Catholic Church on Islam and Muḥammad was made in Vatican Council II in 1965. Similarly, Protestantism is certainly not a unified religion, and the variety of opinions became apparent in writings about the Prophet from Grotius onwards. Thus, Baudet's conclusion seems to be an almost total misreading of the circumstances, as writers from both the Roman Catholic and Protestant traditions shared a marked ambivalence towards Muḥammad, and they shared the tendency to brand him with the stigma of impostor and false prophet, a stigma that has taken a long time to be erased.

Roman Catholic and Protestant writers did, nevertheless, differ significantly in their approach to Muḥammad. Although the Qur'ān (the authorship of which was at the time attributed to Muḥammad) was read by only a few Roman Catholics, such as missionaries and Orientalists, it was read by the majority of English Protestants, who had various agendas. For instance, Cromwell used it positively in his correspondence; however, Ross, found in the English translation a suitable weapon with which to attack the Commonwealth. The translation also fuelled Puritan-Anglican controversy, and the Cambridge Platonist Henry More likened the 'enthusiasm' of the 'Sectaries' (that is, the Puritans) to that of 'Mahomet' and his followers.[58] Other Protestant writers such as Sale, who were not members of the clergy, had agendas that were unrelated to sectarian politics, and therefore could recognise some of Muḥammad's more positive qualities.

The extent to which the stated intentions of Bayle and Veyssière De La Croze are genuine is questionable. In the late seventeenth and early eighteenth centuries, writers had begun to extol Islam and Muḥammad in order better to attack Roman Catholics. The pastor Abbadie, wishing to show his deftness with rhetorical devices, appears distinctly anti-Muslim, and the argument of Gagnier, the learned Anglican priest, is weakened by his predilection for the fabulous.[59]

It is clear that some Protestant writers were less hostile to Muḥammad than others. Most likely using the word 'impostor' as a cover (so as not to appear too well-inclined towards Muḥammad), Bayle and Sale seem to give a less distorted view of the Prophet. They initiate the slow process of presenting Muḥammad to a French and English readership as more than a great champion of the unity of God: as both legislator and social reformer. Apart from d'Herbelot, Roman Catholic writers, particularly Bossuet, seem rather lightweight in their argument when compared with Protestant writers, although perhaps some allowance may be made in the case of missionaries, given the cultural and logistical difficulties they may have experienced when living abroad.[60] After grappling with serious theological and social issues readers could find some relief in literature of the imagination.

Notes

1. See P. H. Coles, *The Ottoman impact on Europe* (London, 1968), p. 91-98.
2. See M. Bastiaensen, *L'Orient de l'Incroyant* (Brussels,1985), p.25.
3. In *Voyages en Moscovie, en Tartarie, en Perse, aux Indes* (Amsterdam, 1681), pp. 259-260, J. Struys mentions that ten days before the *Ashura* (the voluntary fast-day which is observed on the tenth of Muḥarram to mark the martyrdom of Ḥusayn), the most zealous of the Persians dress in blue, which is their colour of mourning. Cornelis de Bruyn describes a symbolic representation of Ḥusayn's murder played by armed men. He also notes public preaching in the streets, and witnesses a scene where all the spectators burst into tears as they are moved by the eloquence of their preachers. A procession represents the hero, together with seventy-two friends who were killed at the same time. This part of the account sounds particularly authentic, as Shī'ite tradition has it that the general of Yazīd (d. 683), son of Caliph Mu'āwiya, killed Ḥusayn with seventy-two friends at Karbala. See *Voyages par la Moscovie en Perse et aux Indes Orientales* (Amsterdam, 1718), pp. 217-220.
4. A stimulating study of Pascal's polemical techniques is P. Topliss's *The Rhetoric of Pascal* (Leicester, 1966).
5. The Protestant Veyssière de la Croze says exactly the opposite with regard to the methods adopted by the promoters of Islam and Christianity to spread their faith. In 1707, he published his *Réflexions historiques et critiques sur le Mahométisme et sur le Socinianisme* (see below).
6. One of the few missionaries who recorded his impressions of the *'āshūrā'* was Joseph Labrosse, known as Ange de Saint-Joseph in the Carmelite order to which he belonged. He mentions the Persians who on this occasion wear mourning clothes, do not shave their head or beard, wail day and night and repeat, until they lose consciousness, the words: 'Yā Ḥusayn'. The endless repetition of Ḥusayn's name is indeed striking. See *Souvenirs de la Perse safavide et autres lieux de l'Orient (1664-1678)*, ed. M. Bastiaensen (Brussels, 1985), pp. 156-157.

7. See Martin Lings, *Muhammad. His Life based on the earliest sources* (London, 1983), p. 335. Lings was quoting the Qur'ānic commentator Ibn Kathīr's *al-Bidāya wa al-Nihāya*, vol. 5, p. 209.
8. W.M. Watt, *What is Islam?* (London, 1968), p.157.
9. See the Persian and European version, translated and annotated by M. Bastiaensen, under the title *Souvenirs de la Perse safavide et autres lieux de l'Orient* (Brussels, 1985). M. Bastiaensen wisely refrains from reproducing the three European texts: instead he combines them into one (French) and uses the Italian version (starting point of the *Gazophilacium*) as the base text.
10. Under the entry 'Le Coran' (pp. 142-143, ed. Bastiaensen), the author, after having pointed out that Persian scholars reduce all the miracles attributed to Muḥammad to the single eloquence of the Qur'ān, goes on to describe many other so-called miracles.
11. See the commentary of M. Bastiaensen on this quotation, in *Souvenirs*, p. 208, n. 283.
12. See Ibn Hishām's recension of Ibn Isḥāq's *Sīrat Rasūl Allāh*, translated as *The Life of Muhammad* by A. Guillaume (Oxford, 1955), pp. 78-81.
13. Nau would not have been aware of a *fatwa* by the great religious leader Ibn Taymiyya (1263-1328) where he argues that the recluse in an hermitage should be left alone but that the sword should strike at a kind of nest to be found in the middle of the heads of certain people. He was referring to the tonsure of monks. See *Ibn Taymiyyah. Le Statut des moines*, text, ed. and trans. Nasreddin Lebatelier (Beirut,1997).
14. Galland provided a partial translation of the *Kashf* in manuscript as 'Catalogue d'Histoires Arabes, Persanes et Turques'. See Bibliothèque Nationale de France, Fonds Français 6160.
15. The quotations here are from *Bibliothèque orientale* (La Haye,1777).
16. *Le Coran*, text, trans, and commentary by Si Hamza Boubakeur (Paris,1978), 2 vols. Boubakeur, ii: 2122, commentary on *Sūra* 92, l. 20. Unless otherwise stated, all quotations and references to the Quran are from *The Quran*, text, trans. and commentary by Yusuf Ali (New York, 1946), 2 vols.
17. See *Le Coran*, ed. Boubakeur, vol. 1, p.345, commentary on *Sūra* 4, l.159. This is a far cry from the attack on Muḥammad and Muslims in English eschatological writings. According to the prophecies of Daniel and Revelation, the latter are turned into beasts that Jesus will destroy at his second coming. See Matar, *Islam in Britain*, p. 159. A whole community is thus bestialised. It is worth remembering that in seventeenth- and eighteenth-century France and England satirists such as Boileau, Dryden and Voltaire were in the habit of using animal imagery against their personal opponents. See my book *Voltaire and English Literature* (1979), especially pp. 162-233.
18. John of Damascus (J. P. Migne, ed.), *Opera Patrologia* (New York, 1899), vol. 94, pp. 678-780.
19. The Cambridge Platonist Benjamin Whichcote was more lenient towards the Muslims' reading of 'comforter'. He states that 'the Mahometans acknowledge

all that is related regarding Christ, only that what Christ said of sending the Spirit and another comforter is meant of Mahomet', *The Works of the Learned Benjamin Whichcote*, 4 vols., vol. 3, p.33.

20. *The Life of Muhammad*, trans. A. Guillaume, p. 301.
21. *Le Coran*, ed. Boubakeur, i, p. 581, commentary on l. 9. Muhammad 'Abduh, quoted by Desmombynes, supports the metaphorical interpretation (see below, Chapter 5).
22. See the article 'Ummi' by R. Paret in the *Shorter Encyclopedia of Islam* and W. Montgomery Watt, *Introduction to the Quran* (Edinburgh, 1970), pp. 33-36.
23. Published in 4 volumes in Paris in 1726 with Fontenelle's 'Approbation', this work betrays the crusading spirit of its author, who at the beginning refers to the Knights of St. John and their fight against the first 'infidels' and their religion.
24. Vertot gives the impression that the five daily prayers had been prescribed from the very beginning of Muḥammad's preaching, whereas they became established only after Muḥammad's *Night Journey*, that is, after 619-620. See Caussin de Perceval's remark, below.
25. There might be some basis to Saint-Pierre's comment regarding Abū Sufyān, as the latter (an inveterate enemy of the Prophet) may have shown some opportunism in his late conversion to Islam. At any rate, the opponents of the Umayyads, from which he descended, may have taken this view. However, see Savary's comments (below) for a real understanding of Muḥammad's intention.
26. Endowments, University of Cambridge. pp.173-174. See A.M.A.H. Kararah 'Simon Ockley : His Contribution to Arabic Studies and Influence on Western Thought', Ph.D. thesis, University of Cambridge, 1955.
27. On Pococke and Sale (below), see 'The Mysteries of Islam' by I. R. Netton, in *Exoticism in the Enlightenment*, eds. G. S. Rousseau and Roy Porter (Manchester, 1990), pp. 23-45.
28. See the article on Pococke by G. J. Toomer in the Oxford Dictionary of National Biography (Oxford, 2004). We also learn from it that Pococke published an Arabic translation of the Anglican catechism at his own expense in 1671, and produced an abbreviated Arabic version of the Book of Common Prayer, published by O.U.P in 1674.
29. *Islam in Britain 1588-1685*, p. 82. See also, pp. 73-81.
30. See B.N.F., ff. 6094, ff. 118-119.
31. It was reviewed in the Dutch periodical *Bibliothèque universelle* in 1686, but had little impact in France. Writing (in English) to his friend Thierot from England in February 1727, Voltaire scathingly remarked 'that Damn'd book ...is an example of nonsense from one end to the other ... and very distasteful to the French nation who dislikes madness itself when madness is languishing and flat' Best. D. 310, from *Correspondence and related documents*, ed. Th. Besterman in *The Complete Works of Voltaire*, vols 85-135 (Geneva, Banbury and Oxford (1968-77).

32. Although he was to depart from Qur'ānic teaching further on, Ibn Rushd starts his *Faṣāl al-Maqāl* (*The Harmony of Religion and Philosophy*) with showers of praise on God and on his servant and messenger Muḥammad.
33. See Shelly Ekhtiar, '*Hayy Ibn Yaqzan* : the Eighteenth-Century Reception of an Oriental Self-Taught Philosopher' in *Studies on Voltaire and the Eighteenth Century* (Oxford, 1992), vol. 302, pp. 217-245.
34. Matar, *Islam in Britain*, pp. 101-103. Montesquieu carried out a similar process of 'de-Islamicisation' in letters 1 and 16 of the *Lettres Persanes*. In their critical editions, both Antoine Adam and Paul Verniere note that the reference in letter 1 to devotions on the tomb of the virgin who has given birth to twelve prophets can be traced back to Jean Chardin. In the *Voyages en Perse* (1686) the latter translates the prayers offered by pilgrims at the tomb of Fatima, daughter of Mūsā al-Kāẓim, at Kom. The editors do not make it clear that the Chardin text reproduces some twelve lines of praise to Muḥammad (iii, 513). For his attack on pilgrimages and the cult of the Virgin Mary, Montesquieu discards these references. A somewhat similar method is used in letter 16, where the aim is to convey the oriental flavour of the poem by the Persian poet Hassan Casy (Al-Ḥasan b.al-Khaṣīb), translated by Chardin as *Eloge de Hali*. The poem inscribed on the tomb of Abbas II at Kom has seven songs: the first is entirely devoted to Muḥammad (ii, 61). There is no trace of this song in letter 16.
35. It was published by private subscription under the auspices of an Islamic Society in London in 1911, from a manuscript copied by Charles Hornby in 1705. The manuscript version is variously entitled *The History of the Saracens and of Mahomet*, British Library, Sloane 1709 and *The rise and progress of Mahometanism*, British Library, Harleian 6189. I use both the manuscript and printed versions as there are some variants between them.
36. Published version, p.142.
37. Martin Lings, *Muhammad.His life based on the earliest sources* (London,1983), pp.17, 29.
38. 'The Treatment of Arab History by Prideaux, Ockley and Sale', in *Historians of the Middle East*, ed. B. Lewis and P. M. Holt (London, 1962), p. 292.
39. See Ruth Whelan's article on him in the ODNB. The article, however, makes no mention of Abbadie's *Traité de la divinité de notre seigneur Jésus-Christ* (1690).
40. See Le Coran, ed. Boubakeur, vol.1, p.219.
41. See P. M. Holt's 'The Treatment of Arab History by Prideaux, Ockley and Sale', in *Historians of the Middle East*, p. 294.
42. R. Irwin, *The Lust of Knowing. The Orientalists and their Enemies* (London, 2006), p. 100.
43. *Dictionnaire historique et critique.* Second edition (Rotterdam, 1702), vol.ii,p. 1987. Bayle was referring to the translation by Daniel de Larroque, son of the Protestant minister Mathieu de Larroque, published in Paris in 1699.
44. See W. M. Watt, *Muhammad at Mecca* (Oxford, 1953), p. 329.

45. Recent Western representations of the marriage of the Prophet to 'Ā'isha are often highly critical, and he is accused of paedophilia by those hostile to Islam. Given that the paedophilia of some Roman Catholic priests and other men has been uncovered in the last decades, it is quite possible that some Western critics wish to tarnish the reputation of Muḥammad by associating him with it. One may understand their bewilderment at ancient Arab mores, but there is no link between Muḥammad and paedophilia. Although the Prophet married 'Ā'isha when she was very young, his other wives were mature in years, some being widows. 'Ā'isha was given to him in marriage by Abū Bakr, his closest friend, destined to become the first Caliph and the pillar of Sunnī Islam. 'Ā'isha herself was the transmitter of many *Aḥādīth* from the Prophet and is highly respected in Sunnī Islam.
46. In *Dissertations historiques et critiques sur divers sujets* (Rotterdam, 1707).
47. The other three were Adriaan Reland's *An Abridgment of the Mahometan Religion, A Defence of the Mahometans* and *A Treatise of Bobovius concerning the liturgy of the Turks* (London, 1712).
48. See Al-Bukhārī (ed. and tr. Muḥammad Muhsin Khan), *Sahih* (Medina, 1971), vol. 1, pp. 86-87.
49. See *Le Coran*, ed. Boubakeur, commentary on *Sūra* 62, vol. 2, l. 1909.
50. Rabadān also wrote a poem in celebration of the life of the Prophet: this was carried by Spanish Muslim refugees to Tunisia, where it was performed to music. This poem has been edited by Father José Antonio Lasarte as *Poemas de Mohamad Rabadan*. See L. P. Harvey, *Muslims in Spain. 1500 to 1614* (Chicago, 2005) p. 173.
51. See the article by Ann Thomson, 'Joseph Morgan et le Monde Islamique', *Dix-Huitième Siècle*, no. 27, 1995, pp. 349-363.
52. *La Vie de Mahomet* (1732), p. 1.
53. Leibniz, *Opera omnia* (Geneva,1768), vol. 5, p. 479.
54. E. D. Ross's introduction to Sale's *The Koran* (London,1921), p. x.
55. Voltaire, *Correspondence and related documents*, D. 1588.
56. Quotations are from *The Koran commonly called the Alkoran of Mohammed* (London, 1890).
57. In *Paradise on Earth. Some thoughts on European images of non-European man*, translated from Dutch by Elizabeth Wentholt (New Haven and London), p. 51.
58. In *An Explanation of the grand mystery of God's Laws* (1660), p. 158. See Matar, *Islam in Britain*, p. 105. Voltaire was to make much of the 'enthusiasm' (that is, fanaticism), of the character Mahomet and his followers in the play *Mahomet* (see below).
59. The claim regarding Gagnier's caution in depicting Muḥammad is made by Bernard Lewis in *Islam and the West* (New York, 1993), p. 90.
60. In the *Panegyrique de St François d'Assise* (1652), Bossuet denounces the 'impostures of Mahomet their (the Muslims') false prophet' while in the *Panégyrique de Saint Pierre Nolasque* (1665) he complains about the progress of this 'monstrous religion' (Islam) whose leader is given the title of prophet by Satan.

2

The Imagined Muḥammad from Marana to Voltaire

Marana's *L'Espion dans les cours*

French and English readers who were particularly interested in exoticism would have found their taste well catered for with the publication of Antoine Galland's translation of the *Arabian Nights* into French (between 1704 and 1717), followed by the publication of the *Mille et un Jours, Contes Persans* (1710-1712) of François Pétis De La Croix (1653-1713), the *Aventures d'Abdalla fils d'Hanif* (1712-1714) of the abbé J. P. Bignon and of Montesquieu's epistolary novel, the *Lettres Persanes*.[1] Nevertheless, the first two books also contain some serious philosophical reflections on the fragility of the human condition.

Before the appearance of these major literary texts, other works (of equal merit) that dealt with the Orient or with oriental characters had become available. One of these was Giovanni Paolo Marana's *L'Espion du Grand Seigneur*, two volumes of letters (published in 1684 and 1686), with the first volume published in both Italian and French. Marana (1642-1693) was an Italian journalist of Genoese descent who was well-versed in Islamic culture and who lived in France about 1682-1689.[2] He showed his successors, particularly Montesquieu and Voltaire, the potential for the foreign letter series as a genre, since the pseudo-letter could accommodate all types of criticism of a country. The hero of his own epistolary novel, Mahmut, is a Turk visiting Paris, and the fictional letters he sends back to his friends at Constantinople vividly describe what he sees of contemporary politics, culture, manners, and philosophy.

A number of his letters (in whole or in part), and many other passages, reflect images of Islam and its Prophet. Through Mahmut,

Marana was thus able to satisfy the curiosity of those readers who had wanted to know a little more about Muḥammad (whose presence was increasingly noted in literary works), and the views that are offered about Muḥammad in the novel complement the other topics of interest. It is important to bear in mind, however, that *L'Espion* is not primarily a theological treatise. Marana, like Montesquieu in the *Lettres Persanes*, is not writing a book about Islam and Muḥammad. They both have varied interests in society, religion in general, and the 'other'. The epistolary form of these works does not allow them to go deeply into these subjects; when Montesquieu tries to go into some depth on the causes of depopulation in letters 113 to 122, the epistolary form breaks down completely, and the *Lettres Persanes* ceases to be a novel. When referring to Muḥammad himself, however, both writers exploit the taste of their readers for the exotic, by presenting his personality and his teaching (often inaccurate), using a light-hearted and populist approach.

Similar to the other studies discussed in this chapter, *The Turkish Spy* – to give *L'Espion* its English title – is a work of the imagination (a spy tale), and its depiction of Muḥammad cannot be assessed according to strictly historical criteria. Marana depicts Mahmut in disguise as Titus of Moldavia on a mission to spy on Christians and to address secret reports to ministers and officials of the Ottoman Empire. Marana also includes in his book an element of romance, wherein the young Mahmut falls in love with a Greek woman named Daria, who (although married) encourages his advances; in a later episode, Mahmut kills the husband in self-defence. This love affair does not, however, occupy a large portion of the novel. Since Marana allows the spy to project certain views of Muḥammad, it is reasonable to assume that these reflect Sunnī teaching, which was, after all, the dominant religion of the Empire.

There is no doubt that Marana was the author of the first volumes, as 63 of the first 102 letters have survived in manuscript in the original Italian.[3] After the appearance of the French edition of 1686, publication resumed in English under the title *Letters Writ by a Turkish Spy* in 1687. Several volumes (eight in total) appeared in English between 1687 and 1694, making a total of 644 letters. Guido Almansi has shown that it is most likely that Marana was the author of the whole series of letters.[4] The first complete eight-volume English edition of 1694 was retranslated into French, although there are some doubts about the authorship of the last two volumes. This edition later appeared in six volumes (in 1696-1697) under the title *L'Espion dans les cours des princes chrétiens*, with the imprint 'Cologne' on the title page. A six-volume French edition was published in 1715-1716, again with the imprint 'Cologne', probably meaning Amsterdam. In English, editions of the *Letters Writ by a Turkish Spy* continued from 1730 to 1801. Judging by the number of editions of the novel in the late seventeenth and early eighteenth centuries, it can safely be concluded that it had met with the approval of a wider reading public. Marana had probably read accounts of travels to the Middle East and the Ottoman Empire, such as Jean de Thévenot's *Relation d'un Voyage fait au Levant* (1664), Jean Baptiste Tavernier's *Les Six Voyages en Turquie, en Perse et aux Indes* (1676) and Jean Chardin's *Voyages en Perse* (1686). He includes a rebuttal, by Mahmut, of other travellers' observations regarding the lack of education among Muslims.[5]

Mahmut's credentials are firstly presented as those of a Sunnī who believes in the Qur'ān, the Sunna and the writings of the leaders of the four orthodox schools of jurisprudence (that is, the Mālikī, Ḥanbalī, Ḥanafī, and Shafi'ī schools). However, he is fully aware of the existence of Shī'ite Islam. In letter 58 (vol. III), which is addressed to Muḥammad the hermit, who lives in the Prophet's cavern in Arabia Felix (Yemen), he states that he is not one of those destined for eternal punishment: this punishment is reserved for many people on account of the pernicious love they have for 'Alī, which detracts from the respect and veneration they should have for Caliphs 'Umar, 'Uthmān, and Abū Bakr. This exclusion of Muḥammad as worthy of respect, which Marana voices through the character of Mahmut, implies that even the Caliphs are more important than the Prophet.

Some liberty has also been taken with the chronology of the early Caliphate, as Abū Bakr, for example, appears last when he should be first. Marana, in fact, ensures that Mahmut's Sunnite orthodoxy soon crumbles: Mahmut claims that the first Muslims who aspired to perfection abstained from eating meat, and that although he did not forbid its consumption, Muḥammad suggested abstinence as a divine counsel. There is no foundation in Islamic history for this approach that is attributed to Muḥammad.

Mahmut, then, is simply a useful device allowing Marana to make comparisons between Muḥammad and other personalities, in which the Prophet does not present well. In letter 13 (p. 37), which is addressed to a 'sage dervis', Marana invents a trio of the most wicked, villainous, and hateful men: Judas, Muḥammad, and Luther. Marana claims that since the last two were the most impious, they are therefore the most tormented in Hell. The character of Muḥammad in this trio quite possibly references the famous work of his compatriot Dante, the *Divine Comedy* (1306-1321), with which many of his cultured readers would have been familiar. In Canto XXVIII of the *Inferno*, Dante places Muḥammad in the eighth of the ninth circles of Hell, where he is mutilated and endlessly cleft in two from his chin.

The 'sage dervis' is later informed of the Duc de Guise who, while at the head of Charles IX's army, followed a precept reminiscent of that found in the Book of Common Prayer 'doing unto others as you would have done unto you'. He set an example to the whole of France by forgiving the Calvinist fanatic who wanted to kill him because of his religion. Mahmut then complains that 'our Muḥammad', far from displaying similar generous feelings, promoted in his teaching a rule against Christians (who had otherwise never offended him): that 'infidels' should be killed or chained until they have paid ransom. Marana may have in mind *Sūra* 9, l. 5, which allows the killing of pagans. However, it is clear that this verse has nothing to do with Christians. Similar to verse 3, this refers to pagan Arabs who had broken their word. Verse 29, on the other hand, does state that the People of the Book (Jews and Christians) who do not acknowledge the religion of truth must pay tax.

The spy loses his Muslim faith, although he reminds his cousin Fousi (vol. i, letter 3) of the first pillar of Islam, that is, that there is no God but Allah, and that Muḥammad is his Prophet. He has doubts, which are conveyed in letter 12, where he refers to the sacrilege he is committing by acting contrary to the precepts of Muḥammad expressed in 'his' Alcoran. This use of the possessive suggests that Mahmut cannot be a true Muslim, since a Muslim will never attribute the authorship of the Qur'ān to Muḥammad.

Mahmut makes some feeble attempt at rapprochement between Christianity and Islam, but rather than accentuating common elements, he succeeds only in widening the gap between Christ and Muḥammad. For instance, he reasons more like an anti-Christian polemicist when he stresses the 'great difference between… Jesus crucified with all the ignominies possible, as these infidels do believe, and a Muḥammad immortal and triumphant, a great legislator and the angular stone of the first empire of the world '. The emphasis is on victory and worldly achievement, and Muḥammad scores at Christ's expense. Mahmut's words are not in the spirit of Islamic teaching, which does not talk of an immortal Muḥammad, and emphasises instead his humanity.

In letter 11, addressed to a doctor friend, Mahmut confesses that he is not satisfied with many things pertaining to religion. While he would gladly believe that Muḥammad, as God's messenger, was sincere and perfect, Muḥammad's successors are seen as weak and subject to error, and Mahmut looks back with nostalgic regret at the time of the 'great legislator'. Yet the attitude of *The Turkish Spy* towards the Prophet is full of ambiguity, varying from letter to letter, and its hero brandishes a double-edged sword. Writing to the Jew Nathan Ben Saddi (vol. ii, letter 103), Mahmut says that his native country (which he claims to be Arabia) was favoured by the presence of Ibrāhīm. Ibrāhīm had transmitted to his posterity the light of God,[6] which passed through successive generations until it reached Muḥammad 'our holy legislator'. At this point Mahmut is allowed to write like a pious Muslim, and he refers to the frequent revelations of the angel Gabriel which were given to Muḥammad. Yet agency for every act is transferred from God to Gabriel: thus as God's ambassador Gabriel provides Muḥammad with victory and honour, the new title of the 'seal of the prophets', transport to heaven and the glorification of his tomb (which is visited by the faithful of all nations). There is, however, a hint in this letter of that which particularly interests Mahmut, namely, the notion of the legendary Muḥammad, and this is further developed in other letters.

In an earlier letter (vol. i, l.13) a Jesuit had been allowed to laugh at Muḥammad, who apparently deified his camel and put it in heaven. In vol. iii, letter 102, Muḥammad is transformed into a new Orpheus: he apparently began his mission by preaching to lions and tigers which became tame on hearing his powerful voice. These wild beasts came to kneel before him and brought him food night and day; however, Islamic tradition has recorded no such events in the life of Muḥammad. Marana obviously uses Mahmut to devalue the Prophet and strip him of his halo of sanctity, by associating him with the pagan legends of Orpheus and Romulus, in which animals figure prominently. Mahmut's next remark begins on a less controversial note, as Muḥammad praises the Creator of all things, utters many blessings and prays for all men to become true believers. However, this apparently genuine prayer degenerates into grotesque exaggeration. At his prophet's expense, Mahmut claims that God would no doubt have listened to his prayer had the Devil not taken away from the angel part of Muḥammad's prayer to God, so that an imperfect prayer reached heaven. Nevertheless, the spy maliciously adds, most men became believers. To sustain the mockery, the miraculous completely takes over: according to Mahmut, meteors fought on the Prophet's behalf and thunder, lightning, a hailstorm, and balls of fire destroyed the troops of the infidels. So the Muslim army won without striking a blow, and the empires of the wicked fell into the hands of the true believers. This parodies the Qur'ān, *Sūra* 8, l. 17 (where, according to d'Herbelot, angels fought for the Prophet), is intended to compromise Muḥammad's credibility as a rational leader (see Chapters 1 and 5).

In another letter to Nathan (vol. iv, l. 56), Mahmut suggests it is pointless to draw a parallel between the miracles of Moses, and those of Muḥammad, due to the difference in circumstances. Initially, his approach seems authentic, because he stresses that Muḥammad had not been sent to accomplish miracles, but to preach the unity of God, the resurrection of the dead, the joys of Paradise, and the torments of Hell. However, his attitude to Muḥammad then becomes ambivalent, for his initial statement is merely a pretext to emphasise the miraculous element in Muḥammad's biography. Mahmut attributes to Muḥammad miracles which he never claimed to have performed. For instance, supposedly afraid that doubts might be raised about the truth of his religion, Muḥammad distinguished himself by the supernatural favours that were granted him. One of these, it is alleged, occurred when he was circumcised at birth: as soon as he began to breathe he started talking, saluted his mother, and made the declaration of faith. Likewise, trees and stones purportedly together proclaimed him to be an apostle. In another miracle, he was rescued from the Jews by two angels, when lights fell from a synagogue in Syria. Despite his earlier refusal to draw a parallel between Moses and Muḥammad, Mahmut cannot resist the temptation to compare the descent of the moon at Muḥammad's prayer with the confusion on Mount Sinai when the commandments were given to Moses. Mahmut produces an impressive list of miracles, all tending to heap ridicule on the Prophet, and when he refers to these miracles, it is only to cast doubt on their authenticity. In this way, Marana's picture of the legendary Muḥammad corresponds with that of Gagnier in his *Vie de Mahomet*.

Mahmut is subject to fluctuations in religious beliefs, and he flirts with Christianity, materialism, deism, and agnosticism at various points throughout the narrative. It is therefore difficult to say whether Marana intended for him to represent a particular religious viewpoint. He certainly starts off as a Sunnī Muslim, though his Sunnism is fleeting. In letter 78, addressed to Abdel Melec Muli Omar, President of the College of Sciences at Fez, Mahmut argues that the diversity of religious beliefs professed by people leads him to think that religion is simply a matter of education, and that believers are devoted to the sacred fables of their priests and hold to them firmly, sometimes at the expense of their lives. Moreover, he suggests that all these various cults have been invented by politicians, who have shaped them to fit the inclinations of the people they intend to deceive. Mahmut finds a semblance of truth and falsehood in all religions, and therefore he does not know which one to believe. While he insinuates that they are simply impostures, he is not allowed to develop this thought fully within the text.

By touching on issues such as educational determinism and the human origin of religions, Mahmut whets the appetite of the reader, who is left wondering who will open this field of investigation after Marana and address some of the issues raised in *The Turkish Spy*. Potentially, the authors of clandestine texts in the early eighteenth century, unfettered by the restrictions of the epistolary novel, were in a position to provide a fuller development of these ideas. Clandestine literature dealt with various unorthodox thoughts on religion, and one has to remember that it was primarily addressed to a public of connoisseurs. Among these were major figures of the Enlightenment such as Voltaire, Diderot, and Rousseau. This literature had a definite impact on these thinkers.

Muḥammad in clandestine literature

Despite their reservations about Muḥammad, late seventeenth-century French and English writers do not denounce him with the utmost vehemence. This vehemence, rather, is the mark of clandestine texts, especially in the period 1710-1740, when censorship was rigorously pursued in France.[7] Nevertheless, given that some works were published at a very early date, one can no longer imply that the bulk of this literature waited until the second half of the century (after the breakdown of censorship) to come out into the open. The *Lettre d'Hippocrate à Damagète*, for instance, was published in 1700, and most of the manuscript copies seem to have been based on the printed version. The author of the manuscript *Lettre d'un Médecin Arabe* actually quotes from the work of Jurieu. The dates of composition for many of the texts, particularly those which are characterised by a more frequent and systematic attack on religion in general, are uncertain. Only some of them deal specifically with Muḥammad, who is denounced in this wider context. For instance, *L'Antiquité dévoilée par ses usages* by Nicolas Antoine Boulanger (1722-1759), which may have circulated in manuscript before being published, is more concerned with pilgrimage in Islam, and focuses more on 'Alī than Muḥammad. For this reason, in the search for images of Muḥammad in clandestine texts, a selection is necessary. In particular, the attack against him becomes more sustained in Meslier's *Mémoire* and the *Difficultés sur la religion*.

While the words 'Muḥammad' and the 'Prophet' have almost become synonymous in recent times, for centuries Muḥammad was referred to as an impostor, most notably in an Arab writing, which was an early draft of the clandestine *Traité des trois imposteurs*, a work of the imagination which spread ideas close to those of Enlightenment thinkers. Here Muḥammad is only one of a trio of impostors, the other two being Moses and Jesus. The perception of Muḥammad in this text may well differ from that of texts in which he is the sole object of attack. According to Louis Massignon, the *Traité* dates from the tenth century and its legend became fixed towards 1080. Its origin was not Western and Christian, but oriental and Arabic, the eighteenth-century version being a fantastic reconstruction of the earlier Arabic text.[8] Massignon traced its ideology back to that of the Qarmatian movement of Bahrain, from the late ninth century up until 1076.

Attributing a first version of the work to an Arab source dating back to the tenth century does not raise particular problems. However the texts quoted to support Massignon's writing constitute at best a preliminary draft of the *Traité des trois imposteurs*. They do not mention the main episode of the eighteenth-century *Traité*, namely the story of the man buried alive in a well.[9] As this certainly owes more to blasphemy than to historical accuracy, it is necessary to determine the point at which this episode was added. Towards this end, Patrick Marcolini extends the argument raised in my article on the Arab origins of the *Traité*, suggesting that this episode constitutes the essential element in the passage devoted to 'Mahomet' in the text.[10] He goes on to argue that the *Traité* opened the door to true atheism: not in the timorous version of Diderot or La Mettrie, but in that of Jean Meslier (see below) or the Marquis de Sade (1740-1814). As he points out, Sade's anti-religious rage takes up so many pages that Gilbert Lely has had no difficulty in collecting his fits under the unambiguous title of *Discours contre Dieu* (1980). While unorthodox French writers may have been familiar with the European version of an old Arabic text, the *Traité*, it is not clear whether they actually derived inspiration from it. Certainly, one does not have to wait until Salman Rushdie's *The Satanic Verses* (1988) to read about blasphemy against Islam and the Prophet.

I cannot offer a definitive date for the insertion of the episode in the text and will have to come back to it in due course. The *Traité* was being rewritten in the period 1700-1710, and was published as early as 1719.[11] In the first half of the century, its manuscript copies attracted much attention and are extant in more-or-less complete forms in libraries in Paris and the provinces, London, and St Petersburg. A useful edition of the *Traité des trois imposteurs*, based on a published text of 1777, was produced by Pierre Rétat in 1973.[12] The denigration of Muḥammad is often fed by arguments invoking the *Traité*, to which modern scholarship has deservedly devoted much care.

In a manuscript of the *Traité* in the British Library, dated 1706, and entitled 'Le fameux livre des trois imposteurs', the writer begins with a general attack against religion in which he attributes the origin of all religions as a response to a fear of invisible powers, and created according to preference.[13] He singles out three from the numerous legislators whose rise was witnessed by Arabia and its frontiers – Moses, Jesus and Muḥammad – and, of these three, the most recently occurring was Muḥammad. According to the author, Muḥammad borrowed extensively from Judaism and Christianity in order to establish Islam, and subsequently proclaimed himself the enemy of the older religions. Muḥammad of course made no such proclamation. A tendency to oversimplify is evident throughout the work, and Muḥammad's mission appears in an entirely negative light. Anything that made all three monotheistic religions look like rivals clearly fired the writer's imagination. Abandoning all chronological perspective, the author argues that no sooner had the Christians abolished the laws of Moses than people began to follow a new legislator who rose through the ranks in a way similar to Moses.

In a manuscript of the *Traité* in the Bibliothèque Nationale de France (F. F, 24, 887), there is reference to the 'specious' titles of 'Prophet' and 'messenger of God' given to Muḥammad, who displayed skills similar to those of Moses and Jesus, in making miracles and in pandering to the passions of the populace. At the latter's invitation, Muḥammad allowed himself to be escorted by an ignorant crowd to whom he explained the new 'divine oracles'. This text provides no indication of the progress of later Muslims in the arts and sciences. Instead, it points out that although deceived by the empty promises of the impostor, the people spread his fame and exalted him in such a way that he gradually eclipsed the fame of his predecessors. Yet Muḥammad did not appear capable of founding an empire: he did not excel in politics or in philosophy, and he could not read or write. The author appears to accept the traditional account of the illiterate Muḥammad, adding that the latter vacillated so much that he would have abandoned his project had it not been for the skill of one of his followers. The *Traité* is rather vague about the identity of this follower.

Since the story of the well appears to be the very foundation of Muḥammad's imposture in the *Traité*, it is worth briefly describing this. With the intent to tarnish Muḥammad's reputation, maximum use is made of an extravagant story that circulated extensively in manuscript and published literature.[14] In the text of the *Traité* published by P. Rétat, as in other texts, the reader learns that Muḥammad found himself followed by an ignorant crowd who believed he was divine, and he decided to rid himself of one of his followers who was too close. However, afraid that the leaving person might discover his imposture, Muḥammad felt a need to stop him. To make certain that the man remained, Muḥammad showered him with promises and swore that he wanted to become great only to share power with him. He instructed the follower to hide in an oracle pit and persuaded the rabble that God's voice would proclaim Muḥammad's mission on earth. The man counterfeited the oracle as instructed by Muḥammad and the infatuated crowd heard a voice say: 'I who am your God declare that I have established Muḥammad to be the Prophet of all nations. It is from him that you will learn my true law which has been altered by Jews and Christians.' (p. 76) The man was rewarded with ingratitude by Muḥammad, who had the pit sealed, thus burying him alive. The *Traité* concludes this wild tale with the remark that it was on this heap of stones that the last of the most famous impostors established his law. It is evident that its author made no serious attempt to explain the real foundation of the Islamic community, preferring to depict the early Muslims as the most naïve people in the world. In doing so, this argument chooses to ignore any historical perspective.

This malicious tale persists in a number of other versions of the *Traité*,[15] although it is excluded from a third manuscript of the British Library.[16] With regard to its omission in this version, the translator explains, 'As this writer consulted none but bad authors (seemingly only the lying Greeks) and has from them inserted diverse false facts, I chose to leave it out not being worth transcribing; we having already many far better and withal genuine accounts of this celebrated Arabian legislator'. The translator is aware of the legends that surround Muḥammad and refuses to indulge in them, clearly with some desire to do him justice.

Contrary to the translator's statement, however, the story of the well was not invented by 'bad authors...lying Greeks'; instead, it may be traced back to an Arab source, for a similar story is described by Ibn al-Athīr (1160-1233) in *Al-Kāmil fī al-Tārīkh*, a history of the world from its origin through to 628. The villain in Ibn al-Athīr is the Moroccan reformer Ibn Tūmart (1078-1130). Extracts from al-Athīr's *History* were reproduced by the Baron de Slane in an appendix to his translation of Ibn Khaldūn's *History of North Africa* (1332-1406) under the title of *Histoire des Berbères et des dynasties musulmanes de l'Afrique septentrionale*. It appears from these extracts that during the siege of Tinmal (1121), in the valley of Nafīs in the High Atlas, many thousand inhabitants died at the hands of Ibn Tūmart, who proclaimed himself the 'Mehdi'[17] of the Almohads.[18] In 1125 Ibn Tūmart had recourse to the services of one of his agents, named Bashīr al-Wansharīsī. He feigned astonishment and asked Bashīr what had happened to him. In a scene which filled the spectators with admiration, the latter replied that an angel had cleansed his heart and that God had communicated to him a light by which he could distinguish those destined for paradise from those destined for hell.[19] Bashīr even claimed that God had commanded Ibn Tūmart to have the damned killed and that to prove the truth of his words he had caused many angels to go down into the well. On hearing these words, all the people went to the well. Ibn Tūmart then turned towards the spectators and said: 'This well is pure and sacred, for angels went down there; so we should fill it to prevent it being defiled by garbage'.[20] At this, the spectators quickly threw stones in the well which was filled up.

According to Ibn al-Athīr, this was one of the methods used by Ibn Tūmart to consolidate his power and to rid himself of seven thousand individuals who had offended him. Al-Athīr adds that the story was narrated to him by many Maghribīs of merit, but that the same event is narrated in different ways: in other words, he is alluding to the existence of variations on the story. We do not know who substituted Muḥammad for Ibn Tūmart in the version of the story of the well described in the *Traité des trois imposteurs*, nor do we know when the substitution was made. We do know that the legend of the three impostors, inaugurated between the tenth and eleventh centuries, gained more substance in the first part of the twelfth century because it exploited the machinations of Ibn Tumart, who might either personally, or through the intermediary of his disciples, have tried to compare himself to the Prophet.[21]

The legendary Muḥammad is missing from manuscript 24887 of the B.N.F. Instead, the author gives a partial (but factual) account of Muḥammad's life and mission. Noting that Muḥammad's grandfather, 'Abd al-Muṭṭalib, was the head of one of the most important families of the tribe of the Quraysh (the Banū Hāshim), in which capacity he took part in the wars against the King of Persia and the Emperor of Ethiopia, the author attempts to prove that Muḥammad could not have belonged to the lowest social class. However, as his father died before his grandfather, when Muḥammad was very young, Muḥammad lost the rights to leadership over his tribe. The author exaggerates when he says that Muḥammad, although born a free prince, was reduced to the low condition of a 'garçon de boutique' (f. 72). Nevertheless, he is fairly accurate in determining Muḥammad's age (he makes him thirty at the time of his marriage to Khadīja) and in his statement that his match with the rich widow turned Muḥammad into one of the richest 'bourgeois' of Makka (f. 72).

The picture of Muḥammad that emerges from this manuscript is that of a clever, ambitious opportunist, who spent a long time meditating on his scheme, learning about Moses and Christ from his dealings with Jews in Judea and Christians in Egypt while acting on behalf of his wife; however there is no foundation in Islamic history for the presence of Muḥammad in either of these places. Reports of division among Christians also proved useful to the author's arguments, for it is stated that when Muḥammad was obliged to leave Makka, he went to Madīna in the knowledge that some of the inhabitants who were Arian Christians would join him (f. 74). Muḥammad is thus depicted as casting his net wide to win supporters over to his cause.

At this stage, Muḥammad apparently decided to stop proving his mission using rational means, but instead persuaded his followers to establish Islam by means of the sword. The author does not hesitate to distort Islamic history in order to belittle Muḥammad, and fails to mention that the latter believed he had been given permission to fight the Makkans when they had driven him from his home for worshipping the one true God. However, the author insists that Muḥammad had already strengthened his party by marriage alliances, having married the daughters of four leaders of Madīna. The political implications of Muḥammad's marriage to Zaynab, for instance, are well understood by the author. So are the circumstances favouring Muḥammad's scheme: many Arabs, in their loathing of idol worship had virtually become atheists. So Muḥammad began by leading a solitary and exemplary life, spending much of the day in prayer and meditation. This information is not objectionable in itself, but the author hastens to add that Muḥammad seduced the populace by affecting a very pious exterior, and by talking of revelation and vision. Although the *Traité* points out similarities in the early lives of Moses and Christ, this portrait of Muḥammad as the perfect hypocrite of Western tradition stands out in comparison.

If there is an attempt at comparative religion in the *Traité des trois imposteurs*, it is a farcical one, since the aim is clearly to destroy religion altogether. It contains nothing of the fundamental teachings of Moses, Jesus Christ, or Muḥammad: rather, these individuals are, at best, depicted as political schemers. The authors of the various versions (manuscript or published) put these religious leaders on the same footing for the purpose of denigration and warn their readers that, 'It is not in the writings of the three impostors that one must seek the true idea of God; the apparitions and conferences with the divinity of the first and last, the divine filiation of the second are impostures to be shunned, if one loves the truth'.[22] On the other hand, when distinguishing between the impostors, these authors generally seem to have less aversion to Muḥammad, and they point out that he was more successful than Jesus in that he saw the progress of his law (which he had perfected through hypocrisy and imposture) before his death, something which the son of Mary could not do because of his poverty. Thus, Muḥammad could cherish a hope that Jesus did not have, namely that his law would long survive his death, because he had accommodated it to the genius and passions of his followers, who were born into (and brought up in) ignorance. The author of the *Traité* revels in the ignorance of Muslims, at a time when great efforts were being made by European Orientalists and others to diffuse knowledge of the richness of Arab-Muslim civilisation.

The *Traité* left its imprint on many clandestine texts of the first half of the eighteenth century, including the *Préface sur la religion de M*, which was probably written between 1718 and 1722.[23] This text explicitly refers to *De Tribus Impostoribus*, which it identifies as having a long history of discussion. Claiming that a famous professor of theology from Paris had publicly taught his wide audience that Moses, Jesus, and Muḥammad had been deceivers, the author of the *Préface* goes on to proclaim that the search for truth is the sole object of these studies. Aware of the existence of numerous rivals and imitators of Muḥammad's 'Fourberie', the author is accurately informed about the activities of Moseilama, the most famous of these impostors, who declared himself prophet in the town of Yamāma, and boasted that he had been sent by Heaven to establish worship of the true God and to publish an 'Alcoran' of his own. The criteria for success in this instance are equally valid for the author of this *Préface*, who remarks that these other impostors were less successful than the character who served as their model.[24] In the conclusion to this text, the author accepts that Muḥammad did not enjoy the satisfaction of seeing the downfall of all these fanatics, however, his successors continued the work that Muḥammad would have completed if he had lived longer (f. 165).

The fictitious letter was used as a device in another clandestine text, the *Lettre d'un Médecin Arabe à un fameux professeur de l'Université de*

Halle en Saxe sur les reproches faits à Mahomet, de son recours aux armes, de la pluralité de ses femmes, de l'entretien de ses concubines et de l'Idée de son Paradis.[25] Its author states that travels to Europe were motivated by curiosity about religion, customs, and literature; however, he is not a genuine Arab traveller.[26] He is well aware of the false and unfounded attacks typically made against the Prophet and his religion, and dismisses the charges against Muḥammad relating to force, asserting that Muḥammad's aim was simply to recover the leadership of the town of Makka. The Arab doctor does not, however, display the true spirit of Islam, as he does not justify Muḥammad's conquest on religious grounds.

The author points out that figures such as Alexander, Caesar, William the Conqueror, and Louis XIV are exalted for their military leadership, and that the holy Prophet of Islam never killed anyone simply on account of their religion. He further argues that the levy imposed by Muḥammad on those who refused to follow Islam was not exorbitant, and qualifies Muḥammad's action in this connection as being more humane, equitable than that of any Christian sect: when in a position of power, the latter tended to use this to the utmost severity (p. 10). He relies on Jurieu, whose *Apologie pour la Réformation* is quoted to prove that Muslims are nowhere near as cruel as Catholics. Muḥammad's acceptance of polygamy is defended, on the grounds that the custom of having many wives and concubines prevailed in the East from time immemorial. The author displays wit (if not factual accuracy) at the expense of Islam, in suggesting that Muḥammad received a particular dispensation from heaven in order to beget a great number of young prophets and to multiply his posterity and thereby spread his religion: for each tribe from which he picked a wife soon embraced Islam. This is of course problematic, as there is not the slightest suggestion in Islamic doctrine that other prophets would come after Muḥammad, as he is considered the last.

Another clandestine text identifies a false parallel between Moses and Muḥammad. Purporting to be a letter written from London by Zelim (a Muslim) to Nathan (a rabbi) the *Parallèle entre Mahomet et Moïse le grand libérateur des Juifs* suggests that the religions introduced by Moses and Muḥammad shared similar origins.[27] The Muslim, Zelim, fails to project an authentic image of Islam, omitting any reference to a spiritual significance from the spread of this religion. This author does, however, stress the great differences between Moses and Muḥammad as military commanders. Whereas Muḥammad behaved as Alexander the Great had done in all his conquests, Moses behaved like the Spaniards in America. That is, Muḥammad welcomed with open arms all those who submitted to his law, although he killed the most obstinate of his enemies (the author adds that Muḥammad always spared the lives of the innocent). Muḥammad also urged his followers to avoid applying torment to the conquered, but instead to treat like brothers all those who would follow the Qur'ān. The author of the *Parallèle* criticises the actions of Moses, who ordered the Jews to 'borrow' from their Egyptian friends gold, vases, and clothes to take away with them when they left Egypt. In the text, Zelim challenges Nathan to point to any place in the Qur'ān where God orders Muslims to commit such a perfidious theft. However, this favour enjoyed by Muḥammad and Muslims at the hands of the author is only temporary, as both Moses and Muḥammad are soon subjected to scorn and ridicule.

The *Parallèle* outlines the military achievements of Muḥammad, stating how in the second year of the hijra he attacked a caravan of about a thousand 'Koreishites', killing seventy men and taking the rest prisoners. Doubts are cast as to the significance of this achievement, with the sarcastic remark that God then fought for Muḥammad as he formerly fought for Moses (f. 130). In the letter, the names of Moses and Muḥammad are associated with extravagant miracles, although Zelim states he will not tire Nathan with descriptions of these, his purpose being to talk to Nathan about facts and not ridiculous fiction. On the other hand, Zelim wants Nathan to accept that the frequent conversations Moses had with God are as absurd and as contrary to true piety as those of Muḥammad with the angel Gabriel. In this, he seems to have no intention of being viewed as a genuine representative of Islam, for his ridicule of Moses is not in harmony with Islamic teaching and is offensive to Muslims.

One interesting element in the *Parallèle* is the description of the physical appearance of Muḥammad, which is often omitted in texts about the Prophet. He is described as a man of average build, with a large head, a brown face, a lively complexion, a modest look, and a noble air. He is seen as personable, smooth in conversation, and with a sharp mind. He is also shown to be eloquent and strong, and dauntless in the face of dangers generally feared by others. Zelim insists that this portrait of the Apostle is drawn by a Christian who, being his enemy, can on no account be suspected of having flattered him (f. 131); this reference to a Christian source surely relates to El-Makin, whose *History* had been translated into French (see above), and who was no enemy of Islam. Zelim continues by stating that although Muḥammad had nothing extraordinary about him, his appearance was pleasant and his eyes vivacious: charming modesty accompanied all his actions. These qualities are emphasised (at the expense of others) to account for the desire of Khadīja to marry Muḥammad, indicating that this marriage was a mutual testimony of the most sincere affection, and therefore perfect. So far, Zelim's portrait of Muḥammad is positive, he is presented in a fairly flattering manner and the balance is tilted against Moses. Zelim seems to see little harm in being generous in his assessment of Muḥammad at this stage.

Zelim proceeds to undo this positive representation, however, when outlining the events following Muḥammad's marriage and the commencement of his religious mission. Apparently, after fifteen years of marriage, Muḥammad became subject to epileptic fits that, although present earlier, had become more frequent and longer lasting than during his youth. Writers interested in the biography of Muḥammad, including Bayle, have often referred to the state of Muḥammad at the time of his revelations as epileptic, and Zelim follows these writers in this approach, despite the lack of evidence in support of this view. Zelim claims that the severity of these 'fits' and the idea of such a terrible illness had made Khadīja begin to regret having married Muḥammad (although, once again, there is no foundation for this suggestion). Zelim, in rewriting Muḥammad's biography, claims that the Prophet was terribly upset to find himself despised by the woman he loved. Thus, in order to win back the esteem and affection of Khadīja (and his other wives), which he had lost through a frailty commonly associated with the female sex, Muḥammad decided that the best approach was to persuade them that this terrible illness was in fact spiritual ecstasy. In Zelim's account, Muḥammad then claims that he entered into ecstasy at the sudden apparition of an angel surrounding him, and being unable to stand the splendour and glory of the heavenly messenger, was thrown into saintly convulsions, as had the prophets that preceded him.

This attack in the *Parallèle* bears some resemblance to Voltaire's attack against the pious contortions of Faccio in the pamphlet

'Fanatisme', and the intoxicated zeal of the disciples of the character Mahomet in the play *Mahomet* (see below). Ironically, the 'Muslim' Zelim perpetuates the myth of the hypocrisy of Muḥammad, who is perhaps being used as a convenient weapon against the French 'convulsionnaires' who displayed strong emotions over the tomb of a Jansenist at St Médard. Zelim concludes his account by saying that he will not decide whether Khadīja actually believed, or only pretended to believe Muḥammad about his revelations. Instead of saying that she was the first to embrace Islam (as a Muslim would) Zelim claims that she was the first publicly to declare that Muḥammad had dealings with angels.

The idea that the origin of Islam can be traced back to Muḥammad's marital problems is found in another text, which comes from the cabinet of the abbé Sepher (1710-1781). This work, perhaps dating from an earlier period, is entitled *Recherches de quelques particularités de la vie du prophète Mahomet.*[28] It similarly claims that the desire to retain Khadīja's esteem following his epileptic fits inspired Muḥammad to pass them off as a celestial vision. The author suggests that Muḥammad's audacity and impostures progressed gradually: a more advantageous use of his illness was to play the prophet and thus to distinguish himself from the rest of his nation. In this account, the author is more interested in describing Muḥammad's rise as a leader: that without learning Muḥammad could teach convincingly and gather followers, and that without any fortune and through his own efforts, he could become the prince of the nation.

Muḥammad's next act, according to the author, was to abolish Christianity, hitherto considered well-established and true. This was achieved by the invention of a new religion made up of absurd and incredible tales. However, the spread of Islam took place not in the mountains of Brazil or some wild region where scholarship and true knowledge are unknown, but in the heart of the finest regions of the East, in the most densely populated areas, among the most enlightened and wittiest nations of Asia and Europe and amidst two great religions of the world (p. 4). However civilized these nations were, they did not shrink from believing in Muḥammad's description of paradise. That Muḥammad's success in his mission should be explained in simplistic terms (by citing, for instance, his teaching on paradise) is truly amazing.

The author considers whether Muḥammad, at the beginning of his bogus prophethood wanted to reform religion, or considered this religion merely a means to establish his authority over a whole population. In the opinion of the author, Muḥammad's subsequent acts indicate that he was governed by the latter motive. There is, however, an attempt in the *Recherches* to redress the balance slightly in Muḥammad's favour, albeit temporarily. This gives the evolution of the Arab nation some recognition. Thus, however hateful the domination of Muḥammad may appear to Christians, the text argues that it cannot be considered so criminal when its beginnings are taken into account. It suggests that there is a significant difference between an apostate Christian and a pagan Arab turned Muslim. When the former becomes a Muslim, there is no doubt that they become an object of horror and abomination, but when the latter, an idol-worshipper, abandons idolatry to worship one God, as taught by Muḥammad, they may be excused, as their adopted religion, albeit flawed, still conforms to a greater extent to the truth (p. 33). According to the author, without siding with this unhappy and hateful convert, one might say that a greater evil had been abandoned for a smaller one. Similarly, Leibniz, Veyssière de la Croze, Sale, and others all insisted that the Arab could achieve further progress by becoming a Christian.

The *Recherches* depicts a Muḥammad who tries to please everyone: he retains a little idolatry for the idol-worshipper (the author does not explain what is meant by this), he allows circumcision for the Jew, respect for Jesus for the Christians and countless privileges for libertines and voluptuous people. Hence, the conclusion is entirely negative, as religion has been but the pretext for Muḥammad's ambition, and his prophethood is used for domination. Toward this end, Muḥammad supposedly prepared the Qur'ān over a long period, working on it for twelve to fifteen years, most intensively at the time when he kept himself incommunicado to feign his spiritual retreat. The Qur'ān served Muḥammad's specific purposes, presenting the word of God to sanctify, for instance, his 'incestuous' marriage to Zaynab after her divorce. Muḥammad had hesitated to marry her, but a revelation confirmed that the marriage was authorised (*Sūra* 33, l.37-40). There is nothing new in the criticism: Bayle had famously pronounced the union incestuous. The harvest, as far as Muḥammad's biography is concerned, thus proves fairly meagre in the *Recherches*.

The comparative approach to the study of religion, especially Islam and Christianity, is pursued in a fairly original way by John Toland (1670-1722) in the *Nazarenus*, which also adopts the form of a letter. Published in 1718, the text was written and circulated clandestinely in manuscript translation in the 1700s in France.[29] In the manuscript entitled *Le Nazaréen*, the French reader learns from Toland that it is only in recent times that Christians have been undeceived about the pigeon of Muḥammad, and that his claims of miracles and the suspension of his tomb in mid-air were unknown to Muslims. It seems that Toland has some admiration for Muslims, as he is of the opinion that they generally take greater care than Christians in preserving the integrity of their sacred books.

The remarks by Toland on the authenticity of religious texts are prompted by the mystery surrounding a particular gospel, which he says was attributed to Barnabas but which some Christians declared, along with many other gospels, to be apocryphal. Although he was convinced that the so-called *Gospel of Barnabas* was the work of a Muslim scribe, this text had never achieved the dissemination, in Islamic countries, that Toland claimed.[30] Indeed, Christian scholars believe that it was written in the late sixteenth century or perhaps earlier by a Christian convert to Islam, from an original manuscript in Italian. Entitled 'The True Gospel of Jesus, Called Christ According to the Description of Barnabas his Apostle', it shows Muḥammad expressly named as paraclete (the Comforter) in an apparent reference to John, xiv, 15-18 (and the same reference is also found in Ibn Isḥāq's *Life of Muhammad*, pp. 102-103). W. Montgomery Watt points out that this late text has many additions designed to support Islam at the expense of Christianity, going so far as to make Jesus speak of Muḥammad as the Messiah.[31] Toland insists that some of the fundamental doctrines of Islam originate not in Sergius (the Nestorian monk who is said to have helped Muḥammad), but in the first monuments of the Christian religion (f. 73-74). He develops this point further at the end of *Le Nazaréen*, where he claims that the Muslim belief regarding Christ and his doctrine is not of Muḥammad's invention, for their beliefs are: 'aussi anciennes que le temps des Apôtres, ayant été les sentiments de sectes ou églises entières'(f. 127).

A slightly different attitude is evident in the *Doutes sur les Religions*, translated from an English text in 1739 and attributed to Toland.[32]

In this text, the author sets religions against one another. There is at first some apparent praise of Moses and Muḥammad for having left something in writing behind them, whereas Jesus did not. The writer insinuates, however, that Jesus was actually cleverer than Muḥammad, deliberately leaving the task of writing about his religion to others, so that when this writing is critically examined, no flaws can be attributed directly to him. In each of these three religions, it is a bird, swan, or pigeon which creates the mystery, thus the principle is stressed in the *Doutes* that miracles are recycled through the ages. The author attributes to Muslims the idea that no one rose against Muḥammad in his lifetime, and claims that Muḥammad ordered his followers to remain ignorant, because he clearly saw that the spirit of enquiry would not favour him. There is, of course, absolutely no basis for this claim, but the legend of Islam preaching a doctrine of ignorance dies hard.[33] Equally groundless is the equivalent supposition that Muḥammad turned men into brutes.

This approach of parallel comparison in clandestine literature does not always focus on the three leaders of the monotheist religions, and figures of legendary Roman history are sometimes introduced. Thus, the author of the *Recherches Curieuses de Philosophie*[34] (writing between 1713 and 1714), claims that fear is the basis for a belief in gods. As an example, the author outlines the case of Numa Pompilius, a legislator of the ancient Romans, who, fearing that his republic might be overthrown by maladministration, was forced to make people believe that his laws had been dictated to him by the goddess Egeria. Numa therefore promised that all manner of prosperity would be given to those who observed his laws, and threatened his transgressors with all types of misfortune. It was easy for the author of the *Recherches* to imply that Muḥammad was motivated by the same fear. What he completely lost sight of, however, was the fact that no Islamic empire existed until after Muḥammad's death. Thus, what may have been true of Numa was not applicable to Muḥammad. The author links the divine inspiration of Islam and other revealed scriptures with classical mythology, in order to devalue them further, reminding the reader that fear of shipwrecks made the ancients believe in a Jupiter who hurled thunderbolts and a Neptune who tossed the waves. The conclusion is reached that where there is no fear, it follows that there is neither superstition nor religion.[35]

The manuscript *Divinité de Jésus-Christ détruite*, written by a Spanish Jew, Isaac Orobio, and translated by Henriquez, a Jew settled in Holland, begins by showing the decline of Christianity in Africa, and the corresponding rise of Islam. Orobio is, however, no friend of Islam, expressing no sympathy for 'la loi ridicule de Mahomet', and he states a belief that all Asians have been infected by the doctrine of the impostor Muḥammad. The *Divinité* appeared with another manuscript entitled '*Dissertation sur le Messie*'. Both texts stress that miracles do not suffice to confirm divine truth or to establish the mission of true Prophets.[36] This is merely the prelude to a fierce attack on Muḥammad and Islam, which relies on Western clichés. According to the writers, Muḥammad laid the foundation for his extravagant dogma through fire and sword: a well-trained army introduced the Qur'ān to the barbarians and the leader of the brigands is still revered, as though a great prophet, throughout a large part of the world.[37] Both writers were obviously hostile to Christianity and Islam. They conclude that as both of these religions are the work of men, their followers are forced to follow the will of the stronger.

A more methodical and critical attack against Islam and its Prophet appears in the famous *Mémoire des pensées et sentiments*, written by Jean Meslier, curé of Etrépigny, at some time around 1722. A critical edition was published by J. Deprun, R. Desné, and A. Soboul, who used Manuscript 19460, Fonds Français of the B.N.F as their base text. Unlike many other clandestine writers, Meslier shows no leniency towards Islam or Muḥammad in his general condemnation of all religions, and he seems unable to find many redeeming traits in his depiction of Muḥammad.

The *Mémoire*, better known under the title of *Testament* (which was used by Voltaire when he published extracts from it), invokes the knowledge (or rather the myths) acquired by the West in previous centuries, in order to denounce Muḥammad. Meslier proceeds by using a number of *Preuves* (eight in all) in his systematic denigration of all religions. The tone is set by the first *Preuve*, which is concerned with the 'vanity and falseness of religions which are all merely human inventions'. For Meslier, it is clear that in wishing to pass off purely human laws and institutions as being of supernatural origin, the founders of religions are guilty of error, lies, and imposture. Prior to introducing Muḥammad, he mentions other cases of deceit that has been practised on people by Lycurgus, Draco, and Solon. Meslier continues by arguing that similar to Moses, who published his laws under the name of a God who (he claimed) appeared to him in a glowing bush, the false Prophet Muḥammad established his laws and religion throughout the East by making his followers believe that these had been sent him by the angel Gabriel. Among Meslier's sources for this unfavourable view of Muḥammad were Gabriel Naudé's *Aplogie pour tous les Grands Personages* and the article 'Mahomet' of Moréri's *Le grand dictionnaire historique*.

In order to attack Islam in the fourth *Preuve*, Meslier cites Montaigne, who in the *Apologie de Raymond Sebond* mentions the existence in Islam of children born without fathers (divinely conceived in the womb of virgins). If the virgin birth of Christ is acknowledged in Islam, such an unusual birth is not attributed to other people by Muslims. It is obvious that under the influence of Montaigne, Meslier distorts Muḥammad's teaching. A little later, however, Meslier seems to be slightly more sympathetic towards Muḥammad (or at any rate highly critical of Christians). Meslier examines the Christian scripture wherein the all-powerful and divine Christ has told his followers they will obtain whatever they ask in his name: if they ask a mountain or a tree to move, this will happen. Meslier's conclusion is that if the followers of Christ cannot perform these miracles, they must lack faith; or if they have faith and still cannot perform these miracles, then Christ's promises must be false. Yet, argues Meslier, if Muḥammad had made similar promises to his followers and he was unable to show these miracles, would the 'christicoles' not immediately shout: 'Ah! le fourbe! Ah! L'imposteur! Ah! Les fous de croire un tel imposteur' (I. 311). Meslier's line of argument is that standards which apply to Christians should apply equally to Muslims.

In the seventh *Preuve*, which is concerned with proving the existence of numerous false prophets and false miracles, Meslier adopts a slight change of tactics in belittling Muḥammad. Instead of giving the reader his own opinion of the leaders of the three monotheist religions and of Confucius, each of these is judged by other nations or religious groups. Meslier claims that Moses, 'ce grand législateur égyptien du peuple juif', has always been rejected by all other nations as an impostor, and his miracles were considered to be fables (ii, 358). This is a sweeping generalisation, for it is not correct to state that Muslims regard Moses as an impostor: on the contrary, he is one of the prophets on whom they are urged to bestow salutations of peace. After noting that both Jews and Gentiles regarded Christ as a mad fanatic, Meslier focuses his scorn on the Arab Muḥammad. According to him, Muḥammad is a 'famous prophet of all the Orient' revered by many nations as the greatest, the saintliest and the most faithful servant and friend of God (ii, 359). This string of superlatives is used with irony, to emphasise that Muḥammad is generally regarded as a false prophet and infamous impostor by both Christians and Jews.

In its technique, the *Difficultés sur la religion proposées au père Malebranche*, one of the outstanding monuments of the history of deism, has some affinity with Meslier's *Testament.* A critical edition of the work, which dates from about 1710, was published in 1970 by R. Mortier, who took ms. 1163 of the Bibliothèque Mazarine as his base text. Another critical edition, published in 1982 and reprinted in 1983 by F. Deloffre and M. Menemencioglu, provides a 'composite' text, which relies mainly on ms. 1163 (above) and ms. Sepher of the Public Library at St Petersburg. Deloffre and Menemencioglu attribute the *Difficultés* to Robert Challe, although some doubts persisted for a long time as to its authorship. During his military career, Challe travelled through a number of places, including Spain, Virginia, Quebec, and India, and had many opportunities to undertake a comparative study of religion, which he describes as the 'religions factices'. Although the *Difficultés* is particularly outstanding for the doctrine of natural religion outlined in the fourth and last *Cahier*, which is the first coherent system of deism in France, its anti-Catholic stance is also noticeable.[38]

In the course of this denunciation of Catholicism, certain views of Islam and Muḥammad also emerge. Taking a different approach to Meslier's *Preuves*, Robert Challe deals his hardest blows against religion by means of twenty-one *Vérités*, in the second *Cahier*. Towards the end of the first *Cahier*, Challe lets it be known that the threat of eternal punishment is meaningless to him, regardless of whether it is uttered by mufti or pope, rabbi or Siamese priest. He argues that religious leaders terrorise people into believing that they must stay in their present religion: the Jews claim that God is but the God of the children of Abraham, and the Turks (Muslims) claim that Muḥammad has the key to paradise. Challe counteracts this with the suggestion that no one actually runs any risk in abandoning Christianity, Judaism, paganism, or Mohammedanism until these have been closely examined.[39] When this examination has taken place, people will be in a better position to make up their minds.

Unlike the timid Mahmut in *The Turkish Spy*, Challe boldly proclaims that since God has only decreed a religion of conscience, it follows that the Muslim religion (like Christianity, Hinduism, Buddhism, and Confucianism) has no divine basis. He insinuates that Islam is a human-made religion: while Challe has no doubts about God's power or His justice, he does have doubts about men who claim to speak on God's behalf and books that purport to be His code. Challe asks a series of rhetorical questions that indicate such books are not works of God. He concentrates on the legendary aspects in the biography of Muḥammad, in order to destroy his credibility: it is obvious to him that Muḥammad could not put half the moon in his sleeve, since all the sleeves in the world could not hold a quarter of the moon. In concentrating on these legends, Challe deliberately refuses to distinguish between what the followers of Islam consider to be revelations and myths that have grown up around Muḥammad. That is why he comes back to the story of the moon in the sixteenth *Vérité*, which states that revelation is contaminated by being linked with myths, and provides as an example the account wherein Palinurus asks Aeneas for burial, and a subterranean voice proclaims Muḥammad as Prophet (p. 107). Challe asks if this was the same voice as that of the man who was buried alive in a pit in the *Traité des trois imposteurs*: thus the story persists.

Throughout much of the third *Cahier*, attempts are made, if not to show the superiority of Islam, at least to make it appear no worse than Christianity. Challe outlines a double standard in Roman Catholicism: when a miracle is attributed to a monk, Roman Catholics state that God has empowered the holy practitioner of the miracle, whereas, when a miracle is attributed to a Protestant, a pagan, or a Muslim, it is taken to be a sign of the devil. Challe claims that Christians everywhere depict Muḥammad as coarse, vile, and ignorant, and state that he laid the foundation of his power without any apparent means. Challe concludes that if Muḥammad did acquire some power later, this is no different to the power that is being attained and sustained by Christianity today. At this point, the *Difficultés* draws closer to the *Traité des trois imposteurs*, in stressing that Muḥammad's achievement took place in his very lifetime (and in less than twenty years), whereas Christian power took three centuries to gain a firm foothold.

These clandestine texts share a tendency to oversimplify and to assimilate, using false analogies. It is perhaps easy to reduce all religions to the guiding principle of fear, however, the lack of commitment to the study of socio-cultural causes explains why these clandestine texts rarely show a grasp of evolution among nations. The resulting lack of perspective is perhaps not surprising, since most of the comparisons and parallels have the negative ambition of condemning and destroying revealed religion and replacing it, in some cases, with the religion of their authors. Nevertheless, however negative they may appear at first, the authors of clandestine texts encourage a broadening of the horizon, favouring the relativity of values and morality. Despite their apparent hostility, they stimulate interest in foreign cultures and religions, especially Islam and Muḥammad. An analysis of these texts shows that despite the prejudices and inaccurate information of their authors, Muḥammad is presented in no worse light than Moses or Jesus: despite the epileptic fits that are attributed to him, he often has the upper hand over the latter. Clandestine literature pays homage, however grudgingly, to Muḥammad's achievements, and the charge of using force to spread religion, levelled against him since medieval times, is toned down by the realisation that force is being used in the new world by others.

Voltaire's *Mahomet*

At some point (we do not know exactly when) French writers must have deliberately chosen to neglect Moses and Jesus, as they turned Muḥammad into the sole impostor, to the extent that two famous dictionaries, Furetière's *Dictionnaire universel* (1690) and the *Dictionnaire de l'Académie française* (1694) cited Muḥammad as *the* example to back up their definition of the impostor. Furetière defines the word 'impostor' thus: 'trompeur, affronteur, calomniateur. Mahomet a été un grand imposteur, qui a trompé bien des peuples.' The dictionary of the *Académie* (1740 edition) states : 'l'imposteur est un calomniateur. On le dit aussi de celui qui invente, qui débite une fausse doctrine pour séduire le public: Mahomet était un grand imposteur.' (This definition was also that of the 1789 edition).[40]

By the time he was beginning to write *Mahomet,* Voltaire had acquired more than a basic knowledge of Islam. He had in fact become seriously interested in the Muslim aspects of the Middle East from 1732, when he wrote the tragedy of *Zaïre,* in which he contrasted the mores of Catholicism with those of Islam. Voltaire began *Zulime* in 1739, setting the play in North Africa. As we saw in Chapter 1, he was reading Sale's *The Koran* and its Preliminary Discourse in 1738. He had also read the two biographies of Muḥammad by Boulainviller and Gagnier. Two letters he wrote to Cideville and Pierre Aunillon begin with the Islamic profession of faith, 'There is no God but God and Muḥammad is his Prophet', the Arabic words being quoted in a Western script.[41] Despite the bantering mood, Voltaire had embarked on a real voyage of discovery of Islam and its Prophet. Judging by his letter to the Marquis d'Argenson (on 11th December 1742), he was to read d'Herbelot's *Bibliothèque orientale* and he hoped to locate copies of Chardin's *Voyages en Perse* and Tavernier's *Voyages en Turquie, en Perse et aux Indes.* He concluded his letter thus: 'Si vous avez toutes ces richesses faites moy l'aumône, et je tâcheray d'extraire un peu d'or de toutes ces mines là'.[42] Nevertheless, despite all the efforts Voltaire had made to learn about the Prophet, *Mahomet* evidences little of the riches offered by some of these books: the reason for this should be explored.

It is worth remembering that throughout much of the eighteenth century Muḥammad was not viewed as a prophet in the West. A public brought up on the idea that he was an impostor *par excellence* must have felt some reassurance on finding the idea confirmed as it watched or read *Mahomet.* While this work projects certain images of Muḥammad, the tragedy also reflects Voltaire's preoccupations as a dramatist. Twenty years earlier he had been acutely aware of the problems besetting the French stage in the first decades of the eighteenth century. Like any other ambitious author of his times, he sought to acquire fame by attempting the *grands genres*: that is, epic, tragedy, and comedy. His first play *Oedipe* (1718) had been a resounding success, and one finds in the public and private utterances of the playwright (who was aspiring to be Racine's successor) some interesting observations and some suggestions as to how problems specific to the narrative could be solved. In one sense, although no theorist of the theatre, Voltaire says enough on tragedy in his prefaces, *Dissertations, Discours, Épîtres,* and his correspondence to justify his own attempt to renew Aristotle's *Poetics*. The *Lettres sur Oedipe* (1719) shows the young dramatist's defence of the rights of poetic licence and invention.

More importantly, for our purpose, are Voltaire's thoughts regarding innovation in tragedy in the late 1730s. He thanks La Noue for sending him a copy of his *Mahomet II*, and applauds the changes which the latter brings to the historical character of the hero. He adds that 'une fausseté qui produit au théâtre une belle situation, est préférable en ce cas à toutes les archives de l'univers' (D 1966, 3rd April 1739). In other words, with this precedent in mind, Voltaire the dramatist allows himself to dispense with factual accuracy for the sake of scenic effect in his own *Mahomet*, on which he was to spend so much time between 1739 and 1742. It seems that in writing this letter he wished to continue the defence of poetic creation that he began in the *Lettres*, and to justify the way he treated the hero in *Mahomet* (which, although at first planned for the stage, was subsequently intended for a readership also). Following the performance of *Mahomet* in Lille, in which la Noue played the role of Mahomet, Voltaire told d'Argental that the actor 'avec sa phisionomie de singe a joué le rolle de Mahom bien mieux que n'eût fait Dufrene' (D 2477, 5th May 1741).

Despite the fact that he made substantial pronouncements on the historical figure of Muḥammad throughout his long career, many people choose to judge Voltaire's assessment of Muḥammad only by what he writes in *Mahomet*, and the context in which the play was written is often ignored. It is therefore necessary to bear in mind some background relating to religious unorthodoxy in the French Enlightenment and to Voltaire's literary ambition. In the course of a dialogue with Islam and Muḥammad, which lasted longer than that of any other writer on the same subject, Voltaire showed familiarity with the *Traité des trois imposteurs*. He later decided to put aside the two other 'impostors' in order to concentrate on the third 'impostor' in his tragedy, having referred to the clandestine text in his *Marginalia* as 'a livre dangereux'.[43] As early as 1722, he had been in personal contact with some clandestine thinkers at The Hague who were responsible for the *Traité*'s wide circulation.[44] The contact must have proved useful toward developing his portrayal of the character Mahomet. Voltaire was also, to some extent, influenced by the unorthodox views of Boulainviller, author of the *Vie de Mahomed* (1730) (see below).

Voltaire's aim, in the 1730s, was neither to provide a balanced account of the Prophet, nor to be an impartial historian: the historical Muḥammad was of little interest in *Mahomet.* He believed there he had every justification in tampering with history, which is not such a grave sin after all, when purely literary considerations are taken into account. More serious was his tampering with the response of Pope Benedict XIV, to whom he sent a copy of *Mahomet* with a letter written in Italian (D 3192, 17 August 1745).[45] Voltaire had mixed motives. One of these was to gain Benedict's support for election to the Académie Française: the worse Muḥammad looked, the better Voltaire would appear in the eyes of the Church. In his letter, Voltaire says that he was submitting to the head of the true religion a work composed against the founder of a false and barbarous sect. Seeking the Pope's protection for the play and his blessing for himself, Voltaire claimed that there was no better person to whom he could dedicate this satire of the cruelty and errors of a false prophet. He went to the length of forging part of the Pope's reply (dated 15th September 1745) to his letter.[46] Voltaire made him describe *Mahomet* as a beautiful tragedy, which Benedict had apparently taken great pleasure in reading: Benedict had done no such thing, rather he (along with his successors) maintained a dignified silence, and the original draft of his manuscript reply which has been preserved in the Vatican Archives contains no reference to *Mahomet.*[47] To promote *Mahomet* and himself, Voltaire had substituted the tragedy for the *Poème de Fontenoy*, which he knew the Pope liked. However, this intrigue failed to find favour with the Pope.[48]

Voltaire sent the first act of the tragedy to Frederick the Great in July 1739, claiming that it was written 'sinon dans un bon goût, au moins dans un goût nouveau' (D 2048). He brazenly suggested that he was the first to depict the superstition and fanaticism of the Prophet on stage. When he sent Frederick the last two acts in September, he hinted that the horrors engendered by fanaticism were drawn 'd'un pinceau assez ferme et assez vray' (D 2074). He repeated the suggestion in a later letter to Frederick (D2106, c. 1st November 1739). *Mahomet* even led him to disparage his other play, *Zulime*, for in his letter to the d'Argentals he claimed that there was more novelty and invention in one scene of *Mahomet* than in all the love lamentations of the weak *Zulime* (D 2162, 16th February, 1740). He also claimed that the danger of love (the theme of *Zulime*) is a trite subject in comparison with the danger represented by fanaticism (the subject of *Mahomet*), which was quite new territory. In his letter to Cideville (D 2221, 5th June 1740), Voltaire showed how conscious he was of the eternal problem faced by the writer who seeks originality, when he likened an original idea in the theatre to the discovery of precious ore, exclaiming how happy one would be to strike a new vein in a mine that has been so long exploited. He wondered whether with *Mahomet* he had indeed struck gold from this vein.

From a playwright's point-of-view, a beautiful situation on stage is certainly preferable to the dryness of history. In the preface to *Mariamne* in 1725, Voltaire had argued that one of the fundamental rules of the stage is to depict heroes as they were (or rather as the public imagines them), for it is easier to influence people by using the ideas they have than to influence them by giving them new ones. However, the public also wants characters that arouse pity; if the characters are disagreeable, it is clear that they must be softened, for it is necessary to think of one's public even more than of one's hero. If Voltaire had practised in *Mahomet* what he preached in the preface to *Mariamne, Mahomet* could have been a different (and probably more successful) tragedy.

As many in the audiences that watched performances of *Mahomet* at Lille and Paris, as well as many readers of the play, no doubt considered the Prophet a lecherous villain in real life, it would have been quite in order to tone down his character in the play. There were good precedents for this course of action. Thus Racine claimed in the first preface to *Andromaque* that he had softened the character of Pyrrhus as portrayed by Seneca and Virgil. Voltaire seems to have done the reverse. Privately, he admitted that in his play he had made Muḥammad appear worse than he was (perhaps because he aimed to please Pope Benedict XIV), and in a letter to Frederick, he acknowledges that he could be reproached for being overzealous in making Mahomet commit a crime that Muḥammad did not in fact commit, and that 'Mahomet n'a pas tramé précisément l'espèce de trahison qui fait le sujet de cette tragédie'.[49] He takes up this point again at the time of *Mahomet*'s successful revival in 1751, when he acknowledges to his niece, Mme. Denis, that Muslims had every right to complain, as he had made Mahomet substantially more wicked than Muḥammad was.[50] The conclusion can be drawn that Voltaire, to a greater extent than d'Herbelot, had deliberately created a character that would appeal to the non-Muslims of his time and match their preconceived ideas of the Prophet.

In his letter to Frederick dated 20th December 1740, Voltaire remarks that history simply records that Muḥammad persecuted Abu Softan (that is, Abū Sufyān) whom he calls Zopire in the play, and took away the wife of one of his disciples, Seide (Zayd). Muḥammad did no such thing, for he married Zaynab after her divorce, which leads us to question the history of the Arabs that Voltaire was reading. It has been suggested that for certain aspects of Mahomet's character Voltaire drew both on Boulainviller's *Vie de Mahomed* and Gagnier's *Vie de Mahomet*.[51]

Boulainviller's *Vie de Mahomed* does contain a meeting between Muḥammad and Abū Sufyān, leader of the Makkans and inveterate enemy of the Prophet, which occurred at the suggestion of the latter's uncle, Al-'Abbās. Al-'Abbās persuaded Abū Sufyān to find the Prophet, acknowledge him as his lord and embrace Islam. As soon as 'Umar saw the old enemy of the Prophet, he ran to Muḥammad to ask him for permission to kill Abū Sufyān. Permission for this was refused, and Muḥammad subsequently persuaded Abū Sufyān to become a Muslim. From Abū al-Fidā's *Concise History of Man*, we learn that Muḥammad granted protection to Abū Sufyān on the intervention of his uncle, who also persuaded him to give a degree of privilege to the new convert. Muḥammad decreed that whoever took shelter in Abū Sufyān's house would be spared.[52] Boulainviller's account, as well as this additional information, is authenticated in the much earlier biography of the Prophet written by Ibn Isḥāq (702-768).[53]

A first reading of these biographies may give the impression that they do not contain much material for drama. However, if he had planned to cast Mahomet in the Aristotelian mould, Voltaire would surely have found enough material from the work of Boulainviller. In particular, he could not help noticing, in Boulainviller's account, Muḥammad's generosity towards his principal enemy and his qualities as a leader. Voltaire was well aware that Aristotelian tragedy required a hero with some outstanding qualities, although with some central flaw in his character, who is then placed in circumstances which widen this flaw until it brings about a tragic downfall. Nevertheless, in *Mahomet*, the hero, far from having any outstanding qualities, is a scheming, ambitious, and wicked tyrant. The character Mahomet is exaggerated: hardly any redeeming trait is to be found in this cruel monster.

Voltaire had altered the early version of the play: namely, where Mahomet appeared triumphant and unrepentant to the end, Voltaire decided instead to make the hero feel remorse (Act V, Scene IV). If we are to believe what he says to Cideville, everyone insisted on some slight remorse at the end of the play 'pour l'édification publique'[54] Mahomet's last minute remorse occurs more as an afterthought however, and is not fully integrated with his character. Nothing that Mahomet had previously said or done would lead one to believe that he was capable of such an emotion. Thus, this remorse appears (at best) a passing impression, rather than a permanent trait of character. Cideville may well have made a most apposite comment when he suggested to Voltaire that Mahomet's remorse goes against the idea that one has of his character, adding: 'N'est-ce pas un illustre fourbe qui se joue de dieu et des hommes? Comment accorder ce portrait avec des Remords?'[55] However grateful Voltaire may have been to his friend for suggestions regarding the play, he did not accept those relating to Mahomet's remorse, and this remained in the final version. Yet Cideville felt that there was in *Mahomet* a novelty worthy of Voltaire's genius. He, too, encouraged the stereotyped account of Muḥammad's character to which the West was accustomed.

Spectator and reader alike may wonder where in *Mahomet* the novelty celebrated by Cideville is to be found. As Voltaire had denounced fanaticism (both Muslim and Christian) in *Zaîre*, the return of this critique in *Mahomet* does not appear particularly original. Perhaps Cideville is referring to the subtle attack, through Mahomet, on Jesus, who is not directly mentioned. However, there are only the vaguest of resemblances between the life and words of Jesus and those of Muḥammad: Voltaire's hero enters Makka, for instance, 'l'olive à la main' (Act II, Scene II). Many eighteenth-century critics took *Mahomet* to be a general attack on religion, rather than a specific attack on Christianity. After reading it, the Procureur Joly de Fleury, in the *Observations sur le 'Mahomet' de Voltaire*, written as a result from a request by the Lieutenant de Police , described it as 'comble de l'impiété et de l'irréligion', noting the lines spoken by Mahomet to Zopire (in Act II, Scene V), that is, 'Oui; je connais ton peuple, il a besoin d'erreur, ou véritable ou faux, mon culte est nécessaire.' Fleury suggested that the rest of this scene was indicative of a man who had no conception of God. In fact, Voltaire has made Mahomet's monotheism highly suspect, as his Mahomet resembles more a pagan who believes in oracles. In scene IV, for example, he tells 'Umar that an oracle has promised the universe to 'l'envoyé d'un dieu', whereas in Scene V, he tells Zopire: 'Il faut un nouveau culte, il faut de nouveaux fers./ Il faut un nouveau dieu pour l'aveugle univers' . The God of Islam is not *a* god but *the* God (Allah), and Islam proclaims that He is the same God worshipped in other monotheist religions, just as the religion itself is not new. The God the character Mahomet believes in, however, is almost beyond recognition.

César de Missy, to whom Voltaire had offered the right to publish a London edition of his collected works, including *Mahomet*,[56] seemed to uncritically embrace Voltaire's depiction of the Prophet. He stated he found it strange that the play should be on trial as if it were attacking the Christian religion, given that it removes from the enemies of Christianity one of their favourite commonplaces (which is to turn Muḥammad into a character worthy of contrast with Jesus). In his view, only the enemies of Christianity have legitimate grounds for complaint, for *Mahomet* represents the foundation of 'Mohammedanism' as a work of fraud and violence, having little in common with Christianity.[57] Despite the opinions of Missy, the parallel between Christ and Muḥammad was indeed being made by a discerning few who knew the play. Chesterfield told Crébillon, for example, that under the guise of Mahomet, Voltaire was really attacking Christ. He expressed surprise that nobody had noticed the parallel when *Mahomet* was first performed in Lille in 1741. He describes encountering a good Catholic at this performance, who celebrated the way this impostor and enemy of Christianity was depicted, without identifying the parallels to his own religion.[58]

After its success in Lille, *Mahomet* was performed in Paris on 9th August 1742. However, it was withdrawn in the face of opposition from the Jansenist party led by the Procureur Joly de Fleury. Voltaire complained to Cardinal Fleury about the part played by the 'cabales des convulsionnaires' in the withdrawal of his play.[59] In another letter to Cideville about *Mahomet*, Voltaire notes that 'les bonnes gens ont cru que l'on attaquait St Medard et monsieur St Paris'.[60] By drawing attention to the similarity between Mahomet's followers and the Jansenists, Voltaire injects an element of reality into his imaginary literature, for there is a clear reference in the letter to the real François de Pâris (1690-1727), to the so-called diacre Pâris, a keen Jansenist notorious for the 'miracles' of the *convulsionnaires* on his tomb at the cemetery of Saint-Médard.

Whereas the parallel between Christ and Muḥammad was fairly familiar in clandestine texts, this was not so in *Mahomet*, where Voltaire denounced Catholics so discreetly that he mystified the majority of his readers or playgoers. Much of what he states, even in his private correspondences in the period 1739-1742, does not provide adequate clue about his real intention in the play. For this, one has to go to a contemporary pamphlet about which Voltaire says little: 'Du Fanatisme', which finally became a dictionary article. In this pamphlet there is little to separate it as a work of the imagination from one based on reality, for it describes real events. These events are shown to have a bearing on the imaginary incidents occurring in *Mahomet*, with which it shows a real affinity, as both texts wage war on fanaticism and false miracles.

In *Mahomet*, as in the pamphlet 'Du Fanatisme', Voltaire attacks the *convulsionnaires*. The activities of the 'Protestant géomètre' Nicolas Faccio (referred to in the pamphlet) and his associates, the Camisards or 'French prophets', are broadly comparable to those of the Jansenists on the tomb of deacon Pâris. Faccio's friends had been prosecuted at the charge of the French churches in London, and been condemned by the Queen's Bench to the pillory as common cheats and impostors. In their attempt to bring a dead man back to life with their 'très pieuses contorsions', they may also be compared to Mahomet's disciples, who are thus described by Phanor in Act I, Scene I of the play:

> En ces murs même une troupe égarée,
> Des poisons de l'erreur avec zèle enivrée,
> De ses miracles faux soutient l'illusion,
> Répand le fanatisme et la sédition,
> Appelle son armée, et croit qu'un Dieu terrible,
> L'inspire, le conduit, et le rend invincible.

Again, one notes the reference to Mahomet's special God. In the case of Faccio, his miracle turns out to be false and Voltaire pours contempt on the naïve followers who believe that resurrection can occur infallibly under certain circumstances. Likewise, in *Mahomet*, Voltaire is particularly successful in showing Mahomet's miracle as staged. In

Act V, Scene IV, just when the villain is about to be unmasked, he appeals to God to judge between him and Séide. Séide falls dead, but his death is not due to a miracle: 'Umar had seen to it that Séide took a poison which caused slow death. The people naturally believed that Heaven had worked in Mahomet's favour. All this, of course, stems from Voltaire's fertile imagination.

Voltaire's imagination did not serve him well as dramatist, as it was too closely connected with 'propagande philosophique'. Whereas this tendency to propaganda is mostly restrained in *Zaïre*, leaving the tragic destiny of the character Zaïre to predominate, in *Mahomet* it is the propaganda against fanaticism and religious hypocrisy that is accentuated at the expense of tragedy. Muḥammad has been transformed into a 'hypocritical, love-sick, ambitious and bloodthirsty villain'.[61] *Mahomet* is a tale of love and revenge, wherein Mahomet's desire for revenge is caused by the death of his son at the hands of Zopire (Abū Sufyān). In reality, however, Qāsim (Muḥammad's son), died at an early age.

That Voltaire chose to ignore the fact that Muḥammad adopted a conciliatory approach towards Abu Sufyan (who, although the leader of the Makkans and Muḥammad's inveterate enemy, later became a Muslim), does not by itself constitute a weakness. More of a blemish to the work is the reliance of the plot on a ridiculous love story. In his love for Palmire, Mahomet appears more like a character of comedy than tragedy. Voltaire himself likened Mahomet to Molière's comic character, Tartuffe, in his letter to Frederick (20th December 1740).[62] He expanded on this idea in his letter to César de Missy (1st September 1742) where he described Mahomet as a deceitful character, 'C'est Tartuffe le grand; les fanatiques en ont fait supprimer à Paris les représentations comme les dévots étoufferent l'autre Tartuffe dans sa naissance... J'ay voulu faire voir par cet ouvrage à quels horribles excès le fanatisme peut entraîner des âmes faibles conduites par un fourbe'.[63] From beginning to end, the play produces the effect of a pamphlet on both spectator and reader alike.

The character Mahomet, who performs miracles in the play, is not only completely devoid of the finer traits of psychology, but also sins against verisimilitude. With all his defects, and without any redeeming qualities, it is hardly credible that he should have a following: Mahomet may be viewed as a satanic figure without any of the graces of Satan. Yet he often uses an epic tone of speech, particularly in Act II, Scene

V, where he unveils his plan to Zopire. It is clear that what he has in mind here is the destiny not only of himself, but of Arabia and the whole world:

> Le glaive et l'Alcoran, dans mes sanglantes mains,
> Imposeraient silence au reste des humains…
> Chaque peuple à son tour a brillé sur la terre,
> Par les lois, par les arts, et surtout par la guerre;
> Le temps de l'Arabie est à la fin venu.

Mahomet goes on to say that he will build Arabia on the ruins of the Roman Empire and the weakness of Persia, India and Egypt. Far from displaying originality here, Voltaire has chosen to emphasise the ruthless nature of the conqueror, long attributed to Muḥammad by the West, and to popularise an established view of Islam as a religion preached using violence rather than persuasion.

The impact of form on writers of the imagination

The three sections of the present chapter, based on different genres of writing (namely, the epistolary novel, prose tracts, and verse tragedy) may well give the impression of being discrete and offering only partial assessments of the three impostors. The last part of this observation is justified since the form chosen by the writers prevents them from giving a thorough account of their main protagonists. Yet there is a common thread throughout these texts, which is based on the fertile imagination of their authors. The unifying element is in the negative reflections on the leaders of the monotheist religions central to each of them. Only a brief reference was made to the *Lettres Persanes*, because few of its letters have a direct bearing on Muḥammad. As an epistolary novel it appears superior to *The Turkish Spy*, offering for much of the time multiple points-of-view on a variety of subjects, in comparison with the single viewpoint provided by the one-way correspondence of the latter (Mahmut is always writing to others, but he never receives any reply, or replies are not directly addressed to him). This single point of view is, however, also present in the letters on depopulation (letters 112 to 122 of the *Lettres Persanes*) addressed by Usbek to Rhédi.

Letter 114 attributes the Qur'ānic statement in *Sūra* 2, l. 187 (that 'your wives are your garments') to the Prophet. The Prophet is also credited with a statement based on *Sūra* 2, l. 223: 'Your wives are/ As a tilth unto you/ So approach your tilth…/ But do some good act/ For your souls beforehand'. Montesquieu's criterion for judging Muḥammad in the *Lettres Persanes* appears to have a purely utilitarian and economic (rather than social) basis. If such a criterion were generally applied, the merit of any leader of religion would rest solely on whether their system favoured population growth. In this respect, Muḥammad is depicted less as an impostor and more as a poor legislator.[64] He is condemned not for violation of natural laws, but because he has allowed nature to impose its own law. The letter suggests that nature employs all the force that it is left with to preserve itself; and if hurried, it completely loses its 'vertu productrice et puissance générative'. Islamic polygamy apparently precipitates nature, and as a result of this does nothing to increase the birth rate. The Qur'ānic references to women in letter 114 may appear to create an atmosphere of authenticity, but all these quotations are cited out of context, and do not reflect the true aims of Islam and the Prophet. The purpose of the legislation was not to increase the Muslim population but to safeguard the moral welfare of Muslim women. Islam was not, of course, the only religion to be attacked on economic grounds. In letter 117, for example, both monasticism and the celibacy of priests in Catholic countries are made responsible for the decline in population.

In *The Turkish Spy*, the hero Mahmut begins as a Muslim with impeccable Sunnī credentials, but he soon begins to have doubts about religion and to ask awkward questions, hinting that all religions are based on imposture. The clandestine texts, on the other hand (especially Meslier's *Mémoire* and Challe's *Difficultés sur la Religion*) explicitly denounce religions as having been invented by impostors, who pass off their opinions as divine. The writers of these texts attempt to provide rational explanations for the origins of religion, without examining the socio-cultural factors to any depth.

While the majority of texts in this chapter have been shown to have hostility to Moses and Jesus in equal measure, *Mahomet*, on the other hand, is most hostile to Muḥammad, and seeks to show that far from divine, religion can be manipulated by one man, Mahomet, who (in Act V, Scene IV) even boasts having made God serve his purpose:

> Dieu que j'ai fait servir aux malheurs des humains,
> Adorable instrument de mes affreux desseins.

This incredible character would have us believe that he did all for love (Act V, Scene IV). Even more incredible perhaps is the fact that the play remained part of the regular repertory of the Comédie-Française for more than a century, with 273 performances up to 1852.[65] *Mahomet* must have satisfied the needs of a certain theatre-going public at a certain period in history, just as it must have appealed to readers with their caricatured ideas of Muḥammad.

The form chosen by Voltaire for his attack on Muḥammad in *Mahomet* (French classical tragedy) certainly has an impact on the content of the work, and on our understanding of it. Although *Mahomet* at times imitates epic poetry, and thereby violates some of the rules of this tragic form (thereby ensuring its relegation to its margins), Voltaire still aspired for it be considered alongside the tragedies of Racine or Corneille. Like the masters of French classical tragedy, Voltaire only treats a crucial episode in the life of his main protagonist, so that at least the unity of action could be seen to have been observed. The character Mahomet does not himself die, but causes enough deaths to be damned. It is certainly not in this play that Voltaire's real thoughts on Islam and Muḥammad are to be sought. However, the restrictions imposed by a French classical model did not prove to be a permanent obstacle to Voltaire's aims of doing justice to Muḥammad. Voltaire wrote other texts which enabled him to present a more complete and balanced picture of the Prophet. Writers during the Enlightenment would display a rather positive attitude towards Muḥammad.

Notes

1. In the preface to *Exoticism in the Enlightenment*, the editors, G. S. Rousseau and Roy Porter, suggest that for most untraveled Englishmen (as well as Frenchmen), the 'exotic' actually commenced , as it were, rather close to home: as close as the Dutch lowlands or the Swiss Alps (p. vii-viii). If we accept their suggestion, the Middle East should be classed as the 'remote exotic'. See my review of the book in *British Journal for Eighteenth-Century Studies*, vol.14, no. 2 (1991), pp. 211-212. In the introduction to his critical edition of Voltaire's *Zadig*, G. Ascoli noted that literature of the imagination cashed in on this curiosity for things oriental that was prevalent in the seventeenth century: on stage and in Eastern tales the oriental colour was often superficial, but it was a sign of the literary fashion then in vogue. In his survey of works on the Orient,

Ascoli observed that exotic taste was at its height towards 1745. See *Zadig ou la Destinée. Histoire orientale*, ed. G. Ascoli, revised by J. Fabre (Paris, 1962).

2. See W. H. McBurney, 'The Authorship of *The Turkish Spy*', *PMLA* ,72, pp. 915-935 and J. E. Tucker, 'On the authorship of *The Turkish Spy*: An État Present', *Papers of the Bibliographical Society of America*, 52, pp. 34-57.
3. Bibliothèque Nationale de France, Fonds Italien, 1006,1007.
4. 'L'esploratore Turco' e la Genesi del Romanzo Epistolare Pseudo-Orientale', *Studi Secenteschi*, 7, pp. 35-65.
5. See A.J.Weitzman (ed.), *Letters Writ by a Turkish Spy* (London, 1970), p. xv.
6. The *Lettres Persanes* seeks to portray an even more legendary Muḥammad than *The Turkish Spy*. In the thirty-ninth *Lettre*, Haggi Ibbi says that manifest signs always announce the birth of extraordinary men, adding that nothing is more miraculous than Muḥammad's birth. God having decided to send this great Prophet among the living in order to chain up Satan, created a light a thousand years before Adam. It finally reached Muḥammad as an authentic testimony declaring that he descended from the patriarchs. The earth shook three times, all idols prostrated themselves and the thrones of kings were overthrown , thus heaven could not do more to sanction his divine mission. Writing to Usbek at Erzerun in letter 18, Méhémet-Hali portrays Muḥammad as a magician who apparently created Japhet, Noah's son, out of mud, then asked him to relate the story of the arch.
7. I. O. Wade, *The clandestine organization and diffusion of philosophic ideas in France from 1700 to 1750* (Princeton, 1938).
8. See ' La légende *De Tribus Impostoribus et ses origines islamiques*', *Revue de l'Histoire des Religions*, 82 (1920) pp. 74-78, reprinted in *Opera Minora*, ed. Y. Moubarac (Beirut, 1963).
9. I showed that this story is to be dated later than 1080 in '*Le Traité des trois imposteurs et ses origines arabes*', *Dix-Huitième Siècle* (1996), pp. 169-174.
10. See his article '*Le De Tribus Impostoribus et les origines arabes de l'athéisme philosophique européen*' in *Les Cahiers de l'ATP*, October 2003, pp. 1-10. This academic from the Unversity of Nice upholds the tradition of Professor Marie-Helene Cotoni from the same University, who inspired me to write on clandestine literature with her article 'Ebauches d'Etude Comparative des Religions dans la Littérature Clandestine du XVIIIe Siècle', published in the *Annales de la Faculté des Lettres et Sciences Humaines de Nice*, 22, pp. 81-97.
11. T.Voronova, ed. *Corpus des notes marginales de Voltaire* (Berlin,1979), 1 : A-B, p. 429.
12. Apart from Rétat's edition, St Etienne, other editions of the *Traité* include those by Silvia Berti, *Trattato dei Tre Impostori* (Turin, 1994), and Françoise Charles-Daubert, *Le Traité des trois imposteurs et l'Esprit de Spinoza* (Oxford, 1999).
13. B. L., Add. mss., 12064, f.7v°.
14. See, for instance, G. Naudé, *Apologie pour tous les grands hommes qui ont été accusés de magie* (Paris, 1635), p. 168; P. Bayle, 'Mahomet' in *Dictionnaire historique* and the *Difficultés sur la religion.*
15. B. L., Sloane 2039 ; Bibliothèque municipale de Rouen, 1575.
16. B. L., Stowe 47.

17. In Judaeo-Christian theology the equivalent of a 'Mehdi' would be a messiah. The Shī'ites believe that their hidden imām will return at the right time as the 'Mehdi' (the guide) to right wrongs and establish justice on earth. Some Sunnīs also share this belief in the return of the 'Mehdi' at the end of the world to convert all to Islam.
18. Between 1085 and 1090, a Berber dynasty of North Africa, the Almoravids, controlled the whole of Muslim Spain. An armed insurrection took place against them by another Berber dynasty under the instigation of Ibn Tūmart. Although defeated by the Almoravids in 1123, his successor 'Abd al-Mu'min managed to destroy Almoravid power in North Africa in 1147 and eventually exercised power over Spain. See W. Montgomery Watt, *Islamic Philosopy and Theology* (Edinburgh, 1962), pp. 132-136.
19. The cleansing of his heart while he was young and the receipt of divine light later in his life are the very miracles that happened to Muḥammad, according to Arab legends.
20. Extracts from Ibn al-Athīr in *Histoire des Berbères*, trans. W. M. de Slane (Algiers, 1851), ii. p. 575.
21. See the article of J. F. P. Hopkins on Ibn Tumart in *The Encyclopedia of Islam*, second edition, p. 959.
22. B. L., Sloane 2039,f. 56.
23. Bibliothèque de l'Arsenal, Mss. 2239.
24. There is a close affinity between this attitude and that of the authors who define imposture in various dictionaries (see below).
25. Bibliothèque Mazarine, mss. 1195. Written in 1713 and published in 1714, with the French translation of Anthony Collins's *Discourse on Free Thinking.* I have consulted both the manuscript and the published text, and quote from the latter.
26. For an interesting study of those Muslims who actually travelled to Europe, see B. Lewis, *The Muslim discovery of Europe* (1982) and N. Matar, *Europe through Arab eyes 1578*-1727 (2008).
27. Bibliothèque Municipale de Rouen, mss. 1580.
28. B. M de Rouen, mss. 1124.
29. See B. M. de Rouen, mss. 1554, in Recueil Théologique. The full French title is *Le Nazaréen ou le Christianisme des Juifs, des Gentils et des Mahométans.* The *Nazarenus* is edited by Justin Champion (Oxford, 1999). This edition reproduces both the early French manuscript and the later printed text in English.
30. It was published with an English translation by Laura and Lonsdale Ragg (Oxford, 1907). See B. E. Schwarzbach, 'The Sacred Genealogy of a Voltairean Polemic: the Development of Critical Hypotheses Regarding the Composition of the Canonical and Apocryphal Gospels', *Studies on Voltaire and the Eighteenth Century* (Oxford, 1986), vol. 245, pp.322-323.
31. In *Muslim-Christian Encounters* (London, 1991), p. 117. The late Professor Watt was rather vague about identity when he spoke of an English Deist who had made some use of it to attack the Christian orthodoxy.
32. B.N.F., 24885.
33. In the *Lettres Persanes* also there is nostalgic regret for the happy ignorance of Muḥammad's children. Montesquieu allows Rhédi , in letter 105 to Usbek, to

denounce the sciences and the arts of the West and to wish for the 'aimable simplicité si chérie de notre saint Prophète'. Rhédi pines for the good old times and the tranquility that reigned in the hearts of their forefathers.

34. B.N.F, F.F., 9107.
35. The *Traité des miracles* (written about 1718) has some affinity with the *Dissertation sur le Messie*, since it argues that miracles are not a reliable or infallible method of proving the authenticity of a religion. In Bibliothèque Mazarine, mss 1195, p. 2. the author uses a different technique to devalue the miracles made by Moses, Jesus, and Muḥammad, introducing the Indians and the Chinese, who are allowed to scoff at these miracles (p. 3). This author conveniently forgets that the Indians relied heavily on incredible myths to support their philosophy.
36. Bibliothèque Mazarine, mss 1194, p.9 ; B.N.F, F.F, 14928, p.250.
37. Do, mss. 1194, p. 50; do, mss. 14928, p. 273.
38. See Mortier edition, p. 32.
39. Deloffre and Menemencioglu eds., p. 56.
40. See Olivier-Henri Bonnerot, 'Le Prophète et la Guerre: Mahomet dans la pensée des Lumières', extract from ' La Bataille, l'Armée, la Gloire', Actes du Colloque de Clermont Ferrand, 1983 (Clermont, 1985), p. 70.
41. D 2649, 1st September, 1742 and D 2671, c.October 1742.
42. D2698.
43. See *Corpus des notes marginales de Voltaire*, ed. T. Voronova (Berlin, 1979), vol.1: A-B, p. 429.
44. See M. Jacob, *The Radical Enlightenment: Pantheists, Freemasons and Republicans* (London, 1981), p. 103, quoted by N. Cronk in the Preface to *Le Fanatisme, ou Mahomet le Prophète*, critical edition by C. Todd in *Les Oeuvres Complètes de Voltaire*, Voltaire Foundation (Oxford, 2002), vol. 20 B.
45. This letter was the culmination of a series of letters in the campaign he had orchestrated to win over the Pope and which he addressed to various people in 1745, including a minister, the marquis d'Argenson. Voltaire showed how keen he was to ingratiate himself with the Pope whose protection he sought. The latter actually gave him two medals (D 3111, 3rd May, D 3128, 30th May, D 3193, 17th August).
46. See *Mahomet*, ed. C. Todd, pp. 159-161.
47. See the notes to D 3210(15th September 1745). Pope Benedict XIV appears to have taken a wiser stand than Pope Benedict XVI in a similar situation. In the full text of his lecture delivered at the University of Regensburg, before an academic audience on 12th September 2006, the latter makes a reference to the Byzantine Emperor Manuel II Paleologus, who said to a Persian interlocutor in the 1390s: 'Show me just what Mohammed brought that was new, and there you will find things only evil and inhuman, such as his command to spread by the sword the faith he preached'. Benedict XVI also stated that the emperor must have known that *Sūra* 2, 256 reads: 'There is no compulsion in religion'. But he added that this was one of the *Sūras* of the early period, when Muḥammad was still powerless and under threat, hinting that the latter behaved differently when he was stronger. In fact, this *Sūra* was revealed in the later period in Madīna at about 623. The Islamic position has always been that the wars Muḥammad waged in the last eight years of his life were against pagan

Arabs and in self-defence. Pope Benedict XVI does not seem to have distanced himself sufficiently from the Byzantine emperor.

48. It took nearly two centuries for the cloud under which Pope Benedict XIV lived to be dispelled. Luca di Castro drew attention to Voltaire's forgery in *Due Falsa di Voltaire: la Dedicace del Mahomet et l'Accettazione Papale* (Napoli, 1939) and the *Figaro Littéraire* of 21 September, 1957 published an article by Maurice Chapelan entitled 'Voltaire a Commis un Faux Bref de Benoît XIV et Falsifié une Lettre de Frédéric II'. See the standard biography of Voltaire by R. Pomeau, *Voltaire en son Temps*, 2nd edn. (Oxford and Paris, 1995), i. 470-472. The section covering the years 1734-1749 of Voltaire's biography was written by R. Vaillot and revised by R. Pomeau.
49. D 2386, 20th December 1740.
50. D 4597, 29th October 1751.
51. R. Pomeau, *La Religion de Voltaire* (Paris, 1974), p. 150.
52. See Magdy Gabriel Badir, *Voltaire et l'Islam, Studies on Voltaire and the Eighteenth Century* (Banbury, 1974), vol. CXXV, pp. 127-130.
53. *Sīrat Rasūl Allāh*, translated by A. Guillaume as *The Life of Muhammed* (Oxford, 1955), pp. 547-548. See also Martin Lings, *Muhammad: His life based on the earliest sources* (London, 1983), pp. 295-96 and 308.
54. D2515, 19 July 1741.
55. D2521, 7 August 1741
56. D2648, 1st September 1742.
57. D2578, 18th November 1742.
58. D2653, 6th September 1742.
59. D2644, 22nd August 1742.
60. D 2649, 1st September 1742.
61. See C. Todd, ed. *Le Fanatisme, ou Mahomet le Prophète*, p. 12.
62. D 2386.
63. D 2648.
64. See A. Grosrichard, *Structure du sérail : La Fiction du despotisme asiatique dans l'Occident Classique* (Paris, 1979), pp. 145-146.
65. *Mahomet*, ed. C. Todd, p. 30

3

Muḥammad in the French Enlightenment

The Comte Henri de Boulainviller (1658-1722)

Given their anti-religious bias, many works of the imagination in the late seventeenth and the first half of the eighteenth centuries did in fact present a very negative picture of the Prophet. It does not necessarily follow, however, that all French writings prove equally hostile towards him, and one could predict that some of them at least would do him justice. The general weariness that followed the wars of religion between Roman Catholics and Protestants in France may have contributed, to some extent, to a change in outlook. Two black episodes in the history of French Protestantism (the massacre of St Bartholomew in 1572 and the revocation in 1685 of concessions that had been made to Protestants in the Edict of Nantes) were remembered painfully for a long while afterward. Unsurprisingly, some French thinkers began to develop an interest in the different ways of thinking and behaving offered by non-Western nations, and thus began to turn their attention to the 'other'. Voltaire was one of those who clearly expressed the urge to understand the 'other'. In the Avant-propos to the 'Nouveau Plan d'une Histoire de l'Esprit Humain', published in the *Mercure* in April 1745, he complained that too much attention had been devoted to the Roman Empire and to the ancient Greeks and Romans. He was critical of most universal histories for failing to take into account the existence of other nations.

Thus it was natural that horizons in the Enlightenment period should stretch further than in the Renaissance. This broadening of horizons is evidenced by the attention devoted to distant civilisations and countries, and to religious leaders such as Zoroaster, Buddha,

Confucius, and finally Muḥammad, who was perceived to be the 'founder' of Islam. The major figures of the French Enlightenment (Boulainviller, Voltaire, Diderot, and Rousseau) still maintained their scepticism about religion; however, they were perhaps in a position to provide a better understanding of Muḥammad than Protestant writers such as Jurieu and Bayle who had been bruised by religious dissent. In one of his works, the *Vie de Mahomed*, Boulainviller (whose name is usually spelt Boulainvilliers) frequently extols the virtues of Muḥammad. Before venturing to work on Muḥammad's biography, Boulainviller had completed substantial volumes on French history, published posthumously. These include the *Histoire de l'ancien gouvernement de France* (1727), the *Etat de la France* (1727), and the *Essai sur la noblesse* (1730). He was certainly not inexperienced at scholarly research and writing, as some critics (who are unfamiliar with French civilisation) would have us believe.

While attempting to break with the traditional Western perception of Muḥammad in the *Vie de Mohamed*, Boulainviller was much maligned by Orientalists, especially Gagnier, who dismissed this biography as a simple novel. Admittedly, the biography on which Boulainviller worked from 1718 to 1721, was incomplete. As he concludes it at the first *hijra*, when groups of early Muslims were forced to migrate to Abyssinia in 615, Boulainviller misses out major events affecting the life of the Prophet, including the death in 619 of Khadīja (Muḥammad's first wife), and of Abū Ṭālib (his uncle and protector), the mystical Night Journey, Muḥammad's own *hijra* from Makka to Madīna in 622, the occupation of Makka in 630 and Muḥammad's death in 632. On the other hand, the shorter chronology adopted by Boulainviller has its own merits. Similar to the approach adopted later by Sale in his 'Preliminary Discourse' to his translation of the Qur'ān, Boulainviller spares the reader the details of Muḥammad's military expeditions. He chooses instead to concentrate on Muḥammad's essential teaching and to present his achievements in a new light.

Some critics reproach Boulainviller with having no background in Arabic, despite his own acknowledgement of this, and his clear statements that he was unable to have direct access to Arab sources (p. 7). One may note that the same type of criticism is never levelled at the other masters of the Enlightenment, all of whom lacked knowledge of Arabic. This criticism may even occur as petty, when we remember that millions of Muslims worldwide suffer from the same linguistic deficiency, a point made by Rousseau (see below). Boulainviller made up for his shortcoming by acquiring a solid documentation on Islam and its Prophet, based on material translated from Arabic into European languages. In his biography of Muḥammad, which at first circulated in manuscript form under the title *Histoire de Mahomet et de ses premiers successeurs*, before its publication in 1730 as *Vie de Mahomed*,[1] he shows some familiarity with works dealing with Islam and Muḥammad, citing El-Makin, Edward Pococke (the elder), du Ryer, the Qur'ānic commentators Jalāl al-Dīn al-Suyūṭī and al-Zamakhsharī, the canonical Traditionalists al-Bukhārī and Muslim, as well as d'Herbelot, Marracci, Reland, and Ockley. His reference to the Arab writers, however, is indeed fleeting, and we saw in Chapter 1 that Gagnier felt the need to counteract Boulainviller's *Vie de Mahomed* with a *Vie de Mahomet* (1732), a popular novel partly based on his more learned Latin-Arabic edition of Abū al-Fidā's *Concise History of Man*. The verdict of posterity, however, has been in favour of his rival, to the extent that one may wonder why there has been such a revival of interest in Boulainviller in our times.

After its publication in London, the *Vie de Mahomed* appeared a year later in Amsterdam and it enjoyed a degree of success in Europe, with translations into English, German and Italian. More recently, Norman Daniel has noted that there was 'considerable charm' in the book.[2] Nevertheless, its significance has little to do with charm, and Boulainviller has been better understood by Diego Venturino, who devoted four important studies to him and the Prophet from the 1990s. In 1992 Venturino wrote a doctoral thesis on Boulainviller's religious and political thought, and published an Italian translation of the *Vie de Mahomed* and an article on Boulainviller. In 2000, he further published an article on Muḥammad discussing Boulainviller.[3] Boulainviller has also been discussed by Ann Thomson in an article published in 1997.[4]

The Vie de Mahomed was read by contemporaries, such as Mathieu Marais, as being one of Boulainviller's anti-religious works. Marais suggested that it should be handled with care because of some of the indirect criticisms of the Christian religion to be found in the text. In fact, in the manuscript Boulainviller unambiguously states that Muḥammad attacked Christian doctrine (f. 148) and that he established a religion not only in harmony with what his countrymen knew and felt according to the prevailing customs of the land, but also one that satisfied general human ideas, and thus he won more than half of the population over to his way of thinking in less than forty years (f. 165). In his polemical use of Muḥammad against Christianity, Boulainviller now-and-then feels the need to describe Muḥammad as an impostor and to be negative towards the Arabs: this must be seen as a concession to Christian feelings. This is the kind of tactic that was to be used by Sale in the *Preliminary Discourse*, when he does not wish to appear too well-disposed towards Muḥammad (see above). The description of the Prophet as an impostor is particularly prominent at the beginning of book 1 of the *Vie*, where the Arabs are portrayed as being more destructive than the Goths, and hostile to science. Boulainviller subsequently rehashes the story of the burning of the library at Alexandria on Caliph 'Umar's instructions, and clearly seeks to contribute to the medieval Western tradition of regarding Muḥammad and his followers as promoters of ignorance. However, he later states that the Arabs showed an even greater keenness for the sciences than the Greeks and the Romans: thus the unpromising accusations at the start are soon set aside.

Boulainviller subsequently attempts to dispose of a few myths about Muḥammad and Muslims. He rejects the idea of the miraculous, which Christians in general entertain about Muḥammad, based on their own belief in saints who are capable of performing miracles. Muslims, he argues, are far from having such expectations, although they are convinced of the high vocation of the Prophet on whom they shower blessings of peace. He provides as an example Muḥammad's hanging coffin in the mosque at Madīna, suggesting that this is a fiction more in keeping with Christian ideas regarding saints and their miracles. Boulainviller argues that it betrays such a deep ignorance of the foundations of Islam that it is impossible not to attribute this myth to ignorant monks living in Palestine at the time of the Crusades.

Previous depictions of Muḥammad as an impostor give way to a portrayal of him as a new legislator, whose chief characteristic is the gift of persuasion through which the most sublime heroes of their times in valour, generosity, moderation, and wisdom were converted to his religion (p. 133). One cannot help feeling that Boulainviller sometimes succumbs to the temptation of using hyperbole to portray the Arabs in history, although he does argue that Muḥammad's doctrine need not be shrouded in mystery, and that his conversions occurred without the assistance of any miraculous events. He is amazed at the power of Muḥammad's eloquence which made him defy men and angels to compose anything to equal what he had given the public, that is, the Qur'ān. Nevertheless, he obviously dislikes what he describes as Muḥammad's haughtiness, finding it offensive (p. 134).[5]

It should be pointed out that Boulainviller's technique is not only to attack Christianity but also to describe to his readers his understanding of Islam. He is often alive to its spirit, grasping well Muḥammad's teaching against *shirk* (that is, association), whereby an infinite being has no need of another power to produce an effect (p. 135). In trying to define Islam, he is led to challenge the fundamental basis of Christianity, including the doctrines of the Trinity and the Incarnation. He argues that Muḥammad condemns the Trinity because, 'Christians admit a generation in the Divinity - generation which is obviously useless if it produces the same God' (p. 135).

Boulainviller does his best to rid Islam of the stereotypes with which it was linked, but he cannot refrain from reinforcing some of these. Thus, he claims that the dying Muḥammad, on being consulted by his disciples about which was most essential of the teachings he had left for them, recommends peace: among the practical means of preserving peace he included the need for permanent attention to cleanliness and the precaution for men to enclose and keep their wives separate. This reference to cleanliness echoes the criticism levelled by many western writers at Muslims who spend their time 'washing their bodies in order to purify their souls'. In *The Turkish Spy*, for instance, Marana makes Mahmut say that Muslims follow nature's principles according to which the soul shares in the impurities of the body as long as it stays in it (letter 104 to Nathan). Boulainviller himself questions the link between the jealousy of Muslim men towards their wives, and their attention to cleanliness, with peace and calm. Ignoring the context in which segregation of men and women takes place in the Muslim world, Boulainviller suggests that the seclusion of women, as practised throughout the Orient, is an assured means of excluding them from political intrigues and preventing the storms they have often caused in the world: pleasing their husbands alone will lead to domestic and social peace. In this attitude to segregation in the Muslim world,

Boulainviller says nothing that sets him apart from other Western writers. Such segregation, it may be noted, is not part of the teaching of Muḥammad, who actually favoured the participation of women in religious and social life. At this point in the *Vie de Mahomed,* the approach to Muḥammad remains quite conservative.

Book 2 of the *Vie*, which *inter alia* deals with the genealogy and life of Muḥammad, seems to justify the attention devoted to Boulainviller in contemporary scholarship. Muḥammad is portrayed there as God's instrument for punishing the wicked Christians of the Orient who destroyed religion with their quarrels and mutual animosity (a notion admittedly current with writers such as Grotius).[6] More daring (even scandalous in Christian eyes) is the suggestion made by Boulainviller that Muḥammad is God's agent. Apparently, there was a need for Muḥammad toward achieving the following: (1) the removal of certain Eastern Christians who had compromised religion with their disputes and mutual animosities; (2) the recapture (from the Greeks and Romans) of the pleasant lands of Syria and Egypt, and of those lands hallowed by the Messiah where puerile devotions were encouraged; (3) the submission and punishment of the Persians for the sufferings caused to the victims of their ambition, and; (4) the transmission of knowledge of the unity of God from India to Spain, and the abolition of worship apart from that of God (p. 164).

A credible Prophet is necessary to provide knowledge of the unity of God to the world, and according to Boulainviller, Muḥammad was such a Prophet. Boulainviller takes the opportunity to define the Muslim conception of prophethood: Muslims, he argues, consider the prophetic light to be an internal testimony that provides a constant reminder of the perfect use of reason, which often communicates (to the person experiencing this prophetic light) knowledge of the future, and even the innermost feelings of people. They claim that this light was transmitted to Adam, and from him to all the Prophets, including Muḥammad. It will not completely disappear because it is necessary for the reformation of men. This gift[7] of prophecy is therefore simply understood as the mission to once again teach neglected or forgotten truths (pp. 187-188). Boulainviller minimises the importance of prophesising the future: he even agrees with the Arabs that it is not so much knowledge of the future that distinguishes a Prophet, as the talent of speaking eloquently and steering people clear of error by reminding them of what they owe to truth and justice. In Boulainviller's view, Muḥammad admirably satisfies this requirement.

An anonymous author took up the narrative at the point where Boulainviller's ended. At the end of a new book 3, this author had no hesitation in concluding that Muḥammad was an impostor who had progressed from a humble station in life to become the king of Arabia. Boulainviller clearly differed considerably in opinion with this author, as he devotes several parts of books 1 and 2 to challenging the notion (although he uses the word 'impostor' superficially numerous times to refer to Muḥammad). Claiming that the latter acts as God's instrument in implementing the objectives identified above, Boulainviller finds it difficult to reconcile this fact with the perception of him as a clever impostor full of bodily and intellectual defects. If Muḥammad has defects, he suggests, he cannot be despised because of his great plans for religion and politics, which he carries out with great success. Boulainviller suggests that commonsense dictates that if Muḥammad were an impostor (implying he was not), he must have possessed superior qualities for this to convince others. Furthermore, Boulainviller regards as spurious the debate about Muḥammad's imposture on which Christian-Muslim controversy has focused. Boulainviller suggests that if Muḥammad had the grace of Christian revelation, there would have been no doctrine as plausible and so in conformity with reason, nor one which is so comforting for the just (p. 247). The inference to the reader is that Muḥammad's doctrine indicates that he was indeed no impostor.

Earlier on, Boulainviller had accused Ockley, author of the *History of the Saracens* (1708), of spreading the myth of Muḥammad as impostor: according to Boulainviller the Cambridge Professor had relied too much on Prideaux. He argues that in *The true nature of imposture revealed in the life of the impostor Mohammad*, Prideaux failed to distance himself from the popular idea that makes the so-called Prophet an ignorant and despicable impostor (p. 166).

It is natural that there should have been some reference to Muḥammad's family in the *Vie*. Despite his criticism of Prideaux on the subject of Muḥammad's alleged imposture, Boulainviller is not particularly ill-disposed towards the former when it is a matter of giving accurate details on some members of the Prophet's family.[8] He rejects d'Herbelot's idea that Fāṭima, Muḥammad's daughter, was the daughter of 'Ā'isha (p. 236): in reality, 'Ā'isha never had any children. Boulainviller prefers Prideaux's suggestion that Fāṭima was the daughter of Khadīja (which she in fact was), arguing that 'Ā'isha would not have rejected her own son-in-law 'Alī in favour of a stranger Mu'āwiya, on the question of the Prophet's succession, had she been Fāṭima's mother. In Boulainviller's own words, Prideaux had 'the advantage of verisimilitude'.

In providing further information on Muḥammad's family, Boulainviller seems to have had greater recourse to the Qur'ān than to the *Sīra*, although when he refers to the attack by Muḥammad's enemies (Abū Jahl and his pagan confederates) who taunted him with the loss of his two infant sons, he uses both sources. He is accurate when he gives the name of the Prophet's eldest son as Qāsim, a detail not found in the Qur'ān. He commits minor errors, however, by mentioning Qāsim's death at the age of four instead of two, and referring to Muḥammad's three daughters instead of four. The more important point about Muḥammad's children comes from the Qur'ān and from Qur'ānic commentators. Boulainviller mentions that Muḥammad's enemies nicknamed him 'Abtar', that is, one without posterity. This is an offensive term by which they intended to diminish him. In reply, Boulainviller says, Muḥammad produced *Sūra* 108.[9] In this *Sūra*, it is the person who hates the Prophet who will be without posterity. Boulainviller makes God declare that 'in place of posterity he has given the Prophet the whole world to inherit and all peoples inhabiting it as children who obey the lessons of his doctrine which contains nothing but the truth' (p. 232). His attributing *Sūra* 108 to Muḥammad is understandable: if he had simply stated that this *Sūra* was revealed to Muḥammad, Boulainviller would have sounded like a Muslim, an association he was hoping to avoid.

Boulainviller rejects the Western caricature of Muḥammad seducing his followers through polygamy in this life and through the promise of a sensual paradise in the hereafter, arguing that it would be a complete travesty to suggest that sexual licence was used by Muḥammad to produce a work as great and as solid as that of Islam (p. 169). Boulainviller identifies here the existence of a false reasoning, based on the assumption that before the mission of the 'so-called' Prophet, polygamy did not exist in Arabia, and that it had never been practised in the Orient, which is simply not true.

Boulainviller asserts that Muḥammad must have had great talents (without simply making promises) to be able to hold sway over such a large part of the world, and throughout the *Vie de Mahomed* there is much insistence on these talents. Boulainviller goes so far as to say that to deprive him of these is to satisfy one's hatred of him (p. 179). Like other prophets, he was not sent by God to teach new or mysterious doctrines giving rise to challenges. Rather, Muḥammad is depicted as looking on bishops, priests, and the clergy as a body of men who were using religion to serve their passions and greed: thus they were identified as the source of all the disputes that divided Christianity at that time. The anti-clerical trend in Boulainviller's thought is apparent here: he found it convenient to attribute to Muḥammad ideas which the latter probably never had. Boulainviller thus comes to the most mysterious doctrine, a suggestion that had first occurred in Book 1, but is now made more explicit. Namely, that it is the Incarnation which turns a man into God, by the union of two incompatible natures. Muḥammad believed that the words of Christ and his disciples had been distorted to give them a meaning he never intended. In this way, the entire dogma of Christianity is thus made to rest on a misunderstanding.

Two contrasting elements are striking in Boulainviller's juxtaposition of Muḥammad's teaching with Christ's teaching, and there is a mixture of divergence and convergence between the two. Muḥammad established the doctrine of the unity of God as the basis of all truth in religion, with the corresponding need to fear and love Him. To successfully fulfil this duty to God, one had simply to make a proper use of the reason He has given us. Thus Muḥammad preaches a rational religion, in which Boulainviller sees no trace of mysticism. Boulainviller completely ignores the existence of Sufi aspects in Islam (that is, its mystic elements), claiming that its truths of the unity and supreme power of God can be demonstrated by simple human reason. In this way, Boulainviller turns Islam into a religion very close to eighteenth-century Deism.

This is nevertheless close to Christianity also, since it teaches resurrection and the Day of Judgement which, according to him, are dogmas peculiar to Christianity (p. 224). Acceptance of these dogmas, and of the Virgin birth, mean that Muḥammad adopted the most incredible aspects of Christianity; removed from it were the abuses it had come to contain. Boulainviller claims that what Muḥammad saw in Syria was a form of Christianity hardly distinguishable from paganism. He uses Muḥammad to denounce what he calls shameful superstition: the cult of saints and the worship of images which were being asked to preserve lives and grant victory in battles (p. 220). Yet Muḥammad's moral teaching is shown to be similar to that of Christ.

At times sounding faithful to Muḥammad's teaching, Boulainviller insists that in the Prophet's judgement, the justice of God could never impute to anyone the sin he has not committed. Thus, in Islam there is no original sin and no need for atonement. This is a strong divergence from Christianity, as it denies the redemptive mission that Christians have always attributed to Jesus. Boulainviller then states what he perceives as Muḥammad's fundamental teaching, which is belief in three principles: the existence and unity of God (to the exclusion of other powers), that God as universal creator justly rewards virtue and punishes vice (not only in this life but also in the hereafter), and that, showing pity to those who have gone astray through lack of a teaching, God has personally elevated Muḥammad to be His Prophet. Muḥammad never claimed to be divine. Only modesty (which Khadīja reputedly urged him to overcome) prevented him from carrying out the designs of Providence at an earlier time (Muḥammad had waited three years before publicly proclaiming Islam).

One must not conclude that Boulainviller always attempts to undermine Christian teaching. He claims, for instance, that Muḥammad's visit to the monk Baḥīra in Syria may have laid the foundation for a kind of compassion he frequently displayed for solitary people and monks. He probably exaggerates the effect of these travels on Muḥammad when he credits these with bestowing on him vast amounts of new knowledge, and with transforming the ideas of a camel trader into those of an incomparable statesman and a legislator superior to any that had been produced in ancient Greece (p. 208). Similarly, Muḥammad allegedly learnt the art of warfare from the Persians. Although he had initially acknowledged his lack of Arabic, Boulainviller claims to rely on Arab writers for this information, as it was in their writing that it is argued that God wanted to educate Muḥammad gradually through the pains of hunger, thirst, fatigue, and lack of sleep.

Boulainviller adopts an occasional light-hearted witticism in Muḥammad's biography, and this is seen, for instance, when he comments on the Prophet's marriage (in 628) to Ṣafiyya, a young Jewish woman.[10]

The woman is reported by Boulainviller as saying that Aaron was her father, Moses her uncle and Muḥammad her husband (p. 237). Boulainviller, however, fails to understand the nature of Muḥammad's marriages, as he suggests that the Prophet needed several wives as a distraction or as a relief from his labours. Long before his death, Muḥammad was therefore forced to replace these faded beauties with younger wives. Boulainviller finds it hard to conceive that a Prophet who preached eternal truths which were revealed to him from time to time could have been so carried away by pleasures which are meant for persons with less serious projects. How astonishing, too, that a man with such designs, who needed peace to plan them, should have willingly opted for unrest and exposed himself to domestic troubles and jealousies! Such remarks have nothing to do with an anti-Christian stand; they are rather part of the traditional perception of the Prophet.

Early in the book, Boulainviller argued that reason should allow for a mutual respect of the customs of every land, as every nation has its traditions consecrated by habit. If mutual tolerance had been his main objective, he would have been no different from many other eighteenth-century writers. However, his argument goes far beyond a plea for tolerance. From a Christian point of view, the *Vie de Mahomed* certainly appears subversive, because of the rejection of Christianity's fundamental doctrines. Side-by-side with this subversion, the qualities of the Arabs and their Prophet it displays are striking. These factors may have led Venturino to describe the *Vie de Mahomed* as the first openly pro-Islamic text generated by European culture. Whether it is the first such text may be open to discussion, however, there is no doubt that, on the whole, this biography, though incomplete and often lacking in scholarly apparatus, successfully manages to project the remarkable achievements of Muḥammad. This indicates that the thesis displayed by some scholars such as Edward Said (in *Orientalism*), wherein all French writers were pitted against Islam and the Arabs) is untenable.

What we have from Boulainviller is an eighteenth-century rejection of the theory, made fashionable in our times, of the clash of civilisations. He managed to refute all the Discours and Dissertations and essays of previous French and English writers against Muḥammad, and to inaugurate a French tradition of even-handed reporting on the Prophet.

Voltaire (1694-1778)

Among the writers of the French Enlightenment, Voltaire probably had the longest dialogue with Islam and Muḥammad. His observations were made intermittently from 1716 until almost the end of his long career, the volume of his output in this field being substantial. Voltaire's curiosity about Muḥammad had been fostered by research for his play *Mahomet* (1742) and by the books he had read about Islam. His writings are not always restricted to the personality of Muḥammad, however; among those focusing on the Prophet is the short text *De l'Alcoran et de Mahomet* which was first published in 1748, when it appeared in a collective edition of his works, immediately following *Le Fanatisme, ou Mahomet le Prophète.*[11] It later became section II of the article 'Alcoran ou Plutôt le Koran' in the *Questions sur l'Encyclopédie* (1770), and the same pairing is maintained when the texts are incorporated into the 'Dictionnaire Philosophique' of the Kehl edition of the *Complete Works*. This essay is intimately connected with the tragedy. In spirit it is broadly similar to *Mahomet* and it continues the war waged on the character of the Prophet. Nevertheless, it also has a number of key differences. Despite its brevity, it contains more biographical material on Muḥammad than the much longer play (and his other texts) and is generally grounded in historical fact, including a number of references to incidents in the life of the Prophet. Thus, a glimpse of Muḥammad as he really was in history begins to emerge little by little.

In *De l'Alcoran et de Mahomet*, Voltaire uses those sections of the Qur'ān which shed light on certain episodes in Muḥammad's life. He first wishes to impress the reader that he knows the Qur'ānic text well, accurately quoting from Sale's English version of the Qur'ān (1734) lines taken from *Sūra* 10, where Muḥammad's denigrators are challenged to produce a chapter equalling this *Sūra*. He then gives a faithful rendering of the beginning of *Sūra* 17, based on Sale's version, which refers to the Prophet's Night Journey. In the text of the Qur'ān, the journey stops at the mosque situated in Jerusalem, but in a footnote Sale remarks that from Jerusalem Muḥammad was carried through the seven heavens to the presence of God and brought back again to Makka the same night. Voltaire claims that Muḥammad's disciples (who put together the verses of the Qur'ān after his death) excised the journey to the planets because they dreaded the ridicule of the people, especially that of the philosophers. He had of course read the extensive account given of Muḥammad's Night Journey by Jean Gagnier in *La Vie de Mahomet* (1732). He ignores here the source of these details of the journey, which are based not on the Qur'ān, but on *Ḥadīth* literature. For Muslims, the journey is a great mystical story and is a fitting prelude to the journey of the human soul in its spiritual growth in life. For Voltaire it is simply an example of the excesses of the oriental imagination.

It suits Voltaire's purpose to follow authors writing in the 'tradition dévote'. This tradition is in support of his earlier suggestion that Muḥammad is a charlatan whose preaching rests on lies (such as the story he refers to in *De l'Alcoran* of the splitting of the moon, which he attributes to Muḥammad himself).[12] There is a story in Muḥammad's biography (by Arab writers) wherein a number of disbelievers at one time approached the Prophet and asked him to split the moon in two, as a sign that he was indeed the messenger of God. Many others were also present, including believers and those who remained hesitant. Great was their amazement to see the moon divide into two halves, which drew away from each other until there was a half moon shining brightly on either side of the mountain. Those who had made the demand rejected this optical illusion as mere magic.[13] By omitting all reference to the context in which the moon (as reported by tradition) seems cloven in two, Voltaire turns Muḥammad into a magician. Although the apparent source of the information is Sale, the real source is Gagnier's *Vie de Mahomet* to which Sale refers. Voltaire possessed both works, but he relied more on Gagnier than on Sale.[14] However, he had to appear consistent: having denounced the impostor in his tragedy and having only recently, as a son of the Church, dedicated it to the Pope, he could be expected to betray some hostility to Muḥammad.

Perhaps also to this end, Voltaire claimed that Muḥammad lacked originality. Many of the beliefs and practices confirmed by Muḥammad (such as circumcision, for example) were already well established among the Arabs. In this context, Voltaire also mentions fasting (without saying for how long and when it should be observed), the pilgrimage to Makka (which, according to Voltaire was current four thousand years before Muḥammad), ablutions (which are necessary to health and to cleanliness in a burning hot country where, he claims, clothing was unknown). Four items were lifted from the Magians: (1) the belief in the Day of Judgement; (2) the weighing of men and women by an angel[15]; (3) the belief in a narrow bridge over which one has to pass after death[16] and; (4) *jannat*[17], where the elect will find well-furnished apartments, good beds, and fair maidens with black eyes.[18] All these alleged borrowings from other religions are used by Voltaire to destroy the idea that Muḥammad's mission was divinely inspired and unique. Yet he has to admit that all the sensual pleasures so necessary to those who resurrect with senses cannot, in Islamic teaching, compare with the pleasure of the contemplation of the Supreme Being.[19] He also grudgingly admits the humility of Muḥammad who accepts that he will not go to Paradise by his own merit but by God's will.[20] As often happens with Voltaire, what he gives with one hand he takes away with another. By saying that Muḥammad allowed himself a fifth part of the booty 'par cette pure volonté divine' (p. 337)[21] he implies that there was nothing divine in the latter's actions.

One of Voltaire's aims in *De l'Alcoran et de Mahomet* is to discredit Muḥammad by illustrating how he exploited the people's belief in the supernatural, when he himself had nothing supernatural about him. To support the idea that Muḥammad was an ordinary man Voltaire claims that 'le grand prophète essuya la disgrâce commune à tant de maris'.[22] So Voltaire had recourse to his favourite method of denigration by popularising the scandalous tale linking the name of Muḥammad's wife, 'Ā'isha, with 'Assuan' (that is, Ṣafwān). Voltaire had expressed the same idea, but rather more crudely, in a first draft where he suggests that Muḥammad had a chapter of the Qur'ān come down from heaven to restore his honour.[23] In *De l'Alcoran*, Muḥammad makes the same point, namely that the chapter from heaven affirms that his wife was faithful. This refers to the chapter or *Sūra* 24, which was revealed about a month after an incident which occurred in 627, on the return from the expedition undertaken by Muḥammad against the tribe of the Banū Muṣṭaliq. When the march was ordered, 'Ā'isha was not in her tent, having gone to search for a necklace she had dropped. The next morning she was found by Ṣafwān, who put her on his camel and brought her to the rest of the party, leading the camel on foot. This gave occasion to enemies to raise a malicious scandal. The incident is narrated by Sale and is also recorded by Gagnier. Voltaire uses the episode to hint (with a great deal of irony) that *Sūra* 24, like the other *Sūras*, must have been 'écrit de toute éternité' (p. 340).

Voltaire also hopes to show that in war, as in peace, Muḥammad is a mere mortal. He points out that Muḥammad fights and is wounded like any common soldier. He suggests that revolutions result from small things, for 'un coup de pierre un peu plus fort que celui qu'il reçut dans son premier combat donnait une autre destinée au monde' (p. 341). The reference here is to an incident that took place at the battle of Uḥud, in Madīna in 625. The Muslims were nearly overwhelmed, not so much by superior numbers as by lack of discipline. Muḥammad was wounded in his head and face, and one of his front teeth was knocked out by a stone thrown at him. Nevertheless, he rallied his troops and Abū Sufyān, his opponent, decided to withdraw. Voltaire's source is Gagnier's *Vie de Mahomet* (i. 353-72). Uḥud was not the first battle fought by Muḥammad, and in 624, for example, he had won the battle of Badr, about fifty miles south-west of Madīna.

Tales that had been spread about Muḥammad's sexual behaviour are also used by Voltaire to indulge his own sexual fantasy. He attributes to 'Alī the suggestion that Muḥammad was not in a state usually associated with the dead at the time of his burial. He even suggests that 'Ā'isha exclaimed that if she had known that God had granted this grace to the deceased she would have rushed to him instantly[24]. What this grace was is not clear from the Latin quotation of *De l'Alcoran*, but it is made clear by Voltaire's remark elsewhere.[25] There he invents lurid details about the posthumous condition of the Prophet, adding that all his wives testified to it. From Gagnier's *Vie de Mahomet*, Voltaire notes what Muḥammad is reported to have said about two things that pleased him most in the world: women, and the perfumes which aroused his fervour in prayer. Voltaire simply removed the reference to perfumes in *De l'Alcoran* and made the witty suggestion that there was no reason why grace should not be said by a man with a woman in bed, considering that it is said at table: a beautiful woman being well worth a supper (p.342).

Of less offence to Muslims, but of no less overt wit, is Voltaire's refutation of the commentators who favoured the idea of the exclusion of women from the Islamic Paradise. Voltaire does not find it likely that such a clever man as Muḥammad would wish to be on poor terms with that half of mankind which leads the other half.[26] He gives his own account of a story found in Sale and in Gagnier, about an old woman who pestered the Prophet with enquiries about what one should do to enter Paradise. On being told that Paradise was not meant for old women, she cried, but to comfort her, Muḥammad said that no old woman would be found there because they would become young again (p. 338). When Voltaire states that this comforting doctrine is confirmed in *Sūra* 54, he probably refers to *Sūra* 56, l. 35.[27] This information is derived from Sale, who wrote that Muḥammad had too great a respect for the fair sex to teach a doctrine that excluded women from Paradise.

More mundane matters concerning Muḥammad also interested Voltaire. He took note, for example, of the marriage contract between Muḥammad and Khadīja, details of which he obtained from Gagnier. While he showed some sympathy for what he perceives as lack of subtlety in the terms of the contract, he found a similar simplicity absent from Muḥammad's genealogy, as early Muslims trace back his ancestry to Adam. Furthermore, everything that the Prophet owned has been listed in detail: the number of his swords, lances and shields, horses, mules, and camels, as well as the mare 'Burak' which he used for his ascent to heaven.[28] Voltaire jokingly adds that the latter really belonged to the angel Gabriel who had lent it to him. It is noted that twelve women are included in the number of objects owned by Muḥammad, as if they were mere chattels.

Voltaire lets Muḥammad off lightly for his 'deceit', on the grounds that the Arabs had countless prophets before him and that there was no harm in him contributing to this tradition. He is obviously not true to the spirit of Islam, for this teaches that Muḥammad was the last of the prophets. He then invents a story wherein Muḥammad threatens people with death if they did not believe he had spoken to the angel Gabriel: no such threat is recorded in history. Voltaire shows Muḥammad to be vastly inferior to his hero Confucius[29] who, despite having not experienced revelation, used reason to promote his religion, rather than lies and the sword.

Yet *De l'Alcoran et de Mahomet* does not show Muḥammad in an entirely negative light. Voltaire tries to establish a distinction between Muḥammad's civil laws, which he finds as beneficent (he even appears to justify polygamy), and Muḥammad's method, which Voltaire condemns as deceitful and murderous (p. 338). 'Muḥammad's' Qur'ān, he argues, may not suit our times, but was appropriate for contemporary Arabs. Voltaire seems to have grasped some of the essential teaching of

Muḥammad relating to the unity of God (and the resulting prohibition of idolatry), the necessity of praying and almsgiving, and the banning of usury. He expresses admiration for the fact that Muḥammad removed almost the whole of Asia from idolatry, Voltaire finding it logical that a religion 'si simple et si sage' (p. 335), taught by an ever victorious man (Muḥammad), should subjugate part of the world. The most remarkable aspects of the achievement worthy of admiration are, in his view, related to his humble origins: that a camel owner became high priest, legislator, and ruler, united Arabia, shook the foundations of the Eastern Roman Empire and the Persian Empire, changed the face of part of Europe, half of Asia, and almost the whole of Africa, such that his religion nearly subjugated the whole world. In some ways, *De l'Alcoran* can be said to have provided a solid framework for a more balanced reappraisal of Islam and the Prophet that was to come.

On the other hand, it may be argued Voltaire had begun this reappraisal, which entails a new perspective on the Arab people, even earlier, in the *Mercure* article of April 1745 where he tried hard to rid people of their prejudices against the Arabs.[30] One of the writers he criticised in this article was Bossuet, whose account of Muslims in the *Discours sur l'histoire universelle* is severely censured. When Bossuet speaks of Muslim people, it is to depict them as a swarm of barbarians. Voltaire attempted to redress the balance in their favour in two chapters of the *Essai sur les moeurs*, a vast survey of world history begun in the 1740s and published in 1756. In these chapters, Muḥammad and the Arabs are assessed against other leaders and nations of the world. The perception of Muḥammad himself in the *Essai* bears a strong resemblance to that of *De l'Alcoran*, with the difference that in Voltaire's historical text the context is much wider. In Chapter 6, entitled 'De l'Arabie et de Mahomet', Voltaire could not, of course, be expected to give a full account of Muḥammad's life, although he supports the efforts of Bayle in stripping the Prophet of the legends that had grown up around him, and concentrating instead on the man himself. Using the same irony as in *De l'Alcoran*, he dismisses as pure fable the efforts of writers who trace Muḥammad's ancestry back to Abraham (p. 255). To strengthen his case against these myths, he refers to the superstition and exaggeration of the early Arabs, quoting the example of Muḥammad's grandfather ('Abd al-Muṭṭalib) who vowed to sacrifice one of his children to God, but was advised by a priestess to offer some camels instead. The number of camels offered, initially ten, continued to increase until it eventually reached a hundred.[31]

The account Voltaire gives of the early life of Muḥammad and his marriage to Khadīja is reasonably accurate. At this stage Muḥammad distinguished himself from his countrymen only by eloquence devoid of art and method. With a touch of hyperbole, Voltaire describes Muḥammad as intrepid and as generous as Alexander. He then mentions Muḥammad's fight with (and triumph over) the pagan Makkans (although few details are given of his military campaigns) and his letter to neighbouring princes asking them to join Islam.[32] However, Voltaire overlooks the political and social effects of Muḥammad's subsequent marriages, which he attributes merely to sexual desire, although he takes care to point out that Muḥammad's courage and health were not impaired by his sexual behaviour (p. 256).

In line with Western views of the time, Voltaire depicts Muḥammad as a skilful opportunist who cleverly exploited his ignorant and gullible countrymen by elevating himself to the status of a prophet. Unlike many Western writers, however, Voltaire shows how aware he is of Muḥammad's real intention in re-establishing the simple cult of Abraham (p.256). Indeed, Abraham (Ibrāhīm) enjoys a very high status in Islam: in every prayer, Muslims ask for God's blessings on Muḥammad, recalling the blessings previously bestowed on Ibrāhīm. To confirm Abraham's high status, Voltaire quotes accurately from *Sūra* 3, l. 66-68. Even if Muḥammad claims that he wishes to remind people of the unity of God, he is still, in Voltaire's eyes, an 'enthusiast' (that is, a fanatic of good faith). He deceived himself and others by his imagination and by his imposture in order to establish a doctrine he considered good. A parallel can be drawn here between Voltaire's argument and that of the abbé de Saint-Pierre, who had suggested that Muḥammad was at the outset a fanatic of good faith, but deceived himself before deceiving others (see Chapter 1).

Those who were initially 'deceived' were the immediate members of his family (p. 257). The conversion of 'Umar strengthened Muḥammad, as Voltaire says, but the Muslims were still outnumbered by their enemies. The persecution of the former led to the *hijra* in 622. From being a fugitive, Muḥammad subsequently became a conqueror. Voltaire gives a sketchy account of Muḥammad's battles which were won with small armies but, he adds, also with God's help.

The significant factor is that after the conquest of Makka (630), the whole of Arabia was swayed by Muḥammad's military prowess and powers of persuasion. Yet Muḥammad's last wish, Voltaire claims, was not accomplished (p. 261). He assumes that the Prophet wished 'Alī to be appointed Caliph, however Muḥammad made no recommendation for his succession. Voltaire insinuates that the appointment of Abū Bakr as first Caliph was determined by the ambition of his generals, who hoped that they would soon share in the succession now that their old leader had disappeared. There is little to support this, and most sources indicate that Abū Bakr was elevated to the office on grounds of merit, seniority, and acceptability. Voltaire quickly describes the history of the caliphate from the 'rightly guided' Caliphs, Abū Bakr, 'Umar, 'Uthmān, and 'Alī, to the Umayyad and 'Abbasid Caliphs (p. 266).

Voltaire suggests, in Chapter 7, that writers had copied one another, some attributing the authorship of the Qur'ān to a Nestorian monk called Sergius, and others attributing it to Baḥīra (p. 270). One can in fact read in the *Sīra* of the visit that the Prophet-to-be paid to the monk Baḥira at Bostra, Syria, when he was a young boy accompanying his uncle Abū Ṭālib on a merchant caravan. Baḥīra predicted that great things were in store for him, but there is no suggestion of his having written the Qur'ān for him. Voltaire rejects Baḥīra's authorship, arguing that Muḥammad did not have this monk with him all the time. He suggests rather that the Qur'ān was written during Muḥammad's travels and military campaigns. Voltaire, like many other Western writers, exaggerates Muḥammad's travels, as Muḥammad went to only one country, Syria.

Like these authors, Voltaire also dismisses the idea that Muḥammad was illiterate, claiming that it was based on an equivocal passage in the Qur'ān. By this he means *Sūra* 7, 157, where Muḥammad is referred to as a *nabī al-ummī* (usually translated as an 'unlettered prophet'), in order to stress his divine inspiration.[33] Voltaire finds it incredible that a man who had been for many years a trader, a poet, and a legislator should have ignored what even the children of his tribe had learnt (p. 270). Although he does identify some incoherent statements in the Qur'ān, he also admires some of its sublime passages. In particular, he appreciates the definition of God, which Voltaire attributes to Muḥammad: 'C'est lui qui tient l'être de soi-même, qui n'engendre point et qui n'est point engendré'. Voltaire says that this reply to a question put to the Prophet about Allah is to be found in the last but one chapter of the Qur'ān. In fact, the quote is made up of a combination of *Sūra* 2, l. 255 (where God is described as *al-qayyūm*, self-subsisting), and *Sūra* 112, l. 3 (where He neither begets nor is begotten).

In this chapter, as elsewhere, it is by no means an easy task to separate what Voltaire writes on the man Muḥammad from significant aspects of Islamic civilisation. Voltaire is happy to make more extended use of some of the material he had already used in *De l'Alcoran* (regarding circumcision, ablutions, prayer, fasting, almsgiving, and pilgrimage in Islam), however, he is mistaken in including circumcision among legal requirements enjoined on Muslims: this is not a legal requirement, even though, as he says, it is a common practice among Muslims, as well as among the ancient Egyptians and the Jewish people (p. 273). He brings some precision to the notion of prayer, fasting, and almsgiving. Praying five times a day, for example, may be embarrassing for Muslims, but a created being cannot complain of having to worship the creator five times each day. Fasting was well established among many peoples, including Jews and Christians, although as Voltaire points out, Muḥammad made it very difficult for Muslims during a lunar month in which not even drinking water and smoking are permissible until sunset. Voltaire is aware of the hardship fasting can cause when observed at the height of summer, noting that it is so rigorous that historically the rules have had be relaxed, especially during wars. He might have added that some concessions are also made to travellers and pregnant women at all times. Despite Voltaire's complaint about Islam's lack of originality, he does acknowledge the existence of some original features in it. As he observes, almsgiving is recommended in all religions, but Islam is the only religion which makes it an obligatory, positive, and essential commandment (and he gives the precise percentage (2.5%), in money or goods that a Muslim has to allocate).

Voltaire makes a distinction between positive and negative precepts in Muḥammad's teaching (p. 274). Among the latter, he lists the prohibition against drinking wine, which he had already mentioned in *De l'Alcoran* but which he here describes as new and peculiar to Islam. His remark on its observance and non-observance seems judicious. Few readers would query the suggestion that many Muslims dispense with this rule in temperate climes, that the abstinence was laid down in a burning climate where wine often impaired health and reason, and that it is less of a hardship to the Arabs than to other Muslims living in Europe. Muḥammad, Voltaire argues, could not have foreseen that it would be unbearable to 'his' Muslims living in Macedonia, Bosnia, and Serbia. The prohibition against gambling strikes Voltaire as being unique to Islam and more appropriate for a convent than for a nation. The prohibition against pork consumption is attributed to health reasons in hot climates. According to Voltaire, this prohibition ceased to be reasonable in colder climates where Muslims settled, yet it still persists in the regions.

This short list of prohibitions, together with the brief reference to battles waged by Muslims, led to a caricature of the essence of Muḥammad's achievement: the Prophet, says Voltaire, seemed to have formed a nation whose only raison d'être is to pray, procreate, and fight. Yet Voltaire strikes the right note almost immediately after this, mentioning the true spirit of Islam. As he argues, Islam won respect and trust on account of its laws (which, apart from polygamy, he finds austere), and on account of its doctrine, which is straightforward. Faithful heir to Boulainviller, Voltaire understands well why Islam progressed in the world: it was the dogma of the unity of God, presented without mystery and tailored to suit human intelligence that brought under its law a host of nations, including African Negroes and Indian Ocean Islanders (p. 275).

If, in Chapters 6 and 7, Voltaire offers a fairly different view of Muḥammad than before, it is in part due to his antipathy toward the Jewish people. The purpose of the comparison between the practices of Muḥammad and those of the Jews is not so much to elevate the former as to lower the latter. In Chapter 6, he uses the marriage contract of Muḥammad and Khadīja as a pretext for an assault on the Jews. He claims that one can see from the contract the simplicity of barbaric (or so-called heroic) times. Above all, one can see that despite Muḥammad's people having manners that were in conformity with those of the ancient Hebrews (that is, both communities being keen to run to battle in the name of God, sharing the same desire for booty and spoils), the Arabs, in his opinion, make a better impression than the Jews. Similar in approach to Bayle, who pitted Muslims against Catholics, Voltaire uses his assessment of Muslims to discredit Jews. In nearly every department, the Muslims are made to look superior: in courage, magnanimity, elevation of spirit, and generosity. Voltaire asks why Muḥammad and his successors (who began their conquests in the same way as the Jews), achieved great things, while the Jews were successful only in small matters. He provides the answer himself, suggesting that whereas the Arabs had a policy of integrating other nations with them, the Jews kept to themselves. Echoing the prejudices of some Westerners against Islam, in hinting that it is against the arts, Voltaire nevertheless sees signs of evolution among the Arabs who became the preceptors of Europe in the sciences and the arts in the second century of the *hijra* (pp. 260-61). In a comparison between Muslims and Jews, he has almost lost sight of the former in order to concentrate attention on the latter and belittle them. Thus, Muslim Arabs seem to rise in status, in Voltaire's account, when set against the Jewish people.

When he resumes the comparison at the beginning of Chapter 7 (p. 269), Voltaire dispenses with the myth that the progress of Islam in the world was due to its voluptuous inclinations. However, he again takes the opportunity to show the superiority of Islam to Judaism. Muḥammad is given the credit for reducing the number of wives to four, while David is reported to have had eighteen wives, and Solomon seven hundred wives and three hundred concubines. Voltaire is not strictly accurate in his statement about Muḥammad who, for precise sociological reasons (such as the avoidance of promiscuity and prostitution among women in early Islamic history and elimination of the abuse committed by guardians who had unrestricted control of the property of unmarried women) encouraged his followers to marry up to four wives.[34] However, it is clearly Voltaire's intention that the inescapable conclusion to be drawn from his argument is that Judaism is voluptuous while Islam is austere.

The technique he uses against Jews is deemed equally appropriate for use against Christians. At the end of the chapter, Voltaire, as ambivalent as ever towards Muḥammad, examines Islam from an historical perspective. He argues that its spread over more than half of the world was due not to force of arms, but to enthusiasm, persuasion and, above all, the example of the victors. Muḥammad, in the first battles in Arabia against the enemies of his 'imposture' had his countrymen killed mercilessly. But when Islam was strengthened by preaching and force, the Arabs, in their foreign conquests, never forced their religion on foreigners. As Voltaire states, the latter were given the choice of conversion or the payment of tribute. Although Muḥammad established his dogma by the use of his courage and by his arms, the religion he founded became indulgent and tolerant (p. 275). The reverse is true of Christianity: Jesus himself was humble and peaceful, but Christians have, in Voltaire's opinion, become most intolerant and barbarous. Voltaire may be thinking particularly of Spanish atrocities in the New World.

In the ninth *Remarque pour servir de supplément à l'Essai sur les moeurs* (1763), there is an attempt, on Voltaire's part, to reduce the significance of Muḥammad in world history. Although he admits that the biggest change the world had ever witnessed was the establishment of Islam, Voltaire claims that this revolution (which he grudgingly acknowledges must have been willed by God), was infinitesimal from a global perspective. In a sense, Voltaire's stand is not without logic: after all, Muḥammad and the Arabs constitute only one nation, taking up only two of the hundred and sixty-four chapters of the *Essai*. However, what stands out in this *Remarque* is Voltaire's attempt to distance himself from two writers who had made a significant impact on him: Boulainviller (from whom he took the idea of Muḥammad converting large parts of the world to Islam by preaching the unity of God) and Sale (who taught him much about Islam). Voltaire challenges Boulainviller's thesis that God sustained Muḥammad in order to punish Christians of the East, for that would also mean that God wanted to punish the Parsees and Zoroastrians, who did not foment any civil strife (vol. 2, p. 915-16). It seems strange (and unlikely) to him that God would establish Christianity in the East and in Africa, only to destroy it afterwards. Equally unthinkable is the idea that God would sacrifice the religion announced by his Son in favour of a false religion, that is, Islam.

Voltaire accuses Sale of displaying the weakness that any translator has for the author they have chosen to translate, and he shows no enthusiasm for the idea expressed by the latter that Muḥammad had merit in liberating people from idolatry and superstition (p. 917). He does not share Sale's view that Muḥammad worked for the glory of God in destroying sun worship in Persia and star worship in Arabia. His argument is, rather, that the ancient Persians or Magians worshipped the sun as a symbol of divinity, while the worship of the stars among Arabs was subordinated to that of a supreme God. He believes that, on the whole, the religion of Zoroaster was better than that of Muḥammad, who adopted many of the dogmas of the Persians (p. 916). Voltaire uses the Arabs to challenge God's role in the world, claiming that Muḥammad was as fanatical as Cromwell, but nevertheless greater than he: in fact he was a very great man who formed other great men (p. 918). Voltaire turns him into a type of Cornelian hero, such that Muḥammad had to be a martyr or a conqueror: there was no middle way for him, Muḥammad may have helped Muslims to crush the religion of the Magians and the ancient Arabs, but Voltaire cannot see what glory was given to God in this victory.

Yet a more positive attitude to Muḥammad and Islam emerges at first in Voltaire's contemporary work, the *Catéchisme de l'honnête homme* (1763). This is set in Aleppo, and takes the form of a dialogue between a Greek Basilican monk and an 'honnête homme'. Purporting to be written by Rousseau (whom Voltaire wanted to enlist to his cause), it is really a monologue where Voltaire expounds his views on religious history and extols natural religion, where one must worship and love one's master. Through 'l'honnête homme', Voltaire asserts that Muḥammad's sect, the most dazzling of all sects, is an exception among sects. In the midst of so many human institutions it seemed unique in enjoying God's protection, owing its existence only to victories.[35] This is a sudden change in attitude from Voltaire: contradiction is the trademark he shares with other leaders of the Enlightenment. This change can be partly accounted for by the fact that the *Catéchisme* belongs to a long line of texts Voltaire wrote against the revelation of Holy Scripture, and forms part of his campaign to 'Ecraser l'Infâme' (that is, his campaign against superstition, injustice and fanaticism) of the 1760s.[36]

The *Catéchisme* becomes highly polemical when it draws a parallel between Muḥammad and Jesus. This cannot be considered to be an unbiased parallel, since its aim is to destroy the divinity of Jesus and to present a caricature of him. In his comparison, Voltaire notes that Jesus wrote nothing (Voltaire suggests he was probably illiterate), and was born, lived, and died a Jew, having merely observed Jewish rites. He is belittled as someone who spent his time eating lamb with lettuce, while he abstained from eating pork, griffon, and hare. Moreover, Voltaire notes that Christianity is different in every respect from the religion of Jesus, with only Protestantism remaining close to its source, as it condemns the scandalous and fatal innovations introduced by Roman Catholics (p. 134). In comparison, Voltaire claims, Islam has not changed from how it began under its founder, even twelve hundred years later. Muḥammad's laws remain in their entirety and 'his' Qur'ān is as respected in Persia as it is in Turkey, in Africa, and in India: everywhere it is strictly observed, and the only division in Islam, according to Voltaire, relates to the succession between 'Alī and 'Umar.

There is a curious confusion about the chronology of the Caliphate in Voltaire's mind, as he fails to mention the first and third Caliphs (Abū Bakr and 'Uthmān) and he also fails to point out the schism that occurred between Sunnites and Shiites immediately after Muḥammad's death. He wants to minimise schisms in Islam and to forget what he had written on the subject in texts like 'Du Fanatisme' and the *Essai sur les moeurs.* To put Christians to shame, however, Voltaire makes both characters in the dialogue vouch for the characteristic tolerance of the Muslim people. The 'honnête homme' argues (p. 123) that Muslims may despise Christians but they still tolerate them, while the 'caloyer' admits that the Turks under whom he lives persecute no one, and he elicits from the 'honnête homme' the wish that all the peoples of Europe might follow the example of the Turks.[37]

Thematically linked to the *Catéchisme* is *L'Examen important de Milord Bolingbroke* (1766). This text is attributed to Lord Bolingbroke, and purporting to be a summary of his doctrine, this is perhaps the most virulent denunciation by Voltaire of Christianity (Roman Catholicism in particular) and Judaism.[38] Muḥammad has only an indirect role to play and is used as a convenient weapon for the denigration of Christianity. Although the language of Chapter XXXV of the *Examen* is light-hearted, the objections to Christianity are more damaging. The religion of Muḥammad is represented as being more sensible than Christianity: Islam is superior because of what it avoids doing. This religion is, for example, free from the extravagant blasphemy whereby people say that three gods make one. Voltaire may be referring here to *Sūra* 112, which was probably directed originally against the conception of the three Makkan goddesses, but which was also applicable to the Christian doctrine of the Trinity. He claims that the belief in an all-powerful God was the only dogma taught by Muḥammad and he feels that without the addition of Muḥammad as its Prophet, Islam would have been a religion as pure and as beautiful as that of the cultured Chinese (p. 338). Considering the high status the Chinese often enjoyed with Voltaire, this was no small compliment paid to Islam. He also forgives Muslims for treating Muḥammad as the mouthpiece of God, since, he argues, the Prophet taught the Arabs the unity of God.

Chapter XXXII contains a comparison between the Emperor Julian and Muḥammad, where it is determined that the former was greater than Muḥammad, although destiny favoured the latter. After claiming that Muḥammad destroyed the Christian sect in the whole of Asia and Africa, Voltaire adds that 'un Arabe sans lettres a écrasé la secte d'un Juif sans lettres, ce qu'un grand empereur n'a pu faire'. Both religious leaders are treated with contempt, and the contempt shown to Muḥammad is perhaps only slightly less objectionable than that shown to Jesus. Voltaire has a simple explanation for Muḥammad's victory over Christians: he lived long enough, whereas Jesus' life was too short (p. 325).

In *Le Dîner du comte de Boulainvilliers* (1767) which Voltaire attributed to the satirical poet Saint-Hyacinthe (1684-1746) and which was another of his bitter attacks against Christianity, the compliment paid to Islam is not genuine. Muslim adherents appear, if not superior to Christians, at least no worse.[39] The abbé Couet suggests that Christianity could not have risen so high if it had merely relied on fanaticism and lies, however, the count responds that lies did not prevent Islam from rising higher although they were, at least, 'nobler' lies than those of Christianity. Moreover, the fanaticism of Islam was more generous than that of Christianity. Close in spirit to the *Catéchisme de l'Honnête Homme*, the *Dîner* stresses that Muḥammad wrote and fought, whereas Jesus could neither write nor defend himself: he sweated blood and cried tears when condemned by his judges (p. 376). It is clear, in Voltaire's eyes, that Muḥammad was superior to Jesus, for he combined the courage of Alexander with the intelligence of Numa. This attack against Jesus is offensive not only to Christians, but also to Muslims, who frown on the comparison between Muḥammad and legendary figures.

Voltaire continued to write about Muḥammad in the 1770s. In the article 'Arot et Marot' of the *Questions sur l'Encyclopédie* (part II) he praises those authors such as Reland and Sale who were well disposed towards Islam and Muḥammad, but he censures Gagnier for having spread lies about the latter, as if, he adds, one needed lies to uphold the truth of Christianity against the false Prophet (M. xvii, 383).[40] Despite the fact that he is echoing sentiments often expressed by Christian apologists, Voltaire has merit in attempting to distinguish between Qur'ānic and non-Qur'ānic material. Grotius, too, is censured for having spread scandalous tales about Muḥammad (M. xvii, 384). Yet on one point Voltaire agrees with him, for he maintains that a man who continually received chapters of the Qur'ān from the angel Gabriel was worse than a dreamer: he was an impostor. What is surprising is that in his attempt to defend Muḥammad against Grotius's accusations, he turns the former into a heretic Christian. He makes the point that Qur'ānic teaching on the crucifixion was spread by heretical Christian communities in Syria and Arabia up to Muḥammad's time (M. xvii, 385).

In the first section of 'Alcoran ou Plutôt le Koran', published in the *Questions sur l'Encyclopédie*, Voltaire's judgement on Muḥammad appears fairly balanced. As his interest is partly sociological, he refutes the European writers (including Montesquieu) who had written on the subject of women in Islam. He claims that these writers, in their attempt to win women over to their side, had hinted to the latter that Muḥammad did not consider them to be intelligent animals, rather that they were all slaves according to the laws of the Qur'ān, that they owned no property in this world and that in the next world they would have no place in Paradise (M. xvii, 100). To Voltaire, all this is false (as indeed it is) and yet has become firmly entrenched in European discourse about Islam. As he suggests, one only has to read *Sūras* 2 and 4 of the Qur'ān to dispel this idea.

He invites the reader to examine the legislation referring to women in these texts, in translations by Du Ryer, Marracci, and Sale: he lists eight of the clauses and neatly rearranges them (they are not actually found in that order in the Qur'ān). The last clause is particularly interesting, as it deals with the provision for child maintenance by a man who has repudiated his wife. At the end, Voltaire suggests that the 'Règlements de Mahomet sur les femmes'(M. xvii, 100-101) are sufficient to bring about a reconciliation between women and Muḥammad, who did not treat them as harshly as has been claimed. Thus, we have qualified praise of the Prophet. Similarly, although

Muḥammad is still perceived as an ignorant and an impostor and 'his' Qur'ān is a collection of ridiculous revelations, vague, and incoherent preaching, Voltaire refers with sympathy to the difficulties issuing from Makkan poets and theologians that Muḥammad faced as a preacher. Muḥammad's crime, according to the latter, was to have preached the worship of God and not of the stars: this, according to Voltaire, was the source of his greatness.

Voltaire's thoughts on the part Muḥammad had played in the composition of the Qur'ān are most ambivalent. He dismisses as rumour the charge of the Makkans that Muḥammad sought the assistance (of a learned Jew and a learned Christian), hinting that there were no learned men around at that time. To prove his point, Voltaire reproduces an accurate translation of *Sūra* 16, 101-103, from Sale, in which Muḥammad refutes the charge of forgery, showing that the man with whom he was supposed to be collaborating spoke a foreign tongue. Then, closely following a footnote of Sale, Voltaire identifies the supposed collaborator as a Jew named Bensalen or Bensalon (that is, 'Abdullāh ibn Salām), a learned rabbi who converted to Islam in 623 (M. xvii, 102). He finds it unlikely (though not impossible), that a Jew should have helped Muḥammad to write against Jews.

In one area, however, Voltaire never fluctuates: he has a constant admiration for the doctrine of the unity of God taught by Muḥammad. He quotes *Sūra* 112, which he says offered more to the Orient than Muḥammad's sword. But he then turns Muḥammad into a Jansenist, which is no compliment to the Prophet, considering Voltaire's dislike of Jansenists from the days of *Mahomet*. Voltaire simply states that the body of Muḥammad's doctrine is absolute predestination. He perhaps had no room here to take into account the short dialogue on free-will and predestination between Moses and a servant of God that was initiated in *Sūra* 18 of the Qur'ān (see below) and developed into a full debate in ninth-century Islam, when Islamic thinking was enriched by contact with Greek philosophy.[41]

Voltaire did make some indirect observations on this complex question through the character of the hermit in the chapter devoted to him in *Zadig* (1747). There, Voltaire tried (but did not quite manage) to clearly outline Muḥammad's teaching on the problem of free-will. Difficulties arise which force scholars to discuss Jesrad's explanations on the workings of Providence at some length. Some writers stress

Voltaire's debt to the *Essais de Théodicée* (1710) of Leibniz in trying to explain the involved arguments of Jesrad, others see the influence of the poem *The Hermit* (1722) by Thomas Parnell, and mention the ambiguity of the episode, or speak of Jesrad as the Leibnizian angel.[42] There is a case, however, for studying the chapter in the light of Islamic philosophy, which is, in general, optimistic.[43]

It would not be surprising to find in this passage some echoes of the debate on free-will among Islamic sects, as it is described at section 8 of the 'Preliminary Discourse' to Sale's translation of the Qur'ān. Voltaire, we may remember, had enjoyed the Discourse very much. Even if analogies exist between Jesrad's arguments and Leibniz's, the model for the Voltairian character can be traced back to Islamic tradition (where he is called al-Khiḍr). In his critical edition of *Zadig*, G. Ascoli had, in fact, traced back the source of the Jesrad episode to the Qur'ān, *Sūra* 18, ll. 65-82, but had not explained its significance.[44]

This episode (or its variant) is used by some Muslims to prove that God, who has a global plan, was not bound to do what is best for individuals, because in this He would lose his omnipotence; Voltaire may not have been fully conscious of the significance of the story. In a marginal comment on this part of the section, Mme. Du Châtelet writes: 'I understand not'.[45] Voltaire, too, may have been bewildered. The means used by Jesrad in *Zadig* (which appear no crueler than those of the servant of God (al-Khiḍr) in the Qur'ān to inculcate his lessons) may cause surprise by their violence. One wished that different examples had been made available to explain the existence of evil in the world and prove the omnipotence of God. However, it is this story that has been handed down by the Qur'ān. Even if everything does not appear clear in it and in *Zadig*, Voltaire was at least on the right track: he had laid the foundation for a deeper and more successful analysis of this thorny problem, and this was to be undertaken by Diderot.

Diderot (1713-1784)

One might have expected a fair account of Islam and Muḥammad from Diderot, co-editor with d'Alembert of the *Encyclopédie*, a massive work imbued with the idea of progress. A sure sign of progress was its receptivity to the merits of civilisations other than the Judaeo-Christian (such as Islam). It is true that, like Voltaire and Rousseau,

Diderot did not know any Middle Eastern languages. Moreover, his interest in Islam and Muḥammad did not extend over as long a period as Voltaire's. These handicaps do not, however, constitute a serious obstacle to any writer willing or able to offer a sympathetic view of a foreign culture.[46] Diderot's novel *Les Bijoux indiscrets* (1748) may be discarded in any evaluation of his contribution, as the image reflected in it has more affinity with libertine or even pornographic literature than with Islam.

It seems that Diderot devoted more serious attention to Islam and its Prophet in the late 1750s. Yet, a number of false starts at first diverted him from the right path. An unpleasant surprise awaits the reader who, in attempting to verify Diderot's knowledge of the subject, has the misfortune to start with the article 'Arabes' of the *Encyclopédie*. At first, the 'philosophe' appears to be completely muddled concerning even the most elementary matters. Three times he takes Islam (which he terms 'Islamime'), to be a man, as he misunderstood a sentence from Jacob's Brucker's *Historia critica philosophiae* (1742-44), his acknowledged source for the articles he wrote on Islam for the *Encyclopédie*.[47] Diderot is not, however, to be assessed on the basis of this slip, rather, we can examine his contribution to the popularisation of knowledge regarding Islam and the Prophet in the light of the statement he made to Sophie Volland in his letter of 1st November 1759: 'Je sors des Arabes et des Sarrasins, où j'ai trouvé plus de choses intéressantes que je n'en espérois'.[48] He is referring here to the articles 'Arabes' and 'Sarrasins'.

As the first article deals with the ancient Arabs, the second may perhaps be more relevant. We should also bear in mind that Diderot's perspectives on philosophical and theological questions in 'Sarrasins', new and stimulating as they appear to be, relate to controversies on the problems of free-will and destiny, in which Muḥammad was only occasionally involved personally: the majority of these arose (and were debated) more than two centuries after his death.[49] Those with a deeper and narrower interest in the history of the ideas or the debates concerning free-will might have wished the Qur'ān to develop more fully the short debate that takes place on free-will in *Sūra* 18, and may therefore feel rather disappointed, but given the lateness of these debates in Islam, such readers have perhaps been spared the errors of anachronism. Here we need mention only those occasions when a particular approach towards free-will was attributed to Muḥammad by Diderot.

In the article 'Sarrasins', Diderot gives a fairly precise (albeit incomplete) account of Muslim sects, drawn from Brucker. However, he also propagates Western views of Islam that remain current today, namely, that fatalism is the prevailing opinion of Muslims, who ascribe everything to the power of God and nothing to humanity's free-will. Further in the text, Diderot echoes travellers and other writers by insisting that Muḥammad himself preached fatalism, a doctrine responsible for great courage and contempt for death. Apparently, prudence is useless 'devant celui qui a enchaîné les choses de toute éternité, d'un lien que sa volonté même ne peut relâcher'[50]. However, Muḥammad did not preach any such doctrine. On the other hand, he did include destiny (good or bad), among the tenets of the Muslim creed. Although destiny was determined by God, showing courage on the battlefield and not being afraid of death were not its essential features, as many Western writers seemed to believe. While a person's *ajal* (that is, the term of their life, happiness, and misery) were predetermined by God, there were limits to predestination which concerns only the spiritual state: thus, not the whole of one's life is predetermined[51]. It would be strange if the Prophet went against the teaching of the Qur'ān (which is firmly set against fatalism) with its excuses for evading duties imposed by divine law. Though the Qur'ān vigorously opposes fatalism, it gives frequent expression to the truly religious sense of dependence on God for the power to act and for protection from evil. Determinism is mostly to be found in the Traditions, some of which, it has been suggested, may contain a certain amount of pre-Islamic material adapted to Muslim ideas (*ibid.*)

In the article 'Aschariouns' or 'Aschariens', Diderot discusses the theology of al-Ashʿarī (d. 935), the Sunnite theologian. Al-Ashʿarī believes that God determines everything, acts through general laws which He has established, and is the creator and author of all one's acts. The text owes a considerable debt to d'Herbelot's article on the same subject in the *Bibliothèque orientale*, and is, to some extent, simply a shortened version of this article. The unfortunate result is that any gain in concision occurs at the expense of clarity. Thus, Diderot's quotation from the Qur'ān that, 'dieu vous fera rendre compte de tout ce que vous manifesterez en dehors et de tout ce que vous retiendrez caché en vous-même' (*Sūra* 2, l.284) is not as clear as d'Herbelot's 'et de tout ce que vous tiendrez caché en vous-mêmes'.[52] Diderot attempts to establish a link between Ash'arī and early Islam, claiming that in the time of the Prophet Muslims were frightened by this line, and a deputation headed by Abū Bakr and 'Umar (who were to become the first two Caliphs of Islam) asked Muḥammad for an explanation. If we are to believe Diderot, the latter shirked the issue by giving one of those oblique answers which seem to be the mainstay of leaders of religious sects: Muḥammad referred to the punishment of the Jews and urged Muslims to conform to God's will. Diderot states that to satisfy people's consciences in this, Muḥammad published another verse (Muslims would say that Muḥammad received another revelation). In Diderot's rendering, this is: 'Dieu ne charge l'homme que de ce qu'il peut et ne lui impute que ce qu'il mérite par obéissance ou par rebellion.'[53] He stresses the fact that the Ash'arīs are acutely embarrassed by the knowledge that there is nothing in good or evil acts which belongs to humanity, since everything is determined by God. There is a finer nuance in d'Herbelot, who explains that in Ash'arī's philosophy, human acts are produced by God, but that a person is entirely responsible for the use of these acts, by obeying or not obeying the law.

The question of free-will apart, Diderot's approach to the Prophet can be seen in the article 'Théosophes', where he places Muḥammad alongside Aeschylus, Shakespeare, and Roger Bacon (Vol.8, p. 390). This does not necessarily imply that Diderot is well disposed towards him. Diderot's attitude is as ambivalent as that of many other European writers, for he claims that with Muḥammad the demarcation line between genius and madness is very thin. He attributes the extraordinary and potentially divine intuition with which Muḥammad is credited to some periodic disorder, and cannot accept the idea that such insight is really supernatural.[54] Like other visionaries, Muḥammad falls into a kind of lethargy, but when roused from that state he imagines that he is animated by a divine spirit. What is interesting in this article is the absence of any reference (in comparison with Bayle and many other writers), to Muḥammad's so-called epileptic fit, his 'mal caduc'. Instead, Diderot's simple explanation is that an extraordinary imagination is at the basis of Muḥammad's thoughts and deeds. Although he writes about a group of people, Diderot pinpoints circumstances which, traditionally, have been associated with Muḥammad. In Diderot's opinion, it is times of ignorance and great calamity that give rise to such a genius.

The same ambivalence towards Muḥammad is noticeable in Diderot's letters to Sophie Volland, and in his article 'Sarrasins'. At times Diderot's hostility to Muḥammad is most pronounced. In the letter of 30th October 1759, for example, Muḥammad is ironically described as the best friend of women, and the greatest enemy of reason. In both texts, we are told that the 'holy Prophet' could not read or write. Diderot adds little to our understanding of Islam and the Prophet, claiming that having an illiterate Prophet as its founder encouraged the first Muslims to despise all knowledge. This apparently also encouraged their successors' contempt for knowledge and their stubbornness to a 'mensonge religieux dont ils sont entêtés' (*Oeuvres complètes*, ed. cit., vol. 8 ,p. 230).

Guilty of grotesque exaggeration, Diderot shows Muḥammad as so convinced of the incompatibility of philosophy and religion that he condemned to death anyone who might engage in the liberal arts. Reflecting a traditional Western perception of the Prophet, Diderot depicts him as a skilful opportunist who knew how to exploit the division between the idol worshippers, Sabians, Jews, and Christians who lived in his midst. However, Diderot attempts to be original in his approach to Muḥammad's success in making converts. Instead of the account whereby Muḥammad offered non-Muslims the choice of conversion to Islam or the payment of a tax, Diderot suggests that Muḥammad brought all men to a faith by providing them with only one of two choices: beautiful women or extermination, although Diderot says nothing about the conversion of non-Muslim women to Islam. Clearly, there never was a more fictitious basis for conversion.

Muḥammad allegedly caused enlightened thinking to disappear in the din of battle and in the midst of pleasure. Moreover, a century after the death of the 'furious impostor', people animated with the same spirit were heard shouting that God would punish the Caliph Al-Ma'mūn for having fostered the sciences in the empire at the expense of the 'holy ignorance' of the faithful believers. In 'Sarrasins' Diderot accuses Muḥammad of being the fanatical enemy of reason who 'ajusta comme il put ses sublimes rêveries à quelques lambeaux arrachés des livres des Juifs et des Chrétiens, et mit le couteau sur la gorge de ceux qui balancèrent à regarder ses chapitres comme des ouvrages inspirés' (p. 248). This is the old story of Islam as having its foundations on extracts from the Old and New Testaments which are preached by force. Diderot even charges Muḥammad with preaching anthropomorphic notions about God: an unlikely accusation, given that Islam has for so long been acknowledged as the most disembodied of religions, and the Qur'ān takes so much pain to combat the idea of the Trinity. On the other hand, before talking of Sa'dī at the end of 'Sarrasins', Diderot does acknowledge Muḥammad's achievement in bringing idol worshippers to the knowledge of the unity of God, and in securing the basis of moral law by outlining the distinction of the just from the unjust. Nevertheless, Voltaire is certainly more successful in highlighting Muḥammad's merits than Diderot.

Rousseau (1712-1778)

Like Diderot, Rousseau engaged in a short dialogue with Islam. His thoughts on a subject which roused the interest of many of his contemporaries throughout the century covered a period not exceeding a dozen years, from 1750 to 1762/1763. It seems that his Islamic background was less extensive than that of Boulainviller or Voltaire. He must have certainly leafed through the Qur'ān. If he had perhaps not read d'Herbelot, he had certainly read Raymond Lulle (1235-1315), who studied Arabic and the philosophical works of the thirteenth century, and was the promoter of a spiritual crusade for the conversion of Muslims. Rousseau knew Nicolas Antoine Boulanger (1722- 1759): both the man and his works. Boulanger was an engineer who widened his intellectual horizons by studying the Classics, Hebrew, Arabic, and ancient civilizations. He was particularly interested in tracing the origins of religions and had some curious explanations of the origins of pilgrimages, especially the Islamic pilgrimage to Makka. Rousseau also had a good knowledge of the works of the abbé de Saint-Pierre who, as we know, was not well disposed towards Muḥammad. A disciple of Montesquieu, Rousseau read the travellers of the seventeenth and eighteenth centuries, such as Paul Lucas, Jean-Baptiste Tavernier, and Jean Chardin.

Although Rousseau only evidenced a slight interest in Islam and the Prophet, he deserves some attention for the perspectives he offers on Muḥammad. Some of his contemporaries went so far as to compare him with the latter, mentioning their common *hijra*. Thus, Alexandre Deleyre noted that although Rousseau was no disciple of Muḥammad, they shared a migration.[55] Rousseau had migrated from his native city of Geneva in 1763, his migration being in fact a series of exiles across France and Switzerland. There is not much in common between Muḥammad and Rousseau apart from their migration.

Although Rousseau grants a key place to Muḥammad in his observations, he adopts an elliptical method to do this. One of the men targeted in his remarks on the origin of religions and the role of priests in primitive societies in his *Fragment d'un brouillon du Discours de l'Inégalité* could well be Muḥammad. As is well-known, this fragment (which may have been inspired by Diderot), was excluded from the definitive version. In this part of the text, Rousseau explains how curiosity produced crimes and inspired fanatics. It favoured the arrival of strange men who posed as interpreters of incomprehensible thoughts and claimed to 'assujettir tous les autre à leurs décisions, substituant adroitement leurs maximes absurdes et intéressées à la droite raison'.[56] Rousseau does not reveal his true thoughts on Muḥammad immediately. To understand this delay one needs to refer to the *Essai sur l'origine des langues* (1781).

The *Essai* complements the *Discours sur l'Inégalité* (1755) and brings some clarification to Rousseau's approach to Muḥammad. Chapter 9 deals with differences between primitive languages, and when Rousseau states that the experts who give laws to people and leaders who drag the masses with them must speak Arabic or Persian, he is obviously thinking of the Arab-Muslim world. In his opinion, oriental languages which appear in written form do not have the same function as Western languages. They apparently lose their vitality and their warmth, as only half the sense is to be found in the written words. As an example, Rousseau quotes the Arabic language, and in doing so mentions the name of Muḥammad for the first time. He claims that by reciting the Qur'ān in a voice that was eloquent, rhythmical, resonant, and persuasive, Muḥammad charmed the ear and then the heart.[57] Rousseau implies that Muḥammad played on the emotions of his listeners at the expense of their rational faculties. He speculates that the Arabs who listened would succumb to the rhetoric, passion, and warmth of the language, prostrating themselves before him and exclaiming: 'Grand Prophète Envoyé de Dieu, Menez-nous à la gloire, au martire; nous voulons vaincre ou mourir pour vous' (*ibid.*). Such that, without understanding the full implications of this religion, many people would be prepared to follow this eloquent leader.

It is worth noting that Muḥammad's eloquence (which was often quoted in the eighteenth century) could have reached only the first Muslim community, which was a minority. On the other hand, as Rousseau correctly implies, many persons who later converted to Islam did not understand Arabic. Rousseau, who is so alive to the power of language, perhaps oversimplifies the reasons for the spread of Islam during Muḥammad's time. In referring to people's wish for glory or martyrdom he seems to be investing them with the language used by the heroes of French classical tragedy which does not, however, reflect the reality of Arabia in the seventh century. He completely neglects the spiritual factors involved in the conversion of the pagan Arabs, and provides a too simplistic account of the causes responsible for the spread of Islam in Muḥammad's time.

As Rousseau attaches great importance to the part played by language in the evolution of religions, he comes back to this question in the 'Profession de Foi du Vicaire Savoyard' in book 4 of his famous novel *Emile* (1762). Here, it is no longer a matter of the musicality of verses charming the first Muslims. Rousseau wants to widen the field of his investigation to denounce the three revealed religions. He points out that in the three revelations, the sacred books are written in languages that are not understood by the communities that follow them. For the adherents of Islam, he alleges that neither the Turks nor the Persians understand Arabic, and that modern Arabs themselves do not speak the language of Muḥammad. [58] Rousseau uses mild irony to indicate that Muḥammad has a very simple way of teaching people: which is to speak to them in a language they do not understand! He rejects as unsatisfactory the reply to this objection which asserts that the Qur'ān and other sacred texts are available in translation, for he casts doubts on the faithfulness of such translations and maintains that it is impossible to translate accurately. Indeed, many Muslims would share Rousseau's view on the untranslatable nature of the Qur'ān, but they would disagree with him when he says that God who speaks to people needs no interpreter. In Islam, as in other religions, prophets are sent by God to teach nations the divine message.

It is evident that Rousseau exaggerates when he says that no Turks or Persians know Arabic.[59] However, the general point raised by him, that many Muslims are not proficient in Arabic, is valid. One needs to recognise the modernity of his thought concerning this linguistic weakness which affects a large part of the non-Arab Muslim world. His remarks imply that a lack of Arabic may be a hindrance to a thorough understanding of the Qur'ān and Islamic civilization. These comments about the linguistic deficiency may apply more particularly to non-Arab Muslims, especially those who live within Asia's large communities. Although the piety of many among them has never been in doubt, their knowledge of Arabic is often limited to memorising parts of the Qur'ān without fully understanding their meaning . Yet Arabic remains not only the most important language, both for the study of the sacred text and the *Ḥadīth*, but also for the transmission of Islamic civilization. The linguistic problem which existed at the time of the Prophet, and to which Rousseau drew attention in *Emile* is still with us today.

Rousseau replied to the condemnation of *Emile* by the Archbishop of Paris in 1762, with a *Lettre à Christophe de Beaumont* (1763) in which Muḥammad and his religion are attacked most vehemently. Rousseau begins by making a general attack against newly established faiths which maintain themselves through fanaticism and hypocrisy. He then denounces the narrow-mindedness of leaders, which, in his opinion, causes the misfortune of nations. To support his thesis, he invents the story about a Parsee of Surat who secretly marries a Muslim woman and is condemned to death for refusing to be converted to Islam. Rousseau allows the man full scope to use everything available to him to castigate Islam. The religion itself is censured because its dogmas are made to appear too recent to suit God. The picture of Muḥammad from the story of the Parsee is no longer that of an impostor, but of an upstart, for Rousseau makes the Parsee claim that the sacred books of Zoroaster formed the law of Asia and the whole world twenty centuries before Muḥammad, and that three empires had already come to their end before his judges' empires rose from the void: claims that rely heavily on exaggeration. Moreover, it is claimed that the institutions, laws, and even the virtues of Muslims cause torment and degradation because they include fasts and mutilation. In short, the judges live under the double yoke of despotism and fanaticism. The Parsee's account of Islam and of Muḥammad has a close affinity with Boulanger's in the article 'Guèbres' of the *Encyclopédie*.

A man as full of contradictions as the other leaders of the Enlightenment, Rousseau made his most positive evaluation of Islam and Muḥammad at the same time in the *Contrat Social* (1762). In Chapter 7 of

Book 2, entitled 'Du législateur', he does not specifically name Muḥammad, but it is clear that he has him in mind when he speaks of medieval legends that have been circulated about him. Rousseau points out that not every man can make the gods speak and have people believe him when he says he is the mouthpiece of the gods. Thus, the true miracle that proves the legislator's mission is his great soul. Rousseau argues that anyone can resort to coarse methods to deceive the people and assemble a group of madmen, but such a person will never provide the foundation of an empire, and his extravagant excesses will perish with him. Unlike Voltaire, Rousseau does not betray the slightest hint of anti-Semitism, as he finds the same permanence in the law of Moses as in that of Muḥammad (l'enfant d'Ismael), which has been governing half the world for a thousand years, and asserts that both laws bear witness even today to the greatness of the men who promulgated them. Rousseau thus rejects the idea that these prophets are simply successful impostors, rather, he attributes it to 'l'orgueilleuse philosophie ou l'aveugle esprit de parti'.[60] He admires in the institutions of Moses and Muḥammad that great and powerful genius that presides over lasting creations.

In Chapter 8 of Book 4, Rousseau blames Jesus for establishing a spiritual kingdom on earth (a fact which, he says, not only separated the theological and political systems, but also contributed to the loss of unity in the state and to internal divisions among Christians), as a means to praise Muḥammad for the opposite. He admires the 'vues très saines' of Muḥammad, and now overtly uses his name.[61] Rousseau praises Muḥammad's sound policy in binding together a system which remained the same as that of his immediate successors, and likes the fact that this government united the spiritual with the temporal. In comparison, he deplores the separation of powers taking place with the arrival of the 'barbares' (by this he means the Mongols, who destroyed the Abbasid caliphate in Baghdad in 1258). The strangest remark coming from Rousseau relates to the separation of powers among the Shī'ite Muslims of Persia, as history indicates that the opposite was the case.[62]

The beginnings of an evolution in attitudes to Muḥammad?

Through an exploration of these writers, we can perhaps trace the faint beginnings of an evolution in Enlightenment attitudes towards

Muḥammad, and in some cases individual authors themselves seem to show signs of evolution.

With Boulainviller, of course, it is not possible to talk of evolution, as his work on Muḥammad was the only one he wrote on the subject. However, despite his lack of Arabic, he had ensured that his documentation on Islam was of a high standard. Incomplete as his biography was, he had a fairly sound understanding of the essence of Muḥammad's teachings, and he transmitted this understanding to Voltaire.

Voltaire himself, when he was so inclined, could demonstrate awareness and appreciation of Muḥammad's teaching on the unity of God, moral code, and outstanding achievements over a short period (roughly two decades, 610 to 632). He devoted part of his long career to writing on Islam and Muḥammad, and showed a sustained interest in these. Despite his almost perpetual contradictions and his repetition, one must be deeply grateful to him for having, at frequent intervals, opened new perspectives on Muḥammad that were theological, sociological, and historical.[63] He was probably one of the few writers of his times whose attitude to Muḥammad evolved over the years. His assessment of the Prophet need not rest on his play *Mahomet*, since he began a more serious study of Muḥammad after this had been completed. He made partial amends for his earlier treatment of Muḥammad in the dictionary article *De l'Alcoran et de Mahomet* and in his vast universal history, the *Essai sur les moeurs*. It would, however, be unwise to conclude that he had become pro-Islam and pro-Muḥammad from the 1750s onwards.[64] Even the *Essai*, which testifies to Muḥammad's achievement in various fields, is marred by anti-Jewish sentiment. Heir not only to Boulainviller but also to the Protestant polemicists Jurieu and Bayle, he uses Islam and the Prophet in texts such as the *Catéchisme de l'Honnête Homme* and the *Examen de Milord Bolingbroke* as a springboard for attacks on Judaism and Christianity. The earlier camouflage gives way, in the most militant phase of his career (in the 1760s), to direct parallels or pseudo-parallels between Muḥammad and Jesus, to discredit the latter. The remarks contained in such texts are against the spirit of Islam, as Islam dissociates itself completely from attacks made against all Prophets, especially those of the monotheist religions.

It would not be realistic to expect any evolution in attitudes in the case of Diderot and Rousseau on account of their short-lived interest in Islam and Muḥammad. The spirit of contradiction that seems to dominate Rousseau's thinking might explain why he was capable of denouncing Muḥammad's fanaticism in the *Lettre à Christophe de Beaumont* and eulogising him as a legislator in the *Contrat Social*, almost in the same breath. Yet he and Diderot cannot be dismissed in any evaluation of Islam and the Prophet during the Enlightenment. Although they devote little time to Muḥammad (he is often only indirectly involved in their observations), they raise some fundamental issues. Diderot draws attention to the part played by ninth-century Muslim theologians in the debate on free-will, which originated in the dialogue between Moses and the servant of God (al-Khiḍr) in the Qur'ān. He showed that he understood better than Voltaire the issues at stake. He may have invented a few myths about Islam and Muḥammad, but there was no harm in his popularisation of the thought of Brucker, whose *Critical history of philosophy* (written in Latin) might have been confined to oblivion had it not been for Diderot's use of it in articles for the *Encyclopédie*.

As for Rousseau, his critique of Muḥammad, as preaching in a language not understood by many members of his audience, need not be viewed in an entirely negative light. However painful the lack of Arabic may be in the eyes of many non-Arab Muslims, Rousseau deserves recognition for boldly drawing their attention to it. This issue is of fundamental importance to the majority of the Muslim *umma*, because without Arabic they run the risk of leaving the interpretation of Islam solely to a handful of writers, who may be well-versed in the language in which it was revealed, but lacking a fair-minded approach to the Prophet.

Notes

1. Three complete manuscript copies are to be found at the Bibliothèque Mazarine, Paris, in mss. 1946, 1947 and 1948, and mss. 1949, which contains the first book only. Another copy is in the Bibliothèque Nationale de France, mss. fr. 9049. I quote from the mss. and the printed text.
2. N. Daniel, *Islam and the West: The Making of an Image*, revised edition (Oxford, 1993), p. 310.
3. D. Venturino, *Le Ragioni Della Tradizione. Nobilita e Mondo Moderno nel Pensiero di H. de Boulainvilliers* (Florence, 1992); *Vita di Maometto* (Palermo, 1992) and '*Un Prophète Philosophe? Une Vie de Mahomed* à l'Aube des Lumières' in *Dix-Huitième Siècle*, no. 24, 1992, pp. 321-331 and 'Imposteur ou Législateur ? Le Mahomet des Lumières', SVEC, vol. 2, 2000, pp. 243-262.

4. A. Thomson, 'L'Utilisation de l'Islam dans la littérature clandestine', in *La Philosophie clandestine à l'Age classique*, ed. A. McKenna and A. Mothu (Paris, Oxford, 1997), pp. 247-256.
5. Boulainviller's stance here may be contrasted with his attitude to Muḥammad later (in Book 2) where he shows his appreciation of Muḥammad's humility when in *Sūra* 96, which he quotes, Muḥammad is asked by the angel Gabriel to recite. Muḥammad had replied that he could not. As Boulainviller says, the angel's words (in the Qur'ān) are stripped of all the circumstances surrounding revelation which we only learn from those who collected the sayings and deeds of the Prophet.
6. H. Grotius, *De veritate religionis Christianae*, 1627, tr. Symon Patrick (London,1680), p. 207.
7. D. Venturino believes that Boulainviller, after rejecting Spinoza's conception of prophecy in the name of an orthodox conception in 1695 agrees in the *Vie de Mahomed* with Spinoza's fundamental thesis that prophecy is a natural gift. He points out that, while commenting on the first two chapters of Spinoza's *Tractatus* in his *Extrait du Traité Théologo-Politique de Spinosa* in 1695, Boulainviller had defined the prophet as someone who knows divine revelation by supernatural means. See his 'Un Prophète "philosophe", *Dix-Huitième Siècle*, p. 325.
8. Boulainviller was, however, entirely incorrect when he turned Zayd b. Ḥāritha into the cousin and brother in-law of Muḥammad (p. 274). Zayd was a slave who was freed and later adopted by Muḥammad, some time before the first revelations.
9. In *Sūra* 18, l. 83 is an allusion to Dhū al-Qarnayn, which many take to refer to Alexander the Great (so called from his expeditions to the East and West). Alexander seems to have received a divine mandate to remove idolatry and impiety. Boulainviller states categorically that Muḥammad turned him into a Prophet and argues that in this connection he showed more skill than ignorance on the grounds that he had everything to gain in persuading the Arabs that God sometimes intends Prophets to make extraordinary conquests and to submit a great number of nations through force in order to make them recognise truth, when simple persuasion does not suffice. This may be seen as Boulainviller's indirect justification of the use of force by Muḥammad.
10. W. Muir criticised Muḥammad for not observing the *'idda*, that is, the period of three months waiting required of Muslims before marrying a widowed or divorced woman. See the *Life of Mahomet* (London, 1858), iv, 69. So did S. W. Koelle in *Mohammed and Mohammedanism* (London, 1889), p. 183. M. Lings notes that the seventeen-year old Ṣafiyya, deeply pious since childhood, had not been happily married to Kināna (who ill-treated her). At the expedition to Khaybar in 628, she was given the choice of remaining a Jewess, but she chose Islam and the Prophet. See *Muhammad* (London, 1983), pp. 268-269.
11. See my critical edition in the *Complete Works* of Voltaire (Oxford, 2002), vol 20 B, pp.317-342.
12. *Sūra* 54 does not attribute the splitting of the moon to the Prophet, but simply states: 'The hour of judgement approacheth; and the moon is split asunder' (Sale). In a footnote, Sale says that this passage is expounded in two different ways. Some imagine that the words refer to a famous miracle supposed to have

been performed by Muḥammad, for it is said that on the infidels demanding a sign of him, the moon appeared cloven in two. Others think that the preterite tense is here used in the prophetic style for the future, and that the passage should be rendered 'The moon shall be split asunder', for this, they say, is to happen at the resurrection. This second interpretation is also Djavad Hadidi's in *Voltaire et l'Islam* (Paris, 1974), pp. 86-88.

13. See Martin Lings, *Muhammad*, p. 68.
14. Voltaire made numerous notes on his copy of Sale's Koran ; see *Corpus des notes marginales de Voltaire* (Berlin, 1986), iv. 654-64; a note in the hand of Mme Du Châtelet shows that the volume was read during the Cirey period (*Corpus*, p. 724, note 599).
15. In the Qur'ān there is no question of an angel who will weigh men and women in a big scale, but 'the weighing of men's actions on that day shall be just; and they whose balances laden with their good works shall be heavy, are those who shall be happy'(Sale, Ch. 7).
16. The Qur'ān does not mention a narrow bridge to be crossed after death, but speaks of the straight way (which is often the narrow way, or the steep way), which many people shun (Chapter 1, 90). After Muḥammad's time Muslims came to believe that both rewarded and condemned had to walk across a path or bridge stretched over Hell; the ridge of the bridge was fine as a hair and the wicked fell into Hell. See W. Montgomery Watt, *What is Islam* (London and Beirut 1968), p. 51.
17. The Arabic 'al-jannat', literally 'garden', is the most common term used in the Qur'ān to describe Paradise.Voltaire's understanding of the term (which he uses again in the *Essai sur les moeurs*, ch. 7) is rather particular, however, and is indebted to Sale: 'But all these glories will be eclipsed by the resplendent and ravishing girls of paradise, called, from their large black eyes, *Hūr al-'uyūn*, the enjoyment of whose company will be a principal felicity of the faithful. These, they say, are created, not of clay, as mortal women are, but of pure musk; being, as their prophet often affirms in his *Koran*, free from all natural impurities, defects and inconveniences incident to the sex, of the strictest modesty, and secluded from public view in pavilions of hollow pearls…The name which the *Mohammedans* usually give to this happy mansion, is *al Jannat*, or *the garden*' (*The Koran*, pp. 96-97).
18. The Koran, ch. 56.
19. The Koran, ch. 75.
20. It does not seem that this is specifically mentioned in the *Koran*, but it may be inferred from the beginning of ch.48: 'Verily we have granted thee (Muḥammad) a manifest victory: that God may forgive thee thy preceding and thy subsequent sin… It is he who sendeth down secure tranquility into the hearts of the true believers… that he may lead the true believers of both sexes into gardens beneath which rivers flow, to dwell therein forever' (Sale).
21. Voltaire's source is Sale, *The Koran*, ch. 8: 'And know that whenever ye gain any spoils, a fifth part thereof belongeth unto God, and to the apostle, and his kindred, and the orphans, and the poor , and the traveler.'
22. *De l'Alcoran et de Mahomet*, ed. A. Gunny, *Complete Works of Voltaire* (Oxford, 2002), vol. 20B, p. 340.
23. See the *Notebooks* (*OC*, vol. 81, p. 382).

24. *De l'Alcoran*, p. 341.
25. See the *Notebooks* (vol. 81, p. 383).
26. In the *Essai sur les mœurs* (ch. 7), Voltaire again states that Muslim women are not excluded from Paradise. In fact the Qur'ān teaches not only that women enter Paradise as a reward for their good actions, but that husbands and wives enter together (*Sūra* 43). The question of Muslim women in Paradise preoccupied many European thinkers from the seventeenth century onwards. See my article 'Montesquieu's View of Islam in the *Lettres Persanes*', SVEC 174 (1978), pp. 152-155.
27. 'Verily we have created the *damsels of paradise* by a *peculiar* creation' (Sale). In a footnote to this sentence Sale writes: 'Having created them purposely of finer materials than the females of this world, and subject to none of those inconveniences which are natural to the sex. Some understand this passage of the beatified women; who, though they died old and ugly, shall yet be restored to their youth and beauty in paradise.'
28. 'Burāq' is the name given by tradition to the fabulous animal, represented in pictorial art as a mare with a woman's head and peacock's tail, which the Prophet mounted on the night of his ascension to heaven. It is not mentioned in the Qur'ān which refers to Muḥammad's Night Journey in *Sūras* 17 and 53, but commentators say that Gabriel brought it to Muḥammad in the precincts of the Ka'ba in Makka. See the article 'Burak' in *The Shorter Encyclopedia of Islam* (Leiden, 1974).
29. See the *Notebooks*. After he has stated that Islam is inferior to the Chinese religion, Voltaire remarks that Confucius was all the greater because he was not a prophet (*OC*, vol. 81, p. 139).He stimulates the reader's curiosity for the genuine comparative study between Zoroaster, Confucius, and Muḥammad to be undertaken by the marquis de Pastoret in 1787 (See Chapter 4).
30. Voltaire, *Essai sur les moeurs*, ed R. Pomeau (Paris, 1963), vol. 2, p. 817 Voltaire takes up this point in the Avant-propos to the *Essai sur les mœurs*, vol. 1, p. 196.
31. This story is authenticated in the *Sīra*. See A. Guillaume, *The Life of Muhammad*, pp. 66 68.
32. For a list of the rulers approached, see Lings, pp. 260-261.
33. There is some evolution in Voltaire's thought concerning Muḥammad's learning (or lack thereof). In the seventh of the *Lettres philosophiques* (1734), he spoke of 'l'ignorant Mahomet'. In *De l'Alcoran* (1748) he accuses the monks of having claimed that he was illiterate, and he cannot himself conceive how the leader of the Arabs could not sign his own name.
34. W. M. Watt, *Muhammad at Medina* (Oxford, 1956), p. 274.
35. Voltaire, *Dialogues et anecdotes philosophiques*, ed. R. Naves (Paris, 1966), pp.128-29.
36. See the article by F. S. Eigeldinger in *Dictionaire général de Voltaire*, ed. R. Trousson and J. Vercryusse (Paris, 2003), pp. 178-180.
37. Voltaire's attitude to the Turks may best be described as a seesaw. In 1716, he had sent an epistle to Prince Eugène, praising him for his victory over the Turks at Peterwardein and attacking the 'insolent circumcised'. But in the *Essai sur les moeurs*, as in the *Catéchisme*, he has words of admiration for them. In the late 1760s, as Russia declared war on Turkey, Voltaire regressed. He showed

unconditional fidelity to Catherine II and preached to all Europe the importance of an anti-Turkish crusade to liberate Greece from Turkish oppression. In 1770, one can find echoes (admittedly in a bantering tone), of the spirit of the Crusades, when he writes to the Empress saying that he would have liked to contribute to the killing of a few Turks for her and concluding his letter thus: 'On dit que pour un bon Chrétien c'est une oeuvre fort agéable à Dieu'(D 16575, 11th August 1770).

38. See the critical edition by R. Mortier, *Complete Works of Voltaire* (Oxford, 1987), vol. 62, pp. 127-362 and also his article in *Dictionaire général de Voltaire*, pp.485-490. Voltaire takes the opportunity to refer to the Muslim commentators' account of Muḥammad's journey across the heavens and to rectify the information he had given in *De l'Alcoran,* by pointing out that Muḥammad himself does not speak in 'his' Alcoran of the extravagance attributed to him (p. 228). Prompted by a desire to remove the miraculous from Muḥammad's biography in the article 'Arot et Marot' of the *Questions sur l'Encyclopédie* (1770), he again says that the details of the journey are not given in the Qur'ān. Believing that they are to be found only in Abū al-Fidā, Voltaire draws attention to the lateness of the source. He does not seem to know that a whole chapter of Ibn Isḥāq's *Sīrat* is devoted to the Night Journey. He believes that the story is lacking in authenticity because it was invented by Abū Hurayra, Muḥammad's contemporary.
39. See *Le Dîner du comte de Boulainvilliers*, ed. Ulla Kölving, *Complete Works of Voltaire*, vol. 63A (1990), pp. 291-408.
40. Where a Voltaire text is not available in the Voltaire Foundation edition of the *Complete Works*, I use *Oeuvres Complètes*, ed. L. Moland (Paris, 1877-83). This is referred to as 'M' in the text, and is followed by volume number.
41. The name of the servant of God is Al-Khiḍr: this is found not in the Qur'ān, but in the commentary of the Traditionist Al-Bukhārī on *Sūra* 18.
42. See J. Van den Heuvel, *Voltaire dans ses Contes* (Paris, 1967), pp. 170-179, H. T. Mason, *Voltaire.* (London, 1975), pp. 54-55; his critical edition of *Zadig* in *Complete Works of Voltaire* (Oxford, 2004), vol. 30B, pp. 65-234, and R. Pomeau, *Romans et Contes* (Paris, 1966), p. 28.
43. See my book *Images of Islam in Eighteenth-Century Writings* (London, 1996), pp. 142-144.
44. *Zadig ou la Destinée-histoire orientale*, ed. G. Ascoli, revised by J. Fabre (Paris, 1962), 2 vols.
45. See *Corpus des notes marginales de Voltaire* (1988), vol. 4, p. 657.
46. Despite his loudly proclaimed ignorance of Arabic, Boulainviller, as we saw above, was fairer to Islam and Muḥammad than the Arabist Gagnier was in the 1730s.
47. *Œuvres complètes*, ed. H. Dieckman, J. Proust and J. Varloot (Paris, 1975), vol. 5, pp. 422,423 and 424. In his notes on the articles 'Arabes' and 'Sarrasins', J-C. Vadet gives a detailed account of Diderot' s borrowings from Brucker.
48. *Correspondance*, eds. G. Roth and J. Varloot (Paris, 1953-70), vol. 2, p. 309.
49. See *Images of Islam in Eighteenth-Century Writings*, pp. 163-165.
50. Diderot, *Oeuvres complètes*, ed. cit., vol. 8, pp. 272-273.
51. See W. Montgomery Watt, *Free-Will and Predestination in Early Islam* (London, 1948), p. 25.

52. *Bibliothèque orientale* (Paris, 1777), vol. 1, p. 258.
53. Cf. Qur'ān , *Sūra* 2, l. 286.
54. See J. Proust, *Diderot et l'Encyclopédie* (Paris, 1962), p. 271.
55. *La Correspondance complète de Jean-Jacques Rousseau* (Geneva, Oxford, 1965-89), p. 2760.
56. See R. A. Leigh, 'Manuscrits disparus de Rousseau' in *Annales Jean-Jacques Rousseau* (Geneva, 1905), vol. 34, p. 68 and Rousseau, *Œuvres complètes*, ed . J. Starobinski (Paris, 1964), vol. 3, p. 224.
57. *Essai sur l'origine des langues*, ed. J. Starobinski, in *Œuvres complètes*, vol. 5, p. 409. In his edition of the *Essai* (Bordeaux, 1968), C. Porset believes that the work was composed in 1756, but published in 1781. In the article 'Rousseau et l'Origine des Langues' in the volume *J-J Rousseau. La Transparence et l'Obstacle* (Geneva, 1971), p. 356, J. Starobinski points out that the *Essai* introduces a history of society inside a history of language, but he does not mention Islam or Muḥammad.
58. *Emile*, ed. C. Wirz and P. Burgelin, *Oeuvres complètes,* vol. 4. p. 619. It is true that varied dialects exist throughout contemporary Arab nations, but the written version (which is used everywhere) is that of classical Arabic. Perhaps the classical Arabic is not sufficiently studied.
59. The abbé G. B. Toderini declares that all educated Turks know Arabic and Persian, see *Della Letteratura Turchesca* (Venice, 1787), translated by the abbé de Cournand as *De la littérature des Turcs* (Paris, 1789), vol.1, p. 7.
60. *Contrat Social*, ed. R.Derathé, O.C, vol. 3, p. 384.
61. *Ibid.*, p. 462.
62. The idea of the union of the two powers was noted in the eighteenth century in James Porter's *The religion, laws, government and manners of the Turks* (London, 1768). It has in our times been confirmed by Patricia Crone and Martin Hinds in their book *God's Caliph: religious authority in the first centuries of Islam* (Cambridge, 1986).
63. One (not necessarily negative) effect of his repetitions is that Voltaire has the opportunity of stressing the fundamental teaching of Muḥammad and of correcting mistakes he made. One of these relates to the Night Journey, at first described as originating in the Qur'ān, but later properly attributed to the *Ḥadīth*.
64. Two writers who made valuable contributions to Islamic studies - Djavad Hadidi in *Voltaire et l'Islam* and Diego Venturino in 'Imposteur ou Législateur? Le Mahomet des Lumières' do not seem to have taken into sufficient account the nature of Voltaire's ambivalence and his use of Muḥammad in the polemics against Jesus in the 1760s.

4

Muḥammad in the Age of Empire to 1900

Muḥammad as represented in some historical works

The French Enlightenment masters could be expected to have made some impact on writers of the later eighteenth, if not the nineteenth, century. If this was indeed the case, it is valuable to inquire as to the extent to which these writers have contributed to the formation of the image of Muḥammad in the West.

The abbé Vincent Mignot (1730-1790), was a nephew to Voltaire, and had kept in touch with him. Given this connection, it could be hoped that in some ways he was influenced by his uncle, or might, at any rate, have inherited from him a tradition of broad-minded openness as far as foreign civilisations and personalities were concerned, although sadly this does not seem to have materialized. Mignot's writing was highly rated by two nineteenth-century biographies: Michaud's *Biographie universelle* described him as 'très instruit', while the *Nouvelle biographie générale* mentioned the precision and impartiality he apparently showed in his *Histoire de l'Empire Ottoman depuis son origine jusqu'à la paix de Belgrade en 1740* (1771).[1] The *Histoire* was the fourth volume of Mignot's historical works, and it was translated into English and German, the previous volumes being concerned with various aspects of European history. Mignot took the opportunity to include in it a 'Discours historique sur Mahomet et ses successeurs'. Although he had no knowledge of Arabic, he claims that he used a translation of Turkish historians by Denis-Dominique Cardone (1720-83), Professor of Arabic at the Collège Royal, and that at the Ministry of External

Affairs he consulted the correspondence of French ambassadors to the Porte. Despite these efforts, his contribution on Muḥammad does not seem to deserve the high praise bestowed on him.[2]

Mignot concentrates his attention on Muḥammad; however, he does so to diminish the importance of the Prophet's role in history. Unlike many other Western writers, he displaces Muḥammad as the founder of Islam: instead, he lays responsibility for its establishment on the shoulders of a Jew and a Nestorian monk, neither of whom is referred to by name. These two produced a confused mixture of Judaism and Christianity and 'jetèrent quelques étincelles de vérités dans un abîme de ténèbres' (p. 4). The merit, traditionally associated with Muḥammad, of proclaiming to coarse idolaters a God that was eternal, incorporeal, infinite, and the source of all perfection and justice, was exclusively given to them by Mignot. He argues that a simple and pure worship would not have sufficed to put the impostor on the throne, and that as he wanted to be king, legislator, and prophet, Muḥammad had to win over the people by the miraculous. Towards this end, 'his' Jew provided him with all the wild stories of the Talmud and persuaded him to invent revelations, ecstasies, and conversations with God.

Voltaire's nephew is very critical of the Qur'ān, but his greatest scorn is reserved for Muḥammad himself. He accounts for the bravery of Muslim soldiers by alluding to Muḥammad's insistence on the role of destiny. This is a conception, widely popularized by Diderot and other Western thinkers, whereby no-one remains unaffected by destiny: the soldier who is not destined to die at a certain hour will shrug off the arrows of an entire army. On the other hand, one who has reached their fatal term will not escape death despite every precaution. Mignot's conclusion is that true Muslims abuse the principle of God's prescience, and consider themselves no more in danger in the most murderous battle than at a feast or in their bed. Their courage is also fostered by their Prophet's solemn promise that all those who die sword-in-hand against the 'infidels' will be martyrs, and therefore admitted to Paradise regardless of crimes they may have committed in their lifetime. Mignot did not wish to speak of the strict conditions laid down in the Qur'ān for obtaining Paradise. He does, however, acknowledge that Muḥammad's successors profited more than he from the bloody fanaticism which elevated ferocious soldiers to the rank of apostles and martyrs (p. 13).

Mignot also has little sympathy for Islamic legislation with regard to women. He had, at first, stressed the fact that despite being much younger than his wife Khadīja, Muḥammad did not marry anyone else during her lifetime. But then he points out that the false prophet used the authority of the Qur'ān to marry up to fifteen women simultaneously, while allowing his followers to marry only four wives. The insinuation here is that the legislator bends the rules to suit his own needs and caters for his weaknesses (p. 15). 'Ā'isha's conduct (that is, alleged infidelity), Muḥammad's jealousy, and his scorn for a sex 'auquel ses sens le soumettaient malgré lui' are held responsible for the severity of Qur'ānic law against women. The reasons put forward by Mignot do not take into account the political and social factors governing the Prophet's marriages, or the provisions regarding women that were made in the Qur'ān, to which Voltaire had drawn attention. Mignot suggests that so great is the influence of Muḥammad on Muslims that they behave towards their womenfolk as some savage idol worshippers do towards their domestic deities: they lavish presents on the women, but also imprison and mistreat them (p. 17). The only positive observation of Mignot on the situation of Muslim women is that they were described by Muḥammad as having souls. Perhaps wishing to contradict Montesquieu in the *Lettres persanes* (and other writers with similar opinions to Montesquieu), Mignot states that Muḥammad was not so ridiculous as to refuse a soul to the fair sex he both hated and loved. In many respects, however, Mignot was backward looking, for he shows less affinity, on the whole, with the leaders of the Enlightenment than with the bigoted abbés Vertot and de Saint-Pierre.

Fortunately, we have in his near contemporary, Edward Gibbon (1737-94), a more serious historian, who in some ways helped to change the perception of Islam and Muḥammad in late eighteenth-century Europe. Although he was not an Arabic specialist, even before his time at Magdalen College, Oxford, he had shown an interest in Muḥammad which he later developed by studying Pococke, d'Herbelot, Ockley, Sale, Gagnier, and Boulainviller.[3] The three chapters he devoted to Islam in his *History of the Decline and Fall of the Roman Empire* were as influential as Voltaire's chapters in the *Essai sur les moeurs*. The beginning of Chapter 50 does not, however, appear promising, as the reader is confronted with a cliché: Muḥammad holds the sword in one hand, the

Qur'ān in the other and erects his empire on the ruins of Christianity and Rome.[4] Gibbon is guilty of anachronism and inaccuracy here, for the empire of the Caliphs to which he is referring did not exist in the Prophet's lifetime, and Christianity and Rome did not perish, even if Iraq, Syria and Egypt were conquered after Muḥammad's death. But this cliché quickly disappears: the causes of the decline and fall of the Eastern Empire are attributed to Muḥammad's genius (Gibbon is again inaccurate), the manners of his nation, and the spirit of Islam. Gibbon clearly sees that Islam was one of the most memorable revolutions, which had a lasting impact on the nations of the globe, and which became part of human history and not simply a passing incident (as Bossuet had claimed in the *Discours sur l'histoire universelle*).

Gibbon focuses attention on the ancient Arabs before discussing the Prophet. He admires the freedom and valour of the pre-Islamic Arab who 'enjoys, in some degree, the benefits of society, without forfeiting the prerogatives of nature' (p. 320). Gibbon believes the pre-Islamic Arab is superior to the primitive of Rousseau (in the *Discours sur l'Inégalité*, 1755), being able to enjoy the best of both civilization and nature. He is so carried away in his admiration for the Arabs that he endows them with an unrealistic level of development: Muḥammad's grandfather and ancestors 'reigned like Pericles at Athens, or the Medici in Florence, by the opinion of their wisdom and their integrity' (p. 321). Gibbon states that the use and popularity of oratory among the ancient Arabs is clear evidence of public freedom, and that in its more simple state the Arab nation is free, disdaining base submission to the will of a master. It is fear of dishonour that is identified as making the patient and sober ancient Arab scorn pain, danger, and death.

Yet Gibbon falls back on the traditional Western perception of Islam, claiming that a quite different cause produces the same display of courage in the modern Arab: the spirit of liberty is replaced by the force of destiny. In this respect, Gibbon is no different from Mignot, as he believes that the Qur'ān inculcates, in the most absolute sense, the tenets of fate and predestination. Although the actions of the Arabs are not strictly governed by a belief in these tenets (which would extinguish both industry and virtue), the influence of predestination in every age has, Gibbon argues, exalted their courage. Gibbon's views echo those of Diderot in his major novel of ideas, *Jacques le Fataliste*, written between 1765 and 1784. The eponymous hero Jacques, and many characters in the anecdotes attached to the story of the novel, maintain that the whole notion of vice and virtue is meaningless if one's acts are predetermined. An amoral attitude to life has, however, nothing to do with Muḥammad's teaching.

In the *Decline*, emphasis is finally placed on Muḥammad himself. Here, Muḥammad is separated from other Arabs and a fair attempt is made to distinguish between the various stages of his career. Gibbon rejects the notion that Muḥammad pandered to the prejudices of his countrymen, and points out that practices of the *jāhilīya* (the time of ignorance before Muḥammad) such as abstention from eating pork, and circumcision, were silently transmitted to the posterity of the Arabs and their converts with Qur'ānic sanction.

Gibbon then gives three different images of Muḥammad corresponding to stages in his biography: the solitary of Mount Ḥirā', the preacher of Makka, and the conqueror of Arabia. In connection with the first he dismisses, as an absurd calumny of the Greeks, the story of Muḥammad's epileptic fits. If such fits were founded, they would, in his view, be an object of pity rather than abhorrence. Using Sale's footnote to *Sūra* 73, Gibbon points out in his own footnote that the story of Muḥammad's epilepsy was greedily swallowed by the gross bigotry of Hottinger, Prideaux, and Marracci. He insists that this is stretching too far the meaning of the titles 'The wrapped up, The covered', given to *Sūras* 73-74. Like Ockley, he finds the silence of the Muslim commentators to be conclusive. He also takes the opportunity to rectify the wild guesses of Boulainviller, who appears to him to have indulged his fancy when suggesting that Muḥammad went to the Persian court. With some justification, Gibbon believes in the accuracy of his own enquiry when he notes that Muḥammad's two journeys to Syria were confined to the fairs of Bostra and Damascus.

Despite Gibbon's promise, only glimpses of Muḥammad the preacher appear in the *Decline*. In his highly selective account, Gibbon observes that Muḥammad asserted liberty of conscience and disclaimed the use of religious violence. In a footnote, he refers to numerous verses on toleration to be found in the Qur'ān. In his attempt to excuse Muḥammad's use of force, he argues that in the state of nature every person has the right to defend, by force of arms, their body and possessions, to repel or even to prevent the violence of their enemies and to extend hostilities to a reasonable measure of satisfaction. He depicts with sympathy a Muḥammad despoiled and banished by the injustice of his own countrymen while conducting a peaceful and benevolent mission, stating that 'the injustice of Makka and the choice of Madīna transformed the citizen into a prince, the humble preacher into the leader of armies' (p. 376).

Such statements tend to conceal an ambivalent attitude towards Muḥammad, for there is a violent contrast in Gibbon's mind between Muḥammad at Makka and Muḥammad at Madīna. Gibbon has less sympathy for the prophet of Madīna who, according to him, assumed in 'his' new revelations a fiercer and more sanguinary tone. He concludes that Muḥammad's former moderation must have been the result of weakness. A footnote more explicitly expresses the nature of Gibbon's ambivalence. In it Gibbon speaks of the vehemence of *Sūras* 8-9, while appearing to censure Marracci's attack on Muḥammad. In the text itself he suggests that Muḥammad displayed Hebraic ferocity in his prosecution of religious war, although he admits that the military laws of the Hebrews were more rigid than those of Muḥammad.

An unflattering image of Muḥammad (still current in the West) now appears, and his military campaigns against the opponents of Islam are reduced to the level of petty excursions for the defence of a caravan that prepared his troops for the conquest of Arabia. Gibbon still tries to redress the balance, and thus he represents Muḥammad not simply as a victor who refuses to indulge the passions of his followers, but more importantly as someone who chooses to forgive his opponents and unite factions at Makka. He contemptuously dismisses a suggestion, which he attributes to Voltaire, that Muḥammad behaved abominably after the conquest of Makka in 630. He cannot accept the idea of a leader who imagines and perpetrates the most horrid crimes, since it is neither charitable nor philosophic, resting as it does on mere allegation and not on history. Although he defends the Prophet, he nevertheless censures him for allegedly ordering or approving the assassination of Jews and idolaters who had escaped from the battlefield. He suggests that the repetition of such acts must have gradually stained Muḥammad's character.

Yet Gibbon proclaims that even a philosophical atheist might subscribe to the Muslim creed, 'a creed too sublime perhaps for our present faculties' (p. 339). Particularly appealing to him is that the same 'pure' and 'perfect' version of the religion which was revealed to Muḥammad at Makka and Madīna has been preserved by Indian, African, and Turkish proselytes.[5] Gibbon does not take into account variety in local religious practices. Naturally, Muḥammad would have been pleased if all Indians, Africans, and Turks had faithfully observed the letter and spirit of his teaching. Gibbon is here using a polemical technique which has some affinity with Voltaire's: but whereas Voltaire displays anti-Christian tendencies in the *Catéchisme*, Gibbon is specifically anti-Catholic, for he makes the Islam that has been handed down appear more pure than it really is in order to attack Roman Catholicism. Thus Gibbon presents a far from realistic picture of Islam, by turning it into a monolithic religion and ignoring the existence of, for instance, an Indian or African Islam.

Later studies will challenge the view that Islam is practised in the same way everywhere throughout the Muslim world. For example, William Dalrymple, writing about eighteenth-century India, notes that for all the sadness of Muḥarram and of the events it commemorates, there was a carnival element in the festival celebrated in Hyderabad, and houses were decorated and lit up with oil lamps, as at the Hindu festival of Divali. His conclusion was that (as so often in India and especially in the Deccan) Islam found itself unwittingly absorbed, transformed, and assimilated by an overwhelmingly Hindu environment.[6] The works of Garcin de Tassy, Professor of Urdu at the Ecole spéciale des langues orientales vivantes, include one with a self-explanatory title, the *Mémoire sur des particularités de la religion musulmane dans l'Inde* (1831).[7]

Gibbon deplores the fact that neither Muḥammad nor his followers are sufficiently versed in languages, although he acknowledges the advance made by the Arabs in astronomy, chemistry, and medicine and also pays homage to the transmission of Arabic culture in Umayyad Spain. He adds that Arabic learning continued for about four hundred years 'till the great irruption of Moguls and was coeval with the darkest and most slothful period of European annals' (vol. 6, p. 28). He has a sense of balance: there is nothing objectionable in his assertion that after this period Islamic learning lost momentum, while Western science made great strides. Gibbon insists on the value of foreign languages: if the Arabs had these they would have been able to study Greek and Roman moral political writings and these 'might have gradually unlocked the fetters of Eastern despotism, diffused a liberal spirit of enquiry and toleration and encouraged the Arabian sages to suspect their caliph was a tyrant and their prophet an impostor' (vol. 6, p. 33). Almost surreptitiously, Gibbon has introduced the notion that Muḥammad was an impostor, even if he does not emphasize or frequently revisit this idea. Gibbon nevertheless argues that Muḥammad's system appears to be more pure than Zoroaster's law, more liberal than the law of Moses and 'less inconsistent with reason than the creed of mystery and superstition which in the seventh century disgraced the simplicity of the Gospel' (vol. 6, p. 487).

Claude Emmanuel-Joseph Pierre, Marquis de Pastoret (1756-1840) was another member of the Académie des Inscriptions et Belles Lettres, and he succeeded Volney at the Académie Française in 1820. Pastoret made a more serious attempt at comparative religion than Gibbon and the authors of clandestine literature. His book *Zoroastre, Confucius et Mahomet comparés comme sectaires, législateurs et moralistes* (1787) was awarded a prize by the Académie des Inscriptions in 1785. Only one of the famous trio of impostors of the first half of the eighteenth century remains in it, as Moses and Christ are no longer considered relevant here. Pastoret was perhaps following Voltaire's suggestion that the contribution to society of leaders who did not belong to the Judeo-Christian tradition should be examined.[8] Educated in a legal and historical background[9], Pastoret tends to stress the legal aspects of Islam in *Zoroastre, Confucius et Mahomet*, although he devotes the third section to Muḥammad. Even if the latter is still viewed as an impostor 'sa conduite ne fut sans doute qu'un tissu d'impostures' (p. 271), he is an impostor who has skills, genius, and who is a deep thinker. Pastoret's displays a keen desire to do some justice to the character of Muḥammad. At the beginning of the section he states that the idea of championing Muḥammad's conquests or errors is not the aim of the text, rather, in the manner of Adrian Reland, he wishes to redress some of the accusations made against Muḥammad by writers who had imperfect knowledge, or who had not studied in depth the 'works' of this great man. Despite the occasional errors (starting with the reference to Muḥammad's works) and prejudices, he shows considerable skill in the way in which he rearranges Qur'ānic material for the benefit of his readers, and much of the time closely references the Qur'ān to illustrate his points.

Under the first heading of 'Dogma', the reader is invited to open the Qur'ān in order to witness the Apostle of the Muslims announce the most sublime truths relating to worship and morals (p. 234). Distancing himself from those who accuse Islam of merely aping Christianity for its moral and spiritual teaching, Pastoret suggests that Muslims have maintained what is most plausible and probable in the latter, together with what is most in harmony with the law and light of nature. It is not surprising that in his slightly deist reading of Islam he should find admirable concision in *Sūra* 112 about the unity of God. His description of the Islamic Paradise is notable for the restraint with which he characterises Muḥammad's 'voluptuous imagination' (p. 245). He expatiates on the means by which the Muslim could attain Paradise, which consist in using one's goods piously and putting them to the service of God. Pastoret, quoting *Sūra* 2, l. 190: 'God loveth not transgressors' insists that Muslims are exhorted not to attack first. He takes care to show that Muḥammad did not wish those who did not share his religious beliefs to be pursued relentlessly by force. Pastoret points out that apart from idolatry (against which Muḥammad's imagination does not relent), Muḥammad orders his followers to respect all faiths.

Pastoret has perceptive insights into the Sharī'a laws relating to the part of the body where the punishment for theft should be applied. Referring to *Sūra* 4, l. 141, he says that Muḥammad wished the punishment to fall mainly on the instrument of the crime, and so had the hands of the criminal cut off. Strangely enough, Pastoret includes what he describes as incest under the criminal code. He claims that Muḥammad was not as severe towards incest, suggesting that the latter recognised as legitimate marriage to the widow of an adopted son. It appeared to Pastoret that the Prophet was justifying his own conduct, since he had himself contracted a union which caused controversy. He quotes *Sūra* 33, ll. 4,37 to show that Muḥammad believed he was not guilty but had used a right that was authorized by God. If he had wished to be lenient towards him, Pastoret could have stressed that l. 4 makes it quite clear that there is a difference between adopted sons and the sons of one's own flesh and blood. Pastoret, however, does not do this. He also fails to quote *Sūra* 4, ll. 23-24, which lists the categories of women a man is forbidden to marry, including the 'wives of your sons proceeding from your loins'.

In the fifth section on moral laws, Pastoret refutes as odious the charge that Muḥammad was a monstrous debauchee. He quotes *Sūra*

4, l. 27-8 and 17, l. 32 to show that believers are taught to avoid adultery (which is identified as one of the sins that lead to Hell). The most glowing picture of Muḥammad emerges in this section: not only does he check all types of excesses, he also favours the practice of all the virtues. Pastoret draws attention to a long list of people who arouse Muḥammad's pity and sensitivity: fathers, children, foreigners, travellers, the poor, and all those who are in need but have no help, no liberty, and no fortune (p. 323). To support his case, he refers, for instance, to *Sūra* 4, l. 40 and 17, l. 26, where the believer is commanded to help these people.

Pastoret may have felt too generous when discussing Islam and Muḥammad, for he rescinds some of the praise lavished earlier, when he compares Muḥammad with Zoroaster and Confucius. Pastoret argues that although Muḥammad shows more skill than his predecessors in adopting his teaching to suit the climate and the natural needs of the people to whom he proclaimed his doctrine, nevertheless, Confucius has developed moral principles with more wisdom and depth and Zoroaster was superior to Muḥammad as a legislator. Pastoret asks: 'Did anyone see Confucius behave like Muḥammad who tried to limit polygamy and then in the very eyes of his disciples assumed with God's blessing the privilege of a liberty without limit?' As before, he refers to the Qur'ān (*Sūra* 33, l. 50) to support his view about Muḥammad being allowed exceptional treatment. Pastoret also thinks that Muḥammad was unjust towards Christians, since he accused them of being polytheists and worshippers of images.

The complicated question of free will in Islam is treated rather superficially. Pointing out that Zoroaster was in favour of it, Pastoret claims that it was 'des circonstances intéressées' which forced Muḥammad to reject this concept (p. 407). The particular circumstances Pastoret has in mind were the events of the battle of Uḥud (625). Pastoret claims that that in order to respond to the complaints of his followers (who had escaped the massacre), Muḥammad fabricated the doctrine of predestination and fatalism, so that they might be resigned to their fate. In saying this, Pastoret distorts Qur'ānic teaching. The verses referred to stress that the time of death depends on God. As *Sūra* 2, l. 145 puts it, 'Nor can a soul die except by God's leave, the term being fixed' while *Sūra* 6, l. 2 says: 'He it is who created you from clay and then decreed a stated term'. These verses, like *Sūra* 7, l. 34 (which is about people being prevented from delaying or advancing their appointed term even by an hour), have nothing to do with the battle of Uḥud, rather they state a general principle.

Whereas in clandestine literature of the first half of the eighteenth century (Chapter 2), Muḥammad had appeared in a more favourable light than Moses and Jesus, in Pastoret's work Muḥammad finally sinks lower in esteem in comparison with other religious leaders (Zoroaster and Confucius). Although endowed with a 'superior intelligence' (p. 410), Muḥammad is inferior to Zoroaster as a legislator because his laws lack 'cette liaison sage et combinée' that one finds in the laws of the latter (p. 424). The weakness of Muḥammad's laws, argues Pastoret, is due to the fact that they depended on special circumstances and Muḥammad's passions. Pastoret quotes marriage practices as an example of this, as he is critical of a system that dispenses with parental consent. On the moral plane, too, Muḥammad appears in an unfavourable light. Pastoret points out that both Zoroaster and Muḥammad had preached brotherly love to their disciples and that both had betrayed this principle in their practice. Yet when it comes to giving concrete examples of betrayal, it is Muḥammad whom he singles out. Quoting *Sūra* 8, l. 39, he finds no justification in Muḥammad's ordering of non-believers to be fought and put to death. Pastoret finally grants moral preponderance to Confucius on the grounds that he had made a deeper study of the human heart and that his teaching is acceptable for all ages and nations.

Lives of Muḥammad

The impetus given by Gagnier's and Reiske's scholarly editions of Muḥammad's biography took a long time to gain momentum. Through lack of Arabic, the three historians discussed above would not have been able to take advantage of them even if they had so desired. Claude-Etienne Savary (1750-1788), on the other hand, was in a better position to do so. He possessed some knowledge of Arabic, which probably improved during his stay in Egypt from 1776 to 1779. He published the *Lettres sur l'Egypte* in 1785, also translated a tale from Arabic, and later worked on an Arabic grammar (published by Langlès in 1813). Savary was, however, better known for his translation of the Qur'ān (1783), to which he appended an 'Abrégé' of the Life of

Muḥammad. That may have guaranteed him a wider readership than a 'Life' by itself would have produced. In any case, Savary was faithful to the French tradition of writing on 'l'homme et l'oeuvre' in a single volume. In the 'Abrégé' he focused on Muḥammad independently of world or European history.

Savary claimed that his biography was based on the best Arab writers and the authentic Traditions. He gave more importance to Abū al-Fidā whose 'simple and faithful narrative' (p. 12) impressed him, although he did refer to Ibn Isḥāq, al-Bukhārī, Bayḍāwī, and Jannabī at times. Muḥammad's qualities of wit, sincerity, and love of virtue appear to be based on the late Arab historian's work. He was rather ambivalent towards the Prophet and certainly less well-disposed towards him than Boulainviller, although he understood better than the latter the political dimension of some of Muḥammad's marriages: one in particular he discusses is Muḥammad's marriage to Umm Ḥabība, the daughter of Abū Sufyān.[10] Savary's reasoning sounds plausible when he suggests that Muḥammad hoped that this alliance would disarm him.

Like Rousseau, Savary depicts a Muḥammad who relies more on rhetoric and on the beauty of style and imagery in his preaching, than on the weight of reason, and who uses this rhetoric to 'seduce' the Arabs. Savary claims that the real cause of Muḥammad's success is his policy of dictating the Qur'ān over a period of twenty three years; this is qualified by Savary as a wise precaution, but as such this assessment is not intended to be a compliment. Thus Savary turns Muḥammad into a skilful opportunist who for three years maintained the secrecy of his doctrine and his grand design, until he thought he could count on the blind obedience of the new converts, and announced his 'revelation'. This, of course, is a fanciful reconstruction of what happened during the Prophet's early preaching, for revelations were announced the moment they occurred. Another sign of opportunism, according to Savary, is that as long as Muḥammad thought himself too weak to win a battle, he did not impose on his followers the task of taking up arms. But as soon as he could count on success, he had the order to fight idolaters and the obligation to defend him to death 'sent down from heaven'. Later, however, Savary makes amends for this negative portrayal by arguing that the success of Islam was due to the simple doctrine preached by Muḥammad, which reason could easily conceive (p. 239).

Savary sets out to be fair to Muḥammad, assuming that the best way of achieving this objective is to give a faithful account of the facts and to discard the miracles that had been falsely attributed to Muḥammad by fanatics. However, the *Abrégé* begins by outlining miracles said to have occurred at Muḥammad's birth, then subsequently dismisses other alleged miracles (such as an angel protecting Muḥammad from the sun's rays in the desert). Savary adds that these made no impact on the learned Abū al-Fidā who, despite being a Muslim, did not wish to turn his Prophet's life into a bad legend. He is scathing towards Gagnier and Marracci for adding credence to these tales which are considered apocryphal by Muslims. Muḥammad is to be judged according to his deeds and not according to the visions of fanatics. He points out that far from attributing to himself the power to make miracles, Muḥammad declares at various places in the Qur'ān that God gives this power to those he chooses among his servants, but that he himself is only concerned with preaching.

Muḥammad's Night Journey was, as Savary sensed, a special case. Unlike Gagnier, he shows restraint in his account of this journey, providing an abridged version based on the Traditionists al-Bukhārī and Abū Hurayra, and criticising the Muslim theologians who had written volumes on the subject and indulged their wild imagination. His reliance on a canonical source (such as that of al-Bukhārī) enabled him to grasp one of the essential points of this journey for Muslims. That is, Western readers of his work could thus learn that Muḥammad, after meeting several Prophets in various heavens, finally took advice from Moses, and God granted his plea to reduce the number of daily prayers from fifty to five. But Savary does not remain true to the spirit of Islam for long, since he argues that Muḥammad imagined the Journey simply to validate the new way of praying that he had established (p. 49).

It seems that Savary wanted to make a distinctive contribution to the debate on Muḥammad's lack of learning. He at first suggests that Muḥammad claimed to be illiterate, relying on his natural eloquence to spread his message. Towards the end of the *Abrégé* he reproduces material that can be found in Abū al-Fidā, which apparently confirms his belief that Muḥammad could write. This material was a weak Tradition, often used by the Shiites to strengthen their case about Muḥammad having appointed, in writing, 'Alī as his successor. In any case Sunnī Muslims, who revere any genuine relic of the Prophet, would have piously preserved any material attributed to him if this had indeed existed. It is a fact that, like Emperor Akbar of India, Muḥammad did not write letters himself, but used secretaries.

An earlier episode (the details of which are recorded by Ibn Isḥāq) is also used to prove that Muḥammad could read. In 628, the Quraysh sent an ambassador named Suhayl ibn 'Amr to make a treaty with Muḥammad. After having met with some preliminary objections to the wording of the treaty, Muḥammad then dictated the following to 'Alī: 'These are the terms of the truce between Muḥammad the Messenger of God and Suhayl b. 'Amr'. Suhayl objected to the expression 'messenger of God', so at his insistence, Muḥammad offered to substitute Muḥammad ibn 'Abdullāh for Muḥammad, the Messenger of God, which he did. According to Savary, it was Muḥammad himself who made the substitution by crossing out the words with his pen, although no such information is to be found in Ibn Isḥāq or Abū al-Fidā. Savary maliciously notes that at that moment Muḥammad forgot that he could neither read nor write[11] and he mischievously adds that this forgetting was a miracle. His explanation is that the feigned ignorance was simply a stratagem used by Muḥammad to impart a divine character to his book and that it is probable during the fifteen years spent in solitude he had acquired sufficient knowledge for his design.

Positive images of Muḥammad do, however, frequently appear in the *Abrégé*. Savary acknowledges Muḥammad's ability to achieve conciliation. He points out that as Madīna was divided between the tribes of the Khazraj and Aws, Muḥammad extinguished the flames of ancient hostility among them and preached unity and concord. At a secret meeting of seventy-five Madīnan converts at 'Aqaba at the end of June in 622, for instance, he invited them to swear allegiance to him and to choose twelve leaders among themselves to take charge of their people's affairs. To make his point, Savary now relies on Ibn Isḥāq who, as he says, recorded the names of the twelve leaders. He felt it important to quote the words of the Prophet, namely that the twelve were sureties for their people just as the disciples of Jesus (p. 60). After discussing the division between the Madīnans, Savary referred to that between the *muhājirūn* (the Makkan emigrants who went with Muḥammad to Madīna) and the *anṣār* (Muḥammad's Madīnan followers, the helpers). The first group claimed precedence for having been the first to embrace Islam, while the second thought that this was due to them for having sheltered him. The dissension would have been calamitous, but Muḥammad managed to reconcile them. However, typical of Savary, he says that the latter made a verse (without specifying which) come down from heaven in *Sūra* 3.

Another highly significant episode occurring after the conquest of Makka is used by Savary to show how Muḥammad won over the leaders of the tribes. Savary says that everything gained during the war was sacrificed by Muḥammad to win their affection. He does not actually refer to a recently revealed verse (*Sūra* 9, l. 60) which identifies a new category of persons entitled to benefit from spoils used as alms (such as the poor and the needy), and those whose hearts are to be reconciled (slaves, captives, and debtors). He only mentions that among others Abū Sufyān and his two sons Yazīd and Muʿāwiya were given one hundred camels each, likewise ʿIkrimah, the son of Abū Jahl. Savary points out that the *anṣārī* who had been left out complained to the Prophet, but he does reproduce a version of Abū al-Fidā's text in which Muḥammad answered the complaints of the *anṣārī*. In this text, Muḥammad criticised the latter because they were grumbling about the things of this world by which he had reconciled men's hearts that they may submit to Islam, while they already had the truc faith which promised them eternal happiness. Savary does reference this however, and adds that the ansari, stung by this mild reproach, went away satisfied.

Favourable comments on the Prophet's character are also evident from Savary. Basing himself on Abū al-Fidā, he describes the young Muḥammad, prior to the Revelation, as a man who roused people's admiration with the qualities of his intellect; he was the best at a reply, the most truthful in conversation, the most excellent for fidelity, and the furthest of all from anything base. Hence his name among his countrymen in Makka became synonymous with the faithful. Savary is critical of Arab authors who took delight in representing Muḥammad with all perfections of body and mind, and he preferred ʿAlī's account of him as recorded by Abū al-Fidā who, he felt, was wiser and less partial than others. He attached greater importance to Muḥammad's personal and moral qualities than to his physical traits (which are, nevertheless, also listed). According to this account, Muḥammad received from nature a superior intelligence; he had excellent reasoning faculties and an astonishing memory. He was just towards everyone:

he gave equal treatment to a relative, a stranger, the powerful, and the weak. He neither despised the poor for his poverty nor respected the rich for their riches. He listened patiently to the person who conversed with him and was not the first to leave.

The public aspects of Muḥammad's life are presented with equal sympathy. As Savary tells his readers, Muḥammad had to endure disgrace, exile and proscription, but these only strengthened his resolution. The accumulation of protests and hatred from Jews, Christians, and the Quraysh did not frighten him: his genius was meant to overcome obstacles. He created an order of brotherhood and this order united his countrymen. Forgetting the wars of apostasy waged by Abū Bakr after the Prophet's death, Savary no doubt exaggerates when he claims that Muḥammad established his power on such a solid foundation that Arabia remained faithful to Islam and that his successors simply had to follow the path that he had traced. Savary ends on a very positive note: Muḥammad's laws have survived the ruin of empires, and the wise among the Orientals rightly confer on him the title of Prophet and consider him to be one of the greatest men that ever existed. What then about the wise among the Westerners?

Thomas Carlyle may well have been one of these wise Westerners in the nineteenth century. Although he had no Islamic cultural background, he gave an important public lecture on Islam and Muḥammad entitled 'The Hero as Prophet' in Edinburgh, in May 1840. This was published as part of the series on *Heroes, Hero Worship, and the Heroic in History* (1841) where Carlyle aired his thoughts on human life. He was among the first Westerners to proclaim the sincerity of Muḥammad and the truthfulness of Islam, even if he expressed himself rather pompously in his description of Muḥammad as 'a silent great soul... one of those who cannot *but* be sincere'.[12] Carlyle had to deal with the negative image of Islam and of Muḥammad, which were both seen as enemies of Christian Europe. Inherited from about the eighth century, it has persisted up to the present in some ways. Carlyle rejected the lies which well-meaning zeal had heaped round Muḥammad and the idea that he was a scheming impostor, his religion being a mere mass of quackery and fatuity. He could not understand how millions of Muslims could have been deceived by such fraud. He instead stressed the inner aspect of Islam and the common features it shared with Judaism and Christianity.

The great irony here is that the rather sympathetic interest in Islam and Muḥammad by many eighteenth-century writers had given way, in the political and military fields, to a shift in balance of power in favour of the Western countries which were vying for influence in North Africa and India.[13] Napoleon had invaded Egypt (which he intended to be his passage to India) with an impressive number of scientists and scholars. Yet after the revolt in Cairo the French killed 2500 Egyptians and fired shells into al-Azhar which was then overrun and desecrated. Villages were torched and Napoleon himself ordered the execution of prisoners. In the proclamation to his troops before Alexandria, however, he asked them to respect the muftis and imāms of the Egyptians and to show the same tolerance towards the ceremonies prescribed by the Qur'ān, and towards the mosques as they had shown towards convents and synagogues. He claimed that he respected God, his Prophet and the Qur'ān, and that if he had stayed in the Orient he would have gone on pilgrimage to Makka.[14]

Given that the approach of the nineteenth century by European powers was one of colonialism (although the Germans were less tainted by it at that stage), this speech by Napoleon showed less chauvinism towards the religion of Islam and towards Muḥammad himself than one might have expected. Colonialism, with its inhuman face, coexisted alongside a serious study by some European scholars of the holy book of the Muslims, their Prophet, theology, philosophy, history, and culture. French and German scholars, in particular, were at the cutting-edge of developments in Islamic studies. For example, despite his support for French imperialism, Silvestre de Sacy (1758-1838), produced the monumental *Chrestomathie arabe* in four volumes in 1806 and 1826: this was a collection of texts on various aspects of Arab-Muslim civilization which he edited and translated with extensive commentaries. Gustav Weil's *Mohammed der Prophet* (1843) inaugurated a new phase in biographical writings. While Bugeaud was conquering Algeria, Silvestre de Sacy and his pupils E. Quatremère, F. E. Schultz, and W. McGucklin de Slane were, with their editorial and translation work, revealing the historian and philosopher Ibn Khaldūn (1332-1406) to the world.

Viewed against this background of scholarly activity, the life of Muḥammad, unsurprisingly, continued to fascinate those French and English writers who had some interest in Islam. In a number of cases it was commented on by the same authors who had devoted their time to the study of the Qur'ān. Those interested in different aspects of Islamic civilization could not help making at least a passing reference to the personality of Muḥammad. This was primarily because he continued to be perceived as the 'author' of the Qur'ān, Islam itself being identified with its 'founder' and being absorbed by him.[15] In the *Life of Mahomet*, for example, William Muir suggests that 'Mahomet and the Coran, the author of Islam and the instrument by which he achieved its success are themes worthy the earnest attention of mankind' (vol. 4, p. 324). At the same time, many French and English writers whether they were specialists of Arabic or not could not choose to remain indifferent to Islam and its Prophet when their constant presence was felt in many fields.

As more research was carried out into primary source material, often culminating in critical editions of early Islamic texts, nineteenth-century writers such as Aloys Sprenger (1813-93) and William Muir (1809-1905), as well as later Arabists, including Alfred Guillaume, Montgomery Watt, and Martin Lings, preferred to use the older Arabic sources of the eighth, ninth, and tenth centuries when compiling their biographies of the Prophet. These sources included the *Life of Muhammad* by Ibn Isḥāq, the *Kitāb al-Maghāzī*, a chronicle of his campaigns by al-Wāqidī, the *Kitāb al-Ṭabaqāt al-Kabīr*, a compilation containing material on Muḥammad and a biography of his chief companions by Ibn Sa'd (d.845), secretary of al-Wāqidī, and a section of the *Tārīkh ar-Rusul wa'l-Mulūk* (the History of the Messengers and the Kings, also known as the *Annals*) dealing with the life of Muḥammad by al-Ṭabarī.

Sprenger and Muir recommended that Abū al-Fidā should be rejected from contemporary discourse, perhaps because older source material was now available. Their advice, however, would have come too late for French and English writers of the first half of the nineteenth century (should they have been inclined to listen). Abū al-Fidā's reputation remained intact among them, as it had in the eighteenth century. There was even a deliberate focus on him, with Sédillot deeming Abū al-Fidā to be the best of the Prophet's Arab biographers.[16] The *Concise History* not only provided the basis for Gagnier's and Reiske's editions and Savary's introductory biography to his translation of the Qur'ān, but it was also translated into English by W. M. Murray (an Episcopal clergyman) in 1833 and into French by N. Desvergers (a member of the Council of the Société Asiatique and a Vice-President of the French Geographical Society), in 1837.

Murray appended a preface, an introduction, and an appendix to his translation which (like that of Desvergers) was quite accurate on the whole. He acknowledges that Abū al-Fidā's work is necessarily compiled from older authorities. Murray does use Ibn Isḥāq's *Sīra*, for example; however, he exaggerates by claiming that his translation contains all the leading facts and omits many fabulous and inconsistent stories (and is therefore quite sufficient to provide all the information on the subject): it 'will exhibit the meaning with sufficient correctness without being absolutely literal' (p.38). Whereas Desvergers is happy simply to translate, Murray frequently uses an introduction and footnotes in the appendix in order to rewrite Abū al-Fidā, while at the same time showing hostility to Muḥammad. For instance, Murray finds the Arab historian too discreet in his account of the Night Journey, and so, like Gagnier some hundred years before, says that he wishes to rectify the situation. However, he is only able to achieve this by reinstating the miraculous. He claimed in doing so that he was giving the main circumstances of the affair which, in his view, was simply 'a piece of curiosity' (p. 174). This comment shows that Murray had misunderstood the significance of the Night Journey, which is a landmark in the development of Islam as a religion.

Not satisfied with Abū al-Fidā's report of the incident which occurred in 627, during the return from the expedition undertaken by Muḥammad against the tribe of the Banū Muṣṭaliq (which, as we noted earlier, gave rise to the malicious gossip against 'Ā'isha), Murray wished to 'supply the defect' by giving his own account. He says that Muḥammad claimed a revelation came from heaven. Here he is referring to *Sūra* 24, which clears 'Ā'isha's name. Murray, however, sees in this revelation proof of Muḥammad's dexterity in dealing with his people. He also takes the opportunity to correct Gagnier (who had mentioned Muḥammad going to a cave in Mount Ḥirā') by pointing out that Abū al-Fidā's original text says nothing about a cave: the reference to a cave occurs in the Traditions.

Although he initially criticizes some zealous Christians who 'suffered their prejudices to get the better of their judgement so far as to represent Muḥammad as a monster of wickedness, without allowing him a single virtue' (p. 1), Murray later claims (in a footnote) that Muslim writers have said enough to convince anyone of his duplicity, treachery, cruelty, and ambition (p. 179). Following this, the emphasis is on a cruel Muḥammad. Thus after victory at the battle of Badr (624), for example, he is depicted as showing his revengeful disposition, ordering some of his personal enemies and prisoners to be put to death. At times, however, Murray appears to soften his attack against Muḥammad, but then suggests Muḥammad began to shift responsibility for distasteful deeds to others. Murray writes, for example, that in 627, when Muḥammad wanted to punish the Jewish tribe of Qurayẓa (who were allies of the Aws), he appointed Sa'd ibn Mu'ādh as umpire to judge the case of his confederates, in order to appear personally impartial. When Sa'd had decreed that the men should be slain, their property divided and the women and children made captive, Muḥammad agreed, stating that Sa'd enacted the judgement of God, and consequently many men were beheaded.

Murray also used Muḥammad's treatment of Abū Sufyān to make a point about his leniency towards former enemies. At the time of Abū Sufyān's conversion, Muḥammad's uncle al-'Abbās sought a favour from the Prophet on Abū Sufyān's behalf. Al-'Abbās convinced Muḥammad who said: 'Whosoever enters the house of Abū Sufyān shall be safe'. Murray quotes these words to argue that although Muḥammad destroyed those whom he considered dangerous and troublesome, his general plan was to conciliate by means of kindness and persuasion rather than to resort to the indiscriminate destruction of opponents. Wishing to do him justice, Murray stresses that Muḥammad prohibited his followers to fight or to exercise any violence at the taking of Makka. As he says, Muḥammad was much displeased with Khālid ibn al-Walīd when, contrary to orders, he slew many of the Banū Jadhima; it would appear that Khālid's conduct was prompted by the Jadhima's killing of his uncle.[17]

Unlike Savary, Murray casts doubt on the genuineness of 'Alī's description as found in Abū al-Fidā, on the grounds that Muslim traditions contain a great deal of fiction. Flattering as Muḥammad's mental powers and natural disposition are, he finds these improbable, granted that he was a man of great talents and that his general conduct was calculated to gain the respect of his countrymen. Murray dismisses as fictitious Muḥammad's offer of making amends to those he had hurt, by suggesting that Muslim writers may have simply borrowed the idea from 1 Samuel 12.3 and applied it to their Prophet. Seeing in Muḥammad striking signs of pride and arrogance (instead of justice) throughout his various dealings, Murray challenges Abū Hurayra's account of Muḥammad's early life at subsistence levels, when he feeds on dates and water and deprives himself of a fire for months. Murray suggests that the suppression of hunger, for instance, may apply to a hermit and may have been transferred to a description of the Prophet.

Ten years after his translation of Abū al-Fidā's Life of Muḥammad, Noël Desvergers saw fit to project certain unflattering images of the Prophet in his popularised work, *Arabie* (1847). The format of the book was probably a factor in preventing Desvergers from producing a coherent study. He was certainly less objective in that text than in his translation, although he did use the latter frequently, with the result that there was little new in his evaluation. Among the myths that he propagates here is one that the Prophet had appointed 'Alī to be his successor. Desvergers did not study the question of Muḥammad's succession in depth. Instead he stressed Muḥammad's indebtedness to Christianity. For instance, he used the episode of the early Muslims' flight from persecution in Makka to Abyssinia in 615, to show that Muḥammad had deliberately chosen a Christian country so that his disciples might help bring his teaching into line with what they had learnt from Christian Scriptures. Desvergers no doubt exaggerates when he claims that Muḥammad closely followed the doctrines of the Man-God, whose divine nature he recognised: however it was generally known that Islam denies the divinity of Christ, although it accepts the virgin birth. Desvergers also claims that as long as Muḥammad was persecuted, the divine moral teaching of the Messiah prevailed with him. Later, however, he takes his detailed prescriptions from Moses.

A more balanced study comes from Armand Pierre Caussin de Perceval (1795-1871), a member of the Académie des Inscriptions, Professor of Arabic at the Ecole des Langues Orientales Vivantes, then at the Collège de France. His *Essai sur l'histoire des Arabes*, published in three volumes in 1847-1848, contains interesting views on Muḥammad, especially in volumes 1 and 2 (volume 3 being devoted to Arab tribes). Perceval makes good use of the Arabic manuscripts available at the Bibliothèque Royale (Nationale), especially one entitled *Sīrat*, which is Ibn Isḥāq's (although he does not acknowledge this clearly). Perceval often refers to the *Ta'rīkh Khamīs*, that is, the *Ta'rīkh Al-Khamīs fī Aḥwāl Anfas Nafs*, a very late biography of the Prophet by the Turkish writer Ḥusayn ibn Muḥammad ibn Ḥasan who died in Makka in 1559. He also uses Ṭabarī, Iṣfahānī, Mas'ūdī, Abū al-Fidā, Ibn Khaldūn, Pococke, and Savary.

Despite an unpromising start, where he suggests that Muḥammad's imagination, exalted by meditation and retreat, could have persuaded him that he was the expected Prophet, Caussin felt it would be an injustice to consider Muḥammad merely as a successful and ambitious impostor. In his comments on the early life of Muḥammad, he sheds some new light on the name of the monk Muḥammad met at Bostra. Caussin says that in the *Murūj al-Dhahab* of al-Mas'ūdī (d. 956), a text that was also used by Gagnier, the monk was known among Christians by the name of Jirjīs (George), but that Gagnier had mistakenly read Serjis. Caussin suggests that this reading caused Gagnier to identify Baḥīra with Sergius. Again, writing in a non-polemical manner, he corrects Savary who, he thinks, is mistaken in supposing that Muḥammad freed Zayd ibn Ḥaritha after the latter had embraced Islam. As he says, the manumission and adoption of Zayd by Muḥammad took place before the first revelations: this information, however, is to be found in Ibn Sa'd's work,[18] not in Ibn Isḥāq's *Sīra* (edited by Ibn Hishām) although Ibn Isḥāq is described as the most esteemed of the biographers of the Prophet (vol. 3, p. 331). Caussin understood well Ibn Hishām's high standing among Muslims.

Caussin highlights some more significant aspects of Muḥammad's character and life. He gives details of the latter's marriage to Khadīja, but indicates that what interests him particularly is the fact that Muḥammad's changed circumstances did not lead him to become intoxicated with power, rather his modesty made him use his wife's wealth sparingly. Thus Muḥammad put in a good word for his former wet-nurse Ḥalīma, to whom Khadīja gave forty sheep. Although Caussin later quotes the Tradition wherein Muḥammad is supposed to have asked for pen and paper shortly before his death, he doubts that Muḥammad could read or write. He is, however, convinced that Muḥammad learnt about the principal dogmas of the Jewish and Christian religions in the course of his travels and in the company of Waraqa.

With regard to Muḥammad's succession, Caussin shows great sensitivity to Sunnī Islam, although he is aware of Shī'ī claims on 'Alī's behalf. He uses the information given in Ibn Isḥāq about Khadīja being the first person to believe in Islam and 'Alī the first male believer, followed by Zayd ibn Ḥāritha. He dismisses, however, the Shī'ī claim that Muḥammad uttered words indicating 'Alī as his successor. As he says, there is no such reference in the *Sīra*, although soon after the *hijra*, the Prophet instituted brotherhood among emigrants and helpers, took 'Alī by the hand and said: 'This is my brother' (see A. Guillaume, *The Life of Muhammad*, p.234). In view of the part played in Islamic history by Abū Quḥāfa (that is, Abū Bakr), Caussin is justified in proclaiming that the latter's conversion to Islam was more important than Zayd's.

Caussin indicates that he is not particularly interested in the miracles attributed to Muḥammad, although for the benefit of those who are, he mentions Gagnier's *Vie*, where details of the Night Journey abound. Notwithstanding his opinion on miracles, he understands perfectly well the importance of this episode: more clearly perhaps than Savary, as he points out that it was only after it that the number of daily prayers was definitively fixed in Islam. This is indeed the case, as since the *isrā'* (that is, since 619-620), Muslims have been required to pray five times a day. It is in his account of Muḥammad's life after the *hijra* that Caussin seems particularly well disposed towards the Prophet. He speaks of a mosque laid from the first day on 'piety', referring to *Sūra* 9, l. 108. As he points out, the Prophet joined in the building to encourage the Muslims to continue to work hard.

Caussin then draws attention to the covenant, based on reciprocal obligations, between the Muslims and the Jews, according to which Muḥammad granted the latter religious freedom and the peaceful enjoyment of their property. More importantly perhaps, this covenant stipulates that the Jews of the Banū 'Awf and other tribes, and all those living in Yathrib (Madīna) are one community with the believers, and that the contracting parties are bound to help one another against any attack on Yathrib.[19] Caussin also refers to the conversion of two learned rabbis to Islam ('Abdullāh ibn Sallām and Mukhayriq) who claimed that the coming of Muḥammad had been mentioned in the Torah. He adds, however, that their example was followed by few of their brothers. Caussin suggests that Muḥammad could rely on the devotion of a large number of Muslims and was therefore not worried by the underhanded opposition of a few Muslim hypocrites who spoke against this tolerance. Thus he spared the Jews and he abandoned his policy of moderation towards them only when he recognised the stubbornness of their hatred.

In Madīna, Muḥammad continued to pray towards Jerusalem, as he had done at Makka, for some seventeen months. Unlike other commentators, Caussin does not attribute the change of *qibla* (direction of prayer) to Jewish coolness towards Muḥammad, but he simply refers to Qur'ānic verses authorising the change, and to the temple of Makka as an object of respect to both Muslims and Arab idol worshippers. Like Murray, he mentions the killing of prisoners after the battles of Badr and Uḥud, while stressing Muḥammad's humanity, but he uses an episode at the later battle to show how Muḥammad refrained from an initial inclination to wreak vengeance on Quraysh (who had mutilated the body of his uncle Ḥamza) and instead urged his disciples never to mutilate the bodies of their enemies. In support of this stance, Caussin quotes *Sūra* 16, ll. 126-27, which teaches that there is merit in enduring pain with patience.

The German Orientalist Aloys Sprenger (1813-93) was as learned as Caussin, having held various senior academic posts in India, and he was equally at ease writing in English and German. His works included an English translation of Mas'ūdī's *Murūj al-Dhahab* (1841), an edition of Abū Tammām's *Ḥamāsa* (1845) and *The Life of Mohammad* (1851).[20] Sprenger was much less well disposed towards Muḥammad than Caussin. Aware that Ibn Isḥāq was highly esteemed among Muslims and among other European historians whom he criticised, Sprenger did his best to undermine his reputation.[21] Although he acknowledged the latter's faithful memory, refined taste and elegant style, he wanted him to be considered 'the father of Mohammedan mythology' (p. 69). Fortunately, Sprenger was refuted by William Muir, who used Ibn Khallikān's *Biographical Dictionary* to vindicate Ibn Isḥāq's standing.[22] Sprenger preferred Ibn Sa'd to Ibn Isḥāq: he thought that Ibn Sa'd had produced by far the best biography of Muḥammad. Curiously enough, he claimed that Sunnīs were disgusted with the impartiality of Ibn Sa'd, accusing him of having a Shī'a bias. Ibn Isḥāq included 'Ā'isha among the companions who accepted Islam around 614, and Sprenger points out that she was born at about that time (and hence, as a newborn, was an unlikely convert) and thus urged readers to use the biographer with caution.

Despite identifying this error made by Ibn Isḥāq, Sprenger relied heavily on his research. One of his aims was to show how much Muḥammad learnt from Christians, and towards this end Sprenger even distorts the meaning of Ibn Isḥāq in some cases. Thus, he quotes him as saying that Muḥammad had intercourse with 'Abd al-Raḥmān, a Christian of Yamama. What Ibn Isḥāq actually wrote was that there was a rumour circulating among the rabbis of Madīna to the effect that 'we have heard that a man in Al-Yamāma called al-Raḥmān teaches you' (*Life*, p. 140). In response to this rumour came the revelation in *Sūra* 13, l. 30 which includes the following: 'Thus have we sent thee amongst a people before whom other peoples had passed away... yet do they reject Him the most Gracious.' By omitting all reference to the context and the revelation, Sprenger attributed to Ibn Isḥāq thoughts that would have been far from his mind. Sprenger also used Ibn Isḥāq to show that before the first revelations Zayd ibn 'Amr had considerable influence on the development of monotheist ideas in the Qur'ān where, according to Sprenger, all the sayings of Zayd were literally repeated. Ibn Isḥāq describes Zayd as a man who had sampled Judaism and Christianity, but was not satisfied with either of them (*Life*, p. 103). He adds that when Zayd reached the country of the Lakhmites, he was attacked and killed. Sprenger finds this conclusion very suspicious, although without saying why.

Elsewhere in his *Life of Mohammad,* Sprenger tries to be positive towards the Prophet (at least, to a certain extent). He wants readers to consider Muḥammad from the perspective of the slaves of Makka who saw in him their liberator and converted to Islam, although 'they were superstitious enough to consider his fits... as the consequence of an inspiration' (p.159). Nevertheless, Sprenger also has another agenda: he attempts to show that Muḥammad improved his knowledge of Christianity at the same time, since slaves such as Zayd ibn Ḥāritha and Bilal were of Christian parentage. Despite this agenda, he makes sustained efforts to prove Muḥammad's sincerity. Whereas in his 'The Hero as Prophet' lecture, Thomas Carlyle had (without much evidence) stressed Muḥammad's sincerity, Sprenger adopted a carefully researched argument to come to an ambivalent conclusion. Drawing on his German cultural background, he sees Muḥammad's affinities not with Cromwell but with Goethe. Muḥammad's struggles, he suggests, bear a strange resemblance to the opening scene of Goethe's *Faust*. In both Muḥammad and in Faust he notes an anguish of the mind, and distraction by doubts, which is dispelled by the songs of angels, and this engenders in them a consciousness of their sincerity. Unfortunately, this is not unadulterated sincerity, since after the crisis they blaspheme, sacrifice their faith and their consciousness of God to serve self-aggrandizement.

The story of the 'satanic verses' is retold by Sprenger to prove Muḥammad's sincerity: as tradition has it, when Muḥammad wondered what would induce the leaders of Makka to accept Islam (this was around 615), a revelation came to him: 'Have you considered Al-Lāt and Al-'Uzza, and Manāt, the third, the other?' (*Sūra* 53, l. 19-20). But immediately after this story, as Ṭabarī wrote in his *Tafsīr*, the Prophet's tongue slipped, and by mistake he said the words: 'These are the swans exalted, whose intercession is to be hoped for', which were later corrected by Gabriel[23] (Rāzī rejected this story which is not to be found in the six canonical collections of *Aḥādīth*). The Makkans were delighted by the false verses, but the true continuation of the *Sūra* was soon revealed to Muḥammad. Later, another verse which appears to refer to this episode was revealed: 'God annuls what Satan casts, then God confirms His signs' (*Sūra* 22, l. 52). In Sprenger's words, after having pronounced the satanic verses the following day, Muḥammad 'repented and said the verses were prompted to him by the devil' (p. 185). Nevertheless, by saying that Muḥammad himself rescinded the verses, Sprenger is at the same time attempting to prove that the latter is the author of the Qur'ān. He goes on to say that by deviating from his conviction, Muḥammad might have extricated himself from all persecutions and difficulties, but he disdained to gain this victory at the expense of his conviction. To Sprenger, this was the strongest proof of Muḥammad's sincerity. He also refers to *Sūra* 80, l. 1 where the Prophet is rebuked for having shown impatience towards a blind man ('Abdullāh ibn Maktūm) who had interrupted him, as further evidence of Muḥammad's sincerity.

Sprenger claims that towards the end of Muḥammad's career, it was not conscience, but rather his more sincere friends who saved Muḥammad from compromise. He quotes Zamakhsharī's comment on *Sūra* 17, l. 73, which relates to demands made by the Thaqifites to convert to Islam, including exemption from prayers. According to Sprenger (pp. 186-87), Zamakhshari states that the Prophet remained silent, and 'Umar ibn al-Khaṭṭāb complained that the Thaqifites had filled his heart with contagion. But in Zamakhsharī there is nothing about the Prophet's silence, and 'Umar, addressing the Thaqifites, actually says: 'You have inflamed the heart of our Prophet. May Allah inflame your hearts'.[24] Ibn Isḥāq states that Muḥammad refused the request (*Life*, p. 616). Sprenger even distorts the meaning of the verse, by beginning with the information that Muḥammad had almost been tempted away from that which was revealed to him and adding that 'at the right moment a friend reprehended thee'; the end of verse 73 simply states that they (the Thaqifites, presumably) would have made Muḥammad their friend.

Although Ernest Renan (1823-92) was not a specialist in Arabic to the same extent as Sprenger, he had a sound Islamic cultural background. This enabled him to comment on Islam over a period of some thirty-five years with some authority. His notorious lecture entitled 'L'Islamisme et la Science', delivered at the Sorbonne in 1883, and his controversial remarks on the Arabs made elsewhere, are responsible for his low-standing in the Arab-Muslim world, and yet he provides one of the most stimulating evaluations of Islam and Muḥammad by a Western writer. Renan is, after all, the author of one of the best theses, published in 1852, on Averroes, (that is, Ibn Rushd, 1126-1198). In *L'Avenir de la Science* (1848) Renan still refers to Muḥammad's imposture, but he does stress the historical foundations of Islam. More relevant to our purpose perhaps is the article 'Mahomet et les Origines de l'Islamisme', first published in the *Revue des Deux Mondes* in December 1851, and subsequently reproduced in *Etudes d'histoire religieuse (1857)*. This article has not been fully appreciated by modern commentators: yet its assessment is essential for a balanced appraisal of Renan's perspective on Islam and Muḥammad.

Whereas in *L'Avenir de la Science* Renan hints that Islam is flawed due to its link to the supernatural which renders it irreconcilable with rational European science, in the article he surprises the reader by finding merit in Islam for having, if not virtually abolished the supernatural, at least limited it considerably.[25] He admires the canonical Traditionist al-Bukhārī whom he calls 'l'infatigable', for he says the latter acknowledges that of the 200,000 *Aḥādīth* he had collected, only 7225 seemed to him of sound authenticity (vol. 7, p. 174). Renan's approach to *Ḥadīth* literature appears in harmony with that of modern scholarship, which distinguishes between genuine and spurious *Ḥadīth*.

Although he suggests that European critics could, without appearing too rash, be stricter in the process of eliminating spurious *Ḥadīth*, he admits that these first narratives show many features of the real physiognomy of the Prophet, and are clearly distinct from the pious legends which have been invented by some for the benefit of their readers. He hints that the books and speeches attributed to the founders of other religions are lacking in authenticity: these tell us less about the founders than about the way their disciples conceived the ideal (vol. 7, p. 176). Renan argues that this was not the case with Muḥammad, as the Prophet's biography is an ordinary one without miracles and exaggeration, suggesting that he had good biographers in men like Ibn Hishām and the ancient historians whom he qualifies as 'écrivains sensés'(*ibid.*). On the other hand, the legends surrounding Christian saints, St Francis of Assisi, for example, became much more mythical than those surrounding Muḥammad. The aim of Renan's polemic is clear: it is to paint a more favourable picture of Muḥammad than of Christ and the Christian saints.

Muḥammad's life, Renan admits, is like that of other great founders of religion, in that it is surrounded by fables. He (perhaps unfairly) suggests that these have won the seal of approval only among the Persians, over whom the imagination typically holds sway. Renan says nothing, for instance, about the contribution to the consolidation of Sunnī Islam made by authors of Persian origin such as al-Ṭabarī and al-Ghazālī. He claims instead that under the influence of races foreign to Arabia, the story of Muḥammad has been complicated with tales of miraculous circumstances, which bring it closer to the great legendary myths of the high Orient. As an example of the miraculous, he refers to the popular story of how two angels opened the body of Muḥammad at the age of three, removed his gall stone and inserted the prophetic light.[26] He finds nothing Arab in such exaggerations, which appear typical of Persian taste, adding that such grotesque stories do not detract from the purity of the original Arab tradition in much the same way that the dull exaggeration of the apocryphal gospels does not destroy the incomparable beauty of the canonical gospels (vol. 7, p. 184).

The fables that exist in Islam are, in Renan's view, not fundamental to it: they have to be taken as accessories; they are tolerated rather than sanctified. In this way, these fables are very much like the mythology of the apocrypha, which the Church neither adopted nor rejected. In order to stress the sobriety of the miraculous element in Islamic narrative, Renan then offers a sample of India's mythology dealing with the birth of her heroes. His explanation of the difference in style between India and Arabia is that the latter had reached too great an intellectual refinement to accommodate a supernatural legend in the Indian mould (p. 182). The Arabs therefore appear in a better light here than the Persians and Indians because of their limited use of mythology.

Renan does not entirely eliminate examples of the miraculous in Islam, seeking rather to reduce their significance. He claims that the only time when Muḥammad wanted to imitate the fantasies of other religions was on the occasion of the Night Journey to Jerusalem, but things went so badly that the Prophet hastened to withdraw his ill-advised suggestion by declaring that the miraculous journey, at first presented as real, had only been a dream. This journey, which has a deep spiritual significance in Islam, is taken symbolically, not literally, by most Muslims. In either case, it is not accurate to say that the Prophet changed his mind about this. Renan insists, however, that the legends associated with Muḥammad (and found in his biography by Abū al-Fidā) be reduced to a few stories that are characterised by restraint. Even at the battle of Badr, where angels are reported to have fought on the side of the Muslims, Renan expresses surprise that the combatants used their imagination in such a sober fashion. The conclusion he wishes the reader to draw is that the legendary elements found in Islam always remained sporadic traditions, and are lacking in authority.

The article 'Mahomet' seems to have less sympathy with the inaccessible rigour of supernaturalism associated with the Man-God (Jesus) than with the ordinary humanity and its weaknesses, which characterise Muḥammad. Renan uses an ingenious technique which allows him to evaluate Muḥammad's achievement and to criticise him as great an extent as he sees fit. Renan argues that in the great supernatural legends, everything is settled and absolute (as is proper when God is completely involved), whereas in the life of Muḥammad things are not clear-cut and occur as approximate in a very human (but historically significant) manner. Thus Muḥammad is defeated and makes mistakes. It is perfectly reasonable to say that Muḥammad makes mistakes, and unlike Sprenger, Renan does not use the incident with 'Abdullāh ibn Umm Maktūm as an example (see above). Although Renan refers to circumstances where, he says, the Prophet compromised moral standards for the sake of political expediency, he favours what he considers to be a legitimate criticism of Muḥammad. For this reason, he attacks Voltaire's portrait of Muḥammad in his play *Mahomet*, condemning the ambitious, heartless Machiavellian portrayed there. Renan defends Muḥammad from the accusation of having altered Biblical stories, suggesting that the latter simply reproduced what he had learnt from rabbinical traditions and the apocryphal gospels, especially *L'Evangile de l'enfance*, which he says was preserved only in Arabic. This, of course, implies that Muḥammad read the text, but Renan does not say whether he could read.

Renan's older but distinguished compatriot, Alphonse de Lamartine (1790-1869), was perhaps better known as a Romantic poet and novelist. He was briefly Foreign Minister, and head of the provisional government of the French Republic in 1848. Soon after, he stood as candidate for the Presidency, but his lack of success virtually ended his political career. The financial problems of his last twenty years led the impoverished writer to produce, in quick succession, a number of historical works aimed at a wider public. Among these was the *Histoire de la Turquie* (1854), the first volume of which was devoted to a *Vie de Mahomet*. Lamartine had already shown some interest in Islam, the Ottoman Empire, and Arab culture some twenty years earlier in the *Voyage en Orient* (1835).

The *Voyage*, however, was not a typical travelogue, as Lamartine included in it material which was not connected with travel at all.[27] Thus, he engaged in a discussion about 'Anṭar (ibn Shaddād), the model of the Arabic romance of chivalry, adding fragments of the story to his book. He also proclaimed the need to launch a European colony in the heart of Asia, to bring modern civilization to the birthplace of ancient civilization, and to rebuild a new empire on the ruins of the crumbling Ottoman Empire. His plans for the Middle East were more fully developed in the 'Résumé Politique', which was added onto the end of the *Voyage*. To the Arab-Muslim world, Lamartine might well appear a prophet of doom, since most of his prophecies relating to the handing over of the Arab provinces of the Ottoman Empire to Britain and France had been fulfilled by the time of the First World War and thereafter.

Fortunately, Lamartine's imperialist agenda occupies only a small section of *Voyage*, part of which attempts to promote doctrinal rapprochement between Christianity and Islam. Unlike Christian apologists, Lamartine does not compare Christianity with Islam in order to promote the former at the expense of the latter. His sympathy for the religion of Islam enables him to stress what he perceives as its distinct contribution to civilization: tolerance. Lamartine is not content with stressing the principle of tolerance advocated in Islam, but he takes delight in showing tolerance put into practice on the occasion of his visits to Nazareth and Jerusalem. It is worth pointing out that the emphasis on Islamic tolerance also served Lamartine's polemical objective against Chateaubriand, who had taken the opposite view on the behaviour of Muslims in the *Itinéraire de Paris à Jérusalem* (1811).

With no political ambitions in the 1850s to divert his attention from writing, Lamartine could, in the *Vie de Mahomet*, develop his interest in Islam by concentrating attention on the Prophet himself. Writing such a biography in the wake of other biographies was a formidable challenge for a non-Arabist, although Lamartine did make use of Ibn Isḥāq, Abū al-Fidā (in Desvergers's translation), Caussin de Perceval's *Essai sur l'histoire des Arabes*, and especially al-Ṭabarī. In his edition of the *Vie de Mahomet*, Ali Kurhan drew a clear parallel between Lamartine's text and these Islamic sources.[28] Al-Ṭabarī's *History* or *Annals* was actually translated in 1867-1874 by the Orientalist Hermann Zotenberg (1834-1914), curator of manuscripts at the Bibliothèque Nationale, Paris. Zotenberg chose a shortened Persian version of Ṭabarī compiled by al-Bal'amī (d. 974).[29] Lamartine used his translation, reproducing it almost verbatim in places. An element of mystery seems to prevail here: Lamartine must have gained access to the translation before publication, perhaps with the help of Caussin de Perceval, who himself used al-Ṭabarī extensively. While Ṭabarī properly belongs to the world of Islamic scholarship, thanks to the Zotenberg translation, Lamartine popularized his work on the Prophet which thus reached a much wider public.

French critics did not object to Lamartine's support for the Turks, but they did show indignation at his presentation of the Prophet in the *Vie de Mahomet*.[30] It is not too difficult to understand why. For even more so than in the *Voyage*, Lamartine shows a tendency to overstress the affinities between Christianity and Islam, and the influence of the former on the latter. As an example of Christian influence on Muḥammad, he mentions the latter's alleged visit to a goldsmith named

Jabar on the Makkan hill of Marwa in the early 620s. The latter was a Greek Christian with whom Muḥammad is supposed to have spent hours.[31] The object of their discourse, speculates Lamartine, could only have been about the dogmas and moral teaching of Christianity, towards which Muḥammad and four of his friends were inclined.[32] Lamartine suggests that the conversation must have been painful, because the Greek craftsman had little knowledge of Arabic and Muḥammad no knowledge of Greek, although it would seem that neither were put off by this. Muḥammad was accused by his enemies of having conceived nothing by himself, and of having had the precepts of the Qur'ān written by the Greek. According to Lamartine, Muḥammad replied indirectly to this 'probable supposition' with a verse of 'his' book, that is *Sūra* 16, l.103, which continues as follows: 'The tongue/ Of him they wickedly point to/ Is notably foreign, while this / Is Arabic, pure and clear'.

At the beginning of Muḥammad's mission there was so much similarity in the profession of faith in Islam with that of Christianity, Lamartine claims, that when the first Muslims fled to Abyssinia to avoid persecution, the Abyssinians received them as half Christians! (p. 110).[33] He concludes that in the first thoughts of Muḥammad, Islam was nothing but an Arabic commentary on the Gospel. He makes Muḥammad hesitate for a long while to consider whether he should not proclaim himself Christ's apostle (p. 111), adding that after his vision or dream the writer in Muḥammad was at work. That, however, does not prove that he was knowingly an impostor. So even in Lamartine's thought the word 'impostor' is not far away: the implication is that Muḥammad was an unconscious impostor.

Lamartine is critical of Muḥammad's attitude to women. While admitting that his morality was austere up to the time of his first wife, who bore witness to his mission, he claims that Muḥammad had an inclination for sensual voluptuousness which the loose morals of the Arabs, the climate, the tradition of the desert Patriarchs, even the tolerance of Moses, and his own nature did not allow him to resist. According to him, this tendency was the main weakness of his character and compromised his laws (p. 126). Lamartine deplores what he sees as Muḥammad's rejection of the severe rules of Christian marriage, which were being followed in Syria, and argues that a religious law-giver who claims to be inspired is not authorized to turn human weakness into a virtue. He asserts that Muḥammad maintained an inequality of duties (between man and woman) and continued the degradation of half of humanity. It is not clear how Lamartine worked out that Muḥammad deprived two-thirds of poor men of legitimate wives and two-thirds of women of husbands, only to give the women masters. Nevertheless, his conclusion was that something that degraded half of God's people could not have been divinely inspired. Lamartine suggests that Muḥammad did not go far enough, although he admits that Muḥammad took some positive steps: he initiated the emancipation of women and gave them moral dignity by putting them on an equal footing with men, acknowledging them as in possession of an immortal soul, and forbidding the desert custom of burying women alive. But even if his teaching was that women should be respected as mothers, wives, and daughters, Muḥammad did not dare (or did not wish) to remove the root cause of inequality. Thus, Lamartine states, Muḥammad's social doctrine was later condemned and Christian laws remained superior to his own laws, although Lamartine does finally concede that Muḥammad was effective in consecrating the rights of women to property (p. 207).

The *Vie de Mahomet* devotes more space to Muḥammad at war: his humanity is made to emerge very slowly, as he shows no mercy to his enemies at first. When he was assured of shelter by his allies at Madīna (from 622), the warrior in Muḥammad, in Lamartine's view, replaced the prophet (p. 139). At the battle of Badr, Lamartine attributes to Muḥammad a certain weakness which deprived him of his senses. This information is not found in Ṭabarī, where Muḥammad encourages his soldiers and says to them: 'To obtain Paradise you only have to find martyrdom.'[34] Muḥammad had given instructions that his enemy Abū Jahl should be found and his head brought over to him. This indeed took place, and when Abū Jahl's head was taken to the Prophet, the latter, according to Ṭabarī, prostrated and thanked God (Zotenberg, p. 162). Lamartine's account is virtually the same, except for the embellishment that Muḥammad looked at the head with a 'féroce satisfaction' (p. 148). His return to Madīna was a triumph, but a father's grief poisoned the joy of the warrior: Muḥammad learnt of the death of his daughter Ruqayya, who was married to 'Uthmān ibn 'Affān. He shed tears over her, but Lamartine adds that tears did not soften his vengeance against some of the prisoners, who were his personal enemies. Lamartine follows Ṭabarī closely when he narrates that Muḥammad ignored 'Uqba's plea for his life on the grounds that he had young children to support. Up to now, argues Lamartine, Muḥammad had given himself only the right to preach the unity of God, but henceforth he took the right to strike in his name. From Prophet he became exterminator (p. 149), although Lamartine adds that merciless crimes are rarely attested to in Muḥammad's life.

On the other hand, Lamartine makes many attempts to show Muḥammad's humanity in battle. On conclusion of a truce of ten years with the Quraysh, Muḥammad is likened to Henri IV, King of France, on entering Paris (in 1594), and Lamartine suggests that he treated the vanquished as victors and the victors as vanquished. When Zayd ibn Ḥāritha and Ja'far, 'Alī's brother, died at the battle of Mu'ta in 629, Muḥammad felt more grief, insists Lamartine, at the loss of his friends than defiance at bad fortune. Thus he went to visit Asmā', Ja'far's widow, and asking for Ja'far's two small children to be brought to him, he kissed them and wept over them. When asked by Asmā' why he wept, he simply replied that they no longer had a father (p. 177). On leaving the house of Zayd's widow, Muḥammad met Zayd's daughter (who was unaware of her father's death). He cried in her arms and was asked why he cried. Muḥammad's reply was: 'These are the regrets of a friend at the loss of a friend' (p. 177). At the siege of Ṭā'if (in 630), many women were taken captives and among them was one from the Banū Sa'd ibn Bakr. She turned out to be Shaymā', one of Muḥammad's foster sisters, daughter of Ḥalīma, his wet-nurse, who had long since died. The memory of his childhood and the motherly care he had received from Ḥalīma saddened him and he shed tears on recognising Shaymā', who was given the option of staying with him. She chose to go back to her tribe, loaded with presents from Muḥammad. Here Lamartine again closely follows Ṭabarī.

The way is paved for the *Vie de Mahomet* to end with a glowing tribute to the Prophet. Lamartine felt that no man voluntarily or involuntarily set himself a more sublime objective than Muḥammad who sought to remove the superstitions intervening between creature and creator, thus to restore God to man and man to God, and reinstate the rational and holy idea of the divinity amid the chaos of the material gods of idolatry. Lamartine believes that no man undertook, with such modest resources, a work that was so out of proportion to human forces. He argues that if the ambition of the project, the paucity of the means at Muḥammad's disposal and the immensity of the results are the three criteria by which to measure human genius, no one could dare compare any great man in modern history with Muḥammad. However, he is still haunted by the idea that Muḥammad might be an impostor, while implying the contrary. Lamartine's conclusion is that Muḥammad's internal inspiration was his only imposture (p. 208).

Glowing tributes such as Lamartine's could not be expected from William Muir, who was an Orientalist scholar, Christian apologist, supporter of overseas missions and the future Lieutenant Governor of the North West Provinces, India (1868). In *The Mohammedan Controversy*,[35] Muir had surveyed relations between the West and Islam from the beginning to his own times. Although he acknowledged the West's intellectual debt to Islam during the medieval period, he believed that Britain's duty was to enlighten the people of India, and that Britain must not rest until her millions in the East abandon the false prophet and rallied around that eternal truth which has been brought to light in the Gospel. The major historical event taking place after the publication of this article was the Indian Mutiny of 1857, which was represented by the British as being inspired by Muslims. It is worth remembering that the four volumes of his *Life of Mahomet* (1858) were written before, during, and after the Indian Mutiny.

In the preface to the *Life of Mahomet*, Muir informs readers that his work was undertaken at the suggestion of the Reverend C. G. Pfander, who was 'well-known as a Christian apologist in the controversy with the Mahometans'. Readers could therefore easily guess what was in store for them: the suggestion of Pfander, a German-born missionary of the Church Mission Society, that Muir should produce a biography of the Prophet 'suitable for the perusal of his followers' is clearly a conflict of interests. There is ample evidence to show that Muir failed in his objective of writing a book acceptable to Muslims, despite his use of early Islamic sources such as Ibn Isḥāq, Ibn Hishām, al-Wāqidī, Ibn Sa'd, and al-Ṭabarī, and his recommendation that the early Traditionists should be respected for what they have to say on Muḥammad. Muir's *Life* is even more detailed than Caussin's *Essai*. It is his attitude to Muḥammad that distinguishes Muir (an Englishman) from Lamartine (a Frenchman): while the latter remains fairly neutral, the former is openly hostile to Muḥammad. Muir rejects completely the notion of

Muḥammad having received any revelation, and he claims that because Muḥammad feared that in his 'pseudo-inspiration there should be even appearance of a human colouring' every sentence of the Qur'ān is prefaced by a divine command and 'Mahomet henceforth assumes the name of God (vol. 2, p. 75). He was critical not only of Muḥammad but also, to a lesser extent, of his biographer, Ibn Hishām. In volume 1, in which some 105 pages are devoted to a study of sources, he censures the latter (whom he otherwise expresses appreciation for) for omitting the story of the 'satanic verses' as it is found in Ibn Isḥāq and Ṭabarī.

Muir's unfavourable account of Muḥammad is particularly evident in volumes 2 and 3. Muslim readers are certainly affronted by the story that he narrates about Khadīja's wedding to Muḥammad; apparently, Khadīja, dreading her father's refusal of Muḥammad, got her father drunk, and the old man accepted the wedding while he was under the effect of wine. Muir reproduced the story, despite the reservation expressed by his source, Wāqidī. Likewise, instead of stressing Khadīja's support for Muḥammad, Muir says that descriptions of a voluptuous Paradise in the Qur'ān were almost entirely confined to a time when he was living a chaste and sober life with her (p. 143).

Another story, based on Wāqidī and Ibn Sa'd, is given prominence, in order to illustrate what Muir calls the origin of the law of female inheritance in Islam (vol. 3, p. 197). After the battle of Uḥud, the widow of Sa'd ibn Rabī', who was killed in the battle, sought redress from the Prophet because Sa'd's brother had taken possession of the entire family inheritance, and she needed her share of it in order to marry her two daughters. Muḥammad, moved by the tale, ordered Sa'd's brother to restore to his family their legitimate inheritance. Muir, who frequently quotes the Qur'ān at other times, in this instance prefers to rely on a story and relegates the Qur'ānic provision on inheritance, contained in *Sūra* 4, to a footnote.

Like Murray, Muir does not approve of the concise account of the Night Journey, as given in the Qur'ān. But unlike French biographers (such as Savary and Caussin de Perceval) he failed to grasp its significance to Muslims. Otherwise, he would not have speculated that Muḥammad and his disciples might have been praying five times a day before they left Makka (vol. 3, p. 37). If this had indeed been the case, the Night Journey would have lost much of its *raison d'être*. However, there is nothing controversial in his information that in 624 Muḥammad, after having given alms, went with his followers to the *muṣallā* (that is, place of prayer), outside the city on the Makkan road. What is controversial, is his suggestion that Muḥammad cast off Judaism and its customs by replacing the fast of *'Ashūrā*. Muḥammad promulgated, as a divine command, that Ramaḍān should be the annual fast from the end of 623. Without quoting any source, Muir states that the Muslims followed the Jews in every practice: apparently, they at first fasted from sunrise to sunset like the Jews and abstained day and night from all pleasures throughout the month, until Muḥammad 'checked this ascetic spirit' (vol.3, p. 48).

It is therefore not surprising that Muir's *Life* should give the impression of being written from an entirely Jewish (if not Christian), perspective. The few Jews who were persuaded to convert to Islam by Muḥammad are branded as traitors, but Muir accepts that they were of 'utmost service to his cause and constantly referred to as his witnesses' (vol. 3, p. 36). He argues that Muḥammad's darker shades, as well as the brighter aspects of his character, must be depicted by the faithful historian. But he is not that historian, for he selects particular episodes to show Muḥammad's cruelty to individuals and whole tribes, without paying attention to the context in which they take place. Thus in 628 Muḥammad subjects Kināna, the Jewish prince of Khaybar, to inhuman torture for having concealed his tribe's treasures. Similarly, to darken the character of Muḥammad, Muir recounts the expedition against Umm Kirfa, where the old woman's legs were tied to separate camels which were driven in different directions (vol. 4, p. 13). Like many other Western writers, Muir prefers Muḥammad at Makka to Muḥammad at Madīna. He argues that Muḥammad had no ulterior motive but the reformation of his countrymen at Makka: such that he may have been mistaken as to the means used to achieve his end, but he was of good faith. At Madīna, however, Muir identifies a rapid moral decline and fierce fanaticism in Muḥammad (vol. 4, p. 317).

Yet, without conceding it, Muir actually paints the picture of a Muḥammad who evolves. He sees some fine traits in Muḥammad at the conquest of Makka in 630, which he describes with a singular magnanimity and moderation. He says that it may have been in Muḥammad's interest to forget past injuries, but that this nevertheless required a large and generous heart to forget (vol. 4, p. 133). He adds that Muḥammad was duly rewarded, for the whole population of

Makka adhered to him after this. Muḥammad is also shown to have liberated prisoners from the Banū Tamīm, entertained them hospitably, and sent the chiefs away with rich presents and provisions on their journey (p. 174).

There is also a grudging admission as to the significance of the conquest of Makka. Amongst other things, this meant that Muḥammad had control of the annual pilgrimage and custody of the sacred mosque, although in Muir's eyes, this possession of Makka 'imparted the colour of right to his pretensions' (p. 168). Muir, however, has a true appreciation of the action of Muḥammad in asking Abū Bakr to preside at public prayers in his absence. There is little doubt in his mind that by this nomination Muḥammad intended to signify the delegation of supreme authority to Abū Bakr, 'if not to mark him as his successor after his death' (p. 265). The question of the succession is not as straightforward as Muir makes it appear, but his guess about Muḥammad's intention is not without merit. Muir finally concedes that Muḥammad conferred on his followers the benefits of the unity and infinite perfection of God and a special all-pervading Providence, which became a living principle in their hearts and lives. But, typically, Muir adds that the benefits were purchased at a high price (p. 320).

Like Lamartine, Jules Barthélemy Saint-Hilaire (1805-95) was not an Arabist; he was Professor of Greek and Roman philosophy at the Collège de France, the deputy of Seine-et-Oise, and was briefly Minister of Foreign Affairs (in 1880-1881). His contribution to the formation of the image of Muḥammad in the nineteenth century was not negligible. In *Mahomet et le Coran* (1865), a study he describes, in the 'Avertissement', as more philosophical than historical, he announces that it is based on articles published in the *Journal des Savants*, where he reviewed the works of Sprenger, Muir, and Caussin de Perceval. Here he also used Gustav Weil's *Mohammed der Prophet*. It is how he interprets these sources that remains the relevant question, as in his summary of the biography of Muḥammad the main events are clearly presented and the reader is provided with a useful time-chart such as is not found among the writing of many other biographers.

Following in the steps of Renan (whom he mentions), Saint-Hilaire also stresses the historicity of Muḥammad (p. 27). When he examines Muḥammad's character, he claims that he can easily prove that Muḥammad was the most intelligent and the most clement of contemporary Arabs, and that the religion he preached, though inferior to Christianity, was of immense benefit to the races that adopted it. Moreover, Saint-Hilaire seems to be aware that Muḥammad must never be isolated from his milieu, and he shows appreciation for his kindness and moral rectitude and the fact that he listened more than he spoke. He dismisses Sprenger's account of Muḥammad's alleged epilepsy as irrelevant, since it explains nothing: besides, not all people suffering from hysteria are prophets. Although Saint-Hilaire says that he will not make a forced comparison between Muḥammad and Socrates, this is what he in fact does, and he highlights the sincerity of both (p. 101). He later devotes a separate chapter to the question of Muḥammad's sincerity, drawing encouragement from Nöldeke's views on this in *Geschichte des Qorans* (p. 2).

Saint-Hilaire focuses on certain landmarks in the career of the Prophet. Thus he outlines how, at the first pledge of Aqaba (in 621) when Muḥammad met twelve men of Yathrib from the tribe of the Aws and the Khazraj, he made them swear an oath which is famous in the Muslim world and which, in Saint-Hilaire's view, deserves to be permanently remembered in history: the new Muslims undertook to worship but one God, not to steal, not to kill their children, not to commit adultery, and to abstain from slander. Muḥammad wants them to renounce idolatry and to abandon their barbarous customs. With hindsight, Saint-Hilaire says that one is inclined to laugh at these naïve undertakings, but bearing in mind Muḥammad's times he finds the venture admirable. Before coming to the *hijra* he reminds his readers that at the age of fifty-two Muḥammad had only ten more years in which to achieve all the great deeds that have immortalised his name. The first part of his career turns out to be the most difficult and the most eventful, for it laid the foundations of what was to follow.

Saint-Hilaire says that most historians have acknowledged his unblemished character, even Muir, who was at times extremely severe towards Muḥammad. Saint-Hilaire argues that Muir would have wished Muḥammad dead at the time of the *hijra*, because of his alleged cruelty thereafter: this, he asserts, does injustice to the character of Muḥammad, which remained consistent. Muḥammad may have yielded to political necessities rather than to his passions, but despite being placed under new circumstances he maintained the best part of his virtues (p. 114). Saint-Hilaire uses examples to illustrate Muḥammad's moderation in

630. He quotes Muḥammad's behaviour towards 'Ikrima, the son of Abū Jahl and another Qurayshite, Ṣafwān, on their conversion to Islam, indicating that the Prophet displayed in his encounter with them a moderation that is very rare in victory after long battles, and showed a respect for the vanquished that is unusual among victors, even in the most advanced civilizations. If Muḥammad sometimes deviated, incidents such as that allow Saint-Hilaire to conclude, without being too indulgent towards him, that at these times Muḥammad had been driven by necessity rather than by coarse sentiments.

One of the last assessments of Muḥammad by French writers in the nineteenth century comes from P-Henry Delaporte. The little that is known about him comes from what he expresses in the *Vie de Mahomet* (1874). Delaporte claims to have all the credentials to write a biography: he had been French consul in the Orient, knew Arabic, had access to written Arabic sources, and had consulted the '*ulamā'*. Despite this solid background, he achieved less than he promised, and the main body of the text is particularly disappointing, as it is an endless series of battles, with little commentary. Likewise, Delaporte seems to have been so carried away by his love of the marvellous that he devotes eight chapters of the book to the Night Journey and nearly every chapter is illustrated with a miracle.

In the introduction, however, one may find a rather fair evaluation of Muḥammad's impact on world history. Delaporte points out that the founders of great empires have left behind but a vague memory: Cyrus, Alexander, and Charlemagne are good examples. The 'legislator' of the Arabs is quite different. Perhaps unique in world history, Muḥammad belongs to the present by virtue of the still living creation of his genius. What makes Muḥammad's glory, in Delaporte's view, and sets him apart from founders of world empires, is that he has been able to impart to his work a force that is capable of reacting against factors that modify human institutions, and which lead to the decay of political creations: his law is living and strong even after centuries have passed. Delaporte reckons that if Muḥammad had only been a clever hypocrite, who caused Heaven to intervene as his ambition required, his first step along that course would also have been his last: the good sense of the Arabs would have seen through his tricks, since one cannot deceive a people for an extended period. Muḥammad, however, was driven by a profound conviction. Similarly, Delaporte identifies that the truth on which Muḥammad's law was founded is the dogma of the unity of God and the immortality of the soul, and both of these aspects of religion may have been dormant among Muḥammad's contemporaries and therefore receptive to reawakening.

An interesting point made by Delaporte is that Muslims were Muḥammad's companions (or *ṣaḥāba*, a word recurring among Arab authors), but not his subjects, so that the oath of loyalty was reciprocal and obedience conditional. From a purely religious point-of-view, Muḥammad's character displays astonishing wisdom and power of reasoning, considering prevailing conditions and the customs that must have influenced him. For, while he recommends the strict observance of religious devotions to his followers, he exhorts them to avoid giving too much importance to external rites, in a passage where, in Delaporte's opinion, is summed up the purest moral teaching given (p. 30). This passage, in which the essential teachings of Islam are quoted by Delaporte, is probably made up of various parts of the Qur'ān which he has put together. Delaporte considers that a ray of supreme wisdom must have descended on the Prophet when he declared such a sublime declaration of faith: after reading this exuberant passage, one no longer wonders at the sway Muḥammad held over his contemporaries.

A more negative image of the Prophet is present in *Mohammed and Mohammedanism* (1889) by S. W. Koelle, a German missionary of the Church Mission Society, and Professor of Arabic at Fourah Bay College, Sierra Leone. The learned missionary references Ibn Isḥāq, and shows interest in some of Ibn Isḥāq's more positive remarks towards the Prophet, while remaining hostile to Muḥammad in general. Tracing the development of Muḥammad as Prophet, Koelle initially identifies an inward harmony between the Makkan and Madīnan periods, despite their outward dissimilarity. Later, however, Koelle challenges the Muslim view that Muḥammad's public life was, from beginning to end, one congruous whole, since he detects a radical change of principles in Muḥammad: like Muir, he believes that the ardent preacher, zealous reformer, and austere Prophet of Makka pleading for mere toleration and for bare recognition of his teaching, is in reality the seed and precursor of a military commander and insatiable conqueror. Koelle argues that in both places Muḥammad is essentially the same man: in Makka he is trying to succeed with his plan while in Madīna he actually succeeds. Nevertheless, Koelle sees in Muḥammad a thoughtful and patriotic Arab who realised the full implication of Abyssinian and Persian domination of the Yemen over a number of years, and who therefore concluded that he could rely on Arabs only for the security of his country. Few commendable traits in Muḥammad emerge after these preliminary observations.

Koelle does not believe that Muḥammad received any divine revelations. Thus, the change of *qibla* is identified as having been prompted by prudence: Muḥammad simply waited until the strength of his Arab following increased. The Professor develops Sprenger's comments about Zayd ibn 'Amr, who was a *ḥanīf* (an Arab who, in pre-Islamic times, tended to monotheism), and is alleged to have instructed Muḥammad in religious matters. Reputedly, after the death of Zayd ibn 'Amr, Muḥammad offered this teaching as though it had been derived directly from Heaven. He claims that the Prophet said that people could pray for Zayd's soul. The Muslim view is rather different: Muḥammad praised Zayd, saying that on the day of the Resurrection 'he will be raised as having, in himself alone, the worth of a whole people'.[36] Because of Zayd's high standing in Islam, Koelle goes to the length of suggesting that if Muḥammad had been motivated by religious objectives, he should have followed Zayd and Waraqa in embracing the religion of the man-God Jesus (p. 53). Muḥammad, on the other hand, did not have even the faintest idea of the development and growth of divine revelation, otherwise he could not have supposed that the religion of Abraham could be restored after thousands of years to a position of prominence. No thoughtful person could regard it agreeable to the perfection of God first to reveal His religion, then replace it for a time with the Law and the Gospel, only to alter His previous measures and reintroduce it using Gabriel and a Prophet in Arabia.

Koelle takes every opportunity to show Muḥammad in an unfavourable light. For instance, doubts are cast as to his wisdom as a military commander. Koelle chooses the battle of Uḥud to make this point. Like Muir, he recounts that before this battle Muḥammad had at first taken the advice of the experienced 'Abdullāh ibn Ubayy, who thought that the Muslims should not leave Madīna to fight the Makkans, but then listened to the promptings of others who wanted to fight. He states that Ibn Ubayy responded at once by returning to Madīna with three hundred soldiers (p. 157). The Muslim interpretation is that

Ubayy turned back to Madīna with three hundred of the hypocrites and doubters. Koelle, at the expense of Muḥammad, quotes Ibn Hishām, who states that Muḥammad had said that Gabriel had told him that (his own uncle) Ḥamza was 'written' among the people of the seven heavens.[37] He also quotes Ibn Isḥāq, according to whom Muḥammad had said that all those who had been slain in the path of God would rise on the day of Resurrection, with their wounds emitting blood of musk-like aroma.[38] He rejects the Muslim view that the defeat at Uḥud was due to the disobedience of followers: instead, he traces the defeat back to the rejection of the good advice of a man Muḥammad had 'supplanted' (p. 161).

Koelle is also critical of Muḥammad's attitude to Christians, stating that in Muḥammad's later dealings with them he did not reciprocate the good treatment his followers had received previously from the Christian people of Abyssinia when his followers sought refuge from persecution. Koelle had hoped that he would find Muḥammad to be enlightened on the all-important subject of Christianity: instead, he tried to show its insufficiency and imperfection so as to enhance the superior claims of his own rival system. Koelle quotes Ibn Isḥāq (fairly accurately) to show that this was the aim of Muḥammad in 622 in his theological controversy with the Christians of Najran (Yemen) who sent a deputation, led by their bishop, to him. There was another deputation from them in 631, when they sought to make a pact with the Prophet. A favourable treaty was signed: according to this treaty, in return for the payment of taxes they were to have the full protection of the Islamic state for themselves, their churches, and their other possessions.[39] But in Koelle's opinion, this treaty was imposed on them under humiliating conditions: the Christians from Najran had to give way before Muḥammad's religious dictatorship and their civil rights and national independence had to succumb to the overbearing power of a political despot (p. 138). Koelle has his own interpretation of a later episode, wherein Muḥammad sent messengers to a number of Christian potentates, including the Roman Emperor Heraclius and the Negus of Abyssinia. Koelle guesses that Muḥammad's letters may have made some impression on those recipients who lived near enough to have cause for apprehending that the Prophet might follow them up with measures of violence. Koelle therefore challenges the information, given in Ibn Isḥāq, that these Christian leaders were fully convinced of Muḥammad's divine mission, and dismisses it as gratuitous invention.[40]

The persistence of ambivalence towards Muḥammad

After studying French and English writers' reactions to Muḥammad over a century, it is legitimate to inquire if during this time there has been any evolution in the status of Muḥammad and the way he was perceived in the post-Enlightenment period (up to the end of the nineteenth century). More specifically, we can attempt to determine if the stigma of impostor is still attached to the name of Muḥammad. We may begin to examine this by grouping the writers on the following basis: (1) those who were clergymen or Christian apologists and supporters of Christian missions overseas and; (2) those who had no strong Christian commitment. In accordance with this classification, Mignot, Murray, Sprenger, Muir, and Koelle would belong to the first category and Gibbon, Savary, Pastoret, Caussin de Perceval, Lamartine, Saint-Hilaire, and Delaporte to the second. What should emerge clearly from the above classification is that Muḥammad is, on the whole, more highly regarded by the second class of writers.[41] Yet this classification masks some ambivalence: if Muḥammad gained the status of a legislator among a number of writers such as Gibbon, Caussin de Perceval, and Lamartine (who were well-disposed towards him), even they could not help, openly or surreptitiously, introducing the notion of Muḥammad's imposture into their works, and only in the writing of Saint-Hilaire and Delaporte is this absent. Thus, the rehabilitation of Muḥammad was clearly a drawn-out process in Western writings.[42]

Knowledge of Oriental languages, especially Arabic, and periods of residence in the world of Islam, however desirable in writers, do not always ensure impartiality or sympathy towards the Prophet. Both Sprenger and Muir spent years in India, but contact with Muslims there failed to engender a favourable opinion of the Prophet. However, because of their scholarly research into the Arabic source material dealing with the biography of Muḥammad, and the fact that they passed the fruits of their labours onto others, they cannot be easily dismissed.[43] Muir himself certainly profited from the investigations of Caussin de Perceval, although he lacked the balance displayed by the latter. However, a close analysis of the *Life* may surprise the reader: he does not appear as hostile to Muḥammad as his background would suggest. Towards the end of his book, he did acknowledge, albeit grudgingly, that Muḥammad implanted in his followers the doctrine of the unity of God: the very message Boulainviller proclaimed more than a century earlier.

In the final analysis, estimates of Muḥammad depend on the attitude of their authors. Chronology appears almost meaningless in the nineteenth century: the missionary zeal of Murray against Muḥammad in the 1830s can be matched by that of Koelle in the 1880s. Those who are free from this zeal, and wish to take a more sober approach to Muḥammad's conduct during his military campaigns, stress context and view his acts against a background where he appears more moderate than other commanders. With a shade more restraint, Lamartine's biography would have been even more credible. He certainly exaggerates when he refers to the long and frequent conversations Muḥammad had with Jabar about Christianity, although he did not invent the character. If some see a Cromwell in Muḥammad, others (like Saint-Hilaire) see a Socrates in him. Such divergent views of the Prophet will, it appears, always exist.

Notes

1. With reference to the *Histoire de l'Empire Ottoman*, the *Biographie universelle* claimed that it was much researched and contained important facts culled from the best sources.
2. Joseph de Guignes (1721-1800), Secrétaire-interprète in oriental languages at the Bibliothèque Royale in 1745, was more successful with his *Histoire générale des Huns, des Turks, des Mogols et des autres Tartares occidentaux*, published in four volumes in 1756-58. He was, however, primarily concerned with developments in Islam after the Prophet.
3. See his *Autobiography*, ed. D. A .Saunders (New York, 1961), p. 67.
4. *The History of the Decline*, ed . J. B. Bury (London, 1898-1923), vol. 5, p. 311.
5. In *De la part des peuples sémitiques dans l'histoire de la civilisation* (1862), Renan made a similar claim, arguing that Islam is purer in the Sudan than in Syria, and that superstitious practices have gained little access among the nomadic tribes of Africa.
6. *The White Mughals* (London, 2004), pp. 292-3.
7. See also C. Harrison, *France and Islam in West Africa, 1860-1960* (Cambridge, 1988) and my review of it in *French Studies*, April, 1991, vol. 45, pp. 239-40. One learns that in Upper Senegal and Niger M-F J. Clozel was struck by the influence of ancestral beliefs on African Islam, the survival of local superstitions, belief in spirits and traditions often contrary to the rules of the Qur'ān. A

consensus evolved within the French administration in Afrique Occidentale Française that Islam was very different from the 'orthodox' model of the Arab world: it was much closer to pre-Islamic traditional African beliefs.

8. He did, however, publish *Moïse considéré comme législateur et comme moraliste* in 1788.
9. He published his *Histoire de la législation des anciens peuples* in 9 volumes between 1817-27.
10. For more information on this marriage, see Chapter 5.
11. In *The Life of Mohammad from original sources* (Allahabad, 1851), Aloys Sprenger makes some desperate attempts to prove that Muḥammad could read and write, but he remains unconvincing. One is sceptical about Sprenger's suggestion that the expression which may have been used by Muḥammad in reply to the angel: *mā anā bi-qāri'*, which means 'I am not a reader', implied a refusal in Muḥammad's time. To make his case he relies on Shīʿī commentators. In one instance, he even twists the meaning of the Sunnī Qur'ānic commentator al-Bayḍāwī (d. 1286) with regard to the word 'ummiyūn' in *Sūra* 3, l. 20. He claims that Bayḍāwī explains 'ummiyūn' here as 'those who do not believe in the Bible and who are not of our (Jewish) religion'. In his *Tafsīr*, Bayḍāwī actually says 'those who have no book like the pagans'.
12. T. Carlyle, *On Heroes, Hero Worship and the Heroic in History* (London, 1841), p. 72.
13. With regard to India, the beginning of the shift may be traced back to the series of victories against Moghul/French forces by Clive, followed by the defeat of Tipu Sultan and capture of Seringapatam in 1799. Dalrymple noted that for some three hundred years Europeans coming out to the subcontinent had been assimilating themselves to India in various ways, but that increasingly, from the late 1790s, they felt they had nothing to learn from her. India was then perceived as a suitable venue for ruthless and profitable European expansion (*White Mughals*), p.54.
14. See C. J. Herold, *Bonaparte in Egypt* (New York, 1962), pp. 56, 69 and 186, quoted in W. Watson, *Tricolor and Crescent. France and the Islamic World*, pp. 14, 15 and 156.
15. According to H. Djait in *l'Europe et l'Islam* (Paris, 1978, p. 28) this point was made before Voltaire's *Essai sur les moeurs*. Djait argues that Voltaire's historical perspective in the *Essai* allowed him to distinguish between the Prophet's contribution and later developments in Islam.
16. In *Histoire générale des Arabes* (Paris, 1877, p. 82.) Sédillot (whose preoccupations were primarily scientific) felt it worthwhile to devote a chapter of his book to Muḥammad.
17. See A. Guillaume, *Life of Muhammad*, p.561, n.1. Guillaume shows that this information is not given in Ibn Hishām's recension, but that it is recorded in Ibn Isḥāq, according to Ṭabarī's *History*.
18. See M. Lings, *Life of Muhammad*, p. 51.
19. For the contrasting views of Gaudefroy-Desmombynes, V. Gheorghiu and M. Watt on the 'Constitution' of Madīna, see Chapter 5.
20. He published a German version, in three volumes, entitled *Das Leben und die Lehre des Mohammed* ('The Life and Teachings of Muḥammad', 1861-5).

21. He attributed the view that Ibn Isḥāq attempted to shape Muḥammad's biography according to Christian ideas to Muslim authors: thus he suggested that Ibn Isḥāq followed the Christian tradition of writing biographies (see Chapter 5, below). But he also added that Ibn Isḥāq accepted traditions uncritically, and that he was therefore not relied upon by early writers such as al-Bukhārī and al-Wāqidī. See *The Life of Mohammad*, p. 69, n. 1- 5.
22. *Life of Mahomet* (London, 1858), vol.1, pp. xci-xciii.
23. See Ṭabarī's comment on *Sūra* 22, l.52 in *Tafsīr* (Beirut, 1978), vol.7, pp.131-34.
24. See Zamakhsharī's comment on *Sūra* 17, l. 73 in *Kashshāf*, (Beirut, 1979), vol. 2. p. 460.
25. In *Averroes et l'Avérroïsme* in *Œuvres complètes*, ed. Henriette Psichari (Paris,1947), vol. 3, p. 135, Renan argues that the supernatural hardly appears in the essential teachings of Islam, which is close to the most purified form of deism, a thesis often upheld in the eighteenth century.
26. In *Le Problème de Mahomet* (Paris, 1952), R. Blachère suggests that the legend became more established through Qur'ānic support (see Chapter 5).
27. The full title of the work is *Souvenirs, impressions,pensées et paysages pendant un voyage en Orient* (Paris, 1835), 4 vols.
28. All quotations from the *Vie de Mahomet* are from the edition published by L'Harmattan, (Paris, 2005), in collaboration with the Abdul Aziz Saud al-Babtain Foundation, Kuwait.
29. This translation entitled *La Chronique* has been republished in 1980, 1981, 1983 and 2001. I use the most recent edition.
30. See Ali Kurhan's edition of the *Vie de Mahomet*, pp. 35-41.
31. In a footnote to *Sūra* 16, l. 103, Sale says that the traditions differ about 'the particular person or persons suspected of this confederacy', that is, of having helped Muḥammad. Basing his argument on Zamakhsharī and al-Bayḍāwī, he says one tradition mentions Jabar, a Greek servant of 'Amr ibn al-Ḥadramī who could read and write well; another mentions Jabar and Yaṣār, two slaves who followed the trade of sword-cutler at Makka: they used to read the Pentateuch and Gospel and often had Muḥammad for their auditor when he passed that way. With regard to the beginning of l. 103. 'We know indeed that they say a man teaches him', Al-Bayḍāwī simply says: 'they mean Jabar' and also adds: 'it is said that Jabar and Yasār made swords in Makka, read the Torah and the Gospel and that the Prophet, passing by them, listened to what they read'.
32. These four friends were Waraqa ibn Nawfal, 'Ubaydullāh ibn Jash, Zayd ibn 'Amr, and Uthmān ibn al-Ḥuwayrith: all Christians. Contrary to A. Kurhan's statement (p. 75), Lamartine was not referring to 'Uthmān ibn Affan, the future Caliph, who had never been a Christian. When Muḥammad was young the Qurayshite 'Uthmān ibn al-Ḥuwayrith had converted to Christianity and had tried to make himself King of Makka under Byzantine protection, but had failed. See Maxime Rodinson, *Mohammed* (London, 1991), p. 108. Rodinson's biography originally appeared in French in 1961, the second revised edition in 1968. I prefer the English edition because it allowed Rodinson to use Marsden Jones's edition of the Arabic text of al-Wāqidī.

33. Ṭabarī simply said that the Prophet authorised them to go to Abyssinia, adding that its Christian inhabitants possessed a sacred book and were closer to Muslims than idol worshippers. *La Chronique*, translation Zotenberg (Paris, 2001), vol.2, p.85
34. Ṭabarī, *La Chronique*, trans. Zotenberg, p. 146.
35. Published in *Calcutta Review*, 14 (December, 1845), pp. 418-85.
36. See Martin Lings, *Muhammad*, p. 73.
37. See Guillaume, *Life of Muhammad*, p.756, n. 613. Guillaume adds that Muḥammad and Ḥamza were foster brothers.
38. Lings, *Muhammad*, pp. 324-25.
39. Lings, pp. 324-25.
49. Guillaume reproduces extracts from Ṭabarī from part of the lost work of Ibn Isḥāq, which are omitted by Ibn Hishām. From these both Heraclius and the Negus appear to accept Muḥammad as a Prophet, the latter more clearly. See *The Life of Muhammad*, p. 653, n. 3 and pp. 656-658.
41. In *Victorian Images of Islam* (London, 1992), Clinton Bennett concentrated attention on the writings of six British Christians, and was able to establish a neat category of three writers with conciliatory and another category of three writers with a confrontational approach.
42. The thesis of Paul Hazard, which held sway for a long time, that the progress of Islam and Muḥammad was completed by 1708 when Simon Ockley challenged the notion that the West was superior to the East is no longer tenable. See *La Crise de la conscience européenne.1680-1715* (Paris, 1934), vol. 1, pp. 21-22.
43. W. Muir's criticism of Muḥammad (when he married Ṣafiyya at Khaybar) for not observing the *'idda*, (that is, the period of three months waiting required of Muslims before marrying a divorced or widowed woman) cannot likewise be brushed aside, *Life of Mahomet*, vol. 4, p. 69. Equally critical were Koelle in *Mohammed and Mohammedanism*, p. 183 and Maxime Rodinson, *Mohammed*, p. 254.

5

Sympathy and Scepticism, 1900 to the Present

In his paper on Muḥammad in the Enlightenment, D. Venturino states that for ten centuries the Prophet had to suffer at the hands of Christian intellectuals all the humiliation that they were capable of inflicting on him.[1] While this may have been true up to the period Venturino was surveying, the situation has certainly changed since then. As we noted in the last chapter, the standing of Muḥammad had shown some improvement by the nineteenth century. Yet many writers were still not willing to remove the stigma of impostor attached to his name. Further progress was needed before Muḥammad could be fully accepted as Prophet in the West. His elevation to this did take place in the twentieth century, in both French and English literature, although we do not know exactly when.[2] Biographies of Muḥammad reflecting the traditional Muslim accounts of him have continued to appear until the present, and these have, on the whole, been favourable to him.

There have also been some less positive studies on the Prophet, from those having little regard for Muslim accounts. Doubts relating to the biographical material slowly crept in the minds of some European specialists of Islam, including French- and English-speaking writers.[3] To the latter, the best way to renew modern studies in Islam seemed to challenge accounts of events narrated by Muslim Traditionists and biographers of the Prophet. The Duke of Sermoneta, Leone Caetani (1869-1935), studied the early centuries of Islam and published the *Annali dell'Islam* in ten volumes between 1905 and 1926, although the Belgian Henri Lammens (1862-1937) led the assault against the Traditions. It may be noted, however, that even Lammens, an anti-Islamic

Roman Catholic Jesuit priest, refers to Muḥammad as 'Prophet' in his works. Any satisfaction recorded at Muḥammad's change in status may, however, prove premature: Muḥammad continues to be viewed as an impostor in everything but name by Lammens, although the latter's extremism and prejudices are widely frowned upon not only in the world of Islam but also in the West. [4]

In the shadow of Renan

Renan had stunned the academic world with his pronouncement that Muḥammad could be approached on purely historical terms (see Chapter 4). In the eyes of many scholars, this had seemed to be a challenge worth taking up. In fact, from the early twentieth century onwards, Orientalists have devoted much of their time to responding to Renan and to upholding the opposite view regarding Muḥammad and the origins of Islam. Together with Caetani, Lammens was among the leaders of the school of thought which showed extreme scepticism about the historicity of Muslim accounts of the life of the Prophet. Lammens was the Professor of Arabic literature at the Institut Biblique, Rome, and later at the Roman Catholic University of St Joseph, Beirut. In his paper entitled 'La République marchande de la Mècque vers l'an 600 de notre Ère' (published in 1910), he explains the rise of Islam in political and economic terms.[5] His thesis outlines that in Makka the Quraysh had traded with spice caravans that crossed the Hijaz in the seventh century. Before this was firmly rejected by Professor Patricia Crone, in her highly polemical book, *Meccan trade and the rise of Islam* (1987), the thesis had gained currency with scholars such as Professor Montgomery Watt and Maxime Rodinson. Using this approach, Lammens felt free to attack Islam and its Prophet in the most uncharitable terms. Nevertheless, he cannot be lightly dismissed because of his in-depth knowledge of Islamic sources and the influence he was to have on many later writers.

In 1912, Lammens published *Fatima et les filles de Mahomet. Notes critiques pour l'etude de la Sira*. Although he discusses Muḥammad's family, the subtitle gives an appropriate idea of his real aim: which is not to make an objective analysis of the biography of Muḥammad but to attack him (either directly or indirectly) through his family. He claims that Muḥammad's polemics against infanticide were motivated by his desire to leave heirs issuing from his blood. He also claims that the *Sīra* had never doubted the existence of his four daughters, however, its authors make them disappear prematurely: in multiplying their number the biographers had only thought of the advantage of giving Muḥammad descendants whereas the prolonged co-existence of these, he claims, compromised the unity of the various parts of the great historical novel that the *Sīra* is (p. 7). Much of the book is devoted to challenging the historical foundations of the biography. Lammens cannot understand how 'Uthmān ibn 'Affān could have had precedence over 'Alī, unless he had strong links with Muḥammad. Lammens suggests that to justify the bypassing of 'Ali over the succession, the biographers decided to confer the title of son-in-law on 'Uthmān. He writes as if the latter had never married Ruqayya, the Prophet's daughter, whom the biographers, he says, dispatch to Abyssinia with 'Uthman. He gives the biographers wide-ranging powers over Muḥammad's family: for instance, Ruqayya's marriage is made to take place after the revelation and after her divorce from the son of Abū Lahab, because the Prophet could not be perceived to have given his daughters in marriage to polytheists who are opposed to Islam.[6] Lammens says that another daughter, Zaynab, was married to an unbelieving Umayyad. He expresses feigned surprise at the preference shown by the haughty monotheist Muḥammad for pagan sons-in-law who are rich.[7]

Part of the book is also concerned with reducing the significance of 'Alī in Islamic history. Lammens says that there is little mention of him before the *hijra*, the Shī'ites making him the first believer at Abū Bakr's expense by postponing the latter's conversion. 'Alī, was not the first believer according to Lammens, but rather the first believer among the clan of the Hashimites, and is not seen in any campaigns before Badr (p. 29). Nevertheless, the *Sīra* allows him to catch up. In the *Kitāb al-Maghāzī*, which relates Muḥammad's military campaigns, Al-Wāqidī (whom Lammens describes as a zealous Shī'ite), states that 'Alī killed a large number of the Quraysh at Badr. The gap concerning 'Alī's role in the Makkan period was filled, and his legend came to be an integral part of the official *Sīra*, where Muḥammad appears to preside over the education of his young cousin. Lammens points out that Wāqidī shows Fāṭima, Alī's wife, tending to the wounds of her father in the courtyard of the mosque on his return from the battle of Uḥud, while al-Bukhārī shows her engaging in the same activity on the battlefield, helped by 'Alī. Yet, in Madīna (from which he is frequently absent), Muḥammad preferred to replace him with the blind Ibn Umm Maktūm when such was his need.[8] Muḥammad did not reject the offers of poets to answer the charges of the Qurayshites against him, but when offered the assistance of 'Alī he declined; apparently, 'Alī had ill-treated his sickly wife Fāṭima, compelling her to take shelter at her father's house.[9]

After discussing the story of 'Alī and Fāṭima, Lammens concentrates the attack on Muḥammad. He sees the trace of an important evolution in Muḥammad after the conquest of Khaybar (in 628). As head of state Muḥammad neglects 'Alī and Fāṭima, whom he leaves fairly destitute. The reasons Lammens puts forward for this change is that Muḥammad has aspirations of domination and sovereignty (p. 60). Whereas until now the latter had modestly presided over Friday prayers in his mosque, squatting down on a leather cushion with his back leaning against the trunk of a palm tree, the conqueror of Khaybar and Makka could not remain happy with this 'appareil démocratique' (p. 65). He had perfume spread in the mosque. He and his disciples remembered Abyssinia and Syria where they had seen officers of state sitting on thrones on stage. So under the pretext of allowing the congregation to follow Muḥammad's movements at prayer, they installed the *minbar* (pulpit). Like Murray (see Chapter 4), Lammens does not believe in the asceticism that was purportedly prevalent in early Islam. Most of the Companions, excepting Abū Hurayra, wore silk cloaks obtained from the Yemen. Muḥammad himself preferred the fine silks of Syria, Egypt, and the Yemen (p. 75).

Lammens sees in Muḥammad at Makka an undervalued reformer, who sought popularity, and flattered the masses to gain it. Once he became ruler of the Hijaz, Muḥammad praised the monarchical form of government and adopted the motto 'one God, one Prophet-king'. Lammens gives a very superficial account of *Sharī'a* law when he says that Muḥammad, in a moment of exasperation, prescribes in his Qur'ān (*Sūra* 5, l. 38) that the hand of the thief should be cut. He asserts that Muḥammad did not mean to carry out the threat. Moreover, he asserts that the Prophet had stated that Allah had given him the order (*Sūra* 75, ll. 16-17) to take his time over the edition of the Qur'ān as a separate collection, so that he might revise it at leisure (p. 113): this is mere speculation. The Islamic point of view is that when revelation came it forced on Muḥammad an extreme concentration, verging on suffocation, a condition that was particularly painful to the Prophet who often expressed the resulting tension. The Traditionists al-Bukhārī and Ibn 'Abbās also understand the painful nature of revelation, as they explain that Muḥammad moved his lips because of this pain, although he is enjoined by the revelation not to move 'thy tongue/ Concerning the (Qur'ān)/ To make haste therewith/ It is for Us to collect it /And to recite it'.[10]

In *L'Arabie occidentale avant l'Hégire* (1928), Lammens is perhaps less offensive. The book is as much about Muḥammad at Makka as it is about him at Madīna, although it is not a full biography of the Prophet. At the beginning of his text, Lammens seems surprised that it is Abraham and Moses, rather than Jesus, who most impressed Muḥammad. He points out that in the *mi'rāj* (the Night Journey), the first two Prophets are placed many stations above Jesus. He does not seem to realise that Muslims have been invoking the name of Abraham in their daily prayers from the beginning, and did not wait until their Prophet had settled in Madīna to do this.

Although he stresses Christian influences on Muḥammad before the *hijra*, Lammens is sceptical about the existence of an established Christian community and an ecclesiastical hierarchy in Makka. Muḥammad's grandfather is supposed to have had a conversation at the foot of the Ka'ba with a bishop, who gave him advanced details of the fabulous history of his grandson. Lammens suggests it is pointless to ask who this bishop was and to what Church in Arabia he had been posted, for to do so would be to show undue deference to the creative imagination of the writers of the *Sīra* (which he continues to represent as a work of fiction). He mentions the welcome given to Muḥammad in Ṭā'if by 'Addās (the Christian slave of 'Utba ibn Rabī'a), showing irony at the expense of Sprenger who had described Addās as a monk from Nineveh.[11] He nevertheless admits that Christians kept coming to Makka from outside, and points out that Muḥammad never denied that he often frequented the workshops of Christians in Makka and sought inspiration from this humble milieu. Lammens states he will not spend too much time discussing the reworking, by Muḥammad, of historical and doctrinal material he obtained from these improvised informers. Yet to this reworking is due what Muslims call a 'miracle', that is, to the *i'jāz* (inimitability) of the Qur'ān. Muḥammad, Lammens says, must be thanked for having incidentally informed us about the ethnological origins of his monotheist friends.

After the *hijra*, and in Madīna, it is the Jewish influence on Muḥammad that is stressed. Lammens states that through a more intimate contact with the Jews there, Muḥammad learnt about the radical distinction between the Old and the New Testament, which he described in the Qur'ān (*Sūras* 3, l. 23 and 4, l. 44) as a part of the Revelation. Nearly everything in Islam seems to have been inspired by the Jews. In Madīna, declares Lammens, Muḥammad was impressed by his visits to the synagogue, and after noting Jewish observances he introduced a less rudimentary form of prayer (p. 58). The Friday prayer which he instituted arose from the Sabbath he observed in the Jewish diaspora to Madīna. Lammens adds that signs of tolerance towards Christians, whether indigenous or foreign, should be noted. One of the reasons for this is that Christians did not impose on their newly converted members a legislation that was as antipathetic to Arab independence as the Talmud.[12]

Lammens quotes *Sūra* 3, l. 75 to show how the Jews were infatuated with their superiority over the 'ummiyūn' (the ignorant), yet he makes Muḥammad suffer from an inferiority complex towards them, because of their glorious past.[13] Thus, he imagines that Muḥammad was initially happy with the simple title of messenger or 'warner' (p. 73). He quotes *Sūra* 10, l. 94, where Muḥammad is advised to consult those who had read the Book before him. Muḥammad was suspected by the Makkans of pursuing subversive aims in parallel with his religious reform, and of sowing discord in the state. He was, Lammens suggests, the first among Arabs to propose (in the Madīnan 'constitution' and in the Madīnan *Sūras*) a religious brotherhood based on ties other than blood.[14]

Nevertheless, according to Lammens, the concept of Islam as a world religion only dates from the Caliphate, and was born through contact with non-Muslim scriptural revelations.[15] Its birth was stimulated by the rise of imperialist and chauvinistic theories, which described the Arab people as being destined to gain the spiritual heritage of the nations that had betrayed their trust. Lammens presents the post-*Hijra* period as one of imperialist exaltation; what is strange is that he should seek support for his view from literature of the imagination. He quotes the famous lines from Voltaire's *Mahomet* (Act II, Scene v), in which the character Mahomet predicts that Arabia's time has at last come, as if these came from a historical document and were attributed to Muḥammad. Mahomet's epic tone in the play may be impressive, but it clearly does not deal with history here. In comparison, in his historical work proper, the *Essai sur les moeurs* , Voltaire kept his imagination in check and did not attribute any imperial designs to Muḥammad.

French writer Emile Dermenghem (1892-1971) acknowledges the influence of Lammens, however he shows no animosity to Islam and its Prophet in his book *La Vie de Mahomet* (first published in 1929 and reedited a number of times subsequently). Among his other works are *La Vie des saints musulmans* (1942), *Les plus beaux textes arabes* (1951) (which consists of translations of extracts from Arab authors from the sixth to the twentieth century), and *Mahomet et la Tradition islamique* (1955), all subsequently republished. In *La Vie de Mahomet* Dermenghem mentions the serious attempts made towards dealing with Muḥammad's biography in the nineteenth century (by writers such as Caussin de Perceval, Muir, and Weil) and in the twentieth century (by L. Caetani, L. Massignon, R. Bell, and M. Gaudefroy-Desmombynes). He feels that although these writers have renewed Islamic studies, their works have been above all destructive. Dermenghem thus decides to take a middle course, using original sources and modern critics (p. iv). He is critical of Traditionists, especially al-Bukhārī, who tried to collect the slightest remarks and deeds of the Prophet, and thus made a serious external criticism of the *isnād*s (the chain of transmitters) with no internal criticism of the content. Dermenghem believes that the *Aḥādīth* of the Traditionists created a gap between Christianity and Islam, and that they are often tendentious and therefore suspect (p. 135).

Dermenghem regards the *Sīra* of Ibn Isḥāq, in Ibn Hishām's edition, as the most scholarly, despite the fact that Ibn Hishām believes Mary to be the third person of the Trinity (p. 126). On the other hand, the historical writings of al-Wāqidī, Ibn Sa'd, al-Ṭabarī, and Abū al-Fidā, he believes, share the weaknesses of the *Aḥādīth*. Their authors seek to establish a logical and chronological order which is often difficult to achieve. However, he wants readers to acknowledge that the earliest biographies are not lacking in objectivity, as they do not hide the Prophet's weaknesses; as an example, he refers to the killing, on Muḥammad's orders, of a rich Jew named Sallam ibn Abū al-Ḥuqayq, who had incited his co-religionists of Khaybar against the Muslims in 628.[16] Dermenghem tries to redress Muḥammad's perceived harshness towards Jews, by arguing that one must recognise that they had betrayed him. He nevertheless concludes that after this episode it is difficult to find in the Prophet a model in everything.[17] For this reason, he is critical of Muslim scholars such as Muhammad 'Abduh (1849-1905) in Egypt and Sayyid Ameer Ali (1849-1928) in India, for although they to some extent renewed studies on Muḥammad, they also tend, in Dermenghem's view, to idealise Muḥammad's character.[18]

Rather like Lamartine, Dermenghem does his best to bring Islam and Muḥammad close to Christianity. At times he even exaggerates by suggesting that Muḥammad considered himself a Christian, which was not the case. There is no exaggeration, however, in his saying that Muḥammad was one of the prophets entrusted with calling his people to monotheism and with bringing to it, in Arabic, a book in harmony with the Pentateuch, the Psalms and the Gospel, which he often describes as revealed books. The Qur'ān indeed describes these as part of God's Revelation.

Dermenghem insists on showing that Muḥammad had direct or indirect contact with Christians. Before revelation Muḥammad, he suggests, had been influenced by the *ḥanīf* (monotheist) Zayd ibn 'Amr and Nestorian monks like Baḥīra. Dermenghem makes a strange comment on the latter, claiming that however legendary his story may be in the Muslim tradition, it has something that is real (p. 117):[19] what does this mean?[20] Dermenghem also mentions Christians of Makka, such as Waraqa, who roused Muḥammad's religious conscience before his mission and his meeting with the Greek Jabar. He asserts that Muḥammad did not deny obtaining information from Christians with regard to the Biblical stories, but does not give any source for this conclusion. At the fair of 'Ukāẓ (and at other fairs), Muḥammad met Christian Arabs from Najran and Hira (Mesopotamia), and Dermenghem states, had even heard a famous bishop preach one day. After Khadīja's death in 619, Muḥammad married Sawda ibn Zama whose former husband had become a Christian in Abyssinia.[21] Dermenghem even mentions the fact that Khadīja's hairdresser was an Abyssinian Christian, as if this could have enriched Muḥammad's Christian background!

More seriously, Dermenghem claims, with some further exaggeration, that all the Christian dogmas are found in the Qur'ān, although his point about its recognition of the Eucharist in *Sūra* 5, l.114 is valid. He argues that the beginning of *Sūra* 30, dating from about 615-616 and predicting the victory of the Greeks over the Persians (in 625), shows Muḥammad's Christian sympathies. By juxtaposing these lines with *Sūra* 22, 40 (this is partly a late Makkan, and partly a Madīnan, *Sūra*) he attributes to Muḥammad a rejoicing at the Greek victory, as this prevented the destruction of monasteries and churches where the name of God is frequently invoked. However, there may not be any connection between the Greek victory and the avoidance of destruction of monasteries and churches.

Less controversial aspects of Muḥammad's life are also mentioned in the *Vie de Mahomet*. Dermenghem states that without seeing a socialist in him, one is still struck by the energy with which Muḥammad denounces, especially at the beginning of his mission, the rich unbelievers and the dangers the goods of this world represent for spiritual life. He points out that the sublime also coexisted with the ordinary in Muḥammad's life. Dermenghem could not let Muḥammad's common touch and humanity pass unnoticed. He mentions how Muḥammad allowed his grandsons Ḥasan and Ḥusayn to climb over his shoulder during prayer, and how he pronounced the *shahāda* in their ears. He also narrates how Muḥammad felt strong emotion when, after the battle of Badr, his daughter Zaynab had to offer the necklace she had been given at her wedding to Abū al-ʿĀṣ ibn Rabīʿa as ransom for his liberty. On recognising the jewel, Muḥammad wept and asked Muslims to let his son-in-law go free without paying a ransom.

The impact of Lammens can also be seen in the biography of the Prophet by Tor Andrae (1885-1946), a Swedish Professor at the University of Upsala and Bishop of Linköping.[22] This biography was first published in German in 1932, and was then translated into English (in 1936) and into French (in 1945) as *Mahomet, sa vie et sa doctrine*. Andrae stresses the dependence of Muḥammad on Judeo-Christian traditions. Like Lammens, for instance, he believes that the choice of Friday as the Muslim Sabbath took place during the Prophet's stay in Madīna, and spoke of the touching naiveté of Muḥammad who followed the Judeo-Christian tradition. He states that while in Makka Muḥammad and his disciples only offered the morning and evening prayers, whereas in Madīna another prayer was added at three in the afternoon, in imitation of the Jewish community. It is true that the number of prayers in Islam was initially not fixed, but since 619 (when Muḥammad was still in Makka), pious Muslims have been praying five times a day: they did not wait until they arrived in Madīna to honour Abraham (Ibrāhīm).

In Andrae's view, Muḥammad received the decisive impetus for his own religious mission from the Nestorian Church in Persia. To this Church belonged the Christian Arabs of Hira with whom the Makkans had a close link (p. 90). Yet Muḥammad betrays such an astonishing ignorance of the external forms of Christian worship that Andrae even doubts whether he had ever visited Syria. Andrae says that Muḥammad only speaks once of the Eucharist and then as if it is a real meal, which makes him conclude that Muḥammad had little experience of living Christianity and showed no personal impression of it.

Andrae at first seems to echo Renan's view that Islam appears to be entirely verifiable by history, at least when compared with other great world religions (p. 8). But on three subsequent occasions, he contradicts his earlier statement. He says that we have little historically valid data about the period when Muḥammad was a relatively unimportant man as his acts did not give rise to the same attention he received later (p. 21). Andrae then becomes rather more specific, by suggesting that we cannot give any historical weight to that which Tradition tells us about the Prophet's life before his calling (p. 40). He says that in the crucial years when his vocation was taking shape (that is, between 595 and 610), Muḥammad was a rich man, and his denunciation of avarice, materialism, and hard-heartedness had little to do with personal experience. Finally, according to Andrae, we have little sound information on the Prophet's psychological development in the years between 610 and 622 (p. 112).

The Qur'ān, according to Andrae, is a better source of information on the life of Muḥammad than Tradition. He notes, however, that the longest *Sūra*s are placed at the beginning and that the oldest are at the end. This arrangement makes it difficult to understand the Qur'ān as the principal means of assessing Muḥammad's personality. Andrae is very critical of Muslim exegesis. As an example, he quotes l.16 of *Sūra* 10, which was revealed in the late Makkan period. Muḥammad is made to say: 'A whole lifetime before this/ Have I tarried amongst you'. He says that Muslim exegesis has, very artificially, taken life to mean forty years.[23] What is serious, in his opinion, is that the whole of the chronology of Muḥammad's life before the *hijra* has been made to rest on this weak data.

While portraying some aspects of Muḥammad's life in Madīna, Andrae mentions the practice of plundering of caravans coming from Syria as a means used to obtain resources. This, he suggests, is particularly discouraging to those who like to see in Muḥammad a moral and religious personality. As an example, he quotes the ambush in Nakhla, which took place in the month of Rajab, in the second year of the *hijra* (that is, in January 624) (pp.140-142), which he finds to be a blemish on the Prophet's character. He refers to a sealed letter with Muḥammad's instructions, addressed to 'Abdullāh ibn Jaḥsh, which was to be opened at a later date. According to Andrae, the authentic text of the letter is that given by al-Wāqidī in the *Maghāzī*, and reads: 'Go to the valley of Nakhla and ambush the Quraysh'. He says that the letter was subjected to pious alterations in the hands of the historians, such that in Ibn Hishām it reads: 'Lie in wait there for the Quraysh and find out for us what they are doing'.[24] When the attack took place, Muḥammad said that he had not ordered Ibn Jaḥsh to fight in the sacred month. Andrae's conclusion is that there is some Jesuit casuistry in the reply of Muḥammad, who skilfully engineered Ibn Jash's act without taking responsibility for it. [25]

Towards the end of his study, however, Andrae becomes better disposed towards Muḥammad. He points out that the Prophet did not seek to acquire power or consolidate his position by claiming to have made so-called miracles, although he mentions two exceptions, the miraculous event of the Night Journey and the battle of Badr (where angels are supposed to have taken part on his side). He admires Muḥammad's humility, recalling an episode in which the latter had given a necklace to 'Ā'isha made of pearls taken at the capture of Khaybar. Quoting al-Wāqidī, Andrae states that Muḥammad could not sleep the following night and wanted to take the necklace back to its owner, but he learnt that 'Ā'isha had distributed the pearls to the poor. Andrae says that the frankness with which he acknowledged this fault is to Muḥammad's credit and, for once, to that of Muslim Tradition. He believes that Muḥammad showed as much humility and made enough self-criticism as one could reasonably expect from an Apostle, and that he resisted the temptation of money. He applies to Muḥammad the following words, which the Qur'ān puts in the mouths of all Prophets: 'Our Lord! forgive us / Our sins and anything / We may have done / That transgressed our duty' (*Sūra* 3, l. 147).

The way was paved in France for a more sustained attack than Andrae's on Muslim accounts of the life of Muḥammad. This came from Régis Blachère (1900-1973), Professor at the École Nationale des Langues Orientales, Paris, whose works include the translation of the Qur'ān in three volumes (1947-50), with the first volume being the introduction, and the *Histoire de la littérature arabe des origines à la fin du XVè Siècle de J.C.* (1952), again in three volumes. Despite its fairly serene tone, Blachère's *Le Problème de Mahomet* (1952) produces an iconoclastic effect on the reader.[26] In the introduction, Blachère rejects Renan's view that Muḥammad's biography can be entirely verified in historical sources, an error which he wishes to dispel. Although he concedes that the personality of Muḥammad does not remain covered by the mists in which Zoroaster, Buddha, and Jesus float, he believes that long periods of his life remain impenetrable and that even when Muḥammad stops being a mystery, much uncertainty continues to persist about his thoughts or acts. In his view, the dogmas and laws of Islam were created after Muḥammad.

In the first chapter, which deals with the sources and the chronological problem, Blachère draws some distinction between the *Sīra* and the *Aḥādīth*. He notes, for example, that in the *Sīra* of Ibn Isḥāq , the life of Muḥammad follows a chronological pattern, whereas the sections on the *maghāzī* (military campaigns of Muḥammad), and the virtues and merits of his companions, do not form a continuous biography in the *Ṣaḥīḥ* of the Traditionist al-Bukhārī. This should not seem so surprising, as al-Bukhārī did not set out to write all of Muḥammad's expeditions and his full biography, but to record (among other things) his sayings and deeds, and the beliefs, prayers, and practices of Islam. Although al-Wāqidī in the *maghāzī* and Ibn Sa'd in the *Ṭabaqāt* assembled a documentation having some similarity with al-Bukhārī's, their data, he believes, was more complete in respect of Muḥammad's expeditions and his companions respectively. The documentation was meant to trace the life of Muḥammad in chronological order and they followed Ibn Isḥāq/Ibn Hishām, even if they did not explain the divergences presented by the data. Blachère points out that the oral traditions were slowly handed down over about a century and, as has happened in the case of Jesus, no one thought of recording Muḥammad's life towards the end or soon after. In the course of the slow progress made in this field, the narrative met the disastrous fate that befalls much of what is entrusted to oral transmission.[27] Blachère believes that the data was swollen by apocryphal elements that were inspired by a non-Arab milieu and by the needs of those who were newly converted to Islam from Judaism and Christianity.[28] Thus, when the Traditions were collected between 750 and 890 and submitted to critical examination, it was too late to identify in them the original elements, and too late to remove doubts even within those in which the Traditionists discovered authentic traits.

Blachère claims that the approach of the Traditionists will find a historical allusion everywhere, even where the Qur'ānic text has a general meaning, although he does accept that Tradition can be trusted when there is a transparent allusion (such as in *Sūra* 80, relating to the episode of Ibn Umm Maktūm). He also accepts that in some cases biographical Tradition has preserved some authentic traits of the Makkan period of Muḥammad's mission. However, one has to bear in mind the excesses, involuntary confusion, and pious fraud that must have been brought about by the tendency of Muslim biographers to detect links between the Qur'ān and Traditional data. Blachère notes that from 622 contemporary data of the first generation of Muslims plays a greater role than during Muḥammad's apostleship at Makka. He concludes that, in documents originating in Tradition, everything betrays the effort of the exegetes to historicise traits which, in the Qur'ān, aim only to instruct the faithful. Yet the history of the Arabian Peninsula at the end of the sixth century was known from information circulated orally, then recorded two centuries later by writers who had settled in Madīna or in Iraq. Blachère (who is rather vague about these writers) still believes that material of this type may be used if it is corroborated by other material. The other sources Blachère uses are Byzantine writers. These, he believes, were fairly well informed about the struggles of Arab emirs reigning over the Syrian steppes against their counterparts in Iraq who were the vassals of the Sasanians of Persia (p. 14). Blachère cannot, of course, establish whether Byzantine writers were more reliable or had fewer prejudices than Muslim Traditionists.

Like Lammens, Blachère has a strong preference for the Qur'ān over the *Sīra* as a reliable source for the life of Muḥammad, and he explains why. He says, for example, that through anachronism the *Sīra* (which he calls the biographical tradition) identifies the angel who brought the revelation to Muḥammad as Gabriel, right at the beginning of the apostleship; whereas the Qur'ān has him identified as Gabriel much later, at Madīna. Moreover, the *Sīra* of Ibn Isḥāq/Ibn Hishām contains, in his view, a number of hagiographical stories. He lists among these the Baḥīra episode, and the story of Muḥammad and Abū Bakr taking shelter from their enemies in the cave on Thawr (a mountain some three miles from Makka) in 622. Blachère says that to explain why the Makkans did not discover their intended victims in the last episode, hagiography took up the legend of which Ibn Isḥāq was ignorant, but which appeared in the life of St Felix. The episode is referred to in *Sūra* 9, l. 40. The Night Journey too, he believes, is hagiographical.[29]

Blachère uses the conversion of 'Umar to attack the reliability of the *Sīra*, pointing out that the circumstances of this conversion are recorded in Ibn Isḥāq/Ibn Hishām in two irreconcilable ways: these variant accounts weaken Tradition and thus lessen the worth of Tradition as historical documents. By drawing attention to the fact that the conversion of Ḥamza, Muḥammad's uncle, is described in Tradition (*Sīra*) but not in the Qur'ān, he leaves one with the impression that he would have preferred it to be recorded in the Qur'ān. He says that only two opponents of Muḥammad (Abū Lahab and his wife) are mentioned in the Qur'ān (p.48), forgetting that a description of the lives of various individuals is not in line with its purpose. Biographical tradition ,which he contrasts with the anonymity of Qur'ānic allusions, reveals itself to be better informed (perhaps too well informed) about members of the Makkan oligarchy, such as Abū Jahl and al-Mūghīra, although it keeps quiet about Abū Sufyān or al-'Abbās, Muḥammad's uncle. This alleged omission of the last two is astonishing, as there is frequent mention of their opposition to Muḥammad in the *Sīra*.

Although he is scathing about oral transmission by Muslims, in a later chapter Blachère shows some understanding of what he calls the 'irritating problem of recording revelations in writing' (p. 53). He has no doubt that no-one thought of fixing in writing the very first messages transmitted by Muḥammad, and that for a certain period revelations were entrusted to the sole memory of the faithful. He finds it plausible that in Makka, where Scripture was familiar to many, the idea of noting down revelations occurred to believers who were capable of writing.[30] There is evidence to suggest that this transcription was incomplete and very insecure, due to both the material then in use (scraps of leather, for instance) and the spelling conventions. This latter is the most crucial point: spelling, he recognises, was then so rudimentary that a text could be correctly decoded only if it was known by heart. This is a belated recognition of the validity of the oral tradition. It might have been better perhaps if the Traditions had been collected and written down earlier, but one has to deal with the Islamic world as it was.[31] To Muslims, the lack of contemporary written testimony is not much of a problem. The oral tradition, in the Islam of the first centuries, confers authority on the written text. Thus, it is reading aloud that validates the testimony of many a companion of the Prophet rather than the fact that this was written down: the written text simply acts as an aide-mémoire.

The problem of tracing the life of Muḥammad, then, is connected with that of written Arabic in the early centuries of Islam, and Blachère understands this very well. He finds the idea of recording revealed texts in writing very plausible and he believes this gained ground in early Islam. As evidence, he refers to *Sūra* 19 which dates from 615 and is an account 'Of the Mercy of thy Lord/ To His servant Zakariyā'. These lines reflect, in his view, a written origin. Yet when he describes the strengthening of the Islamic community in Madīna in the period 622-627, Blachère notes that the imperfection of the writing system made it even more indispensable for believers to know the Qur'ānic text by heart, and that some data in the Traditions would lead one to believe that even in this period fragments of revelation were entrusted to the sole memory of believers.

Although he would rather use the Qur'ān to establish the biography of Muḥammad, Blachère relents in his attack on Tradition for the above period when the Islamic community settles in Madīna and is strengthened there.[32] He says that it then has at its disposal for its social and religious life a body of (perhaps oral) texts to which it could appeal in its opposition to the Torah of the Jews of Madīna. In the Madīnan *Sūras*, he argues, the allusions are numerous and clear, and thus bridges can be established between them and the biographical data of Tradition. Through Tradition (here Blachère probably means *Sīra*) one sees many chronological landmarks such as the battles of Badr, Uḥud, the Trench, and the capture of Makka, around which the Qur'ānic revelations are arranged. He seems to suggest that Qur'ān and Tradition support each other in this period, while insisting that the former should remain the essential source of any historical reconstruction of Muḥammad's preaching at Madīna. Blachère's attitude to Tradition has therefore evolved: henceforth greater trust, he believes, may be put in this, as it is supported by the conditions under which Muḥammad will pursue his mission. He suggests the framework is strong enough to make the historian feel secure, even if Muslim apologetics magnify the obstacles Muḥammad had to face. To keep the balance, Muḥammad shows flexibility, tactfulness, humanity, and a steadfastness which, centuries later, still rouse the admiration of every independent person. He does his utmost to give every problem a solution that is not theological in origin but rather dictated by circumstances, and he effectively takes the means at his disposal into account.

A serious work following *Le Problème de Mahomet* was the biography of Muḥammad, *Muhammad at Mecca* (1953), by the Reverend Montgomery Watt (1909-2006), one of the most prolific British scholars of Islam in the twentieth century.[33] Although Blachère (a Marxist) and Watt (a cleric) differ in their attitude to *Sīra* and Tradition, there are affinities between them which Professor Watt did not seem to have realised.[34] In his article 'The Reliability of Ibn Isḥāq's sources'(1983), Watt simply placed Blachère in the camp of Henri Lammens and Carl Heinrich Becker, who believe that the only reliable source for the biography of Muḥammad was the Qur'ān:[35] although he had reservations about the value of the *Sīra*, Blachère did not dismiss it outright.

In *Muhammad at Mecca*, Watt, like Blachère, draws attention to the role of 'Urwa, son of al-Zubayr ibn al-'Awwām (d. 712), one of the earliest Muslims, in assembling scattered materials for the biography of Muḥammad.[36] 'Urwa was a grandson of Caliph Abu Bakr and he was in contact with his aunt 'Ā'isha, the Prophet's widow. Some seventy years after the migration of early Muslims to Abyssinia (that is, about 685), he wrote a letter to 'Abd al-Malik ibn Marwān (Caliph between 685 and 705), as the latter wanted accurate knowledge about the prophet's career. A copy of it has been preserved by al-Ṭabarī. In it, there is a reference to Muḥammad's attack against idols, the oppression of Muslims in Makka, and the Prophet's request that some of them go to Abyssinia.[37]

Like Lammens and Blachère, Watt too claims (p. 64) that in the early *Sūras* of the Qur'ān there was no mention of the unity of God, with the apparent exception of *Sūra* 51, l. 51 which states 'And make not another/ An object of worship/ With Allah'. Although Watt says that this is probably a later addition, Islamic scholars read this as a Makkan *Sūra*. It may be pointed out that the above-named European scholars had not lived within Islam, although this is not a criticism of them. If they had, they would have known that the early Makkan *Sūra* 112, which stresses the unity of God, is often recited by Muslims in their daily prayers. In his note on it, the Protestant Sale, for his part, appears more in tune with living Islam: quoting al-Bayḍāwī, he observes that the *Sūra* is 'held in particular veneration by the Mohammedans, and declared by a tradition of their prophet, to be equal in value to a third part of the Koran. It is said to have been revealed in answer to the Koreish, who asked Mohammed concerning the distinguishing attributes of the God he invited them to worship' (*The Koran*, ed. E.D. Ross, p. 595).

Without going deeply into the question of Muḥammad's sincerity (as Sprenger had done), Watt points out that since Carlyle's lecture on Muḥammad in 'Heroes and Hero Worship' the West has been aware that there was a good case for believing in Muḥammad's sincerity. He is convinced that Muḥammad's readiness to undergo persecution for his beliefs, the high moral character of the men who believed in him and looked up to him as leader, and the greatness of his ultimate achievement, all speak for his fundamental integrity (p. 52). He also does not accept that Muḥammad's symptoms at the time of revelation are identical with epilepsy (which leads to mental and physical degeneration), arguing that Muḥammad was in the fullest possession of his faculties to the end (p. 57).

Watt does not find it plausible to imagine Muḥammad inserting verses of his own composition among those which came to him from what he believed was a supernatural source. Yet he thinks that Muḥammad may have done some rearranging of revealed material, and may have tried to induce emending revelations where he felt that a passage needed emendation (p. 53). Although, as he says, it is part of orthodox Muslim theory that some revelations were abrogated by others, no Muslim believes that Muḥammad induced emending revelations: that would be tantamount to saying that he was the author of the Qur'ān. Instead, Watt tries to be fair much of the time. For instance, he says that with regard to the stories of the prophets in the

Qur'ān close parallels may be found between it and Judeo-Christian documents (usually not canonical books of the Bible, but rather rabbinical works, heretical, and apocryphal writings): thus Western writers are led to conclude that the Qur'ān is the work of Muḥammad and that he repeats the stories he had heard. Watt then attempts to put forward the alternative Muslim point of view: that when early Muslims accepted Muḥammad as a prophet they, like Muḥammad himself, became interested in previous prophets, and found out what they could about them. Their knowledge gradually increased, and this is a fact which is reflected in the Qur'ān (p. 84).

Watt's achievement is that, on the whole, he manages to give a balanced assessment of Islamic material dealing with the Prophet's life, even if he may have been mistaken on the question of Makkan trade. Although not betraying any trace of hostility to Islam, he does not, however, hesitate to examine the material critically. An example of this critical approach occurs in his treatment of the statement in Ṭabarī's *Annals*, that after 'Alī, Abū Bakr, and Zayd ibn Ḥāritha, there was an important group of converts introduced to Muḥammad by Abū Bakr in 615 (that is, 'Uthmān ibn 'Affān, al-Zubayr ibn al-'Awwām, 'Abd al-Raḥmān ibn 'Awf, Sa'd ibn Abī Waqqāṣ, and Ṭalḥa ibn 'Ubaydullāh). Watt finds it hardly credible that the same five men should come together with 'Alī more than twenty years later as acknowledged leaders and be nominated by 'Umar to settle the succession.

Watt's *Muhammad at Mecca* begins the slow process of attempting to repair some of the damage already done to the reliability of the *Sīra* in the first half of the twentieth century, and succeeds in buffering it against some of the criticisms by later Orientalists who have little sympathy with Islam. Although Watt states that suspicion exists about claims to early conversion to Islam, he deems the list of early Muslims given by Ibn Isḥāq to be roughly accurate. The word 'roughly' seems appropriate, for Sprenger had already queried the inclusion of the name of 'Ā'isha in the list (see Chapter 4).[38] Watt states, however, that even if the details provided by Ibn Hishām and at-Ṭabarī for the period following the migration to Abyssinia are scanty, they give a fairly accurate picture of the opposition to Muḥammad. The information matches that given in the Qur'ān, although it is not identical with it (p. 117) and though, as he believes, there is an element of exaggeration as regards the persecution of Muslims, the description of Abū Jahl found in Ibn Isḥāq does not seem to be exaggerated.

A year after the publication of the second volume of Watt's biography of Muḥammad, Maurice Gaudefroy-Desmombynes, a Professor at the Ecole des Langues Orientales and a member of the Institut de France, published *Mahomet*. He refers the reader to Andrae and Blachère, adding that his approach differs from the latter in some ways.[39] Gaudefroy-Desmombynes seems fairly well-disposed towards the Prophet on the whole, and aims for a balanced appraisal. Having stated that Muḥammad learnt from Judeo-Christians about the preaching of the ancient prophets of Israel, and of Jesus and the Apostles (p. 67), Gaudefroy-Desmombynes then refers to the emigration of Muslims to Abyssinia. He argues, however, that one must not exaggerate the influence that these contacts may have had on the development of Muḥammad's religious thought, even if the Quraysh had long had commercial and cultural relations with Abyssinia (p. 92). To him, Judeo-Christian influences on Muslim tradition are evident, but these occur after the time of Muḥammad. He mentions Waraqa, as an influence on Muḥammad's early life, who in Muslim writings dies before the revelation so that he avoids being condemned for unbelief. Gaudefroy-Desmombynes is rather vague about the identity of the person responsible for the suggestion of Waraqa's early demise. He points out that the atmosphere prevailing in Makka, and surrounding the meditation of Muḥammad, was favourable to monotheism. As if to refute critics who claimed that Muḥammad altered revelation to suit his purpose, he quotes the Qur'ān, *Sūra* 10, l. 15 to show that the latter could not modify it in any way. He then uses *Sūra* 25, l. 34 to justify the sending down of revelation in fragments: this practice, as he says, helped Muḥammad to remember the verses easily. Again, the importance of the oral tradition in Islam is recognised in this text.

Due importance is given by Gaudefroy-Desmombynes to the impact of Moses on Muḥammad in the Makkan period. He is aware, for example, of the story that Moses advised Muḥammad, during the Night Journey, to ask Allah for a reduction in the number of prayers Muslims have to read daily. He is even convinced that the verses of the Qur'ān in which Muḥammad narrates the stories of the prophets of Israel and information about his own life led him to confuse their mission with his own and therefore to consider his first task to be the conversion of Jews to Islam. There is surely an element of exaggeration in this suggestion, even if Muḥammad may have made overtures to the Jewish people and appreciated their affinities with Muslims, especially their monotheism. Gaudefroy-Desmombynes sees in the late Makkan *Sūra* 7, ll. 157 to 159 the outline of a programme for the conversion of Jews, and says that the Qur'ān henceforth proposes Moses to him as a model, since he is the leader of a people (pp. 106-107).[40]

Gaudefroy-Desmombynes tries to distinguish between the two phases of Muḥammad's career. At Madīna he describes the Prophet as the interpreter of God's commands as well as being a legislator and a judge. He notes that the very form of the Revelation accentuates the transformation it had undergone in the last Makkan *Sūras*, however this remains unspecific here. Gaudefroy-Desmombynes believes that it was in the first months of the Muslim community's installation in Madīna that Muḥammad showed all the resourcefulness of his nature and all the strength of his personality on the lives of one hundred and fifteen persons. Muḥammad established a true community between the emigrants and the newly converted tribes of the Aws and the Khazraj. Gaudefroy-Desmombynes insists that the three Jewish tribes of the Yathrib (Madīna) on whose quick conversion Muḥammad had counted, although not hostile to him, remained firm in their beliefs. He believes Muḥammad made a last attempt to achieve a general union with the Jews by setting up the 'Constitution of Madīna' which, in his opinion, was a 'chef-d'oeuvre de politique internationale' (p. 118.).[41] Gaudefroy-Desmombynes finds it remarkable that Muḥammad settles only what can be settled, namely that he includes the Jewish confederates of Yathrib as part of the *umma*. Soon, however, Muḥammad loses his illusion regarding the conversion of the Jews, and Gaudefroy-Desmombynes feels that the change of *qibla* (direction of Muslim prayer) from Jerusalem to Makka in January 624 was more than a sign of rupture with the latter: it indicated the trend in future relations.

In *Mahomet*, Gaudefroy-Desmombynes claims to offer some new insights into the motives governing Muslims at the raids or battles they engaged in. Without condoning the raids, he tries to explain why they took place. He sees in them a means by which the unity of the Muslim community was strengthened, especially that between the *Muhājirūn* and the *Anṣār*. But above all, he asserts that they were necessary to improve the economic condition of the emigrants, who had no land to cultivate and were therefore dependent upon their hosts. [42] Gaudefroy-Desmombynes views the raid at Nakhla as a bandit's operation, attempted by emigrants who were without any resources. The battle of Badr which followed it subsequently became a battle between believers and unbelievers. He points out that Muḥammad ʿAbduh dismisses the presence of angels at the battles of Badr and Uḥud: in the opinion of the Egyptian writer, divine assistance took the form of spiritual comfort sent to the Prophet. Gaudefroy-Desmombynes, however, suggests that the Muslim community could not give up the idea that precise facts had been provided by Tradition.[43]

Gaudefroy-Desmombynes is even more scathing towards the Arab treatment of the Jews of the Banū Qurayẓa in 627, when Muḥammad sought to punish the allies of the Aws for their treachery. To save their lives and property, the Banū Qurayza were given a few choices (such as converting to Islam), but they found these unpalatable. Gaudefroy-Desmombynes feels that Muḥammad went beyond the limits, shedding blood unnecessarily (p. 152). He considers it to be an ugly episode in the story of Muḥammad, adding ironically that it was an act which was very beneficial to Allah's glory and his Prophet. He appears harsher in his judgement of this than Murray.[44]

Virgil Gheorghiu (1916-1992), the Romanian-born writer, took an entirely different view of the episode in *La Vie de Mahomet*, a work initially published in Romanian, then translated into French in 1962 (and reprinted many times afterwards). [45] He points out that Muḥammad absolutely refused to become involved in the episode. In accordance with the Constitution of Madīna, the latter is supreme arbiter, but he renounces his prerogatives and leaves the task to a man belonging to a clan allied to the Qurayẓa (Saʿd ibn Muʿādh), who was chosen by themselves. All the tribes of Madīna are bound by the Constitution to help one another when Madīna is attacked from outside. The Qurayẓa not only refused to be associated with the defence of their town against the armed enemy of ten thousand from Makka and Khaybar, but they also allied themselves with the enemy. The sentence against them was final. In his *Muhammad*, M. Lings maintains that Saʿd ibn Muʿādh's judgement against the Banū Qurayẓa coincided exactly with Jewish law as regards the treatment of a besieged city, even if it were innocent of treachery.[46]

Gaudefroy-Desmombynes points out that the farewell sermon of the Prophet in 632 (which he says has been preserved in Tradition), indicates that the jurists of Islam consider the ruling noted above to be the rule which all the faithful should follow, and he thinks it likely that it represents the rule of the ninth rather than the seventh century (p. 217). He admits, however, that the sermon has verisimilitude because in its essential aspects it is a commentary of the Qur'ān.[47] The most positive statement he makes on Muḥammad is that after the Makkan years of visions, ecstasies, preaching, and struggle, he engages during a period of ten years in Madīna in the splendid activity of a missionary and a head of state (p. 221).

In the early 1960s, the Roman Catholic Church, as is well-known, convened Vatican Council II, which at the end of its deliberations in 1965 included for the first time an official declaration on the Church's position regarding non-Christian religions such as Islam. This was followed by the Anglican Church statement on Islam at the Lambeth Conference in 1988. There does not seem to have been a similar statement from the Orthodox Churches, whose adherents form the second largest group of Christians in the world, after the Roman Catholics. Without an authoritative official statement from them, a glimpse of Orthodox Church thinking on Muḥammad in the same period can perhaps be found in *La Vie de Mahomet* (1962) by Monsignor Gheorghiu, although he might have claimed that he was writing in a personal capacity. Gheorghiu went into exile when Soviet troops entered Romania in 1944, and in 1948 he settled in France, where he published a number of literary works, including his best-selling novel *De la Vingt-Cinquième Heure à l'Heure Éternelle* in which he denounced Nazism and Communism. Ordained as a priest in 1963, he became the Patriarch of the Romanian Orthodox Church in France in 1971.

On the whole, Gheorghiu seems fairly well disposed towards Islam and the Prophet, even claiming (with some exaggeration) that no one in history pardoned his enemies more fully and more quickly than Muḥammad, and that he always ignored revenge (p. 253). Making an abundant use of Arab sources, especially Ibn Hishām, he does mention Christian influences on Muḥammad, but does not overstress these. He refers to Muḥammad's visit to Baḥīra during the Prophet's formative years. Gheorghiu has no doubt about Baḥīra's existence: the monk appears to him to be a Nonconformist Christian (judging by the discussion between him and the pagans), although in his discussion with the Arabs, Baḥīra strikes him as being a Manichean. If Baḥīra had been happy with Christian discipline, he argues, he would not have lived in a grotto.

Gheorghiu mentions Christian sects who believe that God creator of the universe speaks to all nations in their own language through prophets, such that He has not given the monopoly of his revelations and truth exclusively to Jews and Christians. Yet he is critical of Abū Ṭālib, who had asked that Muḥammad be defended against Jews: it is impossible that they would have killed him because, in his opinion, prophets are (and will be) stoned and killed by their own family and clan for such an act (pp. 54-55). Unlike Sprenger, the Romanian author Gheorghiu takes considerable pains to include 'Ā'isha in the list of early Muslims. His point is that she was born a Muslim because, according to al-Bukhārī, every child is born a monotheist, hence a Muslim. Moreover, she became a Muslim through her father (who was already a Muslim).

At times, however, the instinct of the novelist seems to get the better of Gheorghiu. Thus, in the episode of the angel Gabriel's visit to him, Muḥammad says that he drew close to Khadīja according to the *Sīra*. Whereas, in Gheorghiu's account, she undressed until she was completely uncovered, and then asked Muḥammad to do the same and take her into his arms. She apparently explained to him that the devil would not be slightly embarrassed at the sight of a naked woman who embraces her husband, while an angel, being discreet, would disappear, thereby confirming that he is an angel (p. 80). Gheorghiu's description of events does not match that found in Ibn Hishām (to whom he refers). Yet he feels free to criticise the episode wherein Addas, the Christian slave from Nineveh, is supposed to have fallen in adoration before Muḥammad. He has no doubt that this is a fictionalised account under the influence of the Alids, who were a body of men actively supporting the family or descendants of 'Alī and therefore hostile to the Thaqīfites who were clients of their opponents, the Umayyads (p. 146).

Commentators sometimes draw attention to the political and religious dimension of Muḥammad's marriages, and Gheorghiu has his unique way of looking at some of these. One is discussed in a short chapter entitled 'Un Mariage *In Absentia*'. It takes Gheorghiu a little time to explain what appears to us to be a baffling title, when he is simply referring to Muḥammad's marriage to Umm Ḥabība (about 627/628). At the beginning of the chapter the writer mentions Muḥammad's sole aim, since his return to Madīna, of establishing friendship with Makka, quoting in support the Qur'ān, *Sūra* 60, l. 7 which addresses the Prophet thus: ' Allah will perhaps establish friendship between you and your enemy'. What better way to achieve his aim in 628 than to marry Umm Ḥabība, daughter of Abū Sufyān, his principal enemy and commander of the Makkan forces?[48] Already a Muslim, Umm Ḥabība had been married to 'Ubaydullāh ibn Jaḥsh (who subsequently became a Christian) and migrated with him to Abyssinia during the persecution of Muslims in Makka. She belonged to the powerful clan of the Umayyads. So, by marrying her, Muḥammad becomes related to them, his enemies. As she was in Abyssinia, and as her father and family were likely to oppose the marriage, the Prophet dispatched an ambassador to Abyssinia to ask her hand and to bring her back to Madīna. Apparently fearing that she might be kidnapped, Muḥammad sends a letter to the Negus asking him to marry them *in absentia* and without delay. The idea of kidnapping, absent from the *Sīra*, might again stem from Gheorghiu's penchant for the Romanesque, not to mention the novel of adventure. The marriage was, however celebrated by the Negus in Abyssinia.[49]

At the same time as Gheorghiu's rather sympathetic treatment of Muḥammad, M. Watt made an attempt to protect the *Sīra* from the attacks of the Orientalists in his paper entitled 'The Materials Used by Ibn Isḥāq' (1962).[50] This paper is a complete rejection of the point-of-view held by Lammens and C. H. Becker, who had argued that the *Sīra* is not an independent historical source, but merely *Ḥadīth* material arranged in biographical (and possibly chronological) order: thus the *Sīra* is formed from *tafsīr* (Qur'ān commentary) and *Ḥadīth*. As Watt points out, the *Ḥadīth* collections did not exist at the time of Ibn Isḥāq. Watt does acknowledge that the *Sīra* of Ibn Isḥāq contains sections and small passages which belong to *tafsīr*. The commentaries deal with *Sūra*s 6, 8, 17, and 108. At the end of Ibn Isḥāq's account of the battle of Badr, there is a section on *Sūra* 8, ll. 7-13 that provides precise references to incidents in the battle. The longest commentary is found in the pages which develop the story of the Night Journey. These commentaries are, however, but a fraction of the whole work. Watt insists that in the Qur'ān Muḥammad is identified as a bearer of light and a mere mortal, whereas in the *Sīra* various supernatural powers are attributed to him, presumably in response to Christian criticisms that, unlike Christ, Muḥammad did not perform any miracles.[51]

Watt successfully refutes Blachère, who suggests that although Ibn Isḥāq had been able to hear informants belonging to the second Muslim generation, he had uncritically accommodated everything he heard from them, even those lively tales full of marvellous incidents and candid naiveté which were peddled, especially in Iraq, by storytellers and preachers. Their elaboration of Qur'ānic tales charmed the popular imagination, and Blachère noted that Ibn Isḥāq's compilation enjoyed a certain popularity among slightly cultured people (who did not have exacting standards) while it met with censure from serious critics who were shocked by the secular tone of some of the tales (p. 5). Watt takes an alternate view on the elaboration of Qur'ānic allusions in the *Sīra*. He suggests that these had to be developed into complete stories if the main ideas of the Qur'ān were to be impressed on the minds of simple people (p. 25). He points out that in the *maghāzī*, Ibn Isḥāq gave a list of the expeditions, aims, results, numbers, and names of participants, as well as approximate dates: although the information was usually given without any *isnād* (chain of authorities), and was distinct from anecdotes connected with the expeditions.[52] For the battles of Badr and Uḥud, for example, the *maghāzī* material includes an outline of the course of battle. The crucial point is that little of this material can be derived from the Qur'ān, as most expeditions are not mentioned in it. Watt, however, believes that there is little ground for doubting the truth of the main events of the *maghāzī* which have been passed over by Western scholars.[53]

A completely different approach was followed by Patricia Crone and Michael Cook in their sensational book *Hagarism: the making of the Islamic World* (1977). This was banned in Egypt, where an 'Open Letter to the Pope' asked the latter to put a stop to this kind of publication.[54] Crone and Cook aimed to renew modern studies on Islam and the Prophet, and they admit in their Preface to *Hagarism* (p. vii) that the account they have given of the origins of Islam is not one which any believing Muslim can accept. Yet they claim that this in no way belittles the historical role of Muḥammad, but that rather it presents him in a role quite different from that which he has taken on in the Islamic tradition. Referring to *Sūra* 46, l. 12, which describes the Qur'ān as confirming the book of Moses, they attempt to diminish the significance of Muḥammad's revelation by describing it as a 'mere' attestation of that of Moses (p. 17). Like Blachère, they argue that Muḥammad's life, as recorded in the *Sīra*, is mostly the invention of later generations of Muslim writers.

Going beyond Blachère, Crone and Cook state that Muḥammad was not the Prophet; rather, he was a kind of Messianic figure who led a movement to repossess Jerusalem. According to them, the Prophet was alive at the conquest of Palestine (638). Although they acknowledge that this view is irreconcilable with Islamic accounts of his career (they should also have acknowledged that it is irreconcilable with the verdict of world history, which records 632 as the year of Muḥammad's death), they point out that it finds independent confirmation in the historical traditions of the Jacobites, the Nestorians, and the Samaritans: unfortunately, however, there in nothing that can vouch for the impartiality (and hence the reliability) of the traditions of these peoples.

Banning a book has never been acceptable in the world of free speech, and there can be no objection to the starting-point of Crone and Cook that historians do not have access to written documents issuing from the first Muslim community.[55] If one needs contemporary (or near contemporary) documents, one has to rely on those issuing from Jews, Byzantine and Armenian Christians, and Zoroastrians. Crone and Cook thus mention the earliest account of the Prophet's career, given in an Armenian chronicle written in the 660s and ascribed to Bishop Sebeos. According to this, Muḥammad led a combined Arab-Jewish force, which took Jerusalem from the Eastern Roman Empire. He established a community of Arabs and Jews, and endowed both communities with a birthright to the Holy Land. Contrary to Muslim accounts, Jews, and Saracens (Arabs) were allies up to 640. However, in the *Doctrina Jacobi*, a Greek anti-Jewish tract written between 634 and 640, the Prophet of the Saracens appears as an impostor.[56] The above accounts date from the seventh century and issue from hostile Christian sources dealing with Islam and Muḥammad, so may be noted without being endorsed. They could be no more unbiased than accounts of Muḥammad found in later French epic poetry. Indeed, the further back in time one goes, the further one is from the balanced position of Vatican Council II, even if its statement on Islam is brief and does not purport to be a scholarly appraisal of it.

Perhaps more in keeping with the tradition of medieval debates against Islam and the Prophet, *Hagarism* presents the reader with some extreme conclusions. Because only some Qur'ānic verses (from *Sūra*s 33, l. 56, and 4, l. 171, proclaiming *inter alia* the greatness of God, that He and His angels bless the Prophet) are inscribed on the 'Dome of the Rock' (691) in Jerusalem where Muḥammad is reported as having left his footprint on the Night Journey, Crone and Cook assume that the Qur'ān could not have existed before. They fail to acknowledge that the whole Qur'ān could not possibly be inscribed on a building in Jerusalem just as the whole Bible could not be inscribed on a Church! Since the publication of *Hagarism*, old manuscripts of the Qur'ān in a Codex consisting of many fragments located at BNF, Paris, the National Library of Russia, the Vatican Library and the D.W. Khalili Collection of Islamic Art, London, and dating from the Umayyad period, have been found. A study of these based on spelling and palaeography has led F. Déroche, in his book *La transmission écrite du Coran dans les débuts de l'Islam* (2009), to conclude that the Qur'ānic text appeared in written form as early as the years 650-675, the only missing parts being the beginning and end of *Sūra* 2 .The existence of these manuscripts means that the theories of Crone and Cook, regarding the lateness of the written Qur'ān, are untenable.

With reference to *Sūra* 5, ll. 46-48, wherein the Gospel is sent to Jesus and the Qur'ān to Muḥammad, in both cases confirming previous scriptures, Crone and Cook assert that this was an outright rejection of the oral tradition in favour of a uniquely scriptural foundation for the sacred law in Islam (p. 30). This is a complete misreading of the Qur'ānic text. Every Muslim with a tincture of Islamic culture knows that the Prophet made some of his disciples learn the Qur'ān by heart in his lifetime, so that the text might be preserved. The result is that from early Islam onwards there have always been some Muslims who know the whole Qur'ān by heart. The tradition of memorising it is still alive to this day, and no one in the West has ever suggested that Muslims started learning the Qur'ān by heart centuries after the Prophet. A disadvantage no doubt in this emphasis on memorisation of the Qur'ān is that some, especially non-Arabic speaking Muslims, may know the text by rote, without fully knowing its meaning.

The approach to a reconstruction of Muḥammad's life that is based entirely on non-Muslim sources has been challenged by Montgomery Watt, in his paper entitled 'The Reliability of Ibn Isḥāq's Sources' (1983). He points out that the rejection by Crone and Cook of all the Muslim sources for the early history of Islam, and the postulation of an alternative first phase, have not been well received by scholarly opinion, which does not accept their main conclusions or assumptions. He finds this rejection to be contrary to sound historical methods (p. 34).[57] With regard to the *maghāzī* (expeditions), Watt draws attention to the groups against whom each expedition was directed, their leaders, the number of participants, and, in some cases, their names. He explains why the memory of the expeditions has been preserved: the Arabs took pride in the achievement of the Islamic community, and on a personal level individuals must have liked incidents resounding to the honour of their family or tribe. This material includes an outline for the battle of Badr, and Watt states that virtually none of the *maghāzī* material (which gives some basic information and a detailed outline of what happened in the main battles) can be derived from the Qur'ān, and that it is therefore impossible to discover from it the chronological order of main events. Admittedly, there is a section in the *Ṣaḥīḥ* of the Traditionist al-Bukhārī devoted to *maghāzī*, but the latter does not mention all the expeditions. Watt finds it incredible that a person or a group of persons living in the eighth century could have invented all these details and had them universally accepted. Most incredible of all according to him is that no traces have been left of the process of invention. He therefore concludes that the basic framework can be accepted in the main as reliable and that it is possible to give a coherent account of the sources for Muḥammad's biography and the subsequent history of Islam. In short, he finds nothing to justify the rejection of Ibn Isḥāq, al-Wāqidī and his predecessors.[58]

Hagarism was followed by *Meccan Trade and the Rise of Islam* which registers little or no change in attitude to Muslim sources. In this work, Patricia Crone claims that al-Wāqidī, Ibn Isḥāq, and others used selections from a common pool of storytellers' material.[59] She also claims that while al-Wāqidī did not plagiarise Ibn Isḥāq, he did not offer an independent version of the Prophet's life: if Wāqidī had offered a version different from Ibn Isḥāq's, then would it not have been used as an argument to show that both cannot be trusted? Apparently, therefore, the Arab historians agree on the historicity of events that never took place, such as 'Amr ibn al-'Āṣ's adventures at the Ethiopian court in 615. Like *Hagarism*, *Meccan Trade* argues that without correctives from outside the Islamic tradition (such as papyri, archaeology, and non-Muslim sources) there is little hope of reconstituting the original shapes of the early period (p. 230). The Muslim sources concerning the rise of Islam are still deemed to be of questionable historical value, yet when they fit Crone's thesis (that Makkans did not trade incense, spices, and luxury goods or that they stopped trading outside Makka before the rise of Islam), they seem to be met with approval.[60] Thus, Ibn al- Kalbī (d. 763) and even the Traditionist Ibn 'Abbās are described as eminent early authorities (p. 113). There can be no objection to the view that Muḥammad attacked the foundations of his state, his ancestral gods, and his own ancestors, and that he would have been outlawed or killed for this. More controversial is the stripping of Islam of any spiritual significance and the idea that 'Muḥammad's God endorsed a policy of conquest' (p. 244) with the material interests of Allah and tribesmen coinciding. In support of the idea is a reference to the eve of the battle of Qādisiyya (Iraq), the capital of the Sasanian Persians, when Arab soldiers were told (we are not informed by whom) that if they held out, the foreign country, including its women and children, would be theirs.[61] Crone adds that God could scarcely have been more explicit. It is, of course, rather unlikely that Muḥammad was responsible for words uttered on the occasion of a battle taking place in 636 some four years after his death. The final conclusion of the book is that the convergence of Muḥammad's message with tribal interests is so close that there is a case for the view that his programme might have succeeded at any point in Arabian history: this is a very speculative thesis.

To renew studies on the biography of the Prophet it is not necessary to discard all Muslim sources. Professor Gordon Newby proves this point admirably with regard to the *Sīra*.[62] While using these sources, he not only manages to satisfy the passion for reconstruction that inspires so many Orientalists, but he also adds to our knowledge of the *Sīra*. However, as M. Watt has pointed out, the title of Newby's book *The Making of the Last Prophet. A Reconstruction of the Earliest Biography of Muhammad* (1989) is misleading. Newby only reconstructs the first of three parts of the *Sīra* of Ibn Isḥāq, the *Kitāb al-Mubtada'*, 'The Book of Beginnings' or Genesis.[63] The *Kitāb al-Mubtada'*, the missing first part of Ibn Isḥāq's *Sīra*, was not copied widely enough to survive on its own. Newby thus fulfilled the hope expressed by A. Guillaume in the preface to his translation of Ibn Isḥāq's *Sīrat Rasūl Allah*, that a scholar would one day collect and publish the *Kitāb al-Mubtada'*. Quotations from the *Kitāb* which were preserved by Arab Muslim writers have indeed been collected and translated by Newby.

From the reconstruction of this text, it is possible to see how Ibn Isḥāq placed Muḥammad in the context of world history. Ibn Hishām, his editor, decided to omit the *Mubtada'* on the grounds that it does not mention the Apostle, and that the Qur'ān says nothing about some of the things mentioned by Ibn Isḥāq (Guillaume, *Life*, p. 691, n. 10). An additional reason may have been that by the 760s, the transmission of non-Islamic thought was forbidden to Muslims: the *Mubtada'*, which contained Jewish and Christian material, described all the Prophets mentioned in the Qur'ān but also some who were not mentioned there, and Ibn Hishām wanted to make Islam independent of this type of material. Although he concentrated on Muḥammad, it is not exact to say (as Newby does, p. 8), that Ibn Hishām raised him above other prophets, as this would have been against Qur'ānic teaching (which does not discriminate between them). In any case, the Islamic *umma* seems to have preferred his abridged version to Ibn Isḥāq's longer *Sīra*, although the *Mubtada'* was used by some Arab Muslim historians (especially Ṭabarī in his *Tārīkh*, where he adopted Ibn Isḥāq's perspective on world history).

Newby believes that by means of the reconstructed *Mubtada'* (written some time before 767), one can see an early attempt by Muslims to shape their self-perceptions and understandings in a world where they were outnumbered by Christians, Jews, and Zoroastrians. One can also see Ibn Isḥāq's vision of Islam as a universal religion, the Qur'ān as God's word, and Muḥammad as the last Prophet (p. 1). However, Newby considers that the *Sīra is* not a neutral, dispassionate piece of scholarship, rather a committed text in a polemical debate: it supports the claim that Islam is heir to Judaism and Christianity. It consists of three parts: (1) the *Mubtada'*, which deals with the creation of the world to the beginning of Arabian pre-Islamic history (2) the *Kitāb al-Mabath* (*The Book of Sending Forth* or *The Advent*), which outlines the Arabian events that culminate in the birth and early life of Muḥammad (this book therefore contains stories of Jews, Christians, and pagans foretelling the coming of Muḥammad) and (3) the *Kitāb al-Maghāzī*, which focuses on Muḥammad's life after 622, his career as prophet, community leader, and military commander. To Newby, the third part is the most biographical in the modern, Western sense, although the second part is also biographical. When the reconstructed first part is added to the rest of Ibn Isḥāq's surviving history, the work as a whole gives the impression of being based on an Old Testament/New Testament model. Among material used by Ibn Isḥāq in the *Mubtada'* and in the *Mabath* are the *isrā'iliyyāt*, stories derived from Jewish and Christian sources, which link *Sīra* and Qur'ān to previous Scripture. Ibn Hishām removed the *isrā'iliyyat* and the *Mubtada'* from Ibn Isḥāq's *Sīra* and focused on Muḥammad, starting with his genealogy.

Quotations from the *Mubtada'* have been preserved in al-Maqdisī's *Kitāb al-Bad' wa al-Tārīkh*, al-Baghdādī's *Tārīkh Baghdād*, al-Tha'labī's *Qiṣaṣ al-Anbiyā'*, but more extensively in Ṭabarī's *Tārīkh* (History) and *Tafsīr* (Qur'ān commentary). In Newby's reconstruction it has 28 sections: an introduction to the prophets (by Newby) is followed by the text of the *Mubtadā*, the entry on Moses being the longest, and containing many features which parallel Muḥammad's life. In the entry on al-Khiḍr, he is identified with Jeremiah. While this may have suited Ibn Ishāq's plan to fit the chief characters of his book into a Jewish-Christian scheme, there is no such identification of al-Khiḍr in the Qur'ān, (*Sūra* 18, ll. 65-82). One may therefore see the reason for Ibn Hishām's critical stance towards Ibn Isḥāq. Newby does not make it sufficiently clear that the description of the Prophets in the *Mubtada'* is not based on Jewish-Christian canonical material. An example is the text on Isaiah that announces the coming of Jesus and Muḥammad. According to Newby, this provides an Islamic claim to the prophetic line that had started with Judaism, had continued with Christianity, and was now to serve Islamic ends. This claim is not, however, backed by Old Testament material.

Innovation in Islamic studies is approached differently by G. R. Hawting in *The Idea of Idolatry and the Emergence of Islam* (1999). He takes up the line of enquiry followed by J. Wansbrough in *Qur'ānic Studies* (1977) and *The Sectarian Milieu* (1978) where Wansbrough suggested that the people addressed in the Qur'ān were not inhabitants of Arabia. Hawting even claims that he aims to treat Islam in the same way as the other monotheist religions, and to do justice to it as part of that tradition (p. 10). However, it is difficult to see how justice can be done to Islam when its Prophet's role is reduced almost to nothing, and the thesis of the book asserts that the pagan Arabs attacked in the Qur'ān were all monotheists. The Prophet and Islam itself would have no *raison d'être*. To Hawting, Muslim literature that provides details on the idolatry and polytheism of pre-Islamic Arabs is stereotypical and of questionable value (p. 5). Thus the polytheists and idolaters attacked in the Qur'ān were not real according to him, and the pagan and Arabian identity of the polytheists in the Qur'ān cannot be assumed.[64] Contrary to this, the Muslim view is that the Prophet destroyed real idols in Makka: moreover, these were also found outside Makka (in places such as Ṭā'if, the centre of the worship of the idol al-Lāt). Ṭā'if was captured after Makka.

The Idea of Idolatry argues that Islam is the product of intra-monotheist polemic, which follows a process similar to that of the emergence of the other main divisions of monotheism. Thus, instead of being a Christian heresy (as it had been described in the past), Islam must now be seen as having followed the same pattern as Judaism and Christianity in its development, which took centuries to be completed after its inception in the Arab conquests of the regions of the Fertile Crescent. While it is inevitable that non-Muslims would have made an impact on Muslim Arabs after the conquests (as Hindus did on Muslims in India), to argue that Islam was formed from the interaction of Arabs and conquered peoples is to minimise the role of Muḥammad. The notion of a gradual elaboration of Islam through internal debates seems highly anachronistic: this would turn Islam into a purely human creation (a point made against Judaism and Christianity also by the authors of anti-religious clandestine texts in the eighteenth century) (see Chapter 2).

Hawting points out that the 'Koranic *mushrikūn* (associators) are consistently identified as idolatrous and polytheistic Arab contemporaries of the Prophet and that *shirk* (association) is conflated with idolatry in the traditional material in Wāqidī's account in the *Maghāzī* of the Prophet's destruction of idols round the Ka'ba at the conquest of Mecca' (p. 68). So he claims that in seventh-century Arabian religious polemics, monotheists were being dubbed 'idolaters' by their opponents. The parallel he draws between such polemics and those in post-Reformation Europe is entirely unconvincing. It is clear that when Protestants accuse Catholics of being idolatrous, such as Elizabeth I calling Philip II of Spain the 'chief idolater' (p.74), they are using terms of abuse. Both Catholics and Protestants believe in a Holy Trinity after all, although the former make an extensive use of images in their worship. If one looks at late seventeenth-century France, for example, one sees the adversaries (Bossuet on the Roman Catholic side and Jurieu on the Protestant side) producing well-known texts to set out their case.[65] A similar situation, where two sides debate the issue through written texts, is unthinkable in Arabia at the time of Muḥammad. Moreover, Muslims have never believed that their Prophet, like a latter-day Quixote, was fighting imaginary opponents.[66]

Jonathan Berkey's *The Formation of Islam. Religion and Society in the Near East, 600-1800* (2003) supports the thesis of what may be called the 'school' of Cook and Crone.[67] Indeed, the author gratefully acknowledges his debt to Professor Crone as his mentor in various parts of the book. It is therefore not surprising that he should endorse the view put forward by Hawting, another member of the 'school': that it is quite difficult to know what 'Islam' was a century or so after the start of the Muslim era (since almost all the Muslim sources on the years spanning the Prophet's career were written a century and a half or more after the events they describe), and that they reflect more of what later Muslims wanted to remember than what is necessarily accurate (pp. 39-40).

Berkey goes one step further, by suggesting that the Prophet himself would not have understood the question (if it had been put to him) what it means to be a Muslim, and that his answer would have been quite different from that of a jurist in ninth-century Baghdad or a Sufi mystic in fifteenth- century Cairo (p. ix). Such a suggestion seems naïve: the Prophet might simply have referred his would-be questioner to verses of the Qur'ān about the nature of Islam or the qualities of a Muslim (such as l. 136 of *Sūra* 4). Adrian Reland certainly used such verses when attempting to define Islam in *De Religione Mohammedica Libri Duo* (1705). The definition of Islam or Muslim should never rely solely on the understanding of individual Muslims, however eminent they may be, when an authoritative text providing the definition (the Qur'ān) exists. Moreover, *ijmā'* or consensus of the community has to be taken into account. On the other hand, Berkey tries to make his thesis more acceptable by recognising that Islamic texts were based at least in part on material that circulated orally much earlier.

Berkey does his best to distance himself from the extreme views of some members of his school by showing some sympathy with those who adopt a less sceptical approach to Muslim sources. He accepts earlier, rather than later, dates for the writing down of the various sources, and the fact that surviving documentary evidence complements rather than undermines the narrative derived from literary sources (p. 60). In his view, such evidence should at least be accepted as a framework for inquiry. Thus he rejects the view that the Qur'ān was formed two hundred years or more after the Prophet's death (which he accepts as being in 632 A.D.). Berkey often uses Muslim sources, such as Ṭabarī and Mas'ūdī, in his attempt to show that Islamic civilization gained much from older cultures. (He could easily, and without any controversy, have pointed to the probable influence of Syrians, Palestinians, and Greeks on the custom of veiling among Arabs). He acknowledges Islam's roots in western Arabia (rather than accepting the conclusions of others who locate them in the Fertile Crescent), and accepts that without these roots Islam would not exist. Although he stresses Islam's slow emergence through its encounter with the older religious traditions of Egypt, Syria, and Iraq after the Arab conquests, he admits that the encounter drew on ideas implicit in the Prophet's message and career (p. 68).

Despite his Orientalist background, Berkey, unlike Hawting, somehow manages to enhance the role of the Prophet. He considers that the latter laid the groundwork for a radical approach that was based, through the Qur'ān, on a moral vision consisting of abstract notions of justice, judgement, and mercy. Many will share his view that the acceptance of the Prophet's claim to be the apostle of God formed the basis of identity in the new community, and that to participate in it required, from the beginning, a commitment to an identity resting on the Prophet's religious message rather than on tribal relations.

Berkey does not stop there, as he believes that the Prophet provided Muslims with the linguistic and intellectual means of connecting with Judaism, Christianity, and other religions. Although critical of the suggestions by earlier Western scholars that this borrowing of cultural knowledge by Muslim peoples was a one-way street (he finds the notion naïve), he still puts too much emphasis in his book on external factors leading to the formation of Islam. For instance, he claims that the Crusaders encouraged a renewed focus on Jerusalem, perhaps even stimulating the proliferation of treatises called *faḍā'il al-Quds* (that is, the 'excellences' of Jerusalem). This idea fits in with the point he makes that Islam, like any other abstraction, is a construct and must be reconstructed from the materials available (p. 184). To be faithful to his point, Berkey should have used material dating from much earlier than the time of the Crusades, namely *Sūra* 17, l. 1, which stresses the significance of Jerusalem for Muslims. He could also have remembered a *Ḥadīth* of the Prophet to the effect that 'Whoever wants to see a part of Paradise let him look at *Bayt al-Maqdis*' (that is, Jerusalem).

It seems that the question of change in attitude towards Muḥammad, which was such a major preoccupation for many writers in earlier times, has been superseded by a different issue over the last hundred years. Studies are increasingly concerned with the divergent views that Muslim tradition and Orientalists hold regarding accounts of his life: and there appears to be a wide gap between these two accounts. Many of the studies in the period from the beginning of the twentieth century onwards involve an incessant questioning of the reliability of Muslim sources by many French- and English-speaking writers. For this reason M. Watt and others who uphold the reliability of these sources, while still subjecting them to critical evaluation, stand out as isolated thinkers.

It is worth pointing out that the Roman Catholic priest Henri Lammens (whose hostility to Islam is beyond doubt) was not the only one to challenge the Muslim Traditionists and the biographers of the Prophet. Other French-speaking writers, including R. Blachère and M. Rodinson (who are not overly inimical to Islam) were equally sceptical about Muslim sources, even if they use a less vehement tone than some who belong to what the French might call the 'Anglo-Saxon' school. On the other hand, one is struck by the relatively moderate approach of the Orientalist J. Berkey, who shows some sensitivity to the point-of-view of Muslims (especially with regard to their oral tradition), and by the originality of G. Newby, who seems to accept Islamic sources but looks at them using a unique perspective.

In his Foreword to *Mohammed*, Rodinson states that his aim is to produce a readable book, mainly narrative, adding that it was a risky proceeding because:

> A biography of Mohammed limited only to absolutely unquestioned facts could amount to no more than a few dry pages. Yet it is possible to present a probable, and now and then a highly probable, picture of what that life must have been like; to do so, one must use some information from sources of whose veracity we have little proof (p. x).

He states that although he constantly referred to major sources (such as Ibn Isḥāq, Ṭabarī, Wāqidī, and Ibn Sa'd) and often immersed himself in the ocean of 'tradition', these are far from being certain historical fact. As for the authors of spurious *Aḥādīth*, delightful as they are to read, their dialogues and turns of phrase 'seem more redolent of literary talent than of historical authenticity' (p. xi). In short, he rejects both *Sīra* and *Ḥadīth*, believing that there is nothing of which we can say for certain that it incontestably dates back to the time of the Prophet.

A-L. de Prémare understood too well the sceptical approach of Rodinson, since he felt that the latter's views were tantamount to implying that any biography of the Prophet was worth no more than a novel that one hoped was historical (p. 30). Prémare, following Jacqueline Chabbi's article 'Histoire et Tradition Sacrée: la biographie impossible de Mahomet'[68], entitled the last section of the first chapter of his book 'Une « biographie impossible »?' He also used Harald Motzki to describe the historian's dilemma. Motzki had argued that on the one hand it is not possible to write a historical biography of the Prophet without being accused of using the sources critically, while on the other, when one uses the sources critically it is simply impossible to write a historical biography.[69] Prémare therefore concluded that a historical biography was perhaps impossible, given the nature of Islamic sources. Thus we are presented with some final questions: can no nucleus of factual information be retrieved from Islamic sources by sceptical Western historians? Should Arab-Muslim writers of the early centuries of Islam be assessed according to strictly European criteria of later times? While this first question appears to be unanswered, it could form the basis for further research. In the conclusion, the second question is addressed.

Notes

1. D. Venturino, 'Imposteur ou législateur? Le Mahomet des Lumières', p. 244.
2. The change must have taken place in the 1930s. Writing in this period, Tor Andrae referred to the old prejudices against the 'false prophet', an expression which was applied to Muḥammad in Christian polemics. See *Mahomet, sa vie et sa doctrine*, trans. J. Gaudefroy-Desmombynes (Paris, 1945), pp. 9, 172.
3. In his 'Introduction' to the *Annali dell'Islam* in 1905, L. Caetani came to the pessimistic conclusion that one could find almost nothing true about Muḥammad in the Tradition, and could discard as apocryphal all the Traditional material that is available. R. Blachère finds Caetani's thesis subversive. See *Le Problème de Mahomet* (Paris, 1952), p. 10. Discussion of French- and English-speaking Islamicists follows.
4. In *La Vie de Mahomet* (Paris, 1929), E. Dermenghem recognises the brilliance and ingenious approaches of Lammens's books, but thought they were most partial and distorted by his antipathy to Islam and its Prophet. The Marxist atheist M. Rodinson states that while the majority of Orientalists try to temper their judgements and to highlight Muḥammad's religious fervour, Lammens, with his extensive knowledge of the sources (but with deadly hatred also), still expresses bitter doubts about his sincerity. *Mohammed*, p.312. In 'Islam and Syria in the writings of Henri Lammens', in *Historians of the Middle East*, ed. B. Lewis and P. M. Holt (London, 1962), K. S. Salibi says that Lammens, obsessed by his partiality against Islam, accepted uncritically any material that disparaged the Prophet or favoured the Umayyads (p. 335). R. Irwin felt that Lammens scrutinised material favourable to the Prophet in order to discredit it if possible, and spoke of his hypercritical approach to the sources on early Islam. See *For Lust of Knowing. The Orientalists and their Enemies* (London, 2006), p. 202.
5. Published in *Bulletin de l'Institut Egyptien*, 4 , pp. 23-54.
6. Lammens perceives some ambivalence in Muḥammad's attitude towards the family of his unbelieving uncle Abū Lahab. He notes from the *Musnad* (VI, 432) of the Traditionist Aḥmad ibn Ḥanbal that Muḥammad exchanges affectionate words with Abū Lahab's daughter, saying that she is one of his and he is one of hers. That, according to Lammens, was to defend her against what he calls the earlier but malicious allusions contained in *Sūra* 111, ll. 1-5 against her parents. He points out that Muḥammad attended her wedding.
7. Lammens spots contradictions in the ages of Muḥammad's daughters. If their marriages took place before the revelation how, he wonders, does one account for the claim that Fāṭima was extremely young: before Muḥammad's 'call' none of the sisters could have been more than ten years old. Such contradictions, he argues, justify one's scepticism about the historical significance of the *Sīra* (p. 22).
8. There is a suggestion that Muḥammad preferred Zayd b. Ḥāritha to 'Alī. Lammens says that Muḥammad and Zayd shared everything: on occasion, Zayd would, without hesitation, let him have his wife Zaynab. While Muḥammad's marriage to Zaynab after her divorce from Zayd is documented, Lammens, who is so adept at using Arab sources elsewhere, produces no evidence for this scandalous story.

9. Fāṭima, Lammens points out, who had so little privilege in her lifetime, enjoyed a posthumous glory. He gives further details about this in his article on Fāṭima in the *Encyclopedia of Islam*. Under the influence of the Shī'ite tradition the Sunnīs too seem to have elevated the status of Fāṭima.
10. See Tariq Ramadan, *Muhammad. Vie du Prophète* (Paris, 2007), p. 61.
11. A.Sprenger, *The Life of Mohammad*, p. 99. From Ibn Hishām we learn that to a question from Muḥammad, Addās simply replied that he was a Christian from Nineveh. Lammens later says that Addās's intervention, whether authentic or not, seemed insufficient (he was, after all, a slave) and therefore al-Bukhārī and Ibn Hishām tried by all means to enhance the religious, learned status, and the importance of Waraqa at the beginning of the Revelation.
12. Lammens thinks that some of the criticisms made against Jews in the Qur'ān are due to an imperfect understanding of certain Jewish expressions on the part of Muḥammad (p. 82).
13. The unpopularity of the Jews was due, in Lammens's opinion, not to their religious beliefs but to their separatist tendencies (p. 87).
14. See M. Lecker, *The 'Constitution of Medina'. Muhammad's first legal document* (New Jersey, 2004). In *Muhammad at Medina* (1956), M. Watt notes that the inclusion of Jews in the *umma* is an important argument for dating the document before Badr, that the powers of Muḥammad under the Constitution are slight, but that the provision to refer disputes to him is connected with recognition of him as prophet (pp.226-229).
15. This last point has been taken up enthusiastically by more recent Orientalists such as Wansbrough, Crone, Hawting and Berkey.
16. This incident is recorded by Ibn Hishām. See *The Life of Muhammad*, translation A. Guillaume, p. 482.
17. Yet the Qur'ān tells Muslims that they have in Muḥammad 'a beautiful pattern (of conduct)'. *Sūra* 33, l. 21.
18. Dermenghem may be referring to M. 'Abduh's *Risālat al-Tawḥīd*; English trans. *The Theology of Unity* (London, 1966) and to Sayyid Ameer Ali's *Examinations of the life and teachings of Mohammed* (London, 1873) and *The Spirit of Islam* (London, 1891).
19. In *Meccan Trade and the Rise of Islam*, pp. 219-220, Patricia Crone states that the sources are familiar, with a large number of stories existing as variations on the theme of 'Muḥammad's encounter with representatives of non-Islamic religions who recognise him as a future Prophet'. All these sources, according to her, offer fictitious versions of an event (Muḥammad's meeting with Baḥīra) that never took place. She sought support for her view from an unlikely ally, M. Watt. In *Muhammad at Mecca* (pp. 33-4), Watt argued that stories such as Baḥīra's are almost certainly not true in the realistic sense of the secular historian, for they purport to describe facts to which we might reasonably have expected some reference at later periods of Muḥammad's life, but to which there is no such reference. She then adds that, to Watt, this is not a major problem because the event in question is miraculous and thus to be rejected anyway. What Watt actually says is that they (the stories) certainly express something of the significance of Muḥammad for believing Muslims and in that sense are true for them. One may legitimately wonder whether Watt and

Crone would, for example, reject the resurrection of Jesus as fictitious on the grounds that the canonical Gospels show variations in their account of the event.

20. Editors of critical editions of eighteenth-century texts, for example, would be taken by surprise to learn that when texts of authors show variants they should be rejected.
21. See M. Rodinson, *Mohammed*, p. 134.
22. In other ways, Andrae distances himself from Lammens. He admits that it is much easier to understand religious concepts that are new and foreign, such as those of the Indians and the Chinese, and that to understand Muḥammad one needs to have broad-minded views and a greater spiritual independence (p. 9).
23. This interpretation is actually to be found in Abū al-Fidā's *Life of Muhammad*, Chapter 7.
24. *Life of Muhammad*, trans. A. Guillaume, p. 287. In *Muhammad at Medina* (Oxford,1956), M. Watt remarked that the further clause (in some versions) regarding the bringing back of a report to Muḥammad was clearly a later addition intended to give the word *tarassala* the meaning of 'keep watch' instead of ' lay an ambush'. In this way all responsibility for bloodshed was removed from Muḥammad. The easiest solution with regard to Muḥammad's conduct is, according to him, to hold that after the event Muḥammad discovered that there was a far stronger feeling than he had anticipated. Watt thought that Muḥammad himself had few scruples regarding fighting in sacred months, but that he had to respect the scruples of an important section of his followers (p. 9).
25. M. Rodinson took a neutral position on this matter. He wondered whether Muḥammad had deliberately intended to flout the pagan convention of not fighting during the holy month of Rajab or whether perhaps his lieutenant had taken it upon himself to launch the attack. He found it difficult to conclude, yet he says that Muḥammad bowed to public reaction in Makka and refrained from taking his share of the booty until the revelation of *Sūra* 2, l.217 proclaimed: 'Fighting therein (in the prohibited month)/ Is a grave offence/ But graver is it/ In the sight of Allah/ To prevent access / To the path of Allah'. *Mohammed*, p. 163.
26. It is worth drawing attention to Blachère's tone, because it contrasts with that used by some English-speaking scholars.
27. In an appendix entitled 'The Quest of the Historical Muḥammad', in his book *Muhammad and the origins of Islam* (Albany, 1994), F. E. Peters notes that the Muslim community had a deep and careful interest in preserving revelation, but came to the history of its recipient too long after the memory of the events had faded to dim recollections over many generations: therefore history was embroidered rather than remembered. Islam chose carefully to preserve what it understood to be the words of God, rather than the deeds of Muḥammad and the history of the place in which he lived (p. 265). In other words, from this perspective, the Qur'ān is more authentic than the life of Muḥammad.
28. The irony here is that Blachère echoes views similar to those of Renan, whose thesis on the origins of Islam he set out to refute. In his article 'Mahomet et les Origines de l'Islamisme' (1851) Renan claims that under the influence of races

foreign to Arabia the story of Muḥammad has been complicated by miraculous circumstances, which bring it closer to the legendary myths of the high Orient: one of the foreign races he has in mind is the Persians: see my book *Perceptions of Islam in European Writings* (Leicester, 2004), p. 287.

29. The lengthy accounts of this Journey are to be found in the *Aḥādīth*, not in the Quran. *Sūra* 17 devotes only one verse to it at the beginning.
30. According to al-Balādhurī (d. 892) in *Futūḥ al-Buldān*, the Christian Bishr 'Abd al-Malik learnt the Arabic alphabet from the people of Ḥīra, and when he came to Makka on business he taught it to some Makkans at their request. Balādhurī mentions seven persons who could write it, including the future Caliphs 'Umar, 'Uthmān, and 'Alī. According to Ibn Khallikān (d. 1282) in *Wafayāt*, written Arabic appeared in the Hijaz shortly before the coming of Islam. Even if it existed long before, there is no doubt that only few Arab Muslims knew it. See A-L de Prémare, *Les Fondations de l'Islam. Entre ecriture et histoire* (Paris, 2002), pp. 270-271 and pp. 442-443.
31. Andrae thought that Muḥammad's military commanders were too preoccupied with other matters to think of writing an account of Muḥammad's life in Makka, where he had been subjected to humiliation. *Mahomet, sa Vie et sa Doctrine*, p. 22.
32. Blachère is not always in favour of the Qur'ān. He says, for example, that Muslim exegetes describe in the *Sīra* a legend relating to the early life of Muḥammad whereby two angels seized him, opened his belly, and cleansed his heart (See Guillaume, *Life of Muhammad*, p. 72). Then they find in the Qur'ān in the Makkan *Sūra* 94, ll. 1-3, a reference to 'opening thy breast'. He concludes that the legend has stopped being suspect, being validated by the Qur'ān and taking its place in the life of Muḥammad (p. 11).
33. The first volume was followed by *Muhammad at Medina* (1956). Some of the points in it, such as Jewish influences on Islam in Madīna, had already been made by Lammens.
34. In *Le Problème de Mahomet*, for example, Blachère says that Muslim apologists have exaggerated the obstacles faced by Muḥammad (p. 93), while Watt says that the persecution of Muslims was mild. *Muhammad at Mecca* (p. 119).
35. Watt's paper was published in 1983 as part of the proceedings of a conference entitled 'La Vie du Prophète Mahomet', held at Strasbourg in 1980.
36. In *The Life of Muhammad*, A. Guillaume states that Ibn Isḥāq's biography of the Prophet had no serious rival, but was preceded by several *maghāzī* books. Among his predecessors were a number of writers, especially Urwa who was regarded as the founder of Islamic history. Ibn Sa'd, Ṭabarī and Bukhārī were heavily indebted to the latter (p. xiv).
37. The text of this letter is reproduced in *Muhammad at Mecca*, pp. 100-101.
38. For a different view about 'Ā'isha being a Muslim, see V. Gheorghiu's remarks, below.
39. M. Gaudefroy-Desmombynes, *Mahomet* (Paris, 1957), p. 55. He should also have acknowledged his indebtedness to Lammens when he says that the Traditions seemed to have insisted on the friendship which bound Muḥammad to Zayd ibn Ḥāritha in order to minimise his friendship for 'Alī (p. 79).
40. In *La Vie de Mahomet* (Paris, 2002), V. Gheorghiu notes the prevalence of the opposite tendency among Jews. He says they were convinced that, thanks to

his monotheism and the respect he showed towards the Old Testament and Moses, Muḥammad would soon adopt Judaism (p. 171). On Gheorghiu, see below.

41. V. Gheorghiu read it differently. He described it as a liberal constitution inspired by the same spirit of tolerance as shown by Muḥammad's conduct towards Jews and by the spirit of the Qur'ān. He quotes in support *Sūras* 3, l. 64, 2, l. 62 and 5, l. 69. By following the Gospel, the Pentateuch and divine precepts, the Jews would enjoy all their wealth. Gheorghiu adds that Muḥammad shows unique tolerance in admitting to Paradise men from other religions, and that this tolerance has never been repeated in history by anyone. *Vie de Mahomet*, pp. 182-183. It is of course not Muḥammad who admits eligible people to Paradise but God.
42. Desmombynes later admits, however, that none of the Muslims who were victorious over the Jews at the oasis of Khaybar, situated some 150 kilometres to the north east of Madīna, were willing to settle there and cultivate the lands which had been left empty (p. 172).
43. Yusuf Ali, in his commentary on *Sūra* 8, l. 9, states that the number of angels (a thousand at Badr and five thousand at Uḥud) is probably not to be taken literally: it expresses, in his view, a strength at least equal to that of the enemy.
44. See Chapter 4, above.
45. Translated into French from Romanian by Livia Lamoure and published in 1962, 1970,1999, and 2002. I quote from the last edition, pp. 263-264.
46. Lings (p. 232) reproduces a quotation from Deuteronomy 20:12 which reads: 'When the Lord thy God hath delivered it unto thy hands, thou shalt smite therein with the edge of the sword: but the women, and the little ones, and the cattle, all that is in the city… shalt thou take unto thyself'.
47. In *Mohammed*, M. Rodinson draws attention to the part of the sermon where Muḥammad commends the proper treatment of slaves and preaches brotherhood among Muslims. He notes that according to one version, Muḥammad maintained that all men were equal before Allah, without distinction of social class or racial origin. In it there is a reference to the Madīnan *Sūra* 49, l. 13: 'the noblest of you all in the sight of Allah is the most devout' and Muḥammad's words that 'an Arab is superior to a non-Arab in nothing but devotion'. Rodinson thinks that this version may be suspected of reflecting the preoccupations of a later date, but that the Qur'ānic text it cites is authentic. This denunciation of racism placed in the Prophet's mouth, he adds, has provided a principle which has been more or less largely adhered to in Islamic practice (p. 286).
48. In 626-627 the Banū Musṭaliq, who were allies of Makka and Khaybar, were defeated by Muslim forces. Juwayriyah, daughter of their leader al-Ḥārith, asked Muḥammad to help her buy back her liberty. Instead, Muḥammad asked for her in marriage. Gheorghiu says that at first sight Muḥammad's gesture appears inexplicable, but it is one of those spontaneous acts of skill and courage that fill Muḥammad's biography (p. 250). By this marriage all the members of the clan of the Banū Musṭāliq became related to the Prophet and were freed. In gratitude all became Muslims and offered military alliance to Muḥammad. It was then that the Companions understood why he suddenly decided to marry a slave who could have been his without marriage (pp. 250-251).

49. Ibn Hishām simply says that Muḥammad married Umm Ḥabība after the death of her first husband. Gheorghiu also referred to Ibn Ḥabīb, author of *Muḥabbar*, and to al-Balādhurī, author of *Ansāb al-Ashrāf.* The circumstances of the marriage are much clearer in Martin Lings's biography of the Prophet, wherein Muḥammad did send a message to the Negus, asking him to stand proxy for himself and to ratify the marriage between him and the widow, if she were willing. She chose a kinsman to give her in marriage and he and the Negus solemnised the marriage in the presence of other Muslims. *Muhammad*, p. 259.
50. In *Historians of the Middle East*, ed. B. Lewis and P. M. Holt (London, 1962), pp. 23-34.
51. According to Peters, there is a consistent low-key attempt to demonstrate the authenticity of Muḥammad's calling by the introduction of miracles, a motif that was almost certainly a byproduct of the eighth-century biographers' contact with Jews, and particularly with Christians (p. 263).
52. Watt (p. 31) argues that scholars are not justified in rejecting all anecdotes found in the *Sira*. He quotes as an example the story of Quzman, a hero at the battle of Uḥud. He believes his story was tendentially shaped: for Muḥammad, showing foreknowledge at the start of the battle, said that Quzman (who was to commit suicide later when his pains became unbearable) belonged to the people of Hell since Islam is against suicide. Quzman's death was subsequently reported to the Prophet. See A. Guillaume, *Life of Muhammad*, p. 383. Watt says that the same anecdote is found in al-Bukhārī, without the man's name and that of the expedition in which he took part. In fact, the expedition was that of Khaybar, according to the Traditionist Abū Hurayra. See al-Bukhārī's *Ṣaḥīḥ,* ed. M. M. Khan, vol.8, p.393. The theological version of the *Ṣaḥīḥ* is, Watt argues, derived from the historical version.
53. Watt should have excluded Maxime Rodinson from his criticism, as in the 'Foreword' to his English version of the Prophet's biography Rodinson says that he profited greatly from the edition of the Arabic text of Wāqidī (*Maghāzī*) by Marsden Jones.
54. See H. Goddard, *Christians and Muslims: From double standards to mutual understanding* (London, 1995), p. 13.
55. Alfred–Louis de Prémare points out that compared with Hebrew and Christian history, the history of the origins of Islam is at a disadvantage from the start: for this period, hardly any epigraphic or archaeological data exist that could be used to compare with Islamic sources. Numerous epigraphic data preceding the seventh century relate to the Yemen, but there is nothing on the Hijaz (the cradle of Islam) or even central Arabia: only late literary Islamic material is available. See *Les Fondations de L'Islam. Entre écriture et histoire*, pp. 23-24. Prémare refused to move Islam away from its origins in Makka.
56. A-L de Prémare describes it as a work of Christian apologetics, written in Greek at Carthage, capital of the Byzantine province of Africa, and addressed to Jews. Muḥammad appears in it with sword in hand and in a chariot of war, promising Paradise to his followers (pp. 148-150).
57. In a paper entitled '*Maghāzī and Sīra* in early Islamic scholarship' included in the Strasbourg conference on 'La Vie du Prophète Mahomet', M. Hinds mentions nineteen transmitters and compilers of material regarding the time of

the Prophet who predeceased Ibn Isḥāq. These included 'Urwa ibn al-Zubayr (d. 714), al-Zuhrī (d. 742), and Mūsā ibn 'Uqba (d. 758). He points out that these early compilations were *maghāzī* (military campaigns) and not *Sīra* (p. 57). In his translation of Ibn Isḥāq, A. Guillaume lists some of these writers of *maghāzī* books. See *The Life of Muhammad*, pp. xiv-xvii.

58. A.-L. de Prémare, who has Orientalist sympathies, argues that Islamic sources are important, and that even if they are biased we need them to apprehend some of the elements that have presided over the rise and constitution of Islam (p. 30).
59. The reference here is to *quṣṣāṣ*, popular preachers or storytellers. They produced expanded versions of the Biblical and other stories briefly alluded to in the Qur'ān to satisfy the curiosity of the second or third generation of Muslims. Many of them used dubious sources, although Wahb ibn Munabbih (d. 732) was a serious scholar who knew Jewish and Christian scriptures and wrote a *Kitāb al-Mubtada'* about the lives of the prophets, which may have been used by Ibn Isḥāq when he gave his own version of the book in the original *Sīra* (now incomplete). See A. Guillaume, *The Life of Muhammad*, p. xv and W. M. Watt, *Muslim-Christian Encounters: Perceptions and Misperceptions* (London, 1991), pp. 37-38.
60. Crone's view of Makkan trade seems to be supported by F. E. Peters in his book *Muhammad and the origins of Islam*. He quotes *The Travels of Ali Bey in Morocco, Tripoli... Arabia* (1816). Ali Bey (Domingo Badia y Leyblich), who visited Makka in 1807, made the following remark about Makka: 'Nature has not designed it as a place of commerce, placed in the middle of an extremely barren desert', vol. 2, p. 101. Peters also quotes *Sūra* 14, l. 37 about Makka being 'in a valley without cultivation'.
61. In the *Tārīkh*, Ṭabarī gave the name of the commander who addressed, in the above-quoted terms, the Arab soldiers preparing for battle against the Persians. He was identified as Sa'd ibn Abī Waqqāṣ, who had been appointed by 'Umar ibn al-Khaṭṭab. Sa'd told the soldiers that if they renounced this world and aspired for the hereafter, God would give them both this world and the hereafter. Sa'd was of course not entitled to involve God in the proceedings. See also J. Berkey, *The Formation of Islam. Religion and Society in the Near East, 600-1800* (Cambridge, 2003), p. 73.
62. As John Burton did with regard to the Qur'ān: his conclusions on the text of the Qur'ān, based on a study of Muslim sources, are different from those of traditional Muslims and other Orientalists. Burton saw no need to argue that the Qur'ān was written from the ninth century onwards. In *The Collection of the Qur'ān* (Cambridge,1977), he attempts to show that Muḥammad himself edited and collected Qur'ān texts and that what the Islamic world believes to be a *muṣḥaf* 'Uthmān (the Qur'ānic text according to 'Uthmān's recension) is really a *muṣḥaf* Muḥammad (p. 239).
63. W. M. Watt, *Muslim-Christian Encounters*, pp. 38-40.
64. Following Yehuda Nevo and Judith Koren in their paper 'The Origins of the Muslim Descriptions of the Jahilihi Makkan Sanctuary' in *Journal of Near Eastern Studies*, 49 (1990), pp. 23-44, Hawting argues that the description of the sanctuary at Makka in the *jāhiliyya* (time of ignorance) is based on pagan cultic centres in the Negev desert (p. 40).

65. Bossuet wrote the *Histoire des variations* (1689) and P. Jurieu the *Histoire du Calvinisme et celle du papisme mises en parallèle* (1683). See my book *Images of Islam in Eighteenth-Century Writings* (London, 1996), pp. 65, 72, and 81.
66. Reviewing Hawting's book in *The Times Literary Supplement* of January 26, 2001, P. Crone concluded that never before had anyone shown with such clarity how little 'the so-called polytheism described in the Qur'ān has to do with the Arabian paganism described in the tradition'.
67. See my review of this in *Journal of Islamic Studies*, vol. 15, September 2004, pp. 364-367.
68. Published in *Arabica XLIII* (1996), pp. 189-205.
69. H. Motzki, ed. *The Biography of Muhammad. The Issue of the Sources* (Leiden, 2000), p. xiv.

Conclusion

Some of the fundamental questions raised in the Introduction were concerned with whether the perception and status of Muḥammad evolved in French and English writings over the centuries. The study has shown that they did, albeit slowly, and there are a number of reasons for this slow evolution. The publication of the Qur'ān in the vernacular by du Ryer in France (1647) and its translation in England soon after certainly fostered the development of interest in Islam and the Prophet. Although the English translation was less learned than du Ryer's, it had a wider readership than the latter.

After the retreat of the Ottomans from Vienna occurred in 1683, it would have been legitimate to expect a better appraisal of Muḥammad than before. A positive step was indeed taken by Bayle in his *Dictionnaire historique*. Although his polemical agenda against Roman Catholics is not in doubt, he disposed of a few myths concerning Muḥammad and attempted to concentrate on Muḥammad's historical character and to defend his moral code. Bayle was followed in 1707 by Veyssière de la Croze, who gave a fairly favourable assessment of Muḥammad in his 'Réflexions sur le Mahométisme'.

However, attempts to defend Muḥammad in Western writings must not be seen as gestures of intellectual generosity or openness, as they are often ideologically motivated. The eighteenth-century European deists, for example, liked to turn Muḥammad into an enlightened deist. Nevertheless, an ulterior motive need not always be attributed to Western writers, and some of them at least may be credited with the spirit of enquiry regarding civilizations other than the Greco-Roman, as Voltaire advocated in 1745 when he stated that the time had come for Oriental nations to be given consideration.

Maxime Rodinson surely exaggerates when he argues that the eighteenth century really looked upon the Muslim East and, by implication, upon Muḥammad, through fraternal and understanding eyes.[1] He had not taken into account clandestine literature and the works of writers such as Vertot, Gagnier, and the abbé de Saint-Pierre. Although the word 'impostor' was often applied to Muḥammad not only by the above-mentioned writers but also by Boulainviller, Voltaire, and Diderot (among others), Muḥammad was being increasingly viewed as a 'legislator' by writers such as Gibbon and Pastoret. Voltaire himself cannot be judged solely by *Mahomet*, since he elsewhere gave an informed account of Muḥammad's achievement.

For the character of Muḥammad, the passage from legislator to Prophet was to be a long and arduous process throughout French and English writings. In the post-Enlightenment period up to the end of the nineteenth century, Carlyle's writings excepted (and Carlyle was an isolated case), he did not manage to avoid the stigma of impostor with which he was lumbered. When Arabists Sprenger and Muir mixed with Muslims in India, even this did not increase their sympathy for the Prophet. It can be said that, on the whole, those nineteenth-century writers who were not committed Christians (such as Caussin de Perceval and Lamartine) were more generous towards Muḥammad, although they too still regarded him, explicitly or implicitly, as an impostor.

It would be a serious mistake to take Renan's controversial remarks on Arab science out of context and to be oversensitive to his criticism of Islam. He showed much admiration for the work of the Traditionist al-Bukhārī, who stressed many aspects of Muḥammad's life. Although his thesis that Muḥammad appeared 'in the full light of history' has been challenged from the twentieth century onwards, his point that miracles held greater sway over other religions than Islam remains valid. He may, however, have been unfair to the Persians in suggesting that the few miracles found in Muḥammad's biography were really due to their misrepresentations of the Prophet.

A shift in perspective on Muḥammad gradually became noticeable after the beginning of the twentieth century. Despite the hostility of Lammens and others, Muḥammad was finally recognised as Prophet sometime in the first half of the twentieth century. In 1965, Vatican Council II stressed in positive terms those aspects of his preaching that are acceptable to Christians. Nevertheless, it kept silence over

Muḥammad's claim to divine inspiration, and there still seems to be some ambivalence towards Islam and Muḥammad in Roman Catholic thinking.[2] It is by no accident that in the first four chapters of my book which attempts to reflect what was being noted about Muḥammad for nearly three hundred years (from the 1640s onwards) in French and English literature, the term 'Prophet' is rarely used by Western writers.

One of the conclusions to be drawn from this study is that in a history of Islam (which has spanned more than thirteen centuries) Muḥammad has been considered a Prophet only over the last seventy-five to hundred years in French and English writings. Montgomery Watt attempted to give a plausible explanation for this situation. In the chapter on Muḥammad in *The Cambridge History of Islam* (1977), he argues that the occidental reader faces grave difficulties in attaining a balanced understanding of his historical role, the most serious being the dominant conception that religion is a private matter.[3] He goes on to say that Muḥammad was great, and that his influence was important in the religious, intellectual, economic, social, and political spheres. What is surprising is that he finds it impossible for any occidental to distinguish within Muḥammad's achievement between what is religious and what is non-religious (or secular), as there is no particular reason for the occidental reader to make these distinctions. Certainly the mind of any such reader may not be a *tabula rasa*: many Western readers will have a set of religious beliefs (or no beliefs at all), or a cultural background that is not predisposed to give recognition to what is perceived as remote from their cultural experience. However, as Watt points out, some prejudices are deep-rooted in Western readers (one of them, for example, is that Muḥammad was the incarnation of evil). Separating the facts from the myths abounding in his early life may also account for Muḥammad's slow progress towards recognition as Prophet.

The great paradox to be noted is that no sooner had Muḥammad acquired the status of Prophet than some influential Orientalists renewed, with increased vigour, their attempt to undermine Muslim accounts of his life. A Western account of Muḥammad, however, can hardly be deemed to be more historical than a Muslim account when it replaces the latter by books whose soundness is questionable (such as the Christian apologetic tract, the *Doctrina Jacobi*). In this context, collaboration, or partnership between Muslim scholars and Orientalists becomes virtually impossible. Yet a partnership could be fairly fruitful under certain circumstances: less extreme non-Muslim scholars can benefit from the insights offered by Muslim scholars living within Islam. In Chapter 5, for example, it was shown that Muḥammad's teaching on the unity of God was within reach of ordinary Muslims (in their daily prayers) from the very beginning of his mission.

Muslims, on the other hand, can surely benefit from the commitment and meticulousness of Western scholarship at its best. Although Montgomery Watt shared the doubts of Orientalists about the existence of Baḥīra, for example, and his thesis about Makkan trade may be erroneous, his consistent defence of the reliability of Ibn Isḥāq's sources for the *Life of Muhammad* commands admiration. Watt provided a rather balanced and fair assessment of the Prophet in his numerous works on him. There is a great need for more Western scholars of his integrity to come forward. It is of course understandable that a Western intellectual might feel disoriented on reading Ibn Isḥāq's *Sīra*, which is in part autobiographical (as it includes Muḥammad's infrequent interventions in the narrative). It also contains autobiographical material from persons other than the Prophet, and quotes the testimony of his wives on his illness and death. Strange to a Western reader is the fact that it is interspersed with fairly long extracts of poetry.[4] This is a genre in its own right, and cannot be anachronistically assessed according to the later conventions of European biography (a genre still not recognised or firmly defined at the start of the period under study). Such models in biographical writing as they exist among Arab predecessors of Ibn Isḥāq/Ibn Hishām may not be sufficient to guide the reader.

If full partnership with Orientalists is impossible to achieve in view of their entrenched position, their work cannot be ignored, as it often stimulates debate and widens the perspective of studies on this subject. In the past there have been proper responses to Renan, including those from Muslim writers: a similar scholarly response is essential from the latter today to modern critics of Islam and Muḥammad. The slogan 'burn the book or ban the book' is no substitute for a proper response ('burning the book', incidentally, is not unique to the Muslim world. In the past, this deplorable practice was known in Europe. There is, for example, the notorious case of Volaire's *Lettres philosohiques* which was intended to be burnt publicly.) Part of the confusion created by some modern Orientalists in their evaluation of Muḥammad stems from their attempts to turn Islam into a religion based entirely on written texts. Dismissing the oral tradition in Islam constitutes a profound error on their part.[5] Fortunately, scholars such as Gaudefroy-Desmombynes, R. Blachère, and J. Berkey adopt a more moderate stance on this matter, as they recognise its importance in Islam. Hence, it is natural that Muslims who cannot collaborate fully with Orientalists should at least establish a distinction between the moderates among them and their more extreme colleagues.

One of the consequences of casting doubt on the worth of Muslim accounts of the Prophet, or even rejecting them completely, has been to leave the door wide open for speculation or reconstruction by Orientalists. Muslims do not find it acceptable, for example, that Armenian, Byzantine, Greek, and Syriac accounts of Muḥammad should be given greater weighting than Muslim accounts and therefore supersede the latter. On the other hand, when Gordon Newby painstakingly reconstructs what may have been the original version of the *Sīra* of Ibn Isḥāq on the basis of quotes from reliable Muslim writers such as Tabari, he cannot be dismissed outright. The status of Muḥammad in the reconstructed biography is not diminished by any means, although what one reads is different from the edited and shortened version of Ibn Isḥāq's *Life of Muhammad* by Ibn Hishām. The latter, it should be pointed out, does not claim to have been divinely inspired in its editing. Even if the reconstructed biography is closer to the Judeo-Christian tradition in style,[6] it must be recognised that for once a reconstruction has been based on Arab-Muslim sources. The Muslim community has perfectly good reasons to prefer the shorter version of Ibn Hishām. This, however, is no obstacle to Newby's reconstruction being viewed, perhaps, as the acceptable face of Orientalism.

Notes

1. 'The Western image and Western Studies of Islam' in *The Legacy of Islam*, eds. J. Schacht and E. C. Bosworth (Oxford, 1979), p. 40.
2. Pope John Paul II who has some favourable comments to make on Islam in his book *Crossing the Threshold of Hope* (1994) entitles a chapter 'Muḥammad' when he means Islam, with another chapter, for example, entitled 'Judaism'.
3. *The Cambridge History of Islam*, eds. P. M. Holt, Ann K. S. Lambton and Bernard Lewis, vol. 1 A, p. 30.
4. See A. Cheddadi, *Les Arabes et l'appropriation de l'histoire*, pp. 253, 255-256.

5. In his *In Search of Muhammad*, C. Bennett points out that there is some evidence that Muḥammad encouraged his closest Companions to memorise his sayings, and that they realised the importance of preserving these during the Prophet's own lifetime (p. 25). More importantly perhaps, Bennett should have stressed that Muḥammad made them memorise the Qur'ān.
6. This presents no problem to A. Cheddadi and to myself. The Moroccan scholar points out that Ibn Isḥāq's *Sīra* uses the framework, and certain other aspects of a universal Christian chronicle, although it reveals divergences and distortions from this. See *Les Arabes et l'appropriation de l'histoire*, pp. 228, 229, and 258.

Bibliography

Manuscript sources

LONDON. British Library.

Sloane 1709 History of the Saracens and of Mahomet by Henry Stubbe.
Harleian 6189 The rise and progress of Mahometanism.
Sloane 2039 Manuscriptum De Tribus Impostoribus.
Stowe 47 The famous book entitled De Tribus Impostoribus.

Additional manuscripts

12064 Le fameux livre des trois imposteurs.

PARIS Bibliothèque Mazarine.

1194 Dissertation sur le messie.
1195 Lettre d'un Médecin Arabe à un fameux professeur de l'Université de Halle. Traité des miracles.
1946 Histoire de Mahomet et de ses premiers successeurs. Tome 1.
1947 Histoire de Mahomet et de ses premiers successeurs. Tome 2.
1948 Autre exemplaire complet.
1949 Histoire de Mahomet. Autre exemplaire du Ier livre.
PARIS Biblliothèque Nationale de France. Fonds Français.
24885 Doutes sur les religions.
24887 Dissertations théologiques sur… les trois fameux imposteurs.
9107 Recherches curieuses de philosophie.
14928 Divinité de Jésus-Christ détruite.

PARIS Bibliothèque Nationale de France. Nouvelles acquisitions françaises.

2778 Voltaire. Du Fanatisme.

ROUEN Bibliothèque municipale (Coquebert de Montbret collection).

1124 Recherches de quelques particularitez de la vie du prophète Mahomet.

1554 Le Nazaréen ou le christianisme des Juifs… et des Mahométans.
1580 Parallèle entre Mahomet et Moyse le grand libérateur des Juifs.

Printed sources

Abbadie, J., *Traité de la vérité de la religion Chrétienne.* 2 vols. (Rotterdam, 1684).

———, *Traité de la divinité de notre seigneur Jésus Christ* (Rotterdam, 1690).

Abū al-Fidā, I., *Al-Mukhtaṣar fī akhbār al-bashar*, extracts ed. by J.Gagnier in Arabic and tr. into Latin as *De vita et rebus gestis Mohammedis* (Oxford, 1723).

———, Arabic and Latin version of same extracts ed. as *Annales muslemici* by J. J. Reiske (Leipzig, 1754).

———, 2nd edition, I. G. Adler (ed.), 1789-94, 5 vols.

———, Extracts tr. by W. M. Murray as *Life of Mohammed* (London, 1833).

———, Trans. into French by N. Desvergers as *Vie du Prophète Mahomet* (Paris, 1837).

Almansi, G., "L'esploratore Turco" e la genesi del romanzo epistolare pseudo-Orientale', *Studi secenteschi*, 7, 35-65.

Andrae, T., (tr. J. Gaudefroy-Desmombynes), *Mahomet, sa vie et sa doctrine* (Paris, 1945).

Anon, *Le Traité des trois imposteurs*, Pierre Rétat (ed.) (St-Etienne, 1973).

Anon, *Le Traité des trois imposteurs et l'Esprit de Spinoza*, Françoise Charles-Daubert (ed.) (Oxford, 1999).

Arkoun, M., *Ouvertures sur l'Islam* (Paris, 1989).

Al-Azmeh, A., *Ibn Khaldun in modern scholarship* (London. 1981).

———, *Ibn Khaldun* (London, 1990).

———, *Islams and modernities* (London, 1993).

Badir, M. G., *Voltaire et l'Islam, Studies on Voltaire and the Eighteenth Century*, vol.125, Th. Besterman (ed.) (Banbury, 1974).

Barclay, R., *Apology for the true Christian divinity* (London, 1678).

Barthélemy St-Hilaire, J., *Mahomet et le Coran* (Paris, 1865).

Bastiaensen, M., *L'Orient de l'incroyant* (Brusels, 1984).

Baudet, H., *Paradise on earth. Some thoughts on European images of non-European man*, trans. from Dutch by Elisabeth Wentholt (New- Haven, London, 1965).

Al-Bayḍāwī, *Anwār al-Tanzīl.* The original of 1330, published in Egypt. Reprint (Beirut), in 2 vols. No date given.

Bayle, P., *Dictionnaire historique et critique* (Rotterdam, 1697).

Bennett, C., *In Search of Muhammad* (London, 1998).

Berkey, J., *The Formation of Islam* (Cambridge, 2003).

Blachère, R., *Le Coran, traduction selon un essai de reclassement des sourates* (Paris, 1947-1951), 3 vols.

———, *Le problème de Mahomet* (Paris, 1952).

Bonnerot, O., 'Le Prophète et la guerre: Mahomet dans la pensée des Lumières', in *La Bataille, l'armée, la gloire*, Actes du colloque de Clermont-Ferrand, 1983, Clermont, 1985, pp. 69-80.

Bossuet, J. B., *Discours sur l'histoire universelle* (Paris, 1681).

———, *Histoire des variations* (Paris, 1689).

Boulainviller, H., *Vie de Mahomed* (Paris, 1730).

———, Trans. Diego Venturino as *Vita de Mahometto* (Palermo, 1992).

Brucker, J., *Historia critica philosophiae* (London, 1791).

Bruyn, C. de., *Voyages par la Moscovie en Perse*, 2 vols. (Amsterdam, 1718).

Buaben, J., *Image of the Prophet Muhammad in the West* (Leicester, 1996).

Al-Bukhārī, *Ṣaḥīḥ*, M. M. Khan (ed. and trans.) (Madina, 1971), 9 vols.

———, Krehl, Ludovic (ed.) as *Le Recueil des traditions Mahométanes* (Leiden, 1862-68), 3 vols. Th. W. Juynboll (ed.), vol.4 (Leiden, 1908).

Burton, *The Collection of the Qur'an* (Cambridge, 1977).

Caetani, L., *Annali dell'Islam* (Milan, 1905-26), 10 vols.

Carlyle, T., *On heroes, hero worship and the heroic in history* (London, 1841).

Castel de St Pierre, abbé, *Discours contre le mahométisme* in *Ouvrages de politique* (Paris, 1733).

Caussin de Perceval, A.P., *Essai sur l'histoire des Arabes* (Paris, 1847), 3 vols.

Chardin, J., *Voyages en Perse*.10 vols. (Rouen, 1723).

Cheddadi, A., *Le livre des exemples* (Paris, 2002).

———, *Les Arabes et l'appropriation de l'histoire* (Paris, 2004).

Chinon, G., *Relations nouvelles du Levant* (Lyon, 1671).

Coles, P., *The Ottoman impact on Europe* (London, 1968).

Concile oecuménique Vatican II: Documents conciliaires (Paris, 1965).

Cook, M., *Commanding Right and forbidding Wrong in Islamic Thought* (Cambridge, 2000).

Crone, P. and Cook, M., *Hagarism* (Cambridge, 1977).

Crone, P., *Meccan Trade and the Rise of Islam* (Oxford, 1987).

Dacier, Bon J., *Tableau historique de l'érudition française* (Paris, 1810).

Dalrymple, W., *The White Mughals. Love and betrayal in eighteenth-century India* (London, 2002).

Daniel, N., *Islam and the West*, revised edition (Oxford, 1993).

Deloffre, F. and Menemencioglu, M. (eds.), *Difficultés sur la religion proposées au Père Malebranche* (Oxford, 1983).

Delaporte, H., *Vie de Mahomet* (Paris, 1874).

Dermenghem, E., *Vie de Mahomet* (Paris, 1929).

Déroche, F., *La transmission écrite du Coran dans les débuts de l'Islam. Le codex Parisino-Petropolitanus* (Leiden, 2009)

Desvergers, N., *Arabie* (Paris, 1847).

Dew, N., *Orientalism in Louis XIV's France* (Oxford, 2009).

Diderot, D. G. Roth and J. Varloot (eds.), *Correspondance* (Paris, 1953-70), 16 vols.

———, H. Dieckmann, J., Varloot and J. Proust (eds.), *Oeuvres complètes* (Paris,1975)

Djait, H., *L'Europe et l'Islam* (Paris, 1978).

Du Ryer, A., *L'Alcoran de Mahomet* (Paris, 1647).

Ekhtiar, S., '*Hayy ibn Yaqzan*; the eighteenth-century reception of an oriental self-taught philosopher', in *Studies* (Oxford, 1992), vol. 302, pp. 217-245.

Gagnier, J., *La vie de Mahomet* (Amsterdam, 1732), 2 vols.

Galland, A., Trans. of *Alf laila wa laila* as *Les Mille et une Nuits*, J. Gaulmier (ed.) (Paris, 1965).

Garcin de Tassy, J.-H., *Mémoire sur les particularités de la religion musulmane dans l'Inde* (Paris, 1831).

Gaudefroy-Desmombynes, M., *Mahomet* (Paris, 1957).

Gheorghiu, V., *La Vie de* Mahomet, trans.Livia Lamoure (Mayenne, 2002).

Gibb, H., *Modern Trends in Islam* (Chicago, 1947).

Gibbon, E., *History of the decline and fall of the Roman Empire.* J. B. Bury (ed.) (London, 1898-1923).

Grotius, H., *De veritate religionis Christianae*, trans. S. Patrick (London, 1680).

Gunny, A., *Images of Islam in Eighteenth-Century Writings* (London, 1996).

———, 'Le *Traité des trois imposteurs* et ses origines arabes', in *Dix-Huitième Siècle*, 28 (1996), pp. 169-174.

———, *Perceptions of Islam in European Writings* (Leicester, 2004).

Hadidi, D., *Voltaire et l'Islam* (Paris, 1974).

Hamilton, A. and Richard, F., *André du Ryer and Oriental Studies in Seventeenth-Century France* (Oxford, 2004).

Hawting, G. R., *The Idea of idolatry and the emergence of Islam* (Cambridge, 1999).

Herbelot, B. D'., *Bibliothèque orientale* (Paris,1697, The Hague, 1777).

Holt, P. M. and Lewis, B. (eds.), 'The treatment of Arab history by Prideaux, Ockley and Sale.' in *Historians of the Middle East* (London,1962).

Hopwood, D., *Sexual encounters in the Middle East* (Reading, 1999).

Hourani, A., *A History of the Arab Peoples* (London,1991).

———, *Islam in European Thought* (Cambridge, 1991).

Ibn Isḥāq, *Sīrat Rasūl Allāh* (*Life of Muhammad*) Trans. A. Guillaume (Oxford, 1955).

Ibn Khallikān, *Wafayāt Al-A'yān* trans. M. De Slane as *Biographical Dictionary* (Paris, 1842).

Ibn Ṭufayl, *Ḥayy ibn Yaqẓān*, trans. Edward Pococke (the Younger) as *Philosophus Autodidactus* (London, 1671).

———, trans. Keith, George (London, 1674).

———, *The Improvement of Human Reason*, trans. Simon Ockley (London, 1708).

Ibn Taymiyya, *Le Statut des moines*, text, ed., and trans. by Nasreddin Lebatelier (Beirut, 1997).

Irwin, R., *For Lust of Knowing. The Orientalists and their enemies* (London, 2006).

Jurieu, P., *Histoire du Calvinisme et celle du papisme mises en parallèle* (Rotterdam, 1683).

Labrosse, J., *Gazophylacium linguae Persarum* (*Souvenirs de la Perse safavide*, trans. M. Bastiaensen, originally published 1664-78 (Brussels, 1985).

Lamartine, A de, *La Vie de Mahomet*, vol. 1 of *Histoire de la Turquie*, ed. Ali Kurhan (Paris, 2005).

Lammens, H., *Fatima et les filles de Mahomet* (Rome, 1912).

———, *L'Arabie occidentale avant l'Hégire* (Beirut, 1928).

Lane, E., *Selections from the* Kuran (London, 1843).

Lewis, B., *Islam and the West* (New York, 1993).

———, *The Muslim Discovery of Europe* (London, 1982).

Lings, M., *Muhammad: His life based on the earliest sources* (London, 1983).

Lopez-Morillas, C., 'Yça of Segovia and the Qur'ān among the Mudejars and Moriscos', in *Journal of Islamic Studies*,10, 3 (1999), pp. 277-292

El-Makin, G., *Tārīkh*, trans. T. Erpenius as *Historica saracenica* (Leiden,1625) and P. Vattier as *Histoire mahométane* (Paris, 1657).

McBurney, W. H. E., 'The authorship of *The Turkish Spy*', in *PMLA*, 72, 915-35.

Marana, G. P., *L'espion dans les cours des princes Chrétiens* (Paris, 1696-97), 6 vols.

———, *Letters writ by a Turkish Spy* (London, 1970).

———, '*L'esploratore turco di Govanni Paolo Marana. Letters 1-63*', in *Studi secenteschi*, 9 (1968) to 14 (1973) G. Almansi, D. A. Warren (eds.).

Marcolini, P., 'Le de tribus impostoribus et les origines arabes de l'athéisme européen', in *Les Cahiers de l'ATP*, October 2003, pp.1-10.

Massignon, L., 'La légende "De tribus impostoribus" et ses origines islamiques' in *Opera Minora* (Beirut, 1963), i: 82-85.

Matar, N., *Islam in Britain 1558-1685* (Cambridge, 1998).

———, *Turks, Moors and Englishmen in the Age of Discovery* (New York, 1999).

———, *Britain and Barbary 1589-1689* (Gainesville, Fl. 2005).

———, *Europe through Arab eyes 1578-1727* (New York, 2008)

Meslier, J., *Œuvres*, R. Desné, J. Deprun, and A. Soboul, (eds.) (Paris, 1970), 3vols.

Mignot, V., *Histoire de l'Empire ottoman depuis son origine jusqu'à la paix de Belgrade en 1740* (Paris, 1771).

Montesquieu, C. de Secondat, *Lettres Persanes* (1721), P. Vernière (ed.) (Paris, 1965).

More, H., *An Explanation of the grand mystery of God's Law* (London, 1660).

Moréri, L., *Le grand dictionnaire historique* (Paris, 1683).

Morgan, J., *Mahometism fully explained* (London, 1723).

Muir, W. *Life of Mahomet* (London, 1858), 4 vols.

Nau, M., *L'état présent de la religion mahométane* (Paris, 1684).

Newby, G., *The Making of the last Prophet. A reconstruction of the earliest biography of Muhammad* (Columbia, 1989).

Nöldeke, T., *Geschichte des Quorans* (Leipzig, 1860).

Pascal, B., *Pensées*, Ch. M. des Granges (ed.) (Paris, 1664).

Pastoret, Marquis E., *Zoroastre, Confucius et Mahomet comparés comme sectaires, législateurs et moralistes* (Paris, 1787).

Peters, F. E., *Muhammad and the Origins of Islam* (Albany, 1994).

Pétis de la Croix, F., *Les mille et un jours* (Paris, 1710).

Pococke, E., *Specimen historiae Arabum* (Oxford, 1650).

Pomeau, R., *La Religion de Voltaire* (Paris, 1956, 1974).

———, *Voltaire en son temps* (Oxford, Paris, 1995).

Prémare, A-L de., *Les Fondations de l'Islam* (Paris, 2002).

Prideaux, H., *The true nature of imposture revealed in the life of the impostor Mohammad* (London, 1697).

Qur'ān, trans. André du Ryer (Paris, 1647).

———, trans. Alexander Ross (London,1649)

———, trans. George Sale (London, 1734).

———, trans. Claude Savary (Paris, 1783).

———, trans. Albin Kazimirski (Paris, 1840)

———, trans. Yusuf Ali with text and commentary (New York, 1946), 2 vols.

———, trans. A.J.Arberry (London, 1955).

———, trans. Si Hamza Boubakeur, with text and commentary (Paris, 1978, 1985).

Ramadan, T. *To be a European Muslim* (Leicester, 1999).

———, *Islam, the West and the Challenges of Modernity* (Leicester, 2001).

———, *Muhammad. Vie du Prophète* (Paris, 2007).

Reeves, M., *Muhammad in Europe. A Thousand Years of Myth-Making* (Reading, 2000).

Renan, E., *Oeuvres complètes*, ed. Henriette Psichari (Paris, 1947), 10 vols.

Rodinson, M., *Mahomet* (Paris, 1961). English tr. *Mohammed* (London, 1971).

———, 'The Western image and Western studies of Islam' in *The legacy of Islam*, J. Schacht and C. E. Bosworth (eds.) (Oxford, 1974), p. 62.

Rousseou, G. S. and Porter, R. (eds.) *Exoticism in the Enlightenment* (Manchester, 1990).

Rousseau, J.-J., *Oeuvres complètes* (B. Gagnebin and M. Raymond (eds.) Paris.1964, vols. 3,4, and 5.

———, *Essai sur l'origine des langues,* C.Porset (ed.) (Bordeaux, 1968).

———, *La Correspondance complète de Jean-Jacques Rousseau* R. A. Leigh (ed.) (Oxford, 1965-89), 52 vols.

Rushdie, S., *The Satanic Verses* (London, 1988).

Ruthven, M., *Islam in the World* (Harmondsworth, 2000).

Said, E., *Orientalism*. (London, 1978).

Schoeler, G., *The genesis of literature in Islam. From the aural to the read* (Edinburgh, 2009).

Sédillot, J. A., *Histoire générale des Arabes* (Paris, 1854, 1877).

Sprenger, A., *The Life of Mohammad from original sources* (Allahabad, 1851).

Struys, J., *Voyages en Moscovie, en Perse aux Indes* (Amsterdam, 1681).

Al-Ṭabarī, *Tafsīr* (Beirut, 1978), 10 vols.

———, *Tārīkh al-rusul wa-l-mulūk*. M. de Goeje (ed.) (Leiden, 1885-1889).

———, *La Chronique*, trans. H. Zotenberg (Paris, 1867-1874, 2001), 2 vols.

Thomson, A., 'Joseph Morgan et le monde Islamique', in *Dix-Huitième Siècle*, no.27 (1995), pp. 349-363.

Topliss, Pat., *The Rhetoric of Pascal* (Leicester, 1966).

Venturino, D., *Vita di Mahometto* (Palermo, 1992).

———, *Le ragioni della tradizione. Nobilita e mondo modernonel pensiero di H. de Boulainvilliers* (Florence, 1992).

Venturino, D., 'Un Prophète Philosophe ? Une *Vie de Mahomed* à l'aube des Lumières', in *Dix-Huitième Siècle*, no.24 (1992), pp. 321-31.

Venturino, D., 'Imposteur ou législateur ? Le Mahomet des Lumières', *SVEC* (2000), vol. 2, pp. 243-262.

Vertot, abbé de., 'Dissertation sur l'auteur de l'Alcoran' in *Histoire des chevaliers de Malte* (Paris, 1726), 4 vols.

Veyssière de la Croze, Mathurin, 'Réflexions historiques sur le mahométisme et sur le socinianisme' in *Dissertations historiques et critiques sur divers sujets* (Rotterdam, 1707).

Vitkus, D., *Turning Turk: English theatre in the Multicultural Mediterranean, 1570-1630* (New York, 2003).

Voltaire, F. M. A., *Le Fanatisme ou Mahomet*, C.Todd (ed.), in *Œuvres complètes de Voltaire* (Oxford, 2002), vol 20B.

———, *De l'Alcoran et de Mahomet*, ed A. Gunny, vol. 20B.

———, *Essai sur les mœurs*, ed. R. Pomeau (Paris, 1964), 2 vols.

———, *Zadig*, G. Ascoli (ed.), rev. by J. Fabre (Paris, 1962), 2 vols.

———, *Correspondence and related documents* and *Notebooks* in *Complete Works*, vols. 85-135 and 81-2 (Oxford, 1968-77).

Wade, I.O., *The Clandestine organization and diffusion of philosophic ideas in France from1700 to 1750* (Princeton, 1938).

Wansburgh, J., *Qur'ānic Studies* (Oxford, 1977).

———, *The Sectarian Milieu* (Oxford, 1978).

Al-Wāqidī, *Kitāb al-Maghāzī*, ed. J. Marsden-Jones (London, 1995), 3 vols.

Watson, W., *Tricolor and Crescent. France and the Islamic World* (Wesport, 2003).

Watt, W. M., *Muhammad at Mecca* (Oxford, 1953).

———, *Muhammad at Medina* (Oxford, 1956).

———, 'The materials used by Ibn Isḥāq', in *Historians of the Middle East*, B. Lewis and P. M. Holt (eds.) (London, 1962), pp.23-34.

———, 'The reliability of Ibn Isḥāq's sources', in *La Vie du Prophète Mahomet* (Paris, 1983).

———, *Muḥammad*, in *The Cambridge History of Islam*, P. M. Holt, Ann K. S. Lambton and B. Lewis (eds.) (Cambridge, 1977), vol 1A, pp.20-56.

———, *Bell's Introduction to the Qur'an* (Edinburgh, 1970).

———, *Muslim-Christian Encounters* (London, 1971).

Wentholt, E. (tr.), *Paradise on Earth. Some thoughts on European images of non-European man* (New Heaven and London, 1955).

Whichcote, B., *The works of the learned Benjamin Whichcote* (Aberdeen, 1751), 4 vols.

Index